Readings in the Sociology of the Professions

Edited by :

SHEO KUMAR LAL
AMBIKA CHANDANI

UMED RAJ NAHAR
KIRTI KHANNA

GIAN PUBLISHING HOUSE
DELHI—110007

GIAN PUBLISHING HOUSE,
29/6, Shakti Nagar,
Delhi—110007. Phone : 7213053

ISBN 81-212-0126—8

PRINTED IN INDIA

Published by Mrs. Gayatri Garg for Gian Publishing House, Delhi and Printed by Godwall Printers, Delhi.

Dedicated to the Memory of
Professor M.S.A. Rao

PREFACE

The present volume is the outcome of a National Seminar on *The Sociology of the Professions* held at Jodhpur on October 13-16, 1984 under the auspices of the Department of Sociology, The University of Jodhpur.

The tone of the seminar was set by the eminent social scientist Professor M.S. Gore, Vice-Chancellor of University of Bombay who inaugurated the seminar. It was presided over by Professor Y.B. Damle, President of Indian Sociological Society. Dr. S.N. Mehrotra, Vice-Chancellor of the University of Jodhpur gave reception address. Professor L.P. Vidyarthi, Professor and Head, Department of Anthropology, University of Ranchi gave Valedictory Address which was presided over by Dr. Indra Deva, Professor and Head, Department of Sociology, Ravi Shanker University, Raipur (M.P.).

Sixty-five participants representing various universities, research institutes and professional organisations, in addition to local participants, attended the seminar. In all, forty-six papers were discussed in different sessions. We take this opportunity to thank the scholars who readily conceded to our request and prepared their papers. We are grateful to other participants who made the discussion lively by their comments. Unfortunately, it has not been possible to publish all the papers and discussion points because of the circumstances beyond our control. Twenty-eight papers form part of this book. The papers raise issues relevant to the theme and examine them from different angles. The book has long been in making but once it is in the hands of the readers, they would find that it is one book which provides at least benchmark data on different professions in India at one place. This would help any future researcher in the area of the professions. We shall be more than rewarded if the book stimulates thinking in this sphere irrespective of orientation suggested through various papers.

We are grateful to the University Grants Commission, Indian Council of Social Science Research, Indian Council of Medical Research, New Delhi, and the University of Jodhpur for providing financial assistance to hold this seminar.

We express our sincere thanks to Dr. Ernest Greenwood, Professor Emeritus, University of California, Berkeley (USA) who though could not attend the seminar, contributed to this volume, one of his recent papers which covers the definitional aspects of the professions. Professor Greenwood is a pioneer in the field and his paper is a reconsideration of his earlier position and a critical review of concepts, attributes and approaches for the study of professions. Dr. J.N. Sharma, Professor and Head, Department of English, the University of Jodhpur helped in many ways in our work. We are really grateful to him and to his colleague Dr. Sharad Kumar Rajeemwale for the assistance given to us.

We owe a special debt to Dr. Yogendra Singh, Professor, Centre for the Study of Social Systems, School of Social Sciences, Jawahar Lal Nehru University, New Delhi for introducing this book to the readers.

We also thank M/s Gian Publishing House, Delhi for arranging the publication of this book.

Department of Sociology, The University of Jodhpur, Jodhpur (Rajasthan)

Sheo Kumar Lal, Umed Raj Nahar
Ambika Chandani, Kirti Khanna

FOREWORD

It is heartening to find that sociology in India has been enlarging its concerns both in teaching and research since the beginning of the seventies. The study of professions in India is one such area. From the seventies onwards, massive studies of different dimensions of professions and their roles in the development of our society have been conducted. It was a result of twofold factors : first, the process of modernization and development initiated since Independence had enlarged the social base of professions contributing to its internal differentiation in terms of specialisation, organisation and ideology. Secondly, sociologists began increasingly to realise the significance of professions both as an indicator and as initiator of the processes of modernization. This concern got inevitably mixed with basic commitment of Indian sociologists from the very beginning of this discipline to view concepts in terms their relevance to specific systems and tradtions. It was recognised for example that a viable and worthwhile study of professions in India could not be possible without an appraisal of its concepts in the context of their historical evolution in the tradition and culture of the concerned societies. Even heuristically, the concept of profession must of necessity reflect the culture specific features of its existence in the Indian society.

READINGS IN THE SOCIOLOGY OF THE PROFESSIONS edited by Professor Sheo kumar Lal and his colleagues contains a collection of essays which closely reflect these concerns. The volume has been organised imaginatively so that it throws light both on the issues of theory and typology of professions. The essays in the part I deal mainly with problems of concepts and theories of professions. Theoretical approaches to the study of professions, its attributes, the process of professionalisation and its patterns, and finally the need for rethinking on its conceptual formulation commensurate with the specific cultural-historical features of the Indian society have been examined. Most contributors have raised conceptual issues on the structure and process of professions in India from a comparative analytical perspective and examined it in the context both of its normal and discripant modes of functioning. This is in line with the long standing sociological tradition.

From Part II to VI, the book deals with substantive studies on specific types of professions in India, such as the teaching profession, the scientists and scientific profession, the medical profession, the legal profession and finally professions such as social work and creative arts, especially dancing. There is one essay also on the voluntary organisations dealing with the process of rural development. The readers are bound to benefit from the empirical profile of these various professions, their organisation and structure, their functioning, the problems they encounter and the linkages that they provide to other forms of social structure and organisation in the process of modernization of the Indian society. The issue of linkages assumes great significance when we deal with the role of professions in social development.

Professions aspire to represent values and skills drived from science, technology and rationality embedded in the universalistic humanitarian ideology. As such they have been usually viewed as a rational construct. It is only when we observe them functioning in the specific settings of cultral and social systems that both the limits of the ideological formulation and power of professions in society are revealed. This is where the issue of linkages of profession with other forms of cultural and social institutions in society, such as its social base, composition, belief systems and out look etc. assume significance. The empirical studies of professions in this volume outline some of these linkages and their significance to the structure and functions of various professions in India. Whether it is the teaching profession, scientific profession, medical or legal profession, the effective manner of their discharging professional responsibilities tends to be intimately governed by social origin, class affiliation and ideology of the people in professions. The measures that, therefore, could contribute to the maximization of the efficiency of skill and performance of professions, apart from being intrinsic to its structure, administration, rules and procedures have also to do with the nature of social forces and institutions in the society at large.

This collection of the essays on professions by Professor Lal *et al* amply throws light on many aspects of these problems. It offers a wealth of data and information on professions in India from both a critical and empirical perspective that would serve well the needs of students, administrators and social workers in our country.

YOGENDRA SINGH

Centre for the Study of Social Systems
School of Social Sciences
Jawaharlal Nehru University
New Delhi

EDITORS' INTRODUCTION

The Department of Sociology at the University of Jodhpur provides for the teaching of Sociology of Education and Medical Sociology as optional papers at the M.A. Final level. The syllabi for these papers include tbe study of the medical and teaching professions. Sociology is also taught in the course for the LLB (professional) degree, wherein the legal profession forms part of the syllabus. The department has also provided a full paper on the Sociology of the Professions in the syllabus for the M. Phil. degree. Researches have been conducted in the area of the Sociology of the Professions in the department. The colleagues involved in these activities prepared a scheme to organise a seminar on the Sociology of the Professions to get an idea of the work being done in this field in the country. A circular was sent to various universities and research institutes indicating the intention to hold the seminar. The department received enthusiastic response and, therefore, a National Seminar no the Sociology of the Professions was held here on October 13-16, 1984. We made it clear to the participants that they were free to contribute papers in areas of their interest.

The papers included in this book have been arranged under six heads : I-Profession : Concept and Theory ; II-Teaching Profession ; III-Scientists ; IV-Medical Profession ; V-Legal Profession ; and VI-Miscellaneous. Seven papers have been included under the first head.

Greenwood, who has done major work in this field, has also contributed a paper. It has been included as the first chapter in this book. It may be pointed out that Greenwood, in an earlier article entitled "Attributes of a Profession," published elsewhere in 1957, has presented five attributes distinguishing professions from non-professions. These attributes are : systematic theory, authority, community sanction, ethical codes, and a culture. The approach followed by Greenwood in the article has been termed as the definitional approach by Cullen. Later researches have indicated two distinct perspectives in the study of the professions : (a) Structural Approach and (b) Processual Approach. The structural approach concerns itself with the identification of characteristics which are unique to professions as against non-professions. The work of Greenwood and Goode could be cited as an illustration of this approach. The process of the transformation of a non-profession into a profession is the focus of the processual approach. Wilensky's work is an example of this approach. Greenwood's structural approach came to be criticised by several scholars, especially by followers of the processual approach. In the light of the criticism levelled against his approach, Greenwood reviewed the work of two dozen scholars and he found that certain attributes were actually not the *essential* attributes of a profession. Rather, they were derived ones. He, therefore, made necessary modifications in his earlier position and wrote a paper which has been published in this book under the title "Attributes of a Profession : Revisited" revising his earlier characterisation of a profession. He now emphasises only on three essential attributes of a profession, namely (a) the cognitive or intellectual component of professionalism, (b) collectivity-orientation, and (c) monopolistic components. Drawing attention to the power approach of the professions, he feels that those who are followers of this approach maintain that the structuralists exlude the power aspect from the definition of profession, which is not a fact. The structuralists, as a matter of fact, have incorporated the power element in their professional model. Greenwood's reconsideration is an attempt to present the case in the right perspective.

Dubey, in his key-note address, "The Sociology of the Professions : Major Theoretical Issues," has presented a brief review of the prevalent concepts, attributes and theories in the study of the Sociology of the Professions in the West. He then reviews the Indian situation. According to him, either because of the impact of Indology or colonial rule, or both, Indian scholars have ignored the fact that Indian society was organised around guilds, corporations, occupations and professions, and they interested themselves in micro-level studies of the village, the tribe, etc. But the pioneers of Indian Sociology, such as G.S. Ghurye, Radhakamal Mukherji and D.P. Mukherji did show their interest in the study of the professions. Dubey has divided the studies of the professions in India into three categories : (a) Historical (b) Ethnological and (c) Theoretical. He has also indicated the existing gaps in the study of the professions in India and suggested new areas of studies.

Rajagopalan in his paper "Some Critical Reflections on the Prevailing Outlook of Professions in India," has examined the various definitions of the profession, especially that given by Greenwood. Rajagopalan acknowledges the merits of Greenwood's definition and the underlying meaning, but he seems to have some reservations too. He is of the opinion that professional associations these days are not different from trade unions. Some of these professional organisations are so preoccupied with the activities pertaining to distribution and sharing of power that they hardly find any time for the other essential functions supposed to be performed by them. Pandey in "Whither Professionalism?" deals with the current state of professionalism and speculates on its likely future. He begins with a resume of the theoretical background, then proceeds to explain the process of professionalisation. He also introduces the idea of deprofessionalisation, by which he means the process causing erosion of the essential attributes of a profession. Deprofessionalisation involves dequalification of professional labour, erosion of work autonomy, and class formation. He looks at the possibility of proletarianisation of the professions. He feels that whatever be the situation, the relationship always remains one of domination and subjugation. Gandhi has found gaps between theory and reality. His plea, in his paper, "Professions in Theory and Reality : A Re-Consideration of Theory of Professions in the Light of Some Empirical Evidence," is for continuous examination and re-examination of the prevailing "ideal type" of the professions in view of the existing social situation. Advani is of the opinion that the professions are in a transitional phase. In his paper, "Patterns of Professional Processes", he has pinned faith on some sort of movement which would revitalise the professions so that they could perform the functions to which they proclaim their adherence. Singh argues in his paper, "A Rethinking on the Theory of Sociology of Profession," that in view of the crumbling code of ethics in contemporary society that gives profession a status far superior to that of non-professions, the conventional theories of the sociology of the professions are losing their relevance. In a world which is becoming predominantly materialistic and profit-oriented, the purity of a profession is not free from suspicion. Doctors, lawyers and teachers are now no less self-oriented than businessmen. The idea of self-interest versus disinterestedness is non-rational in the context of the modern occupational structure. Therefore, specification of professional categories is a futile exercise. It is, therefore, necessary in the event of emerging dimensions of various professions to re-define the concept of profession and to evolve a more coherent and contextual methodology for the study of the professions in a changing situation.

Srivastava is of the opinion that university teachers are more and more alienated from their professional role and they find difficulty in identifying themselves with the profession. In his paper, "Sociology of the Professions : An Overview with Analytical Note on University Teaching as a Profession", he has shown that the teaching profession is not free from role-ambivalence and conflict of interest. Nahar has emphasised the need to study the academic profession, particularly the structure of the academic profession, its conflicts, university organisation and its relationship with the outside system. He has explained in detail the scheme of the needed study in his paper, "Teaching in the University System : Needed Area of Research." Khanna in "Career Decision-Making : A Case of University Teachers", has presented the findings of an empirical study indicating the processes of career decision-making. In "The Academic Profession and Social Development", Bhoite notes the low degree of modernisation that his teacher respondents betray. He feels that structural changes should be brought about in the University system so that teachers could modernise themselves to carry forward the task of social development. Rao and Venkararaman in their paper, "A Functional Analysis of Unionism Among College Teachers", have examined the functional implications of the growing phenomenon of unionism among college teachers for their occupational values, role-perception, professionalism and professional orientation. It has been found that unionism, measured in terms of participation in teachers' associations, is a phenomenon to reckon with because of its negative functional implications for higher education in terms of value-orientation and role-perception. Gupta and Rani in their empirical study, "Professional Commitment of School Teachers," have found school teachers professionally committed, while Ruhela's paper, "Professionalisation of School Teachers in India" presents school teachers as disillusioned with their profession.

Chandra's paper, "Indian Scientists and Social System", assesses the social climate, patterns of inter-relationships and life styles of Indian scientists working for national scientific agencies or organisations as also the impact of the social system on their achievement. By and large, social milieu and familial climate contribute positively to the productivity of the scientists but organisational structures shaped on the bureaucratic model function retrogressively. Ramanamma and Bambawale in "Social Structure and Profession of Scientists", point out that structural constraints and insufficient opportunities plague scientists. They appear to support the idea suggested by Rajagopalan, Pandey, Gandhi and Singh that ambivalence creeps in due to a gap between ideology and the reality of the current situation. Srivastava and Toha discuss professional obsolescence which is a comparatively new area of research—especially in India. In a joint paper, "Professional Obsolescence : A Needed Area of Research", they indicate the typology and salient features of professional obsolescence. They emphasize motivational and organisational context of obsolescence. For them, official hurdles, red-tapism and paucity of funds are the major constraints in updating the knowledge and skills of professionals in science and engineering in India.

PART I

PROFESSION : CONCEPT AND THEORY

1

ATTRIBUTES OF A PROFESSION : REVISITED

ERNEST GREENWOOD

INTRODUCTION

The only permanent feature of social phenomena is their impermanence. A tendency to undergo change over time is their prime characteristic. Hence, the population census must be repeated decennially and the cost-of-living index revised periodically. When I was a graduate student, the then current sociology textbooks taught me that juvenile delinquency was a phenomenon largely confined to the lower socio-economic stratum ; that petty theft, drug traffic, violence, vandalism, and unmarried pregnancies were concentrated predominantly in the slum areas (they were not called "ghettoes" then) of large cities ; and that as one traced a line out toward the middle class suburbs, these indicators of social disorganization decreased markedly in relative frequency. But within a generation juvenile delinquency vaulted over the social factors confining it, landing into the suburbs to become a middle-class phenomenon as well. Therefore, empirical generalizations about any social phenomenon should be regularly tested for current verity by reobserving the latter to determine if the phenomenon has changed in the interim. Such regular re-examination is a "should" for another reason. Not only the object observed but those who observe it can and do change over time. A tendency to spawn ever new concepts is a prime characteristic of every field of study. The novel concepts change the perspective of the investigators therein. This leads them to re-observe the same familiar phenomenon, this time identifying hitherto unsuspected properties, and, hence, deriving new or different generalizations about it. That post-Freudian generalizations about the human psyche differ from pre-Freudian ones, is not because human beings changed in the interim, but because Freud's novel concepts changed our perspective upon the latter. Therefore, the emergence of any new idea(s) regarding a phenomenon should prompt a re-examination of currently held generalizations about it.

It was with the above considerations in mind that I undertook to review an article of mine, now two decades old, which was an attempt to ascertain the defining attributes of the professions.[1] The article set-forth five attributes as distinguishing the professions from the non-professions, namely, systematic theory, authority, community sanction, ethical codes, and a culture. The perspective reflected in that article Cullen has called the "definitional approach."[2] Recent students of professionalism, viewing the accumulation of researches into the phenomenon, have identified in these efforts two distinct though related guiding perspectives or as they prefer to call them, theoretical approaches.[3] These are : the profession as structure and professionalization as process. What has been called the definitional is actually subsumable under the structural approach.

Structural versus Processual

The structural approach focuses upon profession *per se*, as is. It is premised on the assumption that professions comprise a class or type structurally distinct from other occupations which, by implication, are non-professional. Thus, the aim of investigations guided by the structural approach is a quest for the essentials differentiating the type from others. More specifically, it is to identify those occupational characteristics which may be said to constitute the distinguishing attributes of professions. The writings of Goode are prime illustrations of the structural approach.[4] My own article is another. The processual approach focuses upon the transformation of a non-professional occupation into a profession. It is premised on the assumption that this is an evolving process consisting of sequential stages through which all would-be professions pass and, furthermore, that the stages are ascertainable. Accordingly, the aim of investigations guided by this approach, is to trace this evolution ; it is to describe what sociologists would call "the natural history" of professionalization, to formulate a model that typifies this process. In addition, it is to identify those social factors, both internal and external to occupations, which facilitate or impede the professionalization process.[5] Wilensky's oft-quoted article on professionalization is a prime illustration of the processual approach.[6]

Investigators employing the processual approach have produced evolutionary models which differ widely regarding the number of stages comprising the professionalization process. On that account the approach has drawn criticism. The critics claim that no two occupations go through the same sequence to become professions, so that it is not possible to construct an evolutionary model which would fit all or even most of the thirty odd existing professions.[7] But so has the structural approach, including my own earlier effort, been the target of criticism.[8] Since they emanate from diverse sources, these criticisms are not always re-enforcing, but at times actually contradictory. Nevertheless, taken singly, each merits consideration. It is this imperative which motivates the present paper. One criticism concerns the validity of the structural approach because of its dubious premise. A second questions the representativeness of the sample studied by structuralists. A third relates to the reliability of the structural approach as a method. A final criticism questions the theoretical adequacy of the structuralist position for its neglect of the attribute of power in professionalism. I will discuss each one of these criticisms in that order, and then conclude with a relevant note regarding the social work profession.

1. ON THE MATTER OF VALIDITY

Critics challenge the validity of the structural approach by questioning its underlying premise that there exists a class of occupations with attributes essentially so different as to merit the label "professional" exclusively. They argue that all occupations are essentially similar. Every occupation is a specific socially approved activity which calls for some skill, which is pursued by a group of persons, which results in something that has a market value because it is in demand, and which, therefore, is a legitimate source of steady income. Hence, as one critic puts it, in essentials the so-called professions are indistinguishable from other occupations, so that there is no logical basis for the proposed differentiation. The only possible difference, if any, between what the structuralists call the professions and the non-professions, is that the former tend on the whole to exhibit in somewhat greater degree certain characteristics which the latter tend on the whole to exhibit in somewhat lesser degree. In other words, there is an occupational continuum : all occupations are distributed along this very same continuum. It is the sociologist who then approaches the latter with his *a priori* structural perspective and proceeds to cut the continuum at some arbitrary point of his own choosing, thereby creating two occupational classes of doubtful validity.[9] In summary, the professional versus non-professional dichotomy has no counter-part in reality.

Commentary

But does the above criticism itself possess validity ? The class of entities called "the professions" is by no means the creature of the sociological imagination. It is a social reality. After all, why does our language contain the term "profession" if not to stand for a distinct class of referents ? Why are there organizations in Western societies termed "professional schools" and "professional associations" ? Clearly because there are professions. As the tertiary (i.e. non-agricultural and non-manufacturing) sector of our economy expands, there is an increase in the white-collar service occupations largely manned by persons with some college education ; for example, real estate and stock broker, insurance and travel agent, business manager and interior decorator. Students of the phenomenon have pointed to the uniform aspiration on the part of members of these occupations to acquire the status and trappings of "profession."[10] Are the latter aspiring after something that is non-existent ? Hardly so. As occupations, the professions have a history which antedates the appearance of sociologists.

The professional versus non-professional dichotomy is an objective fact of social life, which is precisely why sociologists are studying the phenomenon.

It is, of course, true that a continuum exists along which the many occupations may by arrayed with respect to any and all attributes, including those we associate with the professions. To a discussion of this very continuum I devoted a lengthy paragraph in my previous article. So, the existence of an occupational continuum is not at issue here. The issue is really a methodological one : is it in accord with scientific method to focus on the occupations at the poles of this continuum and conceptualize them as two contrasting types, viz., professions versus non-professions ? The answer is that social scientists have been doing just that constantly in describing social regularities. Note such dichotomies as : free-market vs. planned economies, directive vs. non-directive therapies, ascribed vs. achieved statuses, and folk (*gemeinschaft*) vs. mass (*gesellschaft*) societies, to name only a few. The construction of polar types is an accepted procedure premised on the logic that two groups which differ, with regard to a combination of attributes, sufficiently in *degree* are probably different in *kind.* On this issue Freidson, himself a critic of the structural approach, gave the verdict when he wrote that the professions "represent a distinct kind of occupation."[11]

2. ON THE MATTER OF SAMPLE REPRESENTATIVENESS

A second criticism challenges the representativeness of the data from which the structuralists construct their ideal type of profession. The writings of the latter, so the criticism goes, indicate quite clearly that the attributes comprising their model are derived almost entirely from one profession, medicine.[12] The earliest effort to define the attributes of a profession is to be found in the classic paper by Flexner, whose occupational identification was with medicine.[13] The structuralists, so argue the critics, have reverentially followed in Flexner's footsteps since.[14] Pre-occupation with medicine has dominated their studies of professionalism and has, therefore, largely determined the composition of the professional model which these studies have produced.[15] Medicine, however, is atypical.

Medicine in the U.S. is a free, entrepreneurial profession whose practitioners operate, in the main, individually, exercise considerable control over their practice, and are involved in a fee-for-service relationship with their clients.[16] These features of medicine have strongly colored the structuralist's model of the professions as being essentially entrepreneurial and individualistic.[17] The pre-occupation with medicine is explainable on several grounds : its pre-eminent position in the occupational hierarchy ; its great prestige and privileges in society ; and its market monopoly unmatched by any other profession.[18] But its very singularity renders medicine an unrepresentative choice for a case study intended to yield information about professions in general. Some critics, Ritzer among them, contend that the practice of medicine, as it has evolved in the U.S., is really an aberrant case of professionalism.[19] Hence, its repeated use by structuralists as the prototype of the professions yields an erroneous picture of reality.

Commentary

The criticism that the structuralists, including myself, have constructed a professional model derived entirely from medicine, the entrepreneurial profession *nonpareil*, is not quite true. It is true that Flexner, the first structuralist (if he may be so labelled), was affiliated with the medical profession. It so happened that in the early part of this century medical education in the U.S. was chaotic and retarded compared to that in Western Europe. Cognizant of the need for radical reform, the American Medical Association appealed to the Carnegie Foundation for a critical study of the medical schools. To undertake the study, the Foundation engaged Flexner, who was by background an educator and not a physician. The rest is history. The recommendations of the Flexner Report, when implemented, transformed the medical curriculum in the U.S.[20] As a leading architect of professional education in the country, Flexner was subsequently invited to address the then predecessor organization to the National Conference on Social Welfare on the question whether social work was a profession. His classic paper on professional attributes, to which its proponents and opponents repeatedly refer, was delivered on that occasion.

Flexner's approach to his subject was to examine the then generally recognized professions so as to identify their common attributes which might serve him as criteria whereby to gauge social work's claim to professional status. While medicine featured importantly in his analysis, the professions he considered included law, ministry, and engineering as well.[21] In formulating the archetypal profession described in my earlier article, I had uppermost in mind those that had been considered by Flexner plus the professions of the university professor and the research scientist. Goode refers to four professions which have been most used by students of professionalism : law, medicine, ministry, and university teaching.[22] The truth is that structuralists have employed all of the occupations thus far enumerated plus the officialdom of the military and of the civil services. Furthermore, the professions which have been so utilized are not all of the entrepreneurial, fee-for-service kind. Medicine, law, engineering, yes. But the ministry, university teaching, scientific research are bureaucratic professions. In the latter professionals practice as salaried employees in a large organization which assigns tasks to them and subjects them to its rules. Clearly, the structuralist's typical professional cannot be characterized as drawn solely from the entrepreneurial professions generally and the medical profession specifically.

A review of the array of professions actually employed by the structuralists to derive their model indicates that they share one feature in common. All the professions are relatively old, traditional, with long histories. They originated in the pre-industrial era of Western societies ; they came to maturity in the industrial era ; and in the current post-industrial era they constitute what Carr-Saunders has called the "old established professions".[23] As Larson has observed, it is these well established professions that have furnished the elements from which students of professionalism have constructed their ideal types.[24] Such exclusive concentration upon the most mature and established professions requires no elaborate explanation. Precisely because they are mature and established, these professions manifest with maximum clarity the distinguishing attributes of their class. They are the ones clustered at the professional pole of the occupational continuum. They, therefore, comprise the cases most appropriate for observations intended to identify the attributes of a profession.

3. ON THE MATTER OF RELIABILITY

Thirdly, the critics challenge the reliability of the structural approach by pointing to the confusing variation in the results that its use has yielded. They contend that investigators who employ this approach, although conceptualizing the phenomenon of professionalism similarly, nonetheless come up with lists of attributes which differ from one another. A review of the writings of the latter, so argue the critics, reveals not agreement but disagreement regarding the numbers and kinds of attributes characterizing the professions.[25] Which of the several lists available is to be regarded as the attributes distinguishing the professions from the non-professions ? Lortie has criticized sociologists as still not having reached agreement on a single set of criteria for defining a profession.[26]

Commentary

In preparation for this paper I reviewed the writings of two dozen investigators who have concerned themselves with identifying the distinctive attributes of professions.[27] Of these, eighteen published during the 1960s and 1970s, in other words, since the appearance of my earlier article. Hence, the sample reviewed is, in the main, representative of the more recent crop of students of the subject. The review highlights two points.

All together the authors cited a dozen separate and distinct attributes as setting the professions apart from the non-professions. At one extreme an author cited a single attribute as being solely distinctive of a profession, while at the other extreme an author cited nine attributes, with the remaining twenty-two authors distributed in between. The average (median and mode) of the distribution was four attributes cited per author. While many authors cited the identical attribute and while many cited the same number of attributes, no two authors were similar as to both the numbers and the identical attributes cited. Accordingly, the criticism that the structural approach yields a picture of variation among those employing it, contains a truth. However, it does not contain the whole truth, which brings me to the second point highlighted by the review.

Interestingly enough, underneath the variation exists a surprising degree of consensus. Thus, of the dozen attributes cited by our sample, half were cited fewer than six times. Just four attributes alone received well over half of the total citations. Hence, the citations were concentrated around a few attributes. The shape of the distribution here described is comparable to a leptokurtic curve which, while having a large range, actually has a relatively small variance, because of the heavy concentration of frequencies in a few intervals (here discrete categories). Several recent writers have referred to this same anomaly, viz., that although the lists of attributes of the ideal-type profession proffered by students of the phenomenon do vary, nonetheless a certain few attributes keep recurring on every list, thereby indicating an underlying, though obscured, unanimity.[28] Goode summarized it well when he wrote that the characteristics attributed to the professions, on being tabulated, reveal a "hidden similarity...suggesting that their foundation is a shared observation of reality."[29]

The above described anomaly is explainable. The attributes which we associate with the professions are not all of the same logical order. A number of writers have pointed out that certain of these attributes generate other secondary ones ; stated conversely, certain attributes are derived from more basic ones. To illustrate, one-fourth of the authors whom I reviewed cited as a distinguishing attribute that professionals enjoy greater income, prestige and political influence than do non-professionals. This attribute is clearly a derived one, a consequent of professionalism. For an occupation is a profession, not because its members enjoy these advantages, but just the reverse ; the latter derive these advantages, because they are members of a profession. Conceptual clarity, therefore, calls for a dichotomy of professional attributes : the generating or basic ones versus the consequential or derived ones.[30] The basic professional attributes are few and essential, the derived ones are many and varied. Examine the lists of professional attributes proffered by students of the subject and you will find that it is with respect to the derived attributes that they differ so widely. As Goode has suggested, reduce the lists by subtracting from them the derived attributes, and the remaining ones, viz., the basic attributes, will show remarkable and satisfying consistency among them.[31]

If my earlier article is to be faulted, it should be for having failed to propound the distinction between basic and derived professional attributes and for having lumped them together indiscriminately. Actually, the basic attributes reduce to only three. Significantly they are the same three which were most frequently cited by the two dozen authors who were reviewed. What are these attributes ?

Basic Professional Attributes

To begin with, there is the attribute which has been referred to as the cognitive or intellectual component of professionalism.[32] Thus the expertise of the professional is grounded in a body of theory (e.g., physics) or principles (e.g., law) or doctrine (e.g., theology), which is relatively abstract, systematic, and communicable, which is constantly replenished with concepts and data derived from disputation and research, and mastery of which requires higher education that is carefully planned and intellectually demanding. This is what distinguishes a profession from a trade. An apprentice can acquire the skill of his trade by simply watching his master's technique as the latter moves from task to task. A similar didactic approach in the case of a profession would prove entirely inadequate.

A second basic attribute is one which has been varyingly referred to as the collectivity orientation and the normative or service component of professionalism.[33] Thus, the proper performance of the professional role requires that the practitioners renders at all times the highest caliber service of which he is capable, irrespective of the identity and finances of the recipient, and that he invariably subordinates his personal needs and material interests to the latter's welfare, should he be confronted with a choice between them. This is what distinguishes professions from commerce. The maximization of profit is a proper motivation for behaviour in business ; it is inappropriate in a profession.

The third basic attribute is the monopolistic component of professionalism. It is the exclusive privilege of the profession's members, conferred on them by the community and legally sanctioned, to be the sole recognized practitioners of the professional skill. This fact thereby invests them with the control of the following : recruitment and education of neophytes ; accreditation of professional schools ; definition of licensing requirements ; and regulation, evaluation, and when appropriate, censure of the professional behaviour of colleagues. In this regard a profession is comparable to a craft guild, and the modern professions are, indeed, descendants of the medieval guilds.[34]

In my earlier paper the cognitive, normative and monopolistic attributes were conceptualized and termed systematic theory, ethical codes and community sanction, respectively. The present conceptualization and terminology is much more accurate and clear. And for this I am indebted to others whose writings have been so instructive. These three, then, are the essentials of professions and all the other attributes we associate with the latter are derivatives. That professional education is characteristically prolonged and, in fact, unending, is a derivative of the cognitive or intellectual component of professionalism. Similarly, professional autonomy, viz., the practitioner's right to act on his own judgment in given cases without interference from the laity, is a derivative attribute, a consequent of the monopolistic and the service components combined. And from the combination of all three components derives what I referred to in my earlier article as the professional culture.

Within a given profession the three basic attributes are manifest in varying degrees, with the result that a profession may rank higher on one attribute than on another.[35] This phenomenon Cullen has called "status inconsistency."[36] Thus, Toren reminds us, the social work profession has a highly developed service ethic coupled with a considerably less developed fund of scientifically tested knowledge.[37] This suggests that each of the basic attributes constitutes a continuum. This fact, in turn, calls for a revision of our customary conception of professionalism as a one-dimensional (linear) continuum to be replaced by a three-dimensional one. It is into such a three-dimensional space that we must locate the thirty odd existing professions.

4. ON THE MATTER OF THEORETICAL ADEQUACY

A fourth and more fundamental criticism of the structural approach emanates from a new school of investigators who employ a power orientation toward professionalism.[38] The power advocates challenge the professional model proffered by the structuralists as exaggerating the harmony between the professions and the community and conveying no hint of the conflict of interest between them. The structural approach, so the criticism goes, is really rooted in functionalist social theory according to which society is a functioning system, self-corrective, and tending toward equilibrium.[39] Functionalist theory provides a perspective on society as a stable normative order, integrated around universally held values, and organized around compatible social institutions. Hence, functionalism de-emphasizes the existence of intrinsic discord and of necessary conflict in society, and neglects the importance of power as an instrument for redefining social relationships and for rectifying disequilibrium.[40] Rooted in functionalist theory, the structuralists have likewise ignored the element of power in both the evolution and the operation of professions. They have failed to see that the distinguishing difference between professions and non-professions is to be found in the attribute of organized power.[41]

Power Approach to Professions

Power is the capacity of a group to attain its goals in the face of resistances and, once attained, to retain them. Power is latent ; it is manifested as control on the part of the group, both control over its own actions and, correspondingly, control over the actions of others.[42] As applied to occupations, power is maximum collegial control over the content and conditions of work performed by the occupation's members with minimum interference from the laity.[43] Specifically, this means control over recruiting, training, accrediting, licensing, regulating, and disciplining members of the profession, and in effect, excluding all non-members from professional practice and privileges. Freidson, considered the dean of the power school, has argued that the only important and uniform attribute for distinguishing professions from other occupations is their position of legitimate control over work. To be sure, such control over a service market can and does assume varying degrees. Hence, what is customarily referred to as an occupational continuum, is really a power continuum. The professions are the occupations which possess the greatest power to control the conditions of their work, whereas the non-professions possess the least.[44] Thus, as between two collaborative professions, that one is the more professional which controls the other ; good examples are the relationships of physician to nurse and psychiatrist to social worker.

The power approach to professionalism is rooted in social conflict theory according to which society is a collection of rivalrous interest groups, among them occupations, competing for a limited supply of economic goods and prestigious statuses. When a non-professional occupation strives to obtain exclusive control over a service market and thereby to achieve professional status, it invariably encounters strong opposition to its aspirations from other interest groups, especially from some competing occupation intent on the same objective.[45] The resultant competition between the two occupations is essentially a zero-sum game, for the success of one is at the expense of the other.[46] The collective endeavour on the part of the members to elevate their occupation to professional status, Larson has called a "collective [social] mobility project".[47] Their indispensable instrument is the professional association, the organization of which creates a power source.[48] In behalf of its members, the professional association embarks on a prolonged and complex series of transactions with the community so as to establish the boundaries of its service market and to acquire exclusive control over it.[49] The professional association operates as a typical pressure group employing a variety of public relations techniques to influence public policy toward directions in its favour. While the association appeals its case to a wide potential client public, special targets for its persuasion are groups which possess the power to influence the state. The aspiring profession forms organic ties with a segment of the power elite which is able to move the state apparatus to legalize the would be profession's claims. The success of the occupation's drive toward professional status is, thus, largely determined by that group among society's elite which is willing to act as its sponsor. Many of the occupations considered non-professional are such only because they lack the necessary resources to enlist powerful groups in their behalf.[50]

As for the attributes of knowledge and service, do they feature in the power theory at all ? Power advocates point to the fact that an invariable element in the professionalization process is the development by the members of the aspiring profession of an elaborate rationale justifying their claim to professional status. Whatever else it may include, this rationale must revolve around the twin concepts of specialized knowledge and commitment to service.[51] The segment of the power elite whose sponsorship is sought, must be persuaded that the occupation's members possess superior knowledge which gives them a rare skill.[52] But equally important, the sponsor must be persuaded that their commitment to the service ideal is likewise out of the ordinary.[53] No emerging profession can afford to admit harboring motives that are parochial and selfish. Only by conveying an image of competence and altruism can it hope to persuade others that granting it a service monopoly is in the public interest.[54] While the professional association and the trade union resemble each other in goals, which are basically economic for both, they differ widely in the rhetoric they employ. As Haug and Sussman point out, trade unions stress the concepts of equity, grievances, needs, and rights, whereas professional associations stress the concepts of knowledge, performance, service and skill.[55] Actually, it is not demonstrable empirically that the aspiring profession's cognitive and normative attributes are as superior as claimed.[56] However, once having gained recognition as a profession, its claims become *ipso facto* unquestioned. Henceforth the profession is by definition all that it presumes to be. To sum up, the cognitive and the normative are not essential attributes of a profession, but form a rationalization which both motivate and facilitate its efforts to attain and to retain professional status.[57] Hence, from the power perspective these two concepts comprise the "ideology" of professionalism.[58]

Commentary

The power advocates offer a unified theory describing both what a profession is (structure) and how it came to be (process). Instead of the structural and processual approaches, they propose a single, and presumably more sophisticated, approach revolving around the concept of power. In that endeavour they impart to the term "power" a dual meaning, which could generate misunderstanding. As Ritzer has observed, there is power as the motor force in the professionalization process and then there is power as a defining attribute of professions.[59] Actually, the structural and power approaches do have two points of congruence. For one, both approaches are based on the premise that the professions comprise a structurally distinct class, possessing distinguishable attributes. Secondly, both lead to the conclusion that exclusive control over its work is a prime attribute of a profession. The criticism that the structuralists have ignored the attribute of power in professionalism is not substantial. One of the dual meanings imparted to the term "power" by the power advocates is an occupation's exclusive control over the content and conditions of its work. According to this last definition, the structuralists have indeed integrated the attribute of power into their professional model. Although not labeled as "power" the monopolistic component in the structuralist's model symbolizes the concept of power in the meaning of occupational self-control. In this same sense, my earlier article contained forty-three references to "power" broadly conceived. To be sure, in only eight does the word itself appear ; in the remainder synonyms are used (viz., authority, control, dictate, immunity, monopoly and privilege). But none of this is meant to gainsay the sharp antithesis between the structural and power perspectives to professionalism. In the professional model advanced by the power advocates the single and only defining attribute is the monopolistic one. If the structuralists are to be criticized for devaluing "power," then the power advocates are to be criticized for overvaluing it. The power theory of professionalism has the merit and the demerit characteristic of all single-factor explanations of complex phenomena.

The power perspective does have the merit of offering a salutary corrective for the errors to which the structural approach is prone. For one, it compels the structuralists to scrutinize, more than they heretofore have done, the customary sources of their data. These have been by and large the content of publications by and interviews with practitioners of whatever profession is being investigated. But the information thus obtained might well tell us not so much what the profession actually is, but what its members believe it or pretend it or wish it to be. Hence, the face validity of information from such sources requires greater scrutiny than it has perhaps received thus far.[60] Secondly, the power perspective compels a reconsideration of the assumption that, because the professions are essential to the functioning of our society, the interests of the two are, therefore, always compatible. Thus, the lengthy socialization process required for entry into a profession plus its guild-like structure generate a collegial solidarity and a concern for occupational goals which could lead to actions by its members that are profession-centered and conflicting with their responsibility to the community.[61] Also, the profession's monopoly whereby none but its own members may provide a service, is this not a contradiction of the free market principles that govern the distribution of goods and services in our society.[62] Lastly, the power perspective compels the structuralists to question their assumption that the basic attributes of professions are re-enforcing and, accordingly, to prompt them to search for possible anti-theses among them. For example, some students of professionalism have suggested that the expansion of theoretical knowledge and technical expertise in a profession is accompanied by an impersonalization of the service ; that by fostering an increasing absorption on the part of practitioners in the technical aspects of their practice, it results in a diminished concern for their clients as persons. In other words, it is possible that the intellectual component in a profession grows at the expense of the commitment to the service ideal.[63] A similar tension between the service and the monopolistic components has likewise been noted.[64]

Its admitted merit aside, the serious demerit of the power theory is in its single-factor approach to the professions. In positing power as the sole propelling and sustaining factor in professionalism, the power advocates have in their own way over-simplified a complex phenomenon, the very thing for which they criticize the structuralists.[65] Consider briefly what actually is involved in attaining and retaining what Light has aptly characterized as a social contract between the profession and the community. As is true of all such contracts, it has the following features.

First, the contract is the product of a very long series of negotiations between the maturing profession and the community. Wilensky obtained for each of thirteen selected professions the dates of certain crucial events marking stages in the professionalization process.[66] From his data it is deductible that the average (median) time interval from the establishment of the first training school for a nascent profession to the passage of the first licensing legislation, thereby granting it official recognition, is twenty-eight years ; that the average time interval from the organization of its first professional association to the licensing of the profession, is twenty-four years. In other words, the process of professionalization, whereby an aspiring profession achieves its contract with the community, lasts decades. The second feature about the process is that it is completely public. The successes and derelictions of the aspiring profession are topics for review in all media of communication. Its intellectual, ethical and practical claims for a service monopoly are subjects for dissection in legislative hearings and commission reports. It must defend itself against challenges from competing occupations which are threatened by its claims. Goode has amply documented the struggle waged by clinical psychologists during the 1950s and 1960s to gain certification and licensure in the various states against the intense opposition on the part of medically trained psychiatrists.[67]

Third, the basis of every social contract is reciprocity. The profession must be able to offer some *quid pro quo* to obtain the privilege of self-control. What the profession has to offer is a matter not of conjecture but of record, the record of many years' performance. Given the long duration and public character of the professionalization process, there is ample opportunity for all agencies to scrutinize whether the profession has established what Larson has called "its social credit".[68] The community possesses the mechanisms needed to evaluate whether the profession's record demonstrates its members to be, as Goode puts it, responsible masters of their craft.[69] A fourth feature of the social contract between profession and community is that the latter can annul it unilaterally for good cause. If the profession's fund of knowledge is not updated with the times, or if its skills are surpassed by rival occupations, or if its performance comes to have little relation to the needs of society, the service monopoly will be revoked. The very same forces that provided support in the occupation's struggle toward professional status can also withdraw it. From time to time the community subjects given professions to reassessment ; the current public debate over the social role of medicine in the U.S. is a good case in point.[70] Such a reassessment can lead, if not to the termination of the social contract, to its revision resulting in a drastic reduction of the power of the profession concerned.

It is in the light of the above that the power approach should be viewed. Thus, it is undoubtedly true that a powerful sponsor can facilitate an occupation's difficult ascent to professional status and that this has actually been the case for certain professions. But it is more hypothesis than fact that the cognitive and normative elements are generated by the professionalization process primarily as public relations devices for enlisting influential people in high places in the profession's behalf. Several power advocates have gone so far as to characterize professional ethical codes as self-advertisements and frauds.[71] To view the professions through such dark-colored lenses is as simplistic as to view them through rose-tinted ones. Every bit equal to an influential sponsor as a source of power for a profession, is a solid knowledge base combined with a collectivity-orientation. Lacking the latter, resort to the cleverest public relations techniques will hardly persuade anyone, including likely sponsors (who are also potential clients), that the profession possesses what in fact it does not. No occupation can attain and retain professional status on the basis of fraudulent claims. Inasmuch as the efficient functioning of the modern economy and polity is dependent upon professional knowledge and skills, it would be dysfunctional for the community to confer a service monopoly upon an occupation which lacks an adequate cognitive base. And for any authority, including professional authority, to become institutionalized and legitimized, it must, by its very nature, be grounded in a collectivity-orientation.[72]

A NOTE ON THE SOCIAL WORK PROFESSION

The pre-occupation of sociologists with the formulation of a generally acceptable model of the professions has perhaps placed them in the position, doubtless unintended, of being arbitrators of what is and is not a profession.[73] The result has been that the journals of occupations aspiring to professional status are replete with articles which might more appropriately be entitled, "Model, Model on the Wall, Are We a Profession After All ?" A persual of the social work journals over the years yields ample proof of the frequency with which social workers pose this question to themselves. And when they do not, others pose it for them. The answers forthcoming still fail to reflect consensus. Flexner in his classic paper reached the conclusion that social work, as it was practiced in his time, did not meet the criteria for inclusion in the class of professions.[74] In my earlier paper I concluded that social work, while still evolving, nonetheless coincided with my model at sufficient points to warrant its classification among the professions.[75] In the four decades separating the appearances of the two papers social work had, in my view, matured. However, Etzioni, who has studied the less established and newer professions, has reached a negative verdict about social work.[76] On the other hand, Vigilante insists that the current structural model of the professions is inapplicable to social work.[77]

Etzioni and his colleagues have devoted much study to the professions which originated in the late industrial era and are only currently maturing. Included in this group are accounting, administration, counselling, journalism, librarianship, nursing, optometry, pharmacy, social work and teaching. Etzioni points out that these newer professions have understandably been greatly influenced by models which have been derived from studies of the older, well-established professions, and, have, therefore, patterned their own aspirations accordingly. Their collective goal appears to be to achieve a status comparable to that of the established professions.[78] But, Etzioni contends, this aspiration is unrealistic and the goal is unattainable.[79] The reason for this is to be found in what he considers to be the most important component of professionalism, the cognitive. In these newer professions the cognitive infrastructure is relatively weak. The skills employed in their daily work by practitioners in such professions are not grounded in a fully developed theoretical base.[80] What preparatory knowledge they must acquire to qualify professionally is usually not sufficiently abstract, esoteric, organized nor very original. In the case of librarianship, for example, the knowledge consists of large amounts of concrete details.[81] In the case of social work the basic information is a patchwork largely borrowed from the social sciences and allied helping professions. The prognosis that these newer professions will or even can eventually remedy their cognitive deficiencies is not favourable.[82] The plain fact is that these professions are more technical than intellectual disciplines. Their members are urged by Etzioni to recognize the intrinsic imperfections of their professions and to accept a middle status along the occupational continuum above the non-professions but below the old established professions. Etzioni has, therefore, labeled these middle range professions the "semi-professions."[83]

To Vigilante the defect lies not in social work but in the structural model to which social work is constantly compared. In our post-industrial society, so goes his reasoning, the professions have grown both in numbers and variety. The most marked expansion has occurred among what Halmos has called the personal service professions, which includes social work,[84]

The service provided by these professions is a desired change, whether physical, intellectual, psychological or social, in the person of the client/patient. To these newer professions the model of the structuralists is not applicable. The model, having been derived from the old traditional professions, is simply outmoded. To be specific, in the structural model of professionalism there is an exaggerated emphasis on the cognitive, especially the scientific, component. Actually, the presumed superior knowledge of the older professions has become a potent and less than benevolent instrument of social control. By contrast, Vigilante contends, the mark of the true professional is and must be not only nor so much the specialized knowledge that he possesses, but rather what he does with that knowledge, how he uses it.[85] In other words, when classifying an occupation as either a profession or a non-profession, its structural attributes are less important than are the attitudes and behaviours of its members. And the latter, of what do they consist ? On this point Vigilante is not specific, but in this connection Lewis has suggested the following list of attributes : a commitment to the task, a sense of responsibility, a striving for excellence, self-discipline, disinterestedness, and rationality.[86] To summarize, it is not the structure and the organization of the occupation that marks it as a profession, but it is what Hall has called the attitudinal attributes of its members, as reflected in their behaviours in the work setting that makes the distinguishing difference.[87] Posed in such terms, the question whether social work is a profession answers itself.

Etzioni's classification of professions into the full-fledged and the semi-professions is useful. However, it is not new. Years ago Carr-Saunders offered a five-fold classification, with what he labeled "the semi-professions" as one of its categories. The latter, according to him, emphasize precise technical skills rather than theoretical learning, as exemplified in pharmacy and optometry.[88] Etzioni may well have borrowed the label from Carr-Saunders. It is a fact of nature that no class is ever completely homogeneous. The units comprising it invariably differ, either in degree or in kind, with respect to the very attribute(s) that unites them into a class. Hence, the genus sub-divides into species, the type into sub-types. The professions are no exception and attempts to classify them into sub-types merit consideration. Etzioni's negative prognosis regarding the likelihood of a semi-profession evolving to full-fledged status by perfecting its cognitive base may be unduly pessimistic. Transmutation, whereby one social type evolves into another, does occur. Thus, the accountant evolved from the book-keeper, the optometrist from the lens grinder, and the social worker from the friendly visitor. Having themselves evolved from non-professional occupations, cannot certain ones among the semi-professions continue to evolve to full-fledged professions in time ? Goode, accepting Etzioni's classification of social work as a semi-profession, predicts that over the next generation social work will develop a sufficient knowledge base to achieve full professional status.[89]

As for Vigilante, I would not dispute his argument that a certain posture or disposition toward one's work, call it "a professional attitude", is an important attribute of professionalism. I would, however, dispute the implication of his argument that this attribute has been ignored by the structuralists. Far from it, what Lewis lists as the indicators of a distinctive professional attitude are subsumable under the cognitive and the normative components, especially the latter, of the structural model. Thus, my earlier article contained thirty-one references to the professional attitude broadly conceived, i.e., the attitude that members of professions are expected to manifest in their behaviours toward clients, colleagues, and community ; in seven of them terms identical to those on the Lewis list were used. In that same article I devoted a lengthy paragraph to the concept of "calling" in professionalism as manifested in a commitment to one's chosen work and in the personal satisfaction derived from maximal performance.[90] So, the importance of a professional attitude is not in dispute here.

More relevant in this context is Vigilante's perspective upon professionalism as contrasted with Etzioni's and its implications for the social work profession. To Etzioni it is specialized knowledge, the cognitive, which is the principal, the primary component in professionalism ; to Vigilante the cognitive is secondary, subordinate to something more important, a special attitude. In this connection I would strongly caution againts any de-emphasis and downgrading of the knowledge component of professionalism by the leaders of a semi-profession, such as social work, which is already regarded as having a relatively weak cognitive base. To repeat an earlier point, without a solid knowledge base no occupation can lay claim to professional status.[91] The professional is unlike a merchant who has a usable commodity for sale; all he has to offer is his knowledge. As Buckley so well phrased it, without its specialized knowledge a profession would be without a saleable product.[92] It would therefore, be a serious error were social workers to reject as outmoded the knowledge component in the structuralist's model on the grounds that the latter was derived from the now old and traditional professions. As so many others before me have asserted, ours is a knowledge society ; for its efficient functioning it feeds on knowledge, always more and more of it. Hence, I share Vigilante's concern lest professionals employ their esoteric knowledge as a less than benevolent instrument of social control. The remedy for that however, is not to de-emphasize the cognitive but to re-emphasize to normative component in professionalism. The masthead of every professional journal should remind its readers lest they forget that the profession exists by virtue of its social contract with the community. But should the members of any profession begin, from whatever noble motives, to downgrade the importance of knowledge for their craft, they would take the first steps down the road marked "Deprofessionalization."

NOTES AND REFERENCES

1. Greenwood, Ernest, "Attributes of a Profession," *Social Work*, vol. 2, (July 1957) pp. 44-45.
2. Cullen, John B., "Structural Aspects of the Architectural Professions," *Journal of Architectural Education*, vol. 31 (Spring 1978), pp. 18 25.
3. ——, "Professionalism, Licensure, and Examinations," Unpublished, 1977 ; Larson, Magali S., *The Rise of Professionalism, A Sociological Analysis*, University of California Press, 1977 ; Ritzer George, "Professionalisation, Bureaucratisation and Rationalisation," *Social Forces*, vol. 53 (June 1975), pp. 827-34.

4. Goode, William J., "Encroachment, Charlatanism, and the Emerging Professions," *American Sociological Review*, vol. 25 (December 1960), pp. 902 14 ; "The Librarian From Occupation to Profession," in Vollmer, Howard M. and Dr. N. Mills (ed.), *Professionalisation*, Prentice Hall, Englewood Cliffs, N.J., 1966 : "The Theoretical Limits of Professionalisation," Etzioni, Amitai (ed.), *The Semi-Professions and Their Organisation*, Free Press, New York, 1969.
5. Caplow, Theodore, The *Sociology of Work*, University of Minnesota, Minneapolis, 1954, pp. 139-140 ; Denzin, Norman K., and Curtis J. Mettlin, "Incomplete Professionalisation : The Case of Pharmacy," Pavalko, R.M., (ed.), *Sociological Perspectives on Occupations*, F.E. Peacock Publishers, Itasca 1972 ; Hall Richard H., "Professionalisation and Bureaucratisation," *American Sociological Review*, vol. 33, (February 1968), pp. 92-104.
6. Wilensky, Harold L., "The Professionalisation of Everyone ?" *American Journal of Sociology*, vol. 70 (September 1964), pp. 137-58.
7. Goode, *op. cit.*, 1966.
8. Cullen, 1978, *op. cit.*, Daniels, Arlene Kaplan, "How Free Should Profession Be ?" Freidson, Eliot (ed.), *The Professions and Their Prospects*, Sage Publication, Beverly Hills, Calif., 1971 ; Feldbaum, Eleanor G., "Professionalism and Client Orientation," Unpublished, 1977 ; Vigilante, Joseph L., "The Future Dour or Rosy ?" *Social Work*, vol. 17 (July 1972), pp. 3-4.
9. Cullen, 1978, *op. cit.*
10. Laski, Harold J., *The American Democracy*, Viking Press, 1948, p. 564.
11. Freidson E., "The Futures of Professionalism," Stacey, M., *et al.*, (eds.), *Health and the Division of Labour*, Croom Helm, London, 1977.
12. Larson, *op. cit.*, p. xi.
13. Flaxner, Abraham, "Is Social Work a Profession ?" *Proceedings of the National Conference of Charities and Correction*, 1915, pp 576-90.
14. Vigilante, *op. cit.*
15. Reuschmeyer, Dietrich, "Doctors and Lawyers : A Comment on the Theory of Professions," Pavalko, 1972, *op. cit.*
16. Daniels *op. cit.*
17. Engel, Gloria V., and Richard H. Hall, "The Growing Industrialisation of the Professions," Freidson, *op. cit.*
18. Larson, *op. cit.*, p. 38.
19. Ritzer, 1975, *op. cit.*
20. Larson, *op. cit.*, p. 37.
21. Flaxner, *op. cit.*
22. Goode, 1969, *op. cit.*
23. Carr-Saunders, A.M. and P.A. Wilson, "The Emergence of Professions," Nosow, S., and W.H. Form, (eds), *Man Work and Society : A Reader in Sociology of Occupations*, Basic Books, 1962; Reiss, Albert

J. Jr., "Occupational Mobility of Professional Workers," *American Sociological Review*, vol. 20 (December, 1955), pp. 693-700.

24. Larson, *op. cit.*, p 38.
25. Lewis, Lionels S., "The University and Professional Model," Freidson *op. cit.*, 1973.
26. Lortie, Dan C., "The Balance of Control in Elementary School Teaching", Etzioni (ed.) *op. cit.*
27. Those reviewed were : Buckley, John W., "An Exploration of Professional Identity", Stephen E. Loeb (ed.)., *Ethics in the Accounting Profession*, John Wiley, 1978 ; Carr-Saunders and Wilson, *op. cit.*, Reiss, *op. cit.*; Denzin and Mettlin, *op. cit.*; Dyer, Preston M., "How Professional is the BSW Workers ?" *Social Work*, vol. 22, (November 1977), pp. 487-92 ; Epstein, Cynthia F., "Encountering the Male Establishment : Sex-Status Limits on Women's Carcers in the Professions," *American Journal of Sociology*, vol. 75 (May 1970), pp. 965-82; Etzioni, "Preface", Etzioni (ed.), *op. cit.*, Feldbaum, *op. cit.*, Flexner, *op. cit.*, Goode, *op. cit.*, 1960, 1966, 1969 ; Hall, *op. cit.*, Larson, *op. cit.*, Laski, *op. cit.* ; Lewis, *op. cit.* ; Levy, Charles S., "The Context of Social Work Ethics", *Social Work*, vol. 17 (March 1972), pp. 95-101 ; Light, Donalal Jr., "The Structure of Academic Professions", *Sociology of Educations*, vol. 47 (Winter 1974), pp. 2-28; Lorber, Judith, "Review of Professions and Professionalisation" J.A. Jackson (ed.), *Contemporary Sociology*, vol. 1 (November 1972), pp. 533 35 ; Marshall, T.H., "The Recent History of Professionalism in Relation to Social Structure and Social Policy", *Canadian Journal of Economic and Political Science*" vol. 5, (August 1939), pp. 325-40 ; Moore, Wilbert E., "Economic and Professional Institutions", Neil, J. Smelser (ed.), *Sociology : An Introduction*, John Wiley, 1967 ; Nosow, O. Form, *op. cit.*, Parsons, T., "The Professions and Social Structure", *Social Forces*, vol. 17, (May 1939), pp. 457-57 ; Ritzer, *op. cit.* ; Toren, Nina, *Social Work : The Case of a Semi-Profession*, Sage Publications, 1972 : Vollmer and Mills, *op. cit.*, Wilensky, *op. cit.*
28. Freidson, *op. cit.*, 1977 ; Larson, *op. cit.* p. X.
29. Goode, 1969, *op. cit.*
30. Cullen, *op. cit.*, 1977 ; Bukley *op. cit.* ; Goode, 1969 ; Light, 1974.
31. Goode, 1960.
32. Larson, *op. cit.* X.
33 *Ibid.*
34. Nosow and Form, 1962 *op. cit.*
35. Pavalko, *op. cit.*
36. Cullen, 1978.
37. Toren, *op. cit.*
38. Berlant, Jeffrey L., "*Review of the Professions and Their Prospects*", (Eliot Freidson, ed.), *Contemporary Sociology*, vol. 4, (May 1975), pp. 261-63 ; Daniels, *op. cit.*; Freidson, 1977 *op. cit.* ; Ritzer, George, "Power and the Professions", unpublished, 1975.

39. Parsons, T., *The Social System*, Free Press, Glencoe Ill. 1951.
40. Mack, Raymond W., "The Components of Social Conflict", Ralph M. Kramer and Harry Specht (eds.), *Readings in Community Organisation Practice*, Prentice-Hall, 1919.
41. Freidson, "Professions and the Occupational Principle", Freidson (ed.), *op. cit.*
42. Parsons, 1951, *op. cit.*, p. 121.
43. Freidson, 1977, *op. cit.* ; Larson, *op. cit.*, p. xii.
44. Berlant, 1975, *op. cit.* ; Ritzer, 1975.
45. Ritzer, 1975.
46. Goode, 1960, *op. cit.*
47. Larson, *op. cit.*, p. 67.
48. Vollmer and Mills, *op. cit.*,
49. Goode, *op. cit.*, 1969.
50. Berlant, *op. cit.* ; Cullen, 1978, *op. cit.*
51. Daniels, *op. cit.*
52. Cullen, 1978.
53. Zola, Irving Kenneth and Stephen J. Miller, "The Erosion of Medicine from Within", Freidson, 1977, *op. cit.*
54. Freidson, 1977.
55. Haug, Marie R., and Marvin B. Sussman, "Professionalisation and Unionism", Freidson, 1973.
56. Freidson, 1973.
57. Larson, p. xiii.
58. Daniels, *op. cit.* ; Freidson, 1977.
59. Ritzer. *op. cit.*
60. Larson, p. xv.
61. Daniels, *op. cit.*
62. Freidson, *op. cit.*, 1977.
63. Engel, *op, cit.* ; Feldbaum, 1977.
64. Daniels, *op. cit.*
65. Reuschmeyer, Dietrich, "Doctors and Lawyers : A Comment on the Theory of the Professions", Pavalko, 1972, *op. cit.*
66. Wilensky, *op. cit.*
67. Goode, 1960.
68. Larson, *op. cit.*, p. 56.
69. Goode, 1960.
70. Starr, Paul, "Medicine and the Waning of Professional Sovereignity", *Daedalus*, vol. 197 (Winter 1978) pp. 175-92.
71. Daniels, *op. cit.* ; Freidson, 1973.
72. Parson, T., p. 464, *op. cit.*
73. Berlant, *op. cit.*
74. Flaxner, *op. cit.*
75. Greenwood, 1957.
76. Etzioni, 1969, *op. cit.*

77. Vigilante, *op.cit.*
78. Daniels, *op. cit.* ; Larson, *op. cit.*, 38.
79. Etzioni, "Preface", *op. cit* ; Goode.
80. Pavalko, (ed.), *op. cit.*
81. Goode, 1966.
82. Goode, 1969, Lorber, 1972.
83. Etzioni, 1969.
84. Halmos, Paul, "Sociology and the Personal Service Professions," Friedson, 1973, *op. cit.*
85. Vigilante, *op. cit.*
86. Lewis, 1973, *op. cit.*
87. Hall, *op. cit.*
88. Carr-Saunders and Wilson, 1962 *op. cit.* ; Reiss, *op. cit.*
89. Goode, 1969.
90. Greenwood, 1957.
91. Reuschmeyer, *op. cit.* ; Wilensky, *op. cit.*
92. Buckley, 1978,

2

THE SOCIOLOGY OF THE PROFESSIONS : MAJOR THEORETICAL ISSUES

S.M. Dubey

The Sociology of the Professions has emerged as a significant field of study and research within the general frame of sociology. The attention of scholars was drawn to the systematic study of work, occupations and professions with the rise of industrial urbanism in Western Europe. Durkheim in formulating his premises of "division of labour" touched some of the basic issues related with occupations and professions. The emphasis on the need for a separate field to study professions was laid by Carr-Saunders, and Wilson.[1] Among the early authors, Parsons and Marshall also contributed in specifying the concept of "profession."[2] During the last five decades, concerted efforts have been made to analyse occupations and professions from the historical, structural and functional perspectives. The modern professions are closely linked with their pre-industrial settings in Europe. The professions of Western medicine, law and university teaching spread to North America, Latin America, Asia, Africa and Australia from Europe. It is, therefore, essential that in analysing modern professions, their pre-industrial roots in Europe and "dependence" of the "Third World" must be kept in mind. In some of the ancient civilizations like India, China and Arab countries, there is a visible "duality" between traditional and modern professions. At the same time, the functioning of traditional professions has "adjusted" with the demands of the modern professions and the modern professions have adopted to the existing system of health care, resolution of disputes, procedures of imparting education in these traditional societies. This paper has been prepared with the following objectives :—

(a) to understand the historical linkages between the "status professionalism" as existing in pre-industrial setting and "occupational professionalism" as found in the industrial setting in Europe ;
(b) to clarify the concepts and attributes of occupations and professions and to examine the major approaches in the study of professions ;
(c) to explain "professionalisation" and "professionalism" ;
(d) to analyse professional structures as existing in pre-colonial and colonial settings in India ;
(e) to review the major works on professions in India ; and
(f) to indicate emerging trends and research gaps.

For correct understanding of the main issues raised in the sociology of the professions, it is relevant to analyse the historical linkages between the pre-industrial and industrial professional settings in Europe.

The modern professions in Europe are linked with the pre-industrial "status professions". The pre industrial professions were not that significant in the organisation of work though they occupied a high status in the system of stratification. Aristocrates, gentlemen, army officials, clergy, university teachers, lawyers and creative writers belonged to the category of "status professions" in the pre-industrial system. These professions were characterised by high status and their members were supposed not to engage themselves in manual work. They were independent from their employers, clients, economic pressure and even from work.[3] Some of the authors have tried to make a distinction between "status professionalism" and occupational professionalism.[4] The latter is characterised by specialised knowledge, and training. It is coincided with industrial development, technological progress, urban growth and the development of modern labour market in the West. In the medieval period, the universities drew their inspiration from church, as well as, from the guild system.

Professions in pre-industrial Britain were associated with high status clientele. They were patronised by royal court, aristocracy and the nobility. There were certain learned professions linked with church (clergy), universities (teachers), Inns of courts (lawyers) and the Royal Academy of Physicians. In the sixteenth century, the gradual transformation started taking place. Some of the occupations closely linked with guilds started claiming the status of professions. In this category, we may particularly mention, common lawyers, attorneys, barber surgeons, master masons. In the pre-industrial set up, the status of surgeons was much lower than the physicians. The shedding of blood was not approved by the church, therefore, their job was looked down upon. The training in such skills had no regular place in universities. The modern models of professions were derived from pre-industrial criteria of status and pre-industrial ideals, codes and norms linked with the guild system.[5] Apart from the church and the universities which were linked with the learned professions, there was the guild system consisting of the skilled merchants, artisans and the craft men. The members of the different guilds were more rigorously trained than members of the learned professions. The training of learned professions was based on general or theoretical knowledge and their members were the social elite. The guilds were the middle agencies between the authorities, municipalities and the merchants, artisans and the craft men. They may be regarded as the association of specialised workers. Some of the attributes of these guilds, such as, the specialised training, recruitment autonomy, self-governing nature, quality of production and craft ethic, were the sources of the ideology of professionalism which emerged during the nineteenth century.[6]

The first part of the nineteenth century witnessed growing industrialisation, technological progress, scientific development and extension of modernisation. During this period, the ideology of "status professionalism" was gradually transformed into "occupational professionalism." This period witnessed the growth of medicine, law, engineering, teaching, journalism, nursing as modern professions. During this period, professional institutions were more closely linked with work, labour and social stratification. The systematic study of the phenomenon of professions was started by political economists in the eighteenth century in Europe. There were two main bases with emphasis on economic consideration and utility and social moral consideration. According to Spencer, non-coercive division of labour is the basis of modern industrial society.[7] The major bases, for modern professions according to Durkheim is the division of labour expressed through occupations and professions.[8] They are based on material, moral density and increased social solidarity.

There are different schools of thought dealing with professions. A group of authors consider modern professions as the part of industrial work and they try to explain it through the Sociology of Work.[9] Some others tried to develop the Sociology of Occupations which includes the study of professions also.[10] As indicated earlier, a group of authors tried to high-light the need for exclusive study of professions.[11] In the early writings on professions, there was a great deal of discussions on the definition of professions and its distinguishing features. Some others feel that professions cannot be considered as a useful category in sociology because it lacks a distinct referent, and therefore, profession is a term of little scientific value. It is just a symbolic label for a desired status.[12]

Discording the definitional approach and cynicism towards professions, there is growing emphasis on evolving attributes or "ideal types" of professions as prescribed by Max Weber. As regards attributes, professions can be characterised by knowledge-base, specialised training, credentials, licencing, professional code and ethic, service, community-orientation, autonomy and authority for prescription based on theoretical and practical training.

There are two major approaches pertaining to the study of professions :—

(*a*) *Structural-Functional Approach*[13] : The approach found its best exposition in Durkheim's "division of labour" and its function in maintaining "social order" and "cohesion". To avoid "anomic" form of division of labour, Durkheim emphasised on the increasing roles of occupational professional groups and syndicates. They are to his mind a mid-point between the state and the family. He was deriving his inspirations from the communal and corporate ideology of medieval guilds and Roman Collegia. To Durkheim, professions do not represent only the unrestricted economic interests but they are rooted in the moral codes and ethic. Following in Durkheim's footstep, attempt was made to develop the concept of "guild socialism" during the First World War to contain capitalism. A new response against commercialism emerged in the form of professionalism based on moral and communal order. It was believed to provide a sense of power and purpose to individuals. During the inter-war period, special emphasis was laid on contrast between business and profession. Commercial and profit-oriented values related with business were considered as the main cause of the moral degradation of the Western capitalist world and therefore, emphasis was laid on occupational syndicates, guild socialism and professionalism. This point was mainly stressed by Tawney, Saunders and Wilson. On the other hand, Parsons found a great deal of similarities between professions and business. Both were rational, functionally specific and universalistic.

(*b*) *Marxist Approach*[14] : Marxists' view professions as a part of stratification and class structure. In their view, knowledge and professional skills are a commodity having their market value. They can be exchanged for money. It is a fact that professions are based on knowledge and specialised training but the commercial and profit-oriented aspects of professions are concealed in the structural-functional approach of professions.

Theoretically, there are four major aspects of the sociology of the professions which have been focused in recent studies. They may be classified as :—(*i*) concept : (definitions, attributes of professions and occupations) ; (*ii*) process : (professionalisation, education and training, recruitment, licencing, credentials, professional organisations and associations) ; (*iii*) structure : (membership, community, spirit-de corpse) ; (*iv*) professional practices : (professionalism, ideal codes, ethic, ideals).

They may be regarded as cognitive (concept), normative (professionalisation) and evaluative (professionalism) aspects of professions. As regards the question of concepts, definitions and attributes of occupations and professions, we have discussed earlier. With growing claim of different occupations to obtain the status of professions, the definitions and attributes of professions have been changing. Some of the professions, particularly medicine and law acquired the stable status much earlier. The teaching and engineering, has also acquired professional status. They fulfil the attributes of knowledge-base, specialised training, credentials and work autonomy. On the bases of the specialised training, nursing and elementary school teaching claim to attain the status of professions. He prefers to call nursing and elementary school teaching as semi-professions.[15] A growing number of persons with specialised training in medicine, law engineering and teaching have joined salaried jobs in governmental and non-governmental organisations. It is, therefore, that some of the sociologists have tried to classify professions into free-professions (independent practicing lawyers, physicians, surgeons, chartered accountants, architects) and salaried professions (engineers, doctors, university and college teachers, journalists, managers and executives). Due to emergence of salaried class of professionals, the work autonomy an important element of professions—is being eroded day by day. This process has been termed as the bureaucratisation of professions.

Professionalisation indicates increasing claims of occupations to acquire status of professions. Growing specialisation, rising values of expertise, knowledge and skill, modernisation, progressive differentiation and rationalisation of division of labour in industrial society have helped in professionalisation. Through professionalisation the uncommon occupations tend to become real communities whose members share a relatively permanent affiliation and identity, personal commitment, specific interest and general loyalties.[16] A group of Marxist authors believe that the professions, as the part of class system, monopoly over expertise, create structural inequality. Their autonomy depends on links/associations with the ruling class.[17] In the Marxist approach professionalisation is a process by which producers of special services seek to constitute and control a market for their expertise. Professionalisation is, thus, an attempt to translate one order of scarce resource, special energy and skills into another social and economic rewards.[18] The professionalism is used to denote ideology and the value system of professions. The professional ideology in Europe was derived from two diverse traditions—guilds and learned professions. The professional ideology is related with culture and the value system of a society. Social values and the cultural settings, to a great extent, decide attitudes towards work, and provide norms and standards of work, performance and techniques for the application of knowledge.

In view of functionalists, professionalism means observance of codes and ethic, service, community-orientation, affectual-neutrality, rationality and objectivity. According to Marxists professionalism may be characterised by the extension of exchange relations and use value. Thus, the professions are the part of the labour market.[19]

Now, let us have Indian context in view, starting from the ancient period, Indian society was organised around guilds (*Shrenis*), corporations (*Sangha*), occupations and professions. Unfortunately, this fact of Indian society was almost discorded by scholars till the middle of this century. There are two possible academic explanations for such an attitude :

(*a*) Under the impact of indology, there was emphasis on the study of the traditional Hindu ideology (*Dharma, Karma, Punarjanma or re-birth, Purusharthas*), organisational structure (*Varna, Caste, Gotra, Family, Village*) and institutions (*Marriage, Religion, Polity*). In their zeal to explore the textual and ideal notations of Hindu society, indologists ignored the study of work, occupations, professions and their organisational structure i.e., guilds (*Shrenis*) and corporations (*Sangha*).

(*b*) The colonial rule for administrative purpose required detailed reports on caste, tribes and communities, therefore, officially sponsored monographs were prepared on them. This policy, proved to be congenial for anthropological works, dealing with tribes and communities. Thus, guilds, occupations, and professions remained neglected categories.

Historical materials and structural data reveal that the Indian society, since the early period, was organised around occupations (cultivation, craft, manufacturing, construction, business, trade, labour) professional groups (clergy, teachers, astrologers, authors, musicians, artists, architects) and their organisations such as guilds and corporations.[20]

To understand the different aspects of Indian society, indologists, historians and the first generation of sociologists adopted macro-level approach. On the other hand, social anthropologists followed the pattern of micro-level studies (village, tribe), using the methods of intensive fieldwork and participant-observation. By and large, the social anthropological tradition neglected the study of large units (urban communities work, occupations and professions). G.S. Ghurye, R.K. Mukherjee and D.P. Mukherji, the first generation of Indian sociologists showed keen interests in the study of Professions. They fully utilised secondary data and took maximum help of historical materials. In his work *An Introduction to Indian Music*, D.P. Mukherjee, primarily dealing with a form of art, explained the professional and guild aspects of the practitioners of *Hindustani* Music, their links with patrons (Princes, landlords, merchants, middle class), cultural patterns, status symbols, professional training, and their changing professional orientations.[21] Ghurye, in his works *Caste and Class in India* and *Caste, Class and Occupations* used occupation as a category for sociological research. Before the publication of *Caste, Class and Occupations*, he conducted field study on occupations in Bombay.[22] Radha Kamal Mukherjee and Baljeet Singh jointly worked on *A District Town in Transition* where emphasis was laid on the study of occupational structure with the help of census data.[23]

The major Indian works in this field may be divided into three categories (*a*) Historical ; (*b*) Ethnological (study of traditional, professional communities); (*c*) Theoretical (work dealing with modern professions and using concepts and categories of the sociology of professions).

(a) Historical Studies

A few works throw light on the historical, statistical and

organisational status of professions with particular reference to army,[24] medicine[25] and teaching in India.[26] In the nineteenth century, law and partly medicine, started developing as free professions, whereas medicine, civil service, engineering, teaching, nursing and army developed as salaried professions. Christian clergy was added to the existing Hindu priests and Muslim-*Ulema* during this period.

(b) Ethnological Studies

Of late, a number of ethnological studies dealing with several professional communities have been conducted in different parts of India. Since, some of these studies throw light on the pattern and length of training, performance of roles and the relationship between the patrons and clients, they have a value from the point of view of the study of the traditional professions in India. One of the studies makes an interesting study of "Panji and Panjikars of Mithila,"[27] whereas, another study throws light on the socio-economic condition of the *Gangaputra Pandas of Varanasi.*[28] Apart from these two studies conducted in North India, a few studies have been conducted in South India also. Gopalkrishna's study is concerned with the priestly caste of Kerala—the *Nambudris.*[29] Subramaniam studied *Smarthna-Domestic Priests* selected from Mayavaram and two other villages in Madras.[30] The study deals with occupational patterns, education and income of priests and has compared their roles and functions viz-a-viz Brahmans. This study has examined the relationship between the senior and junior priests, their kinship and professional relationship, and teacher-trainees relationship. As regards the training, the priests are trained in a number of *Veda-Pathshalas* (schools) for a period of eight to ten years.

A similar study deals with social organisation of *Dikshitars* the owners, managers and priests of Natraj Temple, living in Chidambaran.[31] Their traditional status, like Nambudris of Kerala, is very high in the caste hierarchy. The above studies reveal that the traditional professions are declining under the impact of modern education, economic pressures and changing perception of status. The sons and daughters of the traditional professional are not found to be interested in their family professions.

(c) Sociological Studies of Modern Professions

In India some of the professions and their members have been studied during the last two decades. The profession of medicine occupies the most attractive field and it has been studied with special reference to social background of doctors, the process of choosing a career, the images of the profession, role-performance, expectations and relationship with clients.[32] There are studies of lawyers and their relationship with their clients.[33] Studies are available on university teachers and intellectuals, their social background, role structure and undergoing modernisation among them.[34] Some attempt has been made to understand the social background of scientists also.[35] Education, professions and mobility has also attracted attention and attempt has been made to understand the rise of professions in the light of modern education, occupational mobility and stratification.[36]

Under the auspices of the Indian Council of Social Science Research trend reports on the Sociology of Law,[37] a monograph on Socio-Legal Research,[38] Sociology of Medicine,[39] and the Sociology of Professions[40] have been prepared. By and large these studies may be divided into two parts :

(*a*) a group of authors have viewed professions as part of stratification system. These studies, by and large took help of the historical materials and secondary data.[41] Ghurye and Dubey supplemented historical materials with field studies.

(*b*) on the other hand, some others have laid emphasis on the study of the normative—evaluative aspects of professions.[42] In these studies, the major emphasis is on the study of roles, role-expectations and role-performance.

Dance and music were important professions in India. Through his perceptive work on Indian music, D.P. Mukherjee has tried to throw light on the guild, procedures of training, class of patrons of musicians performing *Hindustani* music. In the subtle manner, this work breaks new grounds. Its major point may be presented in the form of a paradigm (Table 1).

Similar analysis can be made regarding the traditional medical practitioners, teachers and architects, etc. also.

There are several issues related with "professionalisation" and "professionalism" in India. First of all, they are linked

(TABLE 1)—**PARADIGM**

Origin, Cultural Synthesis, Stages of Transformation, Patrons, Periods, Location of Patrons, Forms of Organisation and Nature of Training of Hindustani Music

(Based on D.P. Mukherjee's work)

1.	Origin and Cultural Synthesis	Folk Music (Northern India)	Religious Music (Traditions of Hindu and Muslims)	Classical Music
2.	Stages of Internal Transformation	Religiosity/ Spirituality	Sumptuous display Bizarre, exotic	Mark of prestige and source of emotional satisfaction
3.	Patrons, Classes and Periods	Priests (at the beginning around four hundred years back)	Princes (Eighteenth century to 1880) Zamindars and Merchants (1880-1930)	Middle Class (after 1930)
4.	Location of Patrons	Temples and Families	(a) Estates Courts in rural surroundings (princes and Zamindars) (b) Urban Centres (Merchants)	Urban Centres (Middle class)
5.	Forms of Organisation	Houses	Guilds	Professional/Formal
6.	Nature of Training	Apprenticeship	Apprenticeship	Music Colleges and Music Universities

with modern education. In Western Europe and Northern America, the ideology of professions adopted itself to the need of industrial capitalism, modern science and technology. On the other hand, colonial rule and modern education helped in the rise and consolidation of modern profession in India. Under the impact of the colonial rule, Western education and English as the medium of instruction, some sort of ''schism'' was created between the traditional professions—already existing in pre-colonial India and the modern professions which emerged under the impact of the colonial rule and Western education. This professional duality is mainly responsible for lowering the position of traditional practitioners of different professions.

The previous century witnessed the emergence of professions, whereas, the current century has experienced the consolidation of professions in India. With the widespread network of universities, medical, engineering and law colleges, there is an increase in the number of professionals. In the same proportion there is a widespread base of clients also. The availability of facilities for professional training has caused occupational change and upward social mobility. Another visible trend in India is the emergence of professional power linked with the formation and consolidation of professional bodies and organisations. There are bodies like Bar Council of India, Medical Council and Press Council of India. They determine the codes, norms and standards for entry, recruitment, performance of roles etc. for members of their professions. They are more concerned with normative aspects of professions. On the other hand, there are organisations of doctors, lawyers, engineers, chartered accountants, university teachers, higher secondary and primary level teachers, journalists etc. which stand to safeguard the professional interests of their members. In the colonial period, there were several confrontations between lawyers and administration. The nationalist press and the colonial administration were at daggers drawn against each other. In the post-Independence period, professional power has been demonstrated quite often.

The "ideal types" of "professionalism" such as, service, codes, community-orientation and fraternity have been eroded by the ideology of free competition, market-orientation, profit motive and exchange relations. There is a visible internal stratification among the professionals.

There are several gaps in professional studies. First of all, no serious sociological attempt has been made to understand the entry procedures, structure and functions of guilds and professions in pre-colonial India. Caste as a "concept" or a "methodological tool" is of little significance in understanding this phenomenon. The structural linkage between the traditional and modern professions is also of significance which has received little sociological attention. Professions of medicine and law have drawn attention for sociological studies but teaching, engineering, journalism are still neglected areas. In the post-Independence period, the recruitment base of professionals has been widened. The constitutional safeguards, policy of protective discrimination and democratisation of education has tremendously contributed in this process. Naturally, the share of disadvantaged groups i.e. Scheduled Castes, Scheduled Tribes, Backward Classes and women have been gradually increasing in professional fields. No attempt has been made for exclusive study of professionals belonging to these groups.

In recent times, management has emerged as an important occupational category. It derives its occupational culture from professions "as well as, bureaucracy the structure and function of emerging occupational culture linked with management, is also a fascinating field for future studies."

NOTES AND REFERENCES

1. Carr-Saunders, A.M., *Professions : Their Organisation and Place in Society*, The Clarendon Press, Oxford, 1928 ; Carr-Saunders, A.N, and Wilson, P.A , *The Professions*, The Clarendon Press, Oxford, 1933.
2. Parsons, T., "Remarks on Education and the Professions," *International Journal of Ethics*, vol. 47, 1937, p. 365; Marshall, T.H., "The Recent History of Profession in Relation to Social Structure and Social Policy", *Canadian Journal of Economics and Political Science*, vol. 5 (August 1939), pp. 325-40.
3. Marshall, *Ibid*.
4. Elliot, Philip, *The Sociology of the Professions*, Macmillan, London, 1972.

5. Larson, M.S., *The Rise of Professionalism*, University of California Press, London, 1977.
6. Mills, C.W., *White Collar*, Oxford University Press, New York, 1956.
7. Spencer, Herbert, *The Principles of Sociology*, Appleton, New York, 1986.
8. Durkheim, Emile, *The Division of Labour in Society*, Macmillan, New York, 1933.
9. Caplow, Theodore, *The Sociology of Work*, University of Minnesota Press, Minneapolis, 1954.
10. Taylore, Lee, *Occupational Sociology*, *Oxford University Press*, New York, 1968 ; Hall, R.H., *Occupations and the Social Structure*, Prentice Hall, Englewood Cliffs, N.J., 1969.
11. Saunders and Wilson, 1933, *op cit.* ; Parsons, T., "The Professions and the Social Structure," *Social Forces*, vol. 17, 1939, pp. 457-67 ; Marshall, *op. cit.*
12. Cogan, Morris L., "The Problem of Defining a Profession," *The Annals of the American Academy of Political and Social Science*, vol. 297, 1955, pp. 105-111 ; Habenstein, R.W., "Critique of Professions as a Sociological Category" *Sociological Quarterly*, vol. 4, 1963, pp. 291-300.
13. Durkheim, *op. cit.*, 1933, Tawney, R.H., *The Acquisitive Society*, Harcourt, Brace, New York, 1920 ; Carr-Saunders, 1928, *op. cit* , Carr-Saunders and Wilson, 1933, *op. cit.* ; Parsons, 1939, *op. cit.*
14. Mills, *op. cit.* ; Larsons, *op. cit.*
15. Etzioni, Amitai, (ed.), *The Semi-Professions and Their Organisation*, Free Press, New York, 1969.
16. Goode, William J., "Community Within a Community : The Profession," *American Sociological Review*, vol. 22, 1957, pp. 194-200; Jackson, J.A., (ed.), Professions and Professionalisation, Cambridge University Press, Cambridge, 1970, pp. 3-15.
17. Polyany, K., *The Great Transformation*, Beacon Press, Boston, 1957 ; Freidson, E., *Professional Dominance*, Atherton, New York, 1970 ; Johnson, T.J., *Professions and Power*, Macmillan, London, 1972 ; Halmos, P., *The Personal Service Society*, Schocken Books, New York 1970 ; Larson, *op. cit.*
18. Larson, *op. cit.*
19. Larson, *op. cit.*
20. Thaper, Romila, *A History of India*, Penguin Books, 1974, pp. 145-159 ; Spear, *A History of India*, Penguin Books, 1973, pp. 47, 95-99 169 and 223.
21. Mukherji, D.P., *An Introduction to Indian Music*, Pune, 1945.
22. Ghurye, G.S., *Caste and Class in India*, 1950.
23. Mukherjee, Radha Kamal, and Baljeet Singh, *A District Town in Transition*, Asia Publishing House, Bombay, 1965.

24. Broom, A., *History of the Rise and Progress of the Bengal Army*, 1850.
25. Royle, J.P., *An Essay on the Antiquity of Hindu Medicine*, 1937 ; Wise, T.A., *Hindu System of Medicine*, 1945 ; *History of Medicine*, 1967 ; Crawford, D.G., *History of Indian Medical Service, 1600-1913*, 1913 ; Henry, *Medical Profession in India*, 1923.
26. Adam, William, *Vernacular Education in Bengal and Bihar*, 1835.
27. Jha, Ugra Nath, *Genealogies and Genealogists of Mithila*, Kishore Vidya Niketan, Varanasi, 1980.
28. Singh, R.B., *Gangaputra Pandas of Varanasi : A Study of Their Social and Economic Conditions*, Unpublished Ph.D. Thesis, Gorakhpur, 1967.
29. Gopal Krishna, Ph.D. Thesis, Madras University, Madras, 1967.
30. Subramaniam, *Smartna : Domestic Priest*. Madras, 1974.
31. Gomathinayagam, 1974.
32. Madan, T.N., "Who Chooses Modern Medicine and Why," *Economic and Political Weekly*, vol. 4, 1969, "Doctors in North Indian City: Recruitment ; Role Perception and Role Performance," Saberwal, Satish (ed.), *Beyond the Village*, Indian Institute of Advanced Study, Simla, 1972 ; Oommen, T.K., *Doctors and Nurses*, Macmillan Delhi, 1978, Venkataratnam, R., *Medical Sociology in Indian Setting*, Macmillan, Madras, 1979.
33. Buxbaum, D.C. (ed.), *Traditional and Modern Legal Institutions in Asia and Africa*, Brill, Leidon ; Das, Veena, "Sociology of Law," *ICSSR Trend Report*, New Delhi, 1973.
34. Shils, E., *The Intellectuals Between Tradition and Modernity : The Indian Situation*, The Hague, 1961 ; Singh, Y., "Academic Role Structure and Modernisation : A Study of University Teachers," Saberwal, *op. cit.*
35. Sri Chandra, *Scientists : A Social Psychological Study*, Oxford and IBH Publishing Co., Bombay, 1970.
36. Dubey, S.M., *Social Mobility among the Professions in a City in Transition*, Popular Prakashan, Bombay, 1975.
37. Das, Veena, *op. cit*
38. Bakshi.
39. Ahluwalia, A., "Sociology of Medicine," *ICSSR Trend Report*, 1972, *op. cit.*
40. Sharma S.L., *Sociology of Professions*, 1980.
41. Ghurye, 1961, *op. cit.* ; Misra B.B., *The Indian Middle Classes*, Oxford University Press, 1961 ; Bakshi, 1975 *op. cit.* ; Dubey, 1975, *op. cit.* ; Jeffery, R., *Western Medicine in India : A Case of Professionalisation*, A Working Paper, 1976.
42. Madan, 1972, *op. cit.* ; Singh, *op. cit.* ; Oommen, *op. cit.* ; Venkatratnam, *op. cit* ; Chandani, Ambika, *The Medical Profession : A Sociological Exploration*, Jainsons, Delhi, 1985 ; Khanna, Kirti, *Academic Role Structure and Modernisation*, Unpublished, Ph. D. Thesis, The University of Jodhpur, Jodhpur.

3

SOME CRITICAL REFLECTIONS ON THE PREVAILING OUTLOOK OF PROFESSIONS IN INDIA

C. RAJAGOPALAN

INTRODUCTION

The emergence of professions and their phenomenal growth in recent times, is generally understood as a natural response to the demands imposed by the ever-increasing process of the division of labour and specialization inherent in modern science and technology. The process of professionalization seems to have so far advanced that its influence now extends even into the political organization. Carr-Saunders had anticipated this development and observed as early as 1928 : "In fact, the entrance of professional associations into questions of public policy, whether on their own initiative or by invitation of the government, is one of the hopeful means of bringing the expert into the service of democracy—perhaps the most important problem in the realm of political organization today."[1]

Parsons also saw in the recent growth of professions, the emergence of a new social force, which he was inclined to regard as a universal trait of all modern societies, including the socialist ones. "It is my view," he observed : "that the professional complex, though obviously incomplete in its development, has already become the most important single component in the structure of modern societies. It has displaced first the "State", in the relatively early modern sense of that term, and more recently, "the capitalistic" organization of the economy. The massive emergence of the professional complex, not the special status of the capitalistic or socialistic modes of organization is the crucial structural development in twentieth century society."[2] The rise of modern professions, according to Parsons, is reminiscent of the process of bureaucratisation earlier, which became an essential feature of both capitalist and communist societies.[3] He tries to substantiate this by stating that "professional men are neither 'capitalists' nor 'workers', nor are they typically governmental administrators or "bureaucrats". They certainly are not independent peasant proprietors, or members of the small urban proprietary groups."[4]

It is clear that the emergence of professions and professionalization was welcomed in the beginning as an indispensable functional requirement designed to meet a vital need in the rapidly and continuously developing modern society. How far this early assessment of the role of professions in modern society has been borne out by subsequent developments, is a question which need to be carefully examined. Parsons' observation tends to convey the misleading impression that professions constitute a great social formation, comparable to the bourgeoise or the managerial class, held together by common interests. It is quite plausible to argue that what are called professions comprise of a multitude of discrete and diversified occupations ranging from divinity to larceny,[5] which have little in common, save the label.

Whatever may be the situation obtaining in the capitalistic societies, professions do not seem to have the same role and to perform the same functions in other types of social systems. It is, therefore, not legitimate to see in the emergence of modern professions, as Parsons does, a process analogous to the development of corporations and the rise of professional management leading to the divorce between the ownership and control of economic enterprises, which is a feature peculiar to the capitalistic society. This incidentally serves as a warning against the possible dangers inherent in attempting universal sociological generalizations which seek to transcend the diversities of social systems. A structural element which is functional in a given social system need not perform an identical function, or for that matter even be functional at all, in a social system of a different type. On the contrary, it is quite possible that it may even prove to be positively dysfunctional. Most studies of sociology of professions in the West presuppose a mature liberal, capitalistic social order as natural and hence they may have little or no relevance to the socialistic or developing societies.

The Meaning of Profession

Before proceeding to examine the role of professions in the contemporary Indian society, which is the main task of this paper, it is essential to have a fairly clear idea of the meaning of professions. The question of what constitutes the essential characteristics of a profession, has been rendered complex by the claims put forth in recent times by a multitude of occupational groups to professional status. While it is easy to cite historical and contemporary examples of what may be regarded as professions *par excellence*, any attempt to conceptualise professions seems to run into serious difficulties.[6] The logical difficulty involved in defining professions also seems to reflect at least in part, the ambiguous and uncertain status of many so-called professions.[7] The clamour for professional status and recognition on the part of many occupational groups, incidentally serves to highlight the salient fact that professions somehow command great prestige in contemporary society and that professional status is a highly sought after value. It is important to go into the roots of this question of why professions are invested with prestige and this question can hardly be answered satisfactorily, so long as the meaning of professions is not properly grasped.

The difficulty involved in defining professions is sometimes sought to be circumvented by substituting it with the term professionalization.[8] It is held that professionalization is not an all or nothing affair, but is essentially a process admitting differences of degree, so that whether a given occupation is a profession or not depends on the extent to which it is professionalized. This view seems to suggest, erroneously enough, that it is easier to define professionalization than profession.

Another attempt to overcome the definitional difficulty has been to conceive of professions as an ideal type. It is, however, important to realise in this context that in any attempt to construct an ideal type of professions, the relative importance of the different constitutive elements may vary from time to time. Some of the occupations which originated as true professions in the past exhibit or share these characteristics to a markedly less extent today, while certain others which were not and, would not have been treated as professions in the past, are now acknowledged to be unmistakably so.

Tracing the evolution of professions, Carr-Saunders has observed that a profession emerges when "a number of persons are found to be practising a definite technique founded upon a specialised training."[9] According to him, "a profession may be defined as an occupation based upon specialised intellectual study and training, the purpose of which is to supply skilled service or advice to others for a definite fee or salary."[10] He goes on to add that in the past the typical or only true professions were those in which the practitioners were free-lancers, who were remunerated by a fee But, today if we were to go by this criterion, a great number of professions will not qualify to be treated as such. He, however, concludes that while certain occupational groups are unambiguously professions, in case of others it is a matter of degree.

Greenwood, who also shares the view that the difference between professions and non-professions is a matter of degree and not quality, has attempted to construct an ideal type of professions in terms of five elements. These are (1) systematic theory, (2) authority, (3) community sanction, (4) ethical codes, and (5) a culture.[11] He is, however, careful to add that some of these characteristics like systematic theory, community sanction and culture are by no means exclusive to professions. This rider suggests that his ideal type is not in any way superior to Carr-Saunders' definition mentioned earlier. Elaborating the last element in his ideal type, Greenwood has observed that what distinguishes a profession from other occupations is the fact that the former implies a career and a career is essentially a *calling*, a life devoted to "good works."[12] To MacIver, the essential characteristics of professions are (a) the ideal of service, (b) an ethical code, and (c) the welfare of society.[13]

It was mentioned earlier that professions command great prestige in society. It may be interesting to inquire into the source of this prestige as it might offer a clue to decipher the meaning of professions. It has already been stated that the emergence of professions is closely associated with the rise of modern science and technology and was a direct response to the demand for specialisation. These specialists sooner or later form associations to protect their interests. Carr-Saunders lists three major motives behind the formation of associations. These are, firstly to secure a monopoly for members of the association to practise that profession; secondly to prescribe and enforce a proper standard of professional and honourable conduct ; and thirdly, to improve the status of the profession, which among other things, is a function of the monetary rewards offered by it.[14] This shows that professional associations share to some extent the characteristics of a guild. This however, is not accidental if it is remembered that the earliest professions were all organised more or less on the lines of the medieval guild.

Professionalization

Two facts seem to emerge clearly from the various attempts to elucidate the meaning of professions. Firstly, profession implies a body of theoretical knowledge, to be acquired through a prescribed course of intellectual training. Secondly, professions are tightly organised bodies, which among other things, set the standards of proficiency, regulate entry into the profession, grant licence for its practice, secure monopoly over its practice, and prescribe a code of conduct for the members in their dealings with one another as well as with the clients.

The first of these characteristics serves to distinguish profession from all manual occupations. Even when the practice of a profession involves some manual work, it is nevertheless founded on a body of theoretical lore. Thus, professions invariably have an intellectual orientation, which distinguishes them from non-professions. It is important to examine carefully this intellectual or theoretical basis of professions, since it has a close bearing on the problem of the proliferation of professions in recent times.[15] There is no doubt that in the beginning the possession of theoretical knowledge definitely served to set apart the amateur and the dilettante from the trained and cultivated professional. This is true especially of medicine and dentistry in the past. However, with the advancement of science and technology which revolutionised the occupational structure, and with which the rise of professions is closely associated, a minimum of formal education, either of the liberal type or of a specialised and technical nature, became an indispensable pre-requisite for entry into most occupations. Consequently, in the modern industrial society, few occupations are open to an uneducated person. In other words, theoretical or intellectual training has become the universal feature of the occupational system of a technologically advanced society,[16] and consequently this factor no longer serves as a satisfactory criterion to distinguish professions from non-professions. This is reflected in the indiscriminate attempts by various occupational groups to Claim professional status, as well as in the universal trend towards scientism and rationalisation.

This process has been aided and accelerated by the second feature of profession mentioned above. One of the powerful means by which most occupational groups seek to get their claim to professional status conceded is organised might, which can sometimes compensate for all other deficiencies including the lack of a body of theoretical knowledge. Though Carr-Saunders had listed the various motives behind the formation of professional associations, all these appear to have been overshadowed by the monopolistic interest which has emerged as the one single dominant trait of professional bodies today. While in the past, initiative to form associations generally came from the most skilled, competent and distinguished practitioners, obviously with a view to keeping the charlatans out and securing the profession a respectable status in society. Today, it is mostly the mediocres and the average members who are eager to form associations, mainly because they are unable to withstand free competition and survive individually and independently. If professional associations have succeeded in containing internal competition, the community at large had to pay a ransom, by way of forfeiting its freedom to reject the services of the professionals.

It was observed earlier that according to Greenwood, a profession comes to occupy a respectable place in society only when it enjoys the sanction of the community. But it must be admitted that there is no explicit procedure for according community sanction to a profession, unless it is through the grant of a charter or by an act of the legislature. This is, however, true of only very few professions like medicine, dentistry, law, etc., and the bulk of professions lack such legislative sanction. The success of most professions, therefore, depends on the extent to which they are able to extort the patronage of the community. In the face of an aggressively organised occupational group which successfully prevents the outsiders from intruding into it, the community is left with no choice but to patronise the organised group, even if the service it renders is of sub-standard quality. Thus, in actual practice, the power and strength of an organization turn out to be the crucial determinant of its prestige. In this respect, a professional association is scarcely distinct from a trade union or a political party, and like the latter its power is in direct proportion to the degree it is free from internecine dissensions and competition from rival organisations. Many professional associations are so busily preoccupied with the quest for power, which is the real source of their prestige, that they are left with little time or inclination to attend to the other functions.[17]

Though professionalization originally began in response to the social and economic impact of modern science and technology, it is not certain if professional associations are able to keep pace with the constant and continuous advancement of modern science. The modern society is characterised by frequent explosion of knowledge accompanied by rapid obsolescence of skill. How far professional associations with their obsession with monopolistic privileges, restrictive practices and the inward-looking guild-like attitude, are geared to meet such transformations is a matter which is indeed open to doubt.[18] Besides, the development of vested interests may often militate against the ready acceptance and absorption of new ideas, lest it undermines the power of those who control the organization. In the absence of competition within the organisation, it is not incumbent upon the members to keep abreast of the developments in their field, since they have a life-time licence to practise the profession, once they are admitted into it. This may pose a serious problem to the clientele, in so far as they will be placed at the mercy of professionals whose skill and knowledge may be highly outdated and this danger is especially acute in a rapidly developing society.

The Classical Professions in India

In the light of the foregoing considerations, it is not certain, if the indiscriminate growth of professions has, after all, been an unmixed blessing, as originally visualised. The discrepancy between the ideal typical conception of profession and the way in which many professions are really found to function in India, is so alarmingly wide as to render their very title to professional status of exceedingly doubtful value. While this is to some extent understandable in the case of the relatively new professions, it can hardly be justified in the case of the oldest professions of medicine, law and teaching. These are not merely the oldest, but at the same time also the true classic model of professions and are often described as the learned professions. A consideration of some of the recent developments within these professions in India might hopefully yield some valuable insight into the problems of professionalization and the role of professions in contemporary society.

Though medicine, law and teaching along with divinity are the oldest and true models of professions, there are important differences among them which is essential to note. Both medicine and law acquired professional status in India under an act of the legislature and therefore their respective professional bodies, viz. the Indian Medical Council (IMC) and the Indian Bar Council (IBC) enjoy statutory recognition. This is lacking in the case of teaching. While the IMC and the IBC are responsible for prescribing and enforcing certain minimum standards in their respective fields, in the case of teaching this responsibility is vested in a variety of bodies, depending on the level and kind of education. Again, while the IMC and the IBC prescribe certain code of conduct for its members, the infringement of which can lead to expulsion from the profession, such a provision is conspicuous by its absence in the teaching profession. Unlike the medical and legal professions, the members of the teaching profession have no scope for independent private practice and therefore they have been reduced to the status of employees. The fact that in spite of these differences, teaching has been counted among the professions right from the beginning, seems to suggest that the most important characteristics are secondary and optional. This conclusion is also further supported by the recent tendency on the part of many occupational groups to advance the claim that their occupations have a theoretical or scientific foundation. But in reality their sole interest in securing professional status is to exercise monopolist control over its practice. These associations show very little concern either for the conduct of their members or for the quality of service they render to the society. In the remainder of this paper I shall attempt to illustrate what has so far been discussed with particular reference to the three classical professions.

In sheer size, legal profession in India is second only to the teaching profession. Yet no profession perhaps presents a more dismal and unedifying picture than the legal profession.[19] Legal education in India has been in a most chaotic and anarchical condition. Most law colleges in the country are part-time evening colleges with hardly any full-time or permanent teaching faculty. There is apparently no limit to the intake of students. The result has been the phenomenal mushrooming of sub-standard institutions and the quality of education imparted in such institutions can easily be imagined.

The legal profession has grown to such phenomenal proportions[20] that the Bar Council and its subsidiaries find it difficult to maintain a surveillance over the conduct of its members. The fact that the bulk of the members of this profession are unable to earn a steady and satisfactory living is one of the root causes many of the evil practices which have crept into it.[21] This problem has been further aggravated by the limited opportunities for salaried employment, which this profession offers.

The phenomenal increase in litigation has burdened the courts with arrears, leading to unconscionable delay in the disposal of cases. Instances are not wanting where cases have not been disposed of, even long after the life-time of the parties. Moreover, so many new legislations are being enacted every year that many lawyers and most judges are blissfully ignorant of many of the new enactments. The professions is also plagued with the problem of attracting suitable candidates to the bench. The remuneration, and working conditions of the judges are so unattractive that a successful lawyer is seldom tempted to enter the bench, which consequently is filled largely with mediocres.

The legal profession is also perhaps the most conservative among all professions.[22] Legislation as an instrument of social change has met with but limited success in India. The normal function of law has been to legalise the changes which have been long under way. The complex procedures involved in initiating a legal process, the devious and dilatory nature of this process, the ruinously expensive nature of litigation, the circumlocutory and obfuscating legal language and the undue emphasis placed on precedents, have all contributed to make law an essentially conservative institution, resistant to change.

Lastly, we may raise a few questions concerning the social role and responsibility of the legal profession. Has the legal profession made any worthwhile contribution to minimise crime or litigation ? What is its contribution to free legal aid especially in a country where the common man is disabled by crippling poverty and inherited ignorance from exercising his ordinary legal rights ? What is the background of the people who enter into this profession and what is their dominant motive ? Does the legal profession continue to command the same respect and confidence as in the past ? With judges' offices going abegging, what respect and prestige does the judiciary command ? These are but a few of the questions which readily come to mind when one reflects upon the professional status of law in the contemporary Indian society.

Unlike law which still continues to be by and large a profession founded on independent private practice, medicine is rapidly becoming employment oriented. To be sure, private practice is very much in vogue, but the bulk of the medical personnel are employees either in the service of the government or private agencies. In sharp contrast to the Bar Council, the Indian Medical Council has been following a restrictive policy ostensibly with a view to preventing the indiscriminate growth of the medical profession. This has exposed the medical profession to the charge of being unresponsive to the needs of the society. In the face of the burgeoning demand for medical practitioners necessitated by the steady growth of population, the stringent conditions laid down by the IMC for the establishment of new medical colleges have been criticised as indirect attempts to safeguard the vested interests of its members. Medicine perhaps offers the best example of a profession which places self-interest above the interest of the society.[23]

Judged in terms of the health needs of the country, the allopathic system has clearly failed to supply adequate number of trained medical personnel. This failure is all the more glaring in the rural areas. The recent attempt to introduce a minimum period of compulsory rural service for all new medical graduates, as is only to be expected, did not find favour with the medical profession. This resistance is easily understandable, if we consider the background and the motivations of the people who succeed in gaining entry into the medical colleges.[24] A recent study has reported evidence of high degree of inbreeding in the medical professions.[25] The medical profession in India has also the dubious distinction of being confronted with the paradoxical situation in which an acute shortage of doctors is found to co-exist with large scale unemployment among medical practitioners.[26] The fact that most medical practitioners look to government and other private agencies for employment instead of thinking in terms of setting up their own private practice points to a significant emerging trend in the orientation of the medical profession.

The indifference of the medical profession to the health needs of the vast rural masses and the criminal abdication of its social responsibility are also evident from its reaction to the proposal for a medical course of a shorter duration, somewhat similar to the L.M.P. of the past. This proposal was aimed at meeting the health needs of the rural population, since it is now well recognised that the five-year M.B.B.S. is too long and too expensive to be within the reach of none but the very affluent, whose aim on completion of the course is to encash their investment as quickly as possible. Once again, the reaction of the IMC was predictably negative.

Another alternative scheme envisaged to meet the shortage of medical personnel and the growing demand for health care was the revival of the indigenous systems of medicine.[27] Some of them like *Ayurveda* are very ancient and have successfully served the health needs of the people for centuries. As a matter of fact, it was only with the introduction of allopathy on which was lavished undue and extravagant governmental patronage that the indigenous systems began to show signs of decline. This scheme also had to encounter stiff and prolonged opposition from organised medical lobbies.[28] Instances such as these serve to expose the underlying philosophy of the medical profession and also provide an insight into the way in which it perceives its role in relation to the larger society.

It was stated earlier that the IMC has been more active and alert in jealously guarding its monopolistic interests by restricting entry into the profession. Recent developments seem to indicate that even this power of the IMC is being rapidly eroded. The rise and spread of a new brand of private medical colleges, where admission is based solely on money power instead of merit or aptitude and the failure of the IMC to stem this pernicious and cancerous development, constitutes a sordid reflection upon the waning prestige of the medical profession in India.[29] The extent of the damage caused to the prestige of the medical profession in India can be gauged from a recent report according to which medical graduates from India are debarred from practice in some foreign countries until they pass a qualifying examination conducted by them. If the present trend in medical education continues unchecked, the day may not be far when medical graduates are denied recognition even in this country, may be not by the IMC, but by the larger society.

Lastly, let me briefly reflect upon the state of the teaching profession. It is not clear whether the teaching profession includes teaching at all levels beginning with the primary or only university and college level teaching. Technically speaking school teaching alone is entitled to be considered as a profession since one of its essential requirement is formal training in teaching and teacher training institutions all over the world are regarded as professional institutions. It was mentioned earlier that teaching in India possesses none of the characteristics conventionally associated with a profession, save perhaps one. In view of these glaring limitations, it is by no means an easy task to make an assessment of its working as a profession. Unlike law and medicine in which there is scope for private practice. teaching profession subsists entirely on salaried employment and mostly under the government.

The teaching profession in India has no central organization comparable to the IMC or the IBC. The teachers are organised according to the institutions in which they are employed and these associations are affiliated to state or national level federations. These teachers associations function like trade unions and whatever power they wield today is derived not so much from their professional standing, as from their tendency for unionisation.[30] Like all trade unions, the teachers associations have been concerned mostly with the economic interests of their members. They have done very little either to improve the image of the teacher or to raise the standard of education in the country. Unlike the legal and the medical profession, the teachers' associations are divided along different political ideologies. This right to espouse and advocate an ideology is obviously derived from the doctrine of academic freedom, which is a distinguishing feature of the teaching profession.

The educational scene in India presents a picture of indiscipline, lawlessness and anarchy. Of late, educational standards have plumetted to an all time low. The students have lost their trust in the teachers and the teachers have lost their credibility. The frequent disturbances and the general atmosphere of tension which mark the climate in the campuses, the growing cult of violence among the students promoted both by professional and teacher politicians, the practice of involving students in the faction fight among the teachers, etc. are but a few of the disturbing developments taking place in the field of education in India.[31] The fact that the teaching profession has rarely expressed any concern or sensitivity to these problems betrays the lack of a sense of social obligation.

Another unique feature of the teaching profession which marks it off from all other professions is that it is singularly free of any vested interests, in so far as it does not seek to exercise any monopolistic privileges. It was mentioned earlier that the teaching profession has not evolved any ethical code to regulate the conduct of its members. With teachers being salaried employees, even the onus of prescribing and maintaining standards of proficiency has been passed on to the organizations employing them. As teachers associations are more effective at the level of the organizations in which they are employed and the larger federations into which they are affiliated, the teachers owe their primary loyalty to these bodies rather than to the profession. In short, the teaching profession offers an excellent example of the kind of transformation which a profession is bound to undergo when it is increasingly bureaucratised and becomes employment oriented. One of the significant trends in this transformation is the gradual replacement of the professional bond by the trade union affinity, which in the long run tends to cut across professional boundaries.[32]

This process can be seen at work in medicine which is being rapidly bureaucratised and turned into salaried employment. Medical practitioners employed in large-scale organization have dual membership and divided loyalty and as the processes of bureaucratisation and unionization gain momentum, their loyalty to the organization-based employees association is likely to claim precedence over their loyalty to the profession.[33]

Conclusions

Professions are witnessing a process of phenomenal growth, the rate of which seems to vary more or less in direct proportion to the advancement in science and technology. This growth includes not only the expansion of the older professions, but also the birth of many new and unheard ones. Besides, many occupational groups are also advancing their claim to professional status. In this process many of the principles and norms which governed professions in the past are found to be either relaxed or completely undermined. Therefore, the attempt to study professions in a dynamic and rapidly developing society in terms of a static conception is bound to prove miserably inadequate and misleading.[34] Side by side with the ongoing changes in the society, there appears to be a corresponding change in the role, relevance and functions of professions as well. It is important not to lose sight of this dynamic character of the growth of professions and professionalization.

Though in principle, professions may be same or similar everywhere, in their actual functioning, they reveal significant differences in different social systems. The role of professions in the socialistic society evidently differs from the manner in which professions function and are organised in a capitalistic society. Likewise, significant differences may be found in the way professions function in the developed and the developing societies.

The progressive transformation of professions from a body of independent practitioners into a class of salaried employees has had damaging effects upon the ethical and social service aspect of professions. This transformation bears close analogy to the process whereby the independent medieval artisans were reduced to the status of wage-earners in the wake of the industrial revolution. The industrial workers are no longer organised on the basis of their trades, but in terms of the plant and industry and are affiliated to the various national and international federations. If the present trend continues, professions are likely to follow the same course and there are unmistakable signs in this direction. The culmination of this process might entail such changes in the very philosophy and practice of professions, which it is difficult to foresee at this juncture.

NOTES AND REFERENCES

1. A.M. Carr-Saunders, and P.A. Wilson, "The Professions", *Encyclopaedia of the Social Science*, 1933 vols. XI-XII, p. 479.
2. Talcott Parsons, "The Professions", *International Encyclopaedia of the Social Sciances*, vol. 12, 1968, p. 545.
3. *Ibid.*
4. *Ibid.*, p. 536.
5. Edwin H. Sutherland, *The Professional Thief*, The University of Chicago Press, Chicago, 1937.
6. According to Seymour, attempts to define a profession in terms of characteristics can easily become an exercise in semantics, Seymour, F.J.C. "What is Professionalism ?" *The A.T.A. Magazine*, vol. 43, No. 10, June 1963, pp. 20-23.
7. *Ibid.*, pp. 126-127.
8. Howard M. Vollmer, and Donald L. Mills (eds.), *Professionalism*, Englewood (Cliffs), N.J. Prentice Hall, 1966.
9. A.M. Carr-Saunders, *Professions : Their Organization and Place in Society*, The Clarendon Press, Oxford, 1928, p. 4.
10. *Ibid.*
11. Earnest Greenwood, "Attributes of a Profession," *Social Work*, vol. 2, no 3, July 1957, pp. 44-45.
12. *Ibid.*
13. Rober MacIver, "The Social Significance of Professional Ethics", *The Annals of the American Academy of Political and Social Science*, vol. 297, January 1955, pp. 118-124.
14. Carr-Saunders, *op. cit.*, p. 6.
15. Carr-Saunders' observation on the official use of the term "Professional Firemen in England" Carr-Saunders, *op. cit.*, p. 4.
16. Nelson N. Foote has called this process as "the Professionalization of Labour", Vollmer and Mills , *op. cit.*, p. 22.
17. A discussion on the politics of professionalization in medicine is found in "The American Medical Association ; Power, Purpose and Politics in Organised Medicine", *The Yale Law Journal*, vol. 63, no. 7, May 1954, pp. 938-947.
18. Hughes had alluded to the same point when he observed : "We have thus an ever increasing number of occupations which aspire to the title, prestige and privileges of professions and a great number of people attempting to improve their lot by gaining the education and other qualifications for entry to professions—and all this is happening in a time when no one can be quite sure that any occupation will maintain its present position for as many years as a

man's normal career ; or that the sciences and arts which one learns will not have become obsolete before one is ready to be retired, even before one has achieved a well-paid, honoured and secure position." Everett C. Hughes, "The Professions in Society", *Canadian Journal of Economics and Political Science*, vol. 26., no. 1, February 1960, pp. 54-61.

19. An incisive discussion of the problems facing the legal profession in India is found in Upendra Baxi, *The Crisis of the Legal Profession*, Vikas Publishing House, Delhi, 1982.
20. India is believed to have the second largest number of lawyers. The number of lawyers in India was about 75,000 in 1958. This figure rose to 99,988 in 1961 and again to 1,47,662 in 1971. A recent estimate places their number at 2,28,000. T.K. Oommen, "The Legal Profession in India : Some Sociological Perspectives", *Indian Bar Review*, vol. 10, no. 1, 1983, pp. 18-19; Marc Gallanter, *Compelling Equalities : Law and the Backward Classes in India* ; Oxford University Press, New Delhi, 1984, pp. 515-516.
21. J.S. Gandhi, *Lawyers and Touts : A Study in the Sociology of Legal Profession*, Hindustan Publication Corporation, New Delhi, 1982.
22. N. Jayaram, "Colonial Legacy and Class Nature of the Legal Profession in India", Paper presented at the National Seminar on *Sociology of the Professions*, University of Jodhpur, 1984.
23. This is in sharp contrast to MacIver's view of profession as a calling whose main purpose is service to the community in which financial and other ulterior considerations are subordinated to the larger goal of the good of the society. MacIver, *op. cit.*, pp. 50-55.
24. N. Jayaram, "Education and Social Structure", Unpublished Ph. D. Thesis, Bangalore University, Bangalore, 1976
25. *Ibid.*
26. In Karnataka State, according to a recent report, as many as 7,000 doctors are unemployed.
27. For a detailed account of the attempt to revive *Ayurveda*, Leslie, Charles, "The Professionalization of Indigenous Medicine", Milton Singer (ed.), *Entrepreneurship and Modernization of Occupational Cultures in South East Asia*, Duke University, 1973.
28. Compare this with the organised opposition which Chiropratic in America met with from the American Medical Association and the Drug interests. W.I. Wardwell, "Strain in a Marginal Social Role", *The American Journal of Sociology*, vol. 61, no. 1, July 1955, pp. 23-28; G. Sivaramkrishnan "Sociology ot Indigeneous Medicine", Unpublished Ph. D. Thesis, Bangalore University, Bangalore, 1980.
29. The very propriety of treating medical practice in India as a profession has been called in question by Jeffrey on the ground that it is under state control. Roger Jeffrey, "Allopathic Medicine in

India : A case of Deprofessionalization", *Economic and Political Weekly*, vol. 13, no. 3 January 20, 1978, pp. 191-203.

30. N. Jayaram and G. Sivaramakrishnan "Teachers and Unionism : The Organization of the Academic Profession", Suma Chitnis, and Philip G. Altbach (eds.), *The Indian Academic Profession*, Macmillan, Delhi, 1979, pp. 105-33.
31. For a discussion of the limitations of present-day teaching as a profession, Seymour, *op. cit.*, pp. 126-129.
32. N S. Timasheff, "Business and the Professions in Liberal, Facist and Communist Society", *The American Journal of Sociology*, vol. 45, no. 6, 1940, pp. 883-889.
33. *Ibid.*, p. 61.
34. Seymour, *op. cit.*, pp. 126-127.

4

WHITHER PROFESSIONALISM ?

RAJENDRA PANDEY

INTRODUCTION

Occupational groupings, which could succeed in defining themselves as a 'profession' in the historical process and which the outside world accepted and reified occupy a special class in the family of occupations.[1] Professions have risen to prominence and occupy a position of importance in modern urbanized society that is unprecedented in history.[2] But professions are not new among the occupations the recorded history of mankind bears testimony to the fact that they existed in almost all societies.[3] Nevertheless, professions as a distinct occupational grouping and professionals as a distinct social group emerged as a concomitant of prodigious socio-economic changes that took place since the Renaissance through the Industrial Revolution onto the post-Second World War era. The professions and the professionals (almost coterminous with that of 'middle class') of the day, in all their manifestations, are a unique social reality. Not surprising, therefore, that both sociologists of professions and theorists of class structure have become increasingly interested in the work and class identity of the growing stratum of professional employees.

Ever since profession shot into prominence in the modern society, professionalism far exceeded professions : the aura of professionalism became persuasive and pervasive, and professionalism a model for most workers in commercial and industrial jobs.[4] It has now become a common place of this sub-sociology that professions offer a great service to the society. Interesting and pragmatically useful though this insight is, it is but one side of a phenomenon of much broader significance. If one appreciates the rise of professionalism, then he ought properly to investigate also the opposite processes that by their presence lead to the negative, opposite consequences, such as dequalification of professional labour and the erosion of the characteristics of professionals. Our assumption is that professionalization as a historical process carries within it a contrary tendency of deprofessionalization and this paper attempts to analyse this aspect of profession.

Discussions on the process of deprofessionalization remain, by and large, neglected by the mainstream literature on the sociology of profession. The past literature of the sociology of professions deals mainly with two aspects of professions, namely, the broad field of the sociology of professions and certain isolated characteristics of the broad field. The literature concerned with the broad field of this sub-sociology is characterized by two fundamental themes : listing the attributes of professions.[5] Once the broad field of the sociology of professions is laid bare, other scholars try to lay their hands on whatever details of this sub-sociology is available ; of course, barring deprofessionalization. For example, there are studies of socialization process of professionals ;[6] inter-professional negotiations ;[7] establishment and maintenance of power of certain occupational groups over others, the public and their client ;[8] social restructuring of professional dominance sustained through control of the division of labour ;[9] place of professions and semi-professions within society ;[10] and inter-relationship of patriarchy and professions ;[11] and the list goes on. That is to say, this listing does not exhaust the studies of this sub-sociology ; indeed, the literature on the various aspects of professions is quite diverse.[12] However, in the vast and ever-growing literature on professions, reflections on the process of deprofessionalization are few and far between. Even the critical studies of the place of professions in the society fail to show its relationship with the class formation.[13] It seems that scholars retreat from class analysis of professionals to an empiricism of time bound appearances. But the past few years have witnessed a growth in the attention paid to this neglected aspect of professions.

In the recent discussion of the professionalization/deprofessionalization, scholars split roughly into two camps. In the first are those who perceive that the professionalization is deep-rooted and the professions are, to borrow a phrase from Mary Jo Bane used in a different context. 'Here to Stay'.[14] Professionalization is on the march, professionals are struggling hard to gain the advantages of being professional, and professions are not being mechanized and rationalized. The overall changes have revealed the traditional character of professions. Freidson states :

> "It seems to be implicit in discussions of the prototypical worker of the post-industrial society that knowledge-based work, the work of the middle class experts, professionals and technicians, is by its very nature *not* amenable to the mechanization and rationalization which industrial production and commerce have undergone over the past century."[15]

The importance of professionals in advanced societies is highlighted by Bell and other "post-industrial" theorists who identify the salaried professionals as the major protagonist of the coming post-industrial society.[16]

Arrayed against them are those who contend that "deprofessionalization rather than professionalization is the trend of the future."[17] Endorsing Haug's observations above Oppenheimer and his associates say : "professionalization as a historical process of formation of segments of the middle class also carries, especially in the present phase of development, its specific contrary tendency, deprofessionalization."[18] In other words, it is contended that the profession and all that it stands for is in a process of deep decline because of decadence. However, the employed professional is recognized as a key new actor in contemporary capitalism by Marxist theorists as well, including theorists of the "new working class", "professional managerial class", "new petty bourgeoisie class" and others.[19]

Despite difference between the two viewpoints, there is broad agreement among them on three points. First, that the number of professionals has exploded in all advanced societies in the twentieth century and this labour force has become the part of the productive apparatus increasingly based on science and science-based technologies. Second, the growth has been mainly among salaried rather than independent professionals reflecting declining opportunities for self-employment in certain professions and the increased direct dependency of professionals on the financial and institutional resources of corporations and the State.[20] Third that professionals have created, what Marx remarked, conflict between mental and manual labour.[21] The professionals are responsible for creating a chasm between the labour of conception and the labour of execution. Under capitalism, the labour of conception dominates that of execution. Those who perform the labour of conception do not simply co-ordinate the labour process but supervise it as well, and, thus, create hierarchy. Gorz writes : "all those whose job it is, because of their technical qualification, to supervise the smooth running production in fact work to reproduce the hierarchical division of labour and capitalist relations of production."[22]

Be as it may, these two viewpoints concerning professionalization/deprofessionalization have contradictory implications for the way in which this institution is to be understood today. In between these two polar interpretations is the moderate view that social changes had a massive impact on the professions but they have shown themselves to be remarkably adaptable institution, but which is nevertheless in a state of crisis.

The intent of this paper is to evaluate the concept of profession, examine the process of professionalization, and discuss the process of deprofessionalization. We will follow the Marxian approach in the analysis of professions.[23] By profession we mean positions defined within the technical relations of production and by class both a set of relationship in dynamic interaction at any point in time as well as a historical process.

PROFESSIONALIZATION

Development of Professions

The precise details of the genesis of professions are no where assembled, nor is their social history recorded. Historically, the professions date back to ancient and pre-literate times. They were numbered few then, consisting primarily of divinity, law, and physique and were regarded "free professions," for, they tended to be free from organizational restraints. The early practitioners of religion, law and medicine were among the progenitors of the professions.[24] These early professionals were not characterized by training and organizations.[25] Many activities now performed by professionals were the concern of clergy. Although "The belief that monks and friars were doctors of the Middle Ages is a gigantic delusion,"[26] nevertheless, knowledge and learning for generations remained in the custodial care of the Church.[27]

But conditions have changed since then tremendously. A new occupational awakening developed in response to the specific social context. Universities were born with the Renaissance and became *inter alia*, training centres for professionals. The advanced academic institutions came to be the "custodians of the intellectual capital of mankind."[28] Professionalism as an occupational environment grew with universities and other institutes of higher learning. As these institutions became secularized, professions also began to get freedom.

Once professions became free, they resorted to form an association for mutual aid. Guild organization was the first step along the way of professionalization for many occupations. This corporate spirit, writes Unwin : "had become universal among all classes of dwellers in cities before the end of the fifteenth century. The clergy..., the legal, medical, and teaching professions ; the merchant, the shopkeeper and the craftsman... were all entrenched behind the bulwarks of professional association."[29]

Professions developed in the historical process in response to specific social context and they created reality which become part of the social context. Professions are, therefore, not the neutral, objective description of reality. Lasch goes on to attack several studies which overlook this fact and charges them with "ignoring the connection between the rise of modern professionalism and the rise of industrial management...The new historian of professionalism, by treating professionals as a separate class with their interests and identity, repeats the mistake made by earlier students of the 'managerial revolution' who argued that managers constitute a 'new class'."[30]

Brief though this developmental sketch of professions is, it yields interesting insights of various sorts. But the insight most relevant to our present topic is this : the professions developed gradually in response to specific social context and once developed they created a reality which becomes part of that social context. The professionalization is, therefore, part of the larger organization of society. Accordingly, it is often found in a less than pure form. It is noteworthy that professionals are not a new class, they are part of the class formation in the society in historical context. Since the pursuit of these broad questions would exceed our present purpose, we switch our attention to the conceptualization of professions.

Conceptualizing Profession

Before we proceed, let us clarify, in brief, the term 'profession.' But to offer a definition of profession, which will be according to the complete satisfaction of all, is very difficult for various reasons. First of all, the concept of 'profession' has a variety of meaning attached to it. Even the arbiter of most definitional disputes, the dictionary fails to provide a definition which may be unanimously accepted. The main reason is that in vernacular, profession is infrequently a synonym for 'occupation,' meaning thereby any socially patterned means of earning livelihood. But, then, there is little consensus about which occupations are professionals.[31] While we speak of surgeons, lawyers, and chemists as professional, we also speak of professional criminals, gamblers, and prostitutes. But, in the latter case, we are ordinarily referring to finesse with which tasks are accomplished. Even if there could emerge an agreement that only socially approved occupations are professions, it would be difficult to obtain consensus upon the status of different professionals, viz., engineers, teachers, and pharmacists. Socially approved occupations means that practitioners possess a sense of responsibility. This implies not only pride in their craft, but also a moral obligation to perform their occupational tasks at maximum efficiency. The term 'professional,' in fact, differentiates not one but several dimensions, such as amount and kind of training, commitment, and working conditions. Secondly, the group of occupations called profession has been assigned contradictory missions and cultural outlooks. Naturally, therefore, professionals have been diversely labelled, viz., 'new class', 'lackeys of capital', 'leader of service society', and 'misleaders of a dismal bureaucratic future', to cite a few.[32] Finally, the historical background of professions differs tremendously. While some professions can be traced to the hoary past, other occupational titles subsumed under profession appeared (literally) only yesterday.

Despite these and other difficulties in defining 'profession', one can come across various definitions in the literature. For example, *Oxford English Dictionary* defines a profession as "a vocation in which professed knowledge of some department of learning or science is used in its application to affairs of others or in the practice of an art founded on it." While the dictionary definition lays emphasis on intellectualistic dimension of profession, it ignores many others, such as ethical and authority aspects. In sociological terms, "professionalism is one that views a profession as an organized group which is constantly interacting with society that forms its matrix, which performs its social functions through a network of formal and informal relationships and which creates its own sub-culture requiring adjustment to it as a pre-requisite for career success."[33] Or, professions are "those occupations which involve the use of knowledge and techniques by a practitioner directly upon, or on behalf of, a client in order to maintain, or induce in the client a culturally determined and socially approved state of well being."[34] Note that sociological definitions do lay stress on the social aspect of professions but they do so at the cost of ignorance of the individual aspect. Marshall holds that the "essence of professionalism is the individual qualities of the professional" which makes for individual judgement and assumption of individual responsibility not concerned with self-interest, but with the welfare of the client."[35] It is clear, then, that none of these definitions singularly convey the complete view of the concept.

While the foregoing definitions are non-Marxist in orientation, the Marxist definition of profession gives a different flavour. Oppenheimer and his associates write :

> "Until recently, 'professional' meant work involving discretion and judgement so that it is difficult or impossible to standardize or mechanize ; work in which the worker produces an entire product, be it a painting, a surgical operation, a book, a bridge, or, an idea; where the worker's pace, work place conditions, product, its use (even to a degree its price) are largely determined by the worker ; where ideally the source of income is an individually regulated sale of product or service under fairly loose market conditions established by face-to-face bargaining rather than sale of labour time in advance of the creation of anything ; and where the bulk of the income goes to the worker without any bureaucratic intermediary except perhaps an agent (as in the case of an artist). Finally, by implication, professional activity is work involving high levels of training, apprenticeship, or other forms of formalized education....Professionalization is a process by which persons in an occupational category struggle to gain the advantages of being professional."[36]

By 'profession' we mean here those occupations which are based on practice and ideology of people who call their occupation a profession and claim certain prerogatives, and, in exchange, they offer or claim to offer certain services due to expertise they possess by way of specialized training which, in turn, results in creation and control of a protected, or institutional market.

Modern Professionalization

Because of the difficulties inherent in accepting any one definition of profession ; scholars have chosen a different path; they define professions by *criteria*. And, various attempts have been made to itemize the traits of profession which emerged in response to new market opportunities, created by industrialization and urbanization and to the decline of communal warrants of professional probity.[37] From a careful convass of the sociological literature on professions, there appears to be consensus on the following distinguishing attributes of a profession : (1) a body of abstract knowledge, (2) service-orientation, (3) professional authority, (4) community sanction, (5) professional-client relationship, (6) code of ethics, and (7) a professional culture. These organizational strategies were adopted by professionalization leaders foı the creation of a protected or institutional market and for collective occupational and social ascension.

The constitution and control of a protected market requires the creation of a standardized and uniform system of training of professional producers. This was achieved by specific bodies of theoretical-technical knowledge. The *first* fundamental feature of profession thus is the *abstract body of knowledge*. "It is this characteristic, the possession of an intellectual technique acquired by special training, which can be applied to some spheres of everyday life that forms the distinguishing mark of a profession."[38] "A body of knowledge", say Carr-Saunders and Wilson "is concerned with the basic fields of inquiry : scientific, institutional, or aesthetic."[39] Continued employment of the scientific method is nurtured by, and, in turn, reinforces the element of, what Parsons, following Weber, calls, rationality.[40] This could only be achieved in the modern type of university, a training institution which culminates the production of knowledge (the research function) with the standardized production of professional producers (the teaching function). In the evolution of every profession, therefore, there emerges the research and teaching functions. In technological profession a division of labour between theory-oıiented and practice-oriented person evolves.[41] The higher education is, thus, a key variable in professionalization. As this occurs in more and more professions, it becomes a generalized social assumption that all educated people—university trained and certified—are *per se* professionals so that anything they do is professional.

The *second* core characteristic of profession is strong *service orientation* The assumption is that the members of the occupational group called 'professions' utilize their knowledge and superior skills in the behalf of other members of the society.

The professionals are assumed to be altruistic ; for them, their own particular interest is secondary and the interest of other members of the society primary.

The *third* distinctive quality of profession is *professional authority*. The prolonged specialized training in a body of abstract knowledge imparts the professional a type of knowledge that highlights the common man's comparative ignorance. The concept of professionality involves the sense of becoming expert in something recondite and unusual available only to guild members.[42] This creates a sense of uniqueness, of having claim to a special territory forbidden to outsiders. This fact serves as the bastion of professional's authority. It is easy to understand it by drawing a distinction between a 'customer' and a 'client'. A professional occupation has a client, while non-professional occupation a customer. Whereas customer exercises his own judgement about his own welfare in non-professional occupations, the professional dictates the client in professional occupation about what is good or bad for him. For, the client is supposed to be lacking the requisite theoretical knowledge. So the client can know neither his own needs nor can evaluate the calibre of the professional service. The client's subordination to professional authority invests the professional with a 'monopoly of judgement'. However, professional's authority is confined to those specific spheres within which professional has been educated ; it is not limitless. To this Parsons calls "*functional specificity*."[43]

The practical goal of professionalization movements was not only to establish a system of training, but to make it the mandatory point of entry into professional practice—the monopolistic source of legitimate professional producers. It is here where one can notice that the label of 'profession' and associated powers and prerogatives are not given ; they are struggled for and gained through self-interested assertions. Every profession seeks *community sanctions* to its authority. In doing so, every profession gradually comes to enjoy a series of powers and privileges—formal and informal. The formal authority of professions is enforced by the community's State power. Every profession succeeds in taking control over its training centres, achieved through an accrediting process exercised by one of the associations within it. It, then, regulates its schools to their number, location, curriculum content, and prerequisites for entry. This is justified by seemingly objective and universalistic criteria of recruitment and achievement—a meritocratic appeal to expertise. Every profession, in this process, succeeds in declaring others as impostor to those not having been conferred a professional title by an accredited professional school and institutes a licensing system for screening those qualified to practice professional skill. Important privilege enjoyed by professionals is, as we said earlier, privileged communication, shared solely between client and professional, and relative immunity from community judgement on technical matters. The powers and privileges enjoyed by a profession give it monopoly. It, then, becomes easier for a profession to establish that this profession depends on superior skill obtained by specialized training that it delivers a superior service, and that it serves the human needs of sufficient social significance. Note that this monopolization of expertise insured and justified the monopoly of opportunities in a market of services or labour and monopoly of status and privileges. Mechanisms are instituted to regulate control over the supply of both expertise and experts at the point of production. Thus, scarcity of personnel is created and high income and privileged working conditions remain assured.[44]

The fifth quality of profession is the *professional-client relationship*. This relationship revolves around three types of interaction which exists between professional and their clients; characteristics of the participants in the interaction; characteristics determining initiation and termination of the interaction ; and characteristics of interaction itself. First of all, the professional-client relationship hinges on the belief that professional possesses expertise and the client is in need of that expertise. Secondlv, the professional-client relationship is governed by norms which require that the interaction be initiated by the client and the termination of interaction be initiatec by the professional, though the client is generally at liberty to leave the professional at any time and thus terminate the relationship. The time to break off the relationship is either when the client's problem has been solved, or the professional has reached the limits of his capability in aiding the client.[45] Finally, the interaction between client and professional consists of four substantive content : (1) privileged communication ; (2) professional alone capable of interpreting and the client must return to the professional for additional help; (3) decisions of professionals limited to the specific interaction period, confined both to 'here and now' situation and to the particular client ; and (4) unaccountability, that is decisions rendered by the professional not ordinarily appealable to an outside authority.

The *sixth* cachet of profession is the *professional ethics.* The monopoly acquired by a profession vis-a-vis clients and community can be abused in a number of ways. And, if the abuses become widespread and permanent, the community will revoke the profession's monopoly, "The strong is never strong enough", wrote Rousseau, "to be always the master, unless he transforms strength into right, and obedience into duty."[46] Therefore, every profession has a built in professional regulative codes which compels ethical behaviour on the parts of its members. The professions' ethical code is partly formal (written) and partly informal (unwritten). Every profession, through its ethical code, makes the profession's commitment to social service a matter of public record, as these codes carry more altruistic overtones and are public service oriented. While specifics of the ethical code vary among professions, the essentials are uniform. The ethics of professions are usually described in terms of client-professional and colleague-colleague relations. Ethics governing client-professional relations assume cosmopolitanism;[47] emotional neutrality, universalism, and disinterestedness.[48] Ethics governing colleague-colleague relations demand behaviour that is co-operative, equalitarian, and supportive. The consultation-referral custom involves professional colleagues in a system of reciprocity. Members of a profession share technical knowledge with each other and support each other vis-a-vis clientele and community.

The *seventh* trait of professions is that there emerges a *professional culture*, consisting of values, norms and symbols.[49] Every profession operates through a network of formal and informal groups. Among the formal groups are organisations which serve as a meeting ground for client and professionals educational and research centres which replenish professionals and expand the fund of knowledge, and professional associations which promote group interest and aims. Within and around these formal groups, there are a number of informal grouping. This creates cultural configuration for professionals to operate. One of the central concepts of professional culture is career concept. The term 'career' is, as a rule, employed only with reference to a professional occupation. At the heart of the career concept is certain attitude towards work which is peculiarly professional. A career is essentially a *calling*, a life devoted to 'good work'. Professional work is never seen solely as a means to an end, it is seen as an end in itself. It is the devotion to duty itself which imparts the professional activity the service orientation and the element of disinterestedness. To the professional person his work becomes his life.[50]

These, then, are some of the characteristics of professions. However, these criteria do not succeed fully in distinguishing professions from other occupations. True difference between a professional and non-professional occupation is not a qualitative but quantitative one. Strictly speaking ; these attributes are not the exclusive monopoly of the professions; non-professional occupations also possess them, but to a lesser degree. Greenwood seems to us to be right when he says that the occupations in a society be thought as distributing themselves along a continuum. At one end of this continuum are bunched the well-organized and undisputed professions (e.g., physician, professor, scientist); at the opposite end are bunched the least skilled and least attractive occupations (e.g., watchman, truckloader, farm labourer). The remaining occupations, less skilled and less prestigeful than the former, but more so than the latter, are distributed between these two poles. The occupations bunched at the professional pole of the continuum possess to a maximum degree the characteristics succinctly described above.[51]

Occupations which are not officially labelled 'professional', but in which workers take some measure of pride as doing some expert job not readily done by people outside the field, seek to professionalize by emulating existing professions. They try to upgrade their occupation by organizing trade associations, publishing journals, and creating structures for admission and certification. The licencing declares membership limited to those meeting qualifications. These occupations develop a code of ethics for justifying their status as a profession. This further excludes non-members. Thus, the occupation concerned comes to label itself as a 'profession' and becomes a privileged sector. The outside world accepts this set of self-definitions and reifies the concept. The label becomes reality as the rest of the society finds itself excluded from knowledge or skill over which profession has declared its monopoly and for a time, at least, gains a privileged position. In this way, just as some are struggling to upgrade, others are undergoing downgrading, fragmentation and proletarianization.

The professionalization is basically a process of class formation.[52] The excuse of monopoly of know-how claimed by professionals is often said to be 'knowledge explosion' which prevents the layman from commanding the details of any profession. This monopolization of knowledge, skill, or technology protects that particular labour market in a guild-like fashion ; as long as the supply of labour can be limited by the guild itself, till then the price of labour can be kept high. In this manner occupations struggle for upgrading, broader spans of control, and professional status. All these processes create chasm between occupations as professional and non-professional occupations and between them who follow professions and non-professions.

DEPROFESSIONALIZATION

In what has preceded, we discussed the processes of professionalization. In doing so, it was shown how occupations endeavour to be recognised as a 'profession' and how professionals struggle to gain the powers and privileges of being professional. In what follow, we turn our attention to its opposite process of deprofessionalization.

What is meant by deprofessionalization ? Deprofessionalization is a process by which characteristics of professionalism are eroded ; it "involves both dequalification of professional labour and erosion of work autonomy."[53] That is to say, deprofessionalization connotes erosion of the characteristics of profession, dequalification of professional labour, and class formation.

Before we proceed, let us keep in mind that the processes of dequalification, deprofessionalization, and class formation can not be talked about if one is given to the belief that the growth of professionals is inherent in the very nature of modern knowledge, technology, and cultural life. Braverman and many others have forcefully argued that there is nothing *inherent* in knowledge or technology to create 'proletarianized' conditions any more than 'professionalized' conditions.[54] In fact, both professionalized as well as proletarianized conditions are the product of specific political social processes, especially of struggles for class assertion within social structures.[55]

Coming to the deprofessionalization, it must be borne in mind that many of the ideal-typical traits of professionalism were either never gained or lost along the way in a spectrum of professions. Even if it be so, many professions are now moving away from the ideal-typical conditions *towards* their opposite. Note that '*towards*' should not be confused with 'have become'. Let us see how the deprofessionalization process is underway.

First : Professionalism is *an ideology*, that is a set of ideas that deliberately and systematically define objectives for the society and provide some clues as to how they can be achieved. As much as professionals are reproduced from specialized system of public education, so much so an ideology that stresses its autonomy, its separation from, and presumable independence of, "business" or political interests. This autonomy is said to be rooted in the specialized knowledge or 'cultural capital' transmitted by the educational system, along with an emphasis on the obligation of educated persons to attend to the welfare of the collectivity. In this manner, the ideology, of "professionalism" emerges : when we say that professionalism is an ideology, it is not intended to suggest that professionalism is only an ideology, but only that it is that too. Demystifying the professions and their study, Freidson has argued that dedication to service and craftsmanship are not distinctive of professionals and "are more usefully treated as elements of an ideology than as empirical characteristics of individual and collective professional behaviour. Taken as an ideology, they have empirical status as claim about their members made by occupations attempting to gain and maintain professional monopoly and dominance."[56] This ideology may be said to be an important component of the process by which occupations seek to gain and maintain the control over their work and working conditions. Freidson, however, goes too far to minimize the importance of knowledge of the professional. But the fact that professionalism is an ideology does not imply that there is no existence of its special skills and knowledge. Furthermore, even though all occupations seek autonomy, only some of them win the status of profession and why it is so ? It is because of the special skill and knowledge of professions. That is to say, the amount of autonomy won by professions does not depend merely on skill and knowledge but also on ideology. This, then, shows in the professionalism the existence of both knowledge and skill as well as *ideologizing* claims to knowledge and skill. And, both of them perform different functions.[57]

Second: The fact that knowledge and skills are produced by advanced education and that they are significant for production is questioned. And, this takes us to the contemporary discussion of the role of "human capital" in productivity. Scholars are divided into two camps regarding the role of the 'human capital' in the productivity. Some scholars are of the view that higher education is linked with productivity, while others hold that some better educated workers are not necessarily more productive. Schultz, who initiated the modern discussion on "human capital" assumes that higher incomes associated with higher education are due simply to the higher productivity of the more educated.[58] As against this, Gouldner and Collins, among others, do not share this view.[59] Collins argues that increased requirement for schooling are not due primarily to the greater skills required by jobs, or to the skills transmitted by education, but are mainly ways that competing status groups monopolize jobs by imposing their standards on personnel selection.[60] Collins cites studies suggesting that some better educated workers are not necessarily more productive than those less educated.[61] The main activity of schools, he holds, is to teach status cultures, and, thus, socialize persons to gain admission to status groups and their privileges. Collins however, acknowledges that "training in specific professions, such as medicine, engineering, scientific or scholarly research, teaching and law can plausibly be considered vocationally relevant and possibly essential".[62] There is, thus, important convergence between the main thrust of Collin's analysis here and Freidson's analysis of professions earlier. Both question the existence and significance of the special skills, techniques, or knowledge produced by advanced education. The central thrust of the analyses of them both is to question whether skill and technical knowledge is indeed produced by higher education, or whether it is needed.

Third : The monopoly of technical knowledge of various professions is being gradually eroded. It is argued that with the extension of rationalization of the labour process, the technical and skilled mental labour of the past is being simplified, routinized, and deskilled. This is the process of dequalification. Haug writes :

> "To the extent that scientific professional knowledge can be 'codified', it can be broken into bits, stored in a computer memory, and recalled as needed. No longer need it be preserved in the professional's head or in books alone ...And what is put into the electronic machine can be extracted by anyone who knows the output procedures. Command over the stored knowledge is not because one knows it but because one knows how to get it."[63]

It transpires, then, that the information and problem-solving procedures that were once stored in the minds of professionals are now located in the electrical circuits of machines. And there are places where physicians' assistants record patients' symptoms into a computer for diagnosis ; legal assistants instruct the machine to locate precedents, and teaching assistants monitor students in front of teaching machines and so on. These empirical instances thus demonstrate how dequalification process is underway and skilled work is being deskilled. The dequalification process, which is inherent to capitalist development, is now being applied to technical, administrative, and professional labour. The situation has come to such a pass where that professional labour, which in its origin was itself an instrument of dequalification of workers, is now itself the victim of dequalification.

One implication of the processes of dequalification is that processes of proletarianization and embourgeoisification have begun. Remember, proletarianization refers to the complex historical process which produces a working class, locking it into subordination to, and conflict with, a capitalist class. As a continuous process, proletarianization reproduces this working class in new and expanded forms, which rests on the predominant structure of exploitation and on the configuration and outcomes of the class struggle at a given time. Once again, take example of computers. The overall impact of computers is first to remove knowledge, skills, and responsibility from people, and thereby strip them of the powers they once enjoyed. Then by placing greater levels of control in the hands of the systems analysts and managers who command the machines and specialized workers appended to them, a new class of bourgeoisie is being created. In this way, this leads to the formation of two antagonistic classes.

Fourth : Accountability of professionals have now begun. It was pinpointed earlier that professionals are not accountable for their actions, because of their monopoly of knowledge and the ignorance of outside world. But the professional's accountability has now started taking place.[64]

There is two-pronged attack on the professionals' cult of expertise : one is from the side of popular movement (ideological) and the other is from the side of computers (technological). On the one hand, popular movements began to question the professionals' monopoly of knowledge on the technical grounds and, on the other hand, demand is placed for professionals accountability on clients and citizens by the ideological plane.

Professionals have now to face the ideological challenges from both sides in the class struggle : from the side of the dominant class and from the side of lower echelons. On the one hand, professionals are subject to devaluation, and, on the other hand many people are no longer ready to yield to the wishes or opinions of professionals. The professional-client relationship premised on inequality is not acceptable. Now the bungled expertise of professionals seemingly divorced from human concern is often doubted. Furthermore, there is dislike and distrust for professionals' unresponsive posture to popular demands.

Besides or, so to speak, above these ideological onslaughts on professionals' immunity, there is technological assault : computers can now be used in systems of professional accountability. It has become much more easier to check how far the judgements professionals make in the exercise of their expertise are in conformity with the standardised norms and procedures.

To quote Hau g again :

> "The upshot of the technological assault on knowledge claims and the ideological assault on service claims is that professionals no longer have the relatively unchallenged autonomy they often enjoyed in a former period."[65]

A close look at these processes reveals the tendency of class formation. It appears that the delivery of professional service is perhaps on way to being reorganized as a labour process. And, now in the reorganized form, the distribution of professional services is being handled by a larger number of machines, assisted by narrow technicians, and commanded by new elite professionals who more and more resemble managers. This process leads to the class formation by increasing the number of para-professional working class, shrinking the number of professionals, and elevating to some towards the elite professional managers.

Fifth : The service-orientation claim and the claim of being liberal and humanistic by professionals are currently suspected. The general attitude of professions in practice is not altruistic, but of intense individualism. Estimating the significance of the individualist and corporate element of professions, Professor Laski laid the main weight on the former :

> "The individualistic organization of these professions is now fatal to the fulfilment of their function. They cannot, I shall argue, give of their best to the civilization in which they play so large a part so long as their members offer their services for private hire and sale...In the present state of civilization the prospect of fulfilling their end as a profession declines rather than grows."[66]

In other words, so long as the professional works on his own for fees paid directly by his clients, his pacuniary interests will prevent him from fulfilling his social obligations, whatever professional associations may do through their ethical codes to curb the profit motive in their members.[67] Remember, long back Veblen said of businessmen that they care only for "the vendibility of their output ; not its serviceability, the needs of mankind."[68] What Veblen said for businessmen in particular[69] can be safely extended to the professionals in general. As long as the opportunities for money-making in professions is great, till then it is likely to tempt some to deviate from strict professional standards and dilute the service-orientation.

The monopoly enjoyed by professions has been abused most often. The powers and privileges are being used to protect vested interests against the public weal.[70] The professional charges, the price of its services at an unreasonably exorbitant rate. It restricts the numbers entering the occupation and thus creates artificial scarcity of personnel to continue its power and privileges. It dilutes the calibre of its performance without community awareness. It frustrates the forces within the occupation pushing for socially beneficial changes in practices.[71]

Sixth : Professional's control over profession is being whittled away by the states and private corporations control over professions. While the states, are becoming 'Welfare State' private corporations are assuming the work of social service.[72] This institutional centralization by the state and corporation is superseding decentralization leaving less space for work autonomy. The fact of the absorption of social services by the State and private corporations to a large extent has undermined an independent practitioner and fee-for-service organization of the newly born professions and steadily whittled away many professions, say, for example, medicine and law. Professor Laski very nicely describes the condition of professionals under State control :

> "Under Mitler, a body of learned professor, whose vocation was the disinterested service of truth, were there willing to prostitute their scholarship to ends which hundreds of them knew to be mean and false."[73]

And, once the state assumes control over professions it can dictate the standards of service and enslave the collective conscience of the profession. Marshall rightly observes : "The natural foe of professionalism in private life is commerc alism. Its natural foe in public life is Politics, in the less respectable sense of the term."[74]

The prolonged professional training produces, it is argued "a professional conscience and solidarity. The profession claims and aims to become a moral unit."[75] In other words, professionals claim to be moral, liberal, and humanistic in their outlook. And, indeed, in principle as well as in practice, they are expected to be so. But there is a gap between what they claim and what they do. According to Reiff, "Professionals see themselves as liberal and humanistic. They are bureaucratic and technological in practice."[76] And, this is shaped by the organizational context within which they work. Johnson and Donnell state :

> "A needy consumer must face bureaucracy and enter into a subservient relation with the service provider. Service professionals mainly work in bureaucratic structures that have the coercive power to enforce the professional's decision *vis-a-vis* his/her client. Professional expertise and largesse are reinforced and constrained by bureaucratic power. State organized production of human services produces not only the needed service but the mode of the objective and subjective dimensions of its consumption as well. Concretely, in the day to day contacts between ordinary people and professionals the objective structures of social relations are those of marked dependant inequality: social worker/client, teacher/student, doctor/patient, bureaucrat/applicant.... The client's subjective response may be one of submissive deference to what may appear as the natural order of the social world or as is the main feature of the present period, of hostile acquiscence to authority. The professional's attitude may be one of professional (often patronizing) concern of contempt for dependence and ignorance. In either case, the social relations are those of latent and manifest antagonism."[77]

Seventh : Professionalism leads to class formation. The ideal construct of the term 'professional' implies the existence of its opposite, the 'proletarianized' employee for whom an extensive division of labour exists.[78] Whatever their content or level, college degrees build a general protective barrier around the stratum of educated workers, separating them from other large groups of worker without a college degree. It implies that in the very process of occupational groupings upgrading themselves as a profession is inherent in this process of class formation. On the one hand, there emerges supervisory/administrative or technocratic upper layer, and, on the other hand, the rest of others, in relation to that upper layer, becomes downgraded and their work deskilled to form a proletarianizing element within professional ranks. Within many professions, a new hierarchy is developing : at the top, a small group of more highly educated technocrats co-ordinate, supervise, and control employees and, at the bottom, large mass of less educated employees are engaged in fragmented labour. Larson recognizes this tendency in professionalization as that of class formation while writing about the rise of professions in the United States.[79]

In this process of class formation, the professionals are becoming the source of domination instead of servicing the social need. They are for extending, reinforcing, and reproducing the system of class domination. For example, social welfare is organized, as Piven and Cloward put it : "to regulate the poor."[80] Education works, Bowles and Gintis say, according to the correspondence principle : that is, attempts are made to gear schools to the manpower needs of the monopoly capital, to ideological indoctrination, and to the creation of a disciplined and docile labour force.[81]

To be sure, professional comes to stand in opposition not only with less educated employees at the bottom but they also come in conflict with the upper classes at the top. The new class of professionals and the old class of bourgeoisie are initially undifferentiated. The class of professionals originates in a separate class while deriving property advantages in the old bourgeoisie class, or when professions are sponsored by the bourgeoisie class. But the professionals are relatively more educated counter-part of the moneyed class. In the process of gaining privileges and advantages for itself the class of professionals come in conflict with the very bourgeoisie class from which it originated or which created it. In fact, class of professionals is the differentiation of the old class into contentious factions.

It may be interesting to look at the way the contest between the old bourgeoisie class and the new class of professionals emerges. The old moneyed class aims at reproduction of their capital at a minimum profit. This is done within a structure in which all of them must compete with one another. This unrelenting competition exerts pressure to rationalize their productive system and administrative efforts and unceasingly to heighten efficiency, or what Marx called the same as 'revolutionizing' production. But this rationalization is dependant increasingly on the efforts of the professional and its expert skills. It is, thus, inherent in its structural situation that the old class of bourgeoisie must bring the New class into existence.

In doing so, much of the professional class is at first trained under the direct control of old, upper class's firms or enterprises. But the old upper class wants to train professionals at public cost and use them for its own benefit. Owing to this the upper class is separated soon from the reproduction of the professionals with the emergence and development of public system of education whose "costs" are socialized.[82]

The more the professionals' reproduction derives from specialized system of public education, the more this class develops an ideology that stresses its autonomy from the upper class along with an emphasis on the welfare of the collectivity. Professionalism subverts the upper class gradually and gently while not criticizing the upper class overtly. Professionalism is a tacit claim to technical and moral superiority over the old upper class. It implies that the old bourgeoisie lack technical credentials and are guided by motives of commercial venality. Professionalism silently instals the professionals as virtuous and legitimate authority who apply their technical skill with dedicated concern for the society at large. Professionalism makes a focal claim for the legitimacy of the professionals and in this process deauthorizes the old upper class tacitly. On the one side, this is a bid for prestige within the established society, and on the other side, it is a tacit presentation of professionals as an alternative to the old, upper class. In asserting its own claims to authority, professionalism, in effect, devalues the authority of the old bourgeoisie class from which professionals originated or which created them.

The special privilege and powers of the professionals are grounded in their individual control of special cultures, languages, techniques, and the skills resulting from professionalization. The professional class is a 'cultural bourgeoisie' which appropriates privately the advantages of an historically and collectively produced cultural capital.[83]

Scholars are divided among themselves about the status of professionals as a class : for some, they are simply strata occupying contradictory locations,[84] but, for others, they make a class.[85] We are of the view that the professionals lead to class formation. The historical process of professionalization of different occupations serve as a means of "enhancing their market power and preserving their status and autonomy from encroachment by either employers or clients."[86] In this manner, professionalization serves as a principal vehicle in the formation of the 'middle class'—a class between old bourgeoisie and new proletariat class. The middle class can be seen as a constellation of strong occupational sub-cultures, each with its particular ideologies, professional associations, sectional interests, values and norms, and associational patterns which we analysed earlier. The professionals strive to establish their independence from the old bourgeoisie in the sphere of cultural ideology.

Not surprising, professionals antagonize both bourgeoisie and working class. The relation between professionals, bourgeoisie, and working class is strained.[87] Gorz says how professionals' relations, become strained with the working class :

> "They have a monopoly of technical and intellectual skills required by the production process and they *deny* these skills to the workers. Their role is to dequalify workers and to reduce work to manual work pure and simple. They represent the skill and knowledge of which workers have been robbed, the separation between intellectual and manual work, between conception and execution. They enjoy significant financial, social and cultural privileges. They are the workers' most immediate enemy."[88]

The professions develop mechanisms to reproduce the class structure. For a long time, the professions remained almost the exclusive prerogative of the sons of the professionals. Institutions of higher education adopted admission standards (and tution fee) that discriminated against working class applicants whose oppressive class situation frustrated the achievement of the requisite standards. Culturally biased tests screened out persons of different social background. In steady demand of educated labour, operational control of university and professional schools remained in the hands of elite, and the government and private foundations funded these institutions to reproduce the existing social order ; they created equilibrium or supply shortages in the markets for professional labour.

Whether proletarianization of professionals is underway ? Currently, the scholars are divided into two camps on the question of proletarianization of professionals. One group of scholars reject the proletarianized view. The 'post-industrial' theorists, notably Bell advances the notion of 'post-industrial society' to highlight the difference between industrial and professional forms of labour.[89] They argue that salaried professionals, unlike proletarianized industrial workers, maintain exclusive control over their own knowledge base. This helps them to resist managerial encroachment on their autonomy, despite the requirements of co-ordinating their work with others in the organization and carrying out responsibilities in a manner consistent with the objectives of the organization. To them, the analogies between craft proletarianization of the nineteenth century and professional proletarianization of the twentieth century are wrong. Whereas the craft workers of the nineteenth century found their knowledge and skills eroded by new technologies and bodies of scientific knowledge, the professionals of the twentieth century have actually gained power in organizational settings due to the enhanced importance of their own knowledge in organizational decision-making and their continued monopolies of science-based professional skills. Thus, the proletarianized view of professionals is rejected and argued that professionals have become powerful due to increased importance of their knowledge ; and that the monopolies of science-based professional skill continue.[90]

The other group of scholars argues that there is "proletarianization of professional." There are *two* theories that reflect on the process of proletarianization of professionals. One school argues that the signs of proletarianization ought to be found at the level of work conditions, in a parallel with the history of both industrial and clerical work. The publication of Braverman's book, *Labour and Monopoly Capital : The Degradution of Work in the Twentieth Century*, helped turn to the *labour process itself* in its continued subjection to heteronomous rationalization.[91] The proletarianization is used by these scholars lightly as a quasi-equivalent of 'rationalization' or 'industrialization' of the labour process. Following this logic, it is argued that due to introduction of rationalization, the professions are degrading.

The second school discusses proletarianization in terms of origins, evolution, and possible historical role of the new working class. One might distinguish *two* broad varieties in it. One set of theories holds to the basic Marxist assumption, that is, the position of individuals in the social relations of production, their productive activity, contradictory or not, form the basis from which to assess the potential and trajectory of their collective consciousness and behaviour.[92] The main argument of this Marxist school is that widespread dependent employment of the professional labour has led to the 'proletarianization of the professional'.[93] It is argued that the shift from self-employment to employee status among professionals parallels the proletarianization of craft workers in the last century. Since professional markets are profitable and attractive to private capital and sophisticated technology and institutional resources are central to professional production and marketing, professional work becomes vulnerable to the process of industrialization experienced by nineteenth century craft. As the professionals lack the resources to maintain an independent economic position, they are absorbed within large-scale organizational corporate and state bureaucracies and become subject like other employees, to heteronomous management, authority and control, and to gradual degradation of status and control. Precisely because of these reasons, Chomsky insists that contrary to the illusions of post-industrial theorists, power is not shifting into their hands.[94] Marxist theorists further argue that professional autonomy, under the emerging conditions of proletarianization, assumes largely symbolic forms. Of course, professionals do not punch time-clocks and typically are free from extensive supervision, but are subjected in a more profound sense to the underlying region and to constraints of proletarianized labour. Professionals' work is folded into a division of labour conceived and enforced by management and professionals had to work to the imposed rhythms of the organization and procedures and technology subject to administrative approval and review, if not outright dictation. The other set of theories assigns a more determinant role to broadly understood ideology and cultural socialization.[95] However, both varieties of theories and theorists measure the role of professionals against role assigned by Marxism to the industrial proletariat.

CONCLUSIONS

In what has gone before, we analysed the processes of professionalization and deprofessionalization. The professions developed in the historical process in response to the specific social context and have come to be characterized by a body of abstract knowledge, service-orientation, professional authority, community sanction, professional-client relationship, code of ethics, and professional culture. It is argued here that professionalization as a historical process carries within it the contradictory process of deprofessionalization.

The deprofessionalization involves erosion of characteristics of profession, dequalification, and class formation. The process of deprofessionalization is underway in several ways, namely, the erosion of monopoly of technical knowledge, beginning of professional accountability; suspicion in service-orientation; violation of professional code of ethics; refutation of professionals' claim of being liberal and humanitarian; cutting of professionals' control; and creation of class antagonism.

Trends of professionalization may be summarized within the parameters of the improbable, probable, and the possible. It is *improbable* that the deepening crisis will stop the growth of professions. The capitalist system survives on creation of professional class for profit. It is *probable* that conditions within professional occupations will further deteriorate and deprofessionalization process will proceed. It is *possible* that the strata of the professionals, which is pushed towards the working class conditions, will assume more progressive role.

Professionalization is a process; occupations come and go; they are non-professional today, semi-professional tomorrow, and fully professional later on. In the process of making, unmaking, and remaking, some professions lose autonomy and control over their work and become fragmented. Consequently, their lower layers become technically dequalified in the labour process. In other words, some professionals are driven to working class conditions, while others towards, or into, managerial bourgeoisie. There is always polarization between proletarianized and bourgeosified professionals. Despite the changes in the internal structure of the two main classes, the relationship always remains that of exploitation and domination.

NOTES AND REFERENCES

1. Ginsberg, Eli, "The Professionalisation of the U.S. Labour Force", *Scientific American*, vol. 240, no. 3, 1979, pp. 48-53.
2. Parsons, T., "The Professions and Social Structure", *Social Forces*, vol. 17, (May 1939), pp. 457-467.
3. Carr-Saunders, A.M., and P.A., Wilson, *The Professions*, Oxford University Press, London, 1933; Lewis Roy and Angus Maude, *Professional People*, Phoenix House Ltd., London, 1952; Pound, R., *The Lawyers from Antiquity to Modern Times*, West Publishing Co., Saint Paul, 1953 ; Sigerist, H.E., *A History of Medicine*, Oxford University Press, New York, 1951; Whitehead, Alfred North, *Adventures of Ideas*, The Macmillan Co., New York, 1953.
4. Strauss, George, "Professionalism and Occupational Aspirations", *Industrial Relations*, vol. 2, (May 1963), pp. 7-31 ; Marshall, T.N. "The Recent History of Professionalism in Relation to Social Structure and Social Policy", *The Canadian Journal of Economics and Political Science*, vol. 5, (August 1939), pp. 325-340
5. Goode, William J., "Encroachment, Charlatanism and the Emerging Professions : Psychology, Sociology and Medicine", *American Sociological Review*, vol. 25, 1960, pp. 902-914; Carr-Saunders and Wilson *op. cit.*, Check, Neil H., Jr., "The Social Role of Professionals", Mark Abrahamson, *op. cit.*; Goode listed ten traits whereas Carr-Saunders and Wilson distinguished between the established and semi-professionals.
6. Becker, Howard S., B. Geer, E. Hughes, and A. Strauss, *Boy in While*, University of Chicago Press, Chicago, 1961.
7. Strauss, *op. cit.*
8. Johnson, T., *Profession and Power*, Macmillan, New York, 1972.
9. Freidson, E., *Professional Dominance : The Social Structure of Medical Care*, Atherton, New York, 1970.
10. Esland, G., *The Politics of Work and Occupation*, Open University Press, Melton Kaynes 1976.

11. Ehrenreich, B., and D. English, *Complaints and Disorders : The Sexual Politics and Sickness*, Feminist Press, New York, 1973; *Witches, Midwives and Nurses : History of Women Healers*, Feminist Press, New York, 1974; *For Her Own Good : Years of the Exports, Advice to Women*, Pluto Press, London, 1979.
Lorber, J., "Women and Medical Sociology : Invisible Professions and Ubiquitous Patients"; M. Williman, and R.M. Kauter, *Another Voice*, Anchor, New York, 1975; Hearn, Jeffey, "Notes on Patriarchy, Professionalisation, and the semi-professions", *Sociology*, vol. 16, no. 2, 1982, pp. 184-202; Simpson, R.L., and I.H. Simpson, "Woman and Bureaucracy in the Semi-Professions", Etzioni (ed.), *The Semi-profession and Their Organisation*, Free Press, New York, 1969; Marret C.M., "Centralisation in Female Organisations : Reassessing the Evidence", *Social Problems*, vol. 19, 1972, pp. 348-35; Grandjean, R.D., and H.H. Bernal, "Sex and Centralisations in semi-profession", *Sociology of Work and Occupation*, vol. 16, 1979, pp. 84-102; Kanter, B.M., "The Impact of Hierarchical Structure on the Work Behaviour of Women and Men", *Social Problems*, vol. 23, 1976, pp. 415-43.
12. Goode, William J., "Community within a Community : The Professions", *American Sociological Review*, vol. 22, 1957; Bucher, Robert and Anselm, Strauss, "Professions in Process", *American Journal of Sociology*, vol. 56, 1961; Becker, Howard S., and James W. Carper, "Elements of Identification with an Occupation," *American Sociological Review*, Vol. 21, 1956; Merton, R.K., *et. al.* (eds.) *The Student Physician*, Harvard University Press; Cambridge, 1957, Parsons, 1939, *op. cit.*; Hughes. E.C., "Professions in Society", *Canadian Journal of Economic and Political Science*, vol. 26, 1960; Carr-Saunders and Wilson, *op. cit.*
13. Esland, *op. cit.*
14. Bane, Marry Jo, *Here to Stay : American Families in the Twentieth Century*, Basic Books, New York, 1976.
15. Freidson E., *Professionalisation and the Organisation of Middle Class Labour in Post-Industrial Society*, P. Halmos, *Professionalisation and Change*, University of Keel, 1973, pp. 47-60.
16. Bell, Daniel, *The Coming of Post-Industrial Society : A Venture in Social Forecasting*, Arnold Heinemans, New Delhi, 1974; Touraine, A., *The May Movement*, Random House, New York, 1971.
17. Haug, M.R., "Deprofessionalisation : An Alternative Hypothesis for the Future," P. Halmos (ed.), *Professionalisation and Change*, *op. cit.*, pp 195-212.
18. Oppenheimer, Martin, *et. al.*, "Professions and Middle Class Professionalisation/Deprofessionalisation," Dale, L. Johnson, *Class and Social Development : A New Theory of the Middle Class*, Sage Publication, Beverly Hills, 1982, pp. 245-325.
19. Ehrenreich, John, and Barbara Ehrenreich, "The Professional Managerial Class" *Radical America*, vol. 11, no. 3 (March-April

1977), pp. 7-31 ; "The New Left and the Professional Managerial Class", *Radical America*, vol. 11, no. 3 (May-June 1977), pp. 7-22 ; Gouldner, Alvin W., "The Class Project I : A Frame of Reference, Thesis, Conjectures, Arguments, and/or Historical Perspective on the Role of Intellectuals and Intelligentsia in the International Class Contest of the Modern Era", *Theory and Society*, vol. 6, no. 2 (September 1978), pp. 153-203 ; 'The New Class Project II...", vol. 6, no. 3 (November 1978), pp. 343-389 ; Oppenheimer, Martin, "The Political Missions of the Middle Strata", Johnson (ed.) *op. cit.*, Poulantzas, Nicos *Classes in Contemporary Capitalism*, New Left Press, London, 1975.

20. Larson, M.S., *The Rise of Professionalism : A Sociological Analysis*, University of California Press, Berkeley, 1977. Larson shows that the percentage of all professional technical workers who are self-employed declined from 25.9% in 1900 to 18.4% in 1920, 16.9% in 1950, 11.7% in 1960, and 10.6% in 1970, and that there is absolute increased high rate of growth in a number of key professional occupations between 1900 and 1980.
21. Marx, K., *Capital*, vol. I, International Publishers, New York, 1967, p. 508: "As in the natural body head and hand wait upon each other, so the labour process unites the labour of the hand with that of the head. Later on they part company and even become deadly foes."
22. Gorz, Andre, "Technology, Technicians and Class Struggle", Gorz, A. (ed.), *The Division of Labour*, The Harvester Press, Harsock, 1976.
23. There are two approaches to the relationship between occupation and class : Non-Marxist and Marxist. In Non-Marxist view, class is operationalized in terms of a typology of occupations ; Professional and technical occupations constitute the upper middle class. Other white collar occupations comprise the middle class proper, and manual occupations make up the working class. This implies that occupational structure fundamentally determines the class structure. By contrast, Marxist theory adopts a different stance towards relationship between occupation and class. Occupations are understood as positions defined within the *technical* relations of production. Classes, on the other hand, are defined by the social relations of production.
24. Carr-Saunders and Wilson, *op. cit.*; Lewis and Maude, *op. cit.*: Pound, *op. cit* ; Sigerist, *op. cit*; Whitehead, *op. cit.*
25. Carr-Saunders and Wilson, *op. cit.*
26. Coulton, G.G., *Medieval Panorama*, The University Press, Cambridge, 1939, p. 447.
27. Bark, W.C., *Origins of the Medieval World*, Doubleday and Anchor Books, New York, 1960.
28. Clark, Burton R., *Educating the Expert Society*, Chandler, San Francisco, 1962, p. 27.

29. Unwin, George, *The Guilds and Companies of London*, Methuen and Co., London, 1908, p. 172.
30. Lasch, Christopher, "The Siege of the Family," *New York Review*, November 24, 1977 ; *Heaven in a Heartless World : The Family Besieged*, New York, 1977.
31. Here are some examples of occupations called professional : By the end of the eighteenth century (1979) the *Trinnial Directory of London* enumerated professional-type occupational listings, including barristers, attorneys, physicians, surgeons, apothecarieos, chemists and druggists, dentists, opticians, architects, surveyors, auctioners, and accountants, Carr-Saunders and Wilson, 1933 pp. 295-296. By the mid of the twentieth century, the United States Census Bureau 1950, includes, among others, the following : accountant, architect, artist, attorney, clergyman, college professor, dentist engineer, journalist, judge, librarian, natural scientist, social worker, surgeon, and teacher.

    Carr-Saunders differentiates four major types of professions in modern industrial states. The *old established professions* are founded upon the study of a theoretical structure of a department of learning which is used in practice of the art founded on it, and the members of the vocation feel bound to follow a certain mode of behaviour. Religion, law, higher education, and aesthetics are associated with the old established professions. The *new profession* have their own fundamental studies upon which their art is founded. Chemists, engineers, natural and social scientists are examples of the new professions. By way of contrast, the *semi-profession* replace theoretical study of a field of learning by the acquisition of precise technical skill. Technical practice and knowledge is the basis of such semi-professions as nursing, pharmacy, optometry, and social work. There are, also the *would-be-professions*, where members aspire to professional status. Familiarity with modern practice in business and government generally distinguished this group. Personnel directors, sales engineers, business counsellors, funeral directors, and institutional managers are example of vocations where members aspire to professional status Reiss adds a new group of professions, although not identified by Carr-Saunders. A fifth group, the *marginal professions*, is made up largely of those who perform technical assignments associated with professional assignments, e.g., medical and laboratory technicians, tasters, illustrators, draftsman, interpretors, and inspectors.
32. Galbraith, John Kenneth, *American Capitalism*, Houghton Miffin, Boston, 1952 ; Bazelon, David, *Power in America : The Politics of the New Class*, American Library, New York, 1967 ; Touraine, *op. cit.*; Bruce-Briggs, *The New Class*, Transaction Books, New Bruns-

wick, N.J., 1979 ; Mills, C.W., *White Collar*, Oxford University Press, London, 1951.

33. A technology is a professsion whose aim is to achieve controlled changes in natural relationships. Convention draws a distinction between technologists who shape non-human materials and those who deal with human beings. The former are called engineers, and the latter practitioners. Greenwood, Earnest, "Attributes of Profession", *Social Work*, (April 1957), pp. 44-45 ; Hall, Oswald, "The Stages of Medical Career," *American Journal of Soçiology*, vol. 53 (March 1948), pp. 327-336; "Tyres of Medical Career," *American Journal of Sociology*, vol. 55 (November 1949) pp. 243-253 ; "Sociological Research in the Field of Medicine : Progress and Prospects," *American Sociological Review*, vol. 16 (October 1951), pp. 639-644.
34. Chelk, *op. cit.*
35. Marshall, T.N., "Professionalism and Social Policy", William, H. Form. *Men, Work and Society : A Reader in the Sociology of Occupations*, Basic Books, New York, 1962, pp. 225-235.
36. Oppenheimer, *et al*; *op. cit.*
37. Goode, William J., "Encroachment, Charlatanism and the Emerging Professions : Psychology, Sociology and Medicine," *American Sociological Review*, vol. 25, 1960, pp. 902-914 ; Carr-Saunders and Wilson, 1933, *op. cit.*
38. Carr-Saunders A.M., and P.A. Wilson, " The Emergence of Professions", Sigmund Nosow and William H. Form (eds), *Men, Work and Society : A Reader in the Sociology of Occupation*, Basic Books, New York, 1962, pp. 199-206.
39. Carr-Saunders and Wilson, 1933, *op. cit.*
40. Parsons, 1939, *op. cit.*; Weber, Max, *The Theory of Social and Economic Organisation*, The Free Press, Glencoe, Ill., 1947.
41. Ft. note 33, *op. cit.*
42. A somewhat irreverent discussion of this phenomenon is given by Goffman. Goffman, Erving, *Asylums*, Doubleday Anchor Books, New York, 1961.
43. Parson, 1939, *op. cit.*
44. Davis, Kingslay, and Willbert E. Moore, "Some Principles of Stratification", *American Sociological Review*, vol. 10, no. 2, (April 1945), pp. 242-249. In this article, the authors treat scarcity of personnel as a reason for higher reward.
45. Wilensky, Harold L., "The Professionalisation of Everyone?". *American Journal of Sociology*, vol. 70, 1964.
46. Rousseau, Jeen-Jacques, *The Social Contract and Discourses*, E.P. Dutton and Co., New York, 1950.
47 Reissman, Leonard, "A Study of Role Conception in Bureaucracy," *Social Forces*, vol. 77, 1949 ; Merton, R.K. "Patterns of Influence :

Local and Cosmopolitan Influentials", *Social Theory and Social Structure,* The Free Press, Glencoe, Ill. 1957 ; Gouldner, Alvin W., "Cosmopolitan and Locals : Towards an Analysis of Latent Social Roles, *Administrative Science Quarterly,* vol 82, 1957, p. 58.

48. Parsons. *op. cit.* 1939.
49. Bledstein, B. J., *The Culture of Professionalism,* Norton, New York., 1976.
50. Hall, *op. cit.,* 1948 ; Caplow, *op. cit.* ; Form William H., "Toward an Occupational Social Psychology," *Journal of Social Psychology,* vol. 24 (February 1946), pp. 85-99.
51. Greenwood, *op. cit.*
52. Larson. *op. cit* ; Ginsberg, *op. cit.*
53. Oppenheimer. *op. cit.*
54. Braveman, Harry, *Labour and Monopoly Capital : The Degradation of Work in the Twentieth Century,* Monthly Review Press, New York, 1974.
55. Haug, *op. cit.*
56. Gouldner, 1975, *op. cit* p.17; Freidson, E., "The Future of Professionalism", M. Slacey, *et. al. Health and the Division of Labour,* Croom Helm, London, 1977, pp. 32-33. There are two prominent Schools to the study of professions : 'the Chicago School' and the 'Harvard Columbia School.' For an early effort to distinguish between these two schools to the study of professions, Gouldner, and Freidson's work is the productive culmination of the "Chicago-school's ongoing efforts to secularize the study of occupations and to see professions as just another occupation. The Chicago approach minimizes the relevance of skill, craftsmanship, and knowledge for shaping the work and the guild-political behaviour of the professions, tending to suggest that these do not differ consequentially in degree or kind from other occupations. Advanced education is thus here understood not so much as skill and knowledge transmitting, but as legitimations of *privilege* and as techniques for allocating jobs and incomes. Skill, knowledge, and education are thus held to be claimed by professions as a way of enhancing the privilege and autonomy all occupations are said to wait."

57 Gouldner adds two demurrers : (1) That they are so used, however, does not demonstrate that they do not exist. The existence of the ideology of professionalism does not *per force* disprove the existence of its special skills and knowledge, (2) Since all occupations seek autonomy, why is it some win considerably more of it than others. Their skill and knowledge is *one* factor. Granted that the amount of autonomy won does not depend only on the special skills of those seeking it, still, valued skills also constitute important grounding of public power and influence. The ideological dimension of professional claims needs to be insisted upon, but this should not exclude recognition of the special skill and knowledge-base of some

occupations. I would thus distinguish between an occupation's skills and knowledge, on the one hand, and its ideologizing *claims* to skill and knowledge, on the other, and the different *functions* each of these performs ; I would also distinguish between claims to skill knowledge and claims to special dedication to the collective welfare and would note that the absence of the latter does not *per force* demonstrate a lack of the former, Freidson, 1975, *op. cit.*, Goode, 1960, *op. cit.*, Merton 1960, *op. cit.*

58. Schultz, Theodor, "Investment in Human Capital," American Economic Review, (March 1961), Presidential Address to the American Economic Association in 1960 ; "Human Capital", *Encyclopaedia of the Social Sciences*, Vol. 2, New York, 1968.

59. Gouldner, Alvin W., *For Sociology*, Penguin Books, Harmondsworth, Middlesex, 1975, Collins, Randall, "Functional and Conflict Theory of Educational Stratification," J. Karabel, and A.M. Halsey, (eds.), *Power and Ideology in Education*, 1977; Fisher, Irving, *The Nature of Capital and Income*, New York, 1927.

60. Collins, *Ibid.*

61. Eisenhower, David, "Unproductive Labour and Crisis," Dale L. Johnson (ed.) *op. cit.*

62. Collin, *op. cit.*

63. Haug, *op. cit.*

64. Green Field, Harry, *Accountability in Health Facilities*, Praeger, New York, 1975.

65. Haug, *op. cit.*

66. Laski, H.J., "The Decline of the Professions", *Harper's Monthly* Magazine, (November 1935), pp. 565-657.

67. Hughes, E.C., "Dilemmas and Contradictions of Status", *American Journal of Sociology*, Vol. 50, 1945.

68. Veblen, Thorstein, *The Theory of Business Enterprises*, Scribers, New York, 1905.

69. ——, *The Engineers and the Price System*, Kelley, New York, 1920.

70. Flexner, *op. cit.* ; Merton, R.K., "Bureaucratic Structure and Personality," Alvin W. Gouldner, *Studies in Leadership*, Harper and Brothers, New York, 1950, pp. 67-79.

71. Merton, *Ibid.*

72. Professionalisation is inconceivable without at least the tacit approval of those interest groups controlling the ebb and flow of societal resources.

73. Laski, *op. cit.*

74. Marshall, *op. cit*, 1962.

75. Hughes, *op. cit.*
76. Reiff, R., "The Danger of the Techni-pro : Democratising the Human Services Professions", *Social Policy*, vol. 2 (May-June 1971), p. 63.
77. Johnson, Dale L., and Christine, O' Donnell, "Accumulation Crisis and Service Professionals", Economics Education Project (ed) ., *Crisis in the Public Sector 1981*, p. 45.
78. Larson, *op. cit.*
79. Larson, *op. cit.*
80. Piven, F.F., and Richard Cloward, *Regulating the Poor*, Vintage, New York, 1971.
81. Bowls, S., and H. Gintis, *Schooling in Capitalist America : Educational Reform and the Contradictions of Economic Life*, Basic Books, New York, 1975.
82. O'Connor, James, *Corporations and the State*, New York, 1974, pp. 126-128.
83. Gouldner, 1978, I, *op. cit.*
84. Wright, Erik Olin, "Class Boundaries in Advanced Capitalist Societies", *New Left Review*, vol. 90, (July-August 1976), pp. 3-16: *Class, Crisis and State*, Left Books, London, 1978; "Intellectuals and the Working Class", *Insurgent Sociologist*, vol. 3, no. 1, 1978, pp. 5-17 ; Oppenheimer, 1982, *op. cit.*
85. Johnson, *op. cit.*
86. Burries, Val., "Capital Accumulation and the Rise of the New Middle Class", *Review of the Radical Political Economics*, vol. 12 (Spring 1980), pp. 17-34.
87. The class of professionals occupy an intermediate position that its social distance from the proletariat barred it from becoming a decisive ally for the major protagonist of socialist politics ; and/or that its position in the system of production denied it an autonomous and leading political role. Hodges, Donald C., "Old and New Working Classes," *Radical America*, vol. 5, no. 1 (January-February 1971); Moody, Kim, "The American Working Class and Transition", *International Socialist*, 1970; "Can the American Workers be Radicalised", Louise Kapp, *The White Majority*, Random House, New York, 1970.
88. Gorz, *op. cit.*
89. Bell, D., *The Cultural Contradictions of Capital*, Basic Books, New York, 1976.
90. Zeitlin, Maurice, "Corporate Ownership and Control : The Large Corporations and the Capitalist Class", *American Journal of Sociology*, (March 1974), pp. 1073-1119; Lasch, *op. cit.*
91. Braveman, *op. cit.*
92. The best example of this trend is Ehrenreichs, 1977, *op. cit.*
93. Larson, 1977, *op. cit.* ; Larson, M.S., "Professionalisation and Educated Labour", *Theory and Society*, 1980, pp. 131-175; Oppenheimer,

M., "White Collar Revisited,", *Social Policy,* (July-August 1970); "The Proletarianisation of the Professional", *Sociological Review,* vol. 20, 1970 ; Mckinlay, John, "Towards the Proletarianisation of Physicians", Charles Derber, (ed.), *Professionals as Workers : Mental Labour in Advanced Capitalism,* G.K. Hall, Boston, 1982 ; Oppenheimer, *et. al., op. cit.,* Derber, Charles, "Managing Professionals : Ideological Proletarianisation and Post-Industrial Labour", *Theory and Society,* vol. 12, 1983, pp. 309-341 ; Bellaby, Paul, and Patrick, Oribabor, "The Growth of Trade Union Consciousness among General Proletarianisation", *The Sociological Review,* vol. 25, no. 4, 1977.

94. Chomsky, Noam, *American Power and the New Mandarins,* Penguin Books, Harmondsworth, Middlesex, 1969.
95. The best example of this trend is in Gouldner, 1978, I and II. *op. cit.*

5

PROFESSIONS IN THEORY AND REALITY : A RE-CONSIDERATION OF THEORY OF PROFESSIONS IN THE LIGHT OF SOME EMPIRICAL EVIDENCE

J.S. GANDHI

BACKGROUND, ARGUMENT AND THE PROBLEM

Despite their much-acclaimed reflexivity, criticality and objectivity, sociologists have not always found it possible to steer clear of certain intellectual fads that constitute their contemporary cultural tradition. And, in the process, they have not merely disregarded certain crucial process that shaped their societies, but have also uncritically accepted certain *notions*, *cognitions* and *definitions* doled out to them by their intellectual peers from across the professional boundaries. And, having once become a part of their intellectual repertoire, these have often persisted for a long-long time and have even imbued sociologists with a zeal to defend them in a manner in which they would defend their inductively derived conceptual constructions. As a consequence of such indiscretion on the part of some of our fore-fathers in sociology, we have been forced to live with conceptual-dead wood for a long time and still continue to do so.

One such case is that of the sociology of the professions, wherein professions were thought to be a genre distinct from the general run-of-the mill occupations. It has been maintained by pioneers like Durkheim, Carr-Saunders and others that as against occupations and common avocations which were guided by considerations of maximal profit, professions were inspired by a sense of high morality which flowed from the centrality of their ethos or from their *collective conscience*.[1] That is why, collectivity-orientation was thought to be one of their *raison d'etre*. In the same logical continuity, it was hypothesized that professional associations represented the collective conscience of professions and laid down rules and norms for guiding the professional conduct. Much against the fact that existential conditions of professional practice often obviated the professionals from conformity to these norms, it was assumed that these norms exercised a compulsive and automatic influence upon the professionals since these were ingrained in them through the process of extended socialization. That is precisely the rationale behind Durkheimian attribution of *exteriority* and *constraint* to these norms. The vitality of these norms which were supposedly laid down by the professional collectives in a self-conscious manner keeping in view the interests of the wider society was thus thought to be at once a guarantee of their collectivity-orientation and a justification for the *autonomy* which they enjoyed in regulating their own affairs. All these attributions to the professions along with the fact that their knowledge—base was relatively more abstract and systematized as compared to the occupations, led to crystallization of professional *ideal type* constitutive of *collectivity orientation*, *professional control* and *autonomy* and *abstract knowledge-base*. That, ever since the emergence of this *Sociology of the professions* as a distinct area of sociological enquiry, researchers again and again have adequately hearkened to this pristine model of professions, failing to appreciate adequately the *reality* of professional functioning and its existential condition has begun to be recognized only recently. But there is no doubt whatsoever that sociological inquiry has often been constricted by certain *apriori* categories (i.e., attributes of professions) imposed upon sociologists by other professions in society.

In brief, sociologists have identified professional attributes not as suggested by their objective inquiry but because the professions wanted them to so identify. This obviously calls for an understanding of the process of intellectual domination by the professional ethos and kind of culture in which it took place. An exciting field of inquiry indeed ! The questions to be posed under such an inquiry would be : What precisely led to the prevalence of professions' self-projection among sociologists? Was it their superior *esteem* or *power* vis-a-vis the relatively weaker position of sociologists ; or, was it their self-conscious "scientific" inferiority which made them succumb to influence from professionals ?

The preceding exposition should be regarded as constituting a general background to a very limited inquiry being attempted here. Based upon whatever little evidence available on the two main professions—medical and legal profession in the Indian society, we shall try to uncover the nature of professional ori ntations—both towards professionals themselves and towards wider society, and then match these with ideal-typical cognitions and orientations as expected according to the conceptual construct of professions. It will then be possible for us to answer the question ; whether the actual professional orientations need to be understood in the light of their existential conditions or that they simply flow from their axiomatic attributes such as collectivity-orientation, professional autonomy, etc.

The term "orientations" in our usage here refers to professional cognitions and perceptions i.e. modes of perceiving the wider socio-political reality and the professions' relationship with such reality.

Professional Orientations : The Evidence

Notwithstanding, a number of studies available on both medical profession[2] and legal profession[3] there is paucity of information on the nature and character of professional cognitions, even though there is ample evidence on some other aspects of professions such as their social background, conditions of practice, professional goals and organizational demands, etc. We shall examine below whatever material is available on this.

(1) We shall start with Madan's study which copiously

reports on doctors' self-image and their cognitive orientations towards society.[4] His study was conducted at All India Institute of Medical Sciences, Delhi during 1975-77 as a part of UNESCO-sponsored study of doctors in India, Malaysia and Sri Lanka. His total sample constituted of 100 doctors out of which only ninety-seven answered. The findings are reported in an anthropological style i.e. through a narrative description of the profession and its conditions, rather than presented in discrete tables.

Despite the fact that all the respondents in Madan's sample were teaching and also in most cases researching at the Institute, the image of doctor *who dealt with the patients* was central to their self-image. Even though, nearly all of them were connected with their professional associations and enjoyed the "intellectual" content of their work curing gave them enormous self-gratification. Many thought that they did not get their due from society and were often ill-treated by public especially politicians. Notwithstanding the importance of their function vis-a-vis the society, they resented that they were not looked upon as humans entitled to ordinary creature-comforts. A majority viewed themselves inferior to civil servants. A substantial number of them were oriented outside the institute, prepared to leave it—whether for going abroad or for a better career within the country, whenever the opportunity arose. The evolution in the goals oi the Institute has not kept pace with an appropriate adjustment in the goals of the professional themselves. As Madan mentions, even though the initial goals of the Institute included developing high-quality teaching and research in the medicine, over a period of time, it came to develop a Centre for Community Medicine. The purpose of teaching under this new programme was "to enable medical students to come to know patients *in sutu* and learn about their social-economic and cultural conditions, and to cultivate a community orientation." Accordingly,..."Each student adopts a few families and visits the field five to six times each semester." The programme is considered as a very important innovation ("the fourth pillar of medical education"), by some of the senior faculty members including the founding director of the institute. But, despite all this, the doctors under study had not shown a corresponding adaptation to this new role and continued to regard it as a "soft choice" or something which is professionally not upto the mark.

Still another casualty at the hands of medical professionals under study was that of *family planning*—another felt-need of the contemporary Indian society. It is not that doctors did not realize the contemporary relevance of this programme but that they could not relate to their profession, its skills, goals and applications. Mainly because they thought that the programme did not involve the employment of any complex professional skills. Instead, they thought it should be the concern of social workers and administrators. Does it not speak of a wilful isolation from an important social concern ? In other words, does it not speak of social irresponsibility instead of conceptually stipulated social responsibility or collectivity-orientation? Another important component of these professionals' self-image is that even though they were critical of the conditions in which the profession was practised such as the politicians' and bureaucrats' domineering control over them, they were not at all critical of the professionals themselves for succumbing to these pressures or for their several unprofessional practices.

All this can be readily appreciated if we recognize that the norms of professional functioning need not be derived from those internalized during the course of professional socialization, or from standards of professional conduct laid down by the professional bodies, but instead come from structure and character of professional situation in which they operate and live.

(2) Another important work which supplies an interesting array of materials falling into the central argument of this paper is *Doctors and Nurses* by Oommen. We shall deal here specifically with the orientations of the doctors, even though these are analysed by him in relation to those of nurses. All the doctors in Oommen's sample were working in the organizational settings of some leading hospitals of Delhi.

It is interesting to note that nearly all the doctors suffered from a sense of relative deprivation vis-a-vis the top bureaucrats which is the same as reported by Madan in his study.

But in Oommen's study ; this inter-professional self-deprivation is associated with a feeling of high professional self-esteem, so that they viewed themselves as more significant than their co-professionals who worked as administrators in the hospital. "An overwhelming majority of doctors and house-surgeons, eighty-six per cent and eighty-eight per cent respectively, ranked themselves at the top in the hospital hiearchy."[5] That, the "professional prestige" is not an abstract, unvarying and monolithic entity but is instead related to the structural conditions of the profession, is brought out by him through its relationship with the professional ranking of a particular hospital where one was working. "...When asked whether there is any prestige associated with working in a particular hospital, sixty-two per cent doctors and sixty-one per cent house-surgeons answered in the affirmative."[6]

Just like Madan, Oommen also found a strong sense of "patient-orientation" among the doctors of his study. On the basis of a variety of responses given by his respondents of their ideal role-perceptions, Oommen classified eighty-four per centas "patient oriented", nineteen percent as "bureaucratic oriented", 4 per cent and two per cent "professional oriented" and "personality oriented" respectively. In still another case, in response to the question : "To whom do you think you are discharging your duties ? Sixty-two per cent mentioned 'patient', nineteen per cent 'myself', sixteen per cent 'nation', other responses being three per cent." Correspondingly, Oommen classified doctors in terms of their reaction to work-situation as "humanitarian" (seventy-nine per cent) and "Bureaucrats" (four per cent). This buttresses his inference on professional orientations.

These predominantly "patient orientations" of the doctors, as against predominantly "bureaucratic" orientations of the nurses in Oommen's study, are interpreted by him in terms of an important trait of the work-situation i.e. a distinct autonomy in professional role-discharge enjoyed by doctors as against the nurses. It is also important to note that doctor's *collectivity-orientation* is confined only to a narrow and close range i.e. upto their patients and does not extend to the wider society. This felt-intimacy of the doctors with their patients can be easily seen to flow from the condition of their work-situation i.e. from frequent interaction which they have with their patients. Nurses' interaction with the patients even though close and intimate is obviously of a "delegated" nature, something which is designed and structured not by themselves but by the doctors whom they are expected to assist professionally. It is clear, thus, that professional orientation is not unitary or monolithic in nature i.e. following automatically from some professional norms, but is instead structured by the elements of the professional situation.

(3) Lastly, we deal with some evidence on the issue adduced by Gandhi.[7] The study analyses the orientations of the lawyers vis-a-vis their own profession as well as judiciary, the *polity* and the *wider society*, as reflected in their deliberations against "the supersession of three Supreme Court Judges by the Government of India and the appointment of Justice A.N. Ray as the Chief Justice of the Supreme Court of India", at a formally organized "All India Convention of Lawyers on the Independence of the Judiciary" in Delhi (between 11-12 August, 1973). Since, the assemblage in question constituted of lawyers and addressed themselves again and again to the same problem, their expression could be legitimately termed as their "collective representations" with regard to specific problem in hand. A broad categorical content-analysis was attempted of various speeches made on this occasion and view-points expressed. These have been analyzed at length elsewhere.[8] For the present argument, however, we shall present only a specific section of the said analysis. For example, it is relevant to recall here that the lawyers regarded themselves as the "strongest bastion" of democratic values and traditions in the country. Accordingly, they felt that they alone could counter, with any effectivity, a threat from the all-powerful State which, through disregarding the time-honoured principle of "seniority" in appointing Chief Justice to Supreme Court of India, was, in fact, encroaching upon the autonomy of the profession. The said appointment by the government, they maintained, was an ominous fore-boding of the things to come; the intended designs of the government of

promoting totalitarianism in the country. All the speakers strongly felt that the practice of handpicking the members of the high judiciary would cut at the roots of the independent judiciary which was intended constitutionally to be a strong bulwark against the autocracy of the government and the executive. A common refrain which ran through all the speeches was that the "protective" role of the profession vis-a-vis the democratic traditions of the country was in continuation of the pioneering role that it had already played all through the independence movement.

All this regard for the social and democratic values could superficially be interpreted as professions "collectivity orientation" which is inherent in it conceptually i.e. according to the theory of professions. But a closer look would uncover some additional characteristics of these professional cognitions and orientations. First of all, lawyers at this conference, thought of society as a regular i.e. static and unchanging entity—the perpetuation of which was the professional duty of lawyers. They nowhere emphasized that the lawyers—whether as lawyers or as judges, should be imbued with a dynamic perspective so as to comprehend the necessity of change. Second; even though strongly critical of government's encroachment on the autonomy of the profession, none of the participant mentioned that the profession should cultivate the requisite criticality and undergo the needed sensitization to the changing social needs. Third, an attitude of self-righteousness reflected in the cognitions of the lawyers smacked of a self-perceived "professional omniscience" which is not a befitting attribute of an intellectual profession.

An analytical view of these cognitions and orientations would reveal that these can be easily appreciated in the light of conditions of professional practice, rather than as derivative of a theoretically stipulated "collectivity-orientation." or "professional autonomy". "First of all, lawyers' concern with the 'tradition' of Constitution as well as with the 'convention' of recruiting judges by seniority follows directly from the logical and ideational basis of their professional practice. Two logical constituents of the lawyers' professional practice stand out prominently, their use of the written word and of the *legal precedent* as the cornerstone of their arguments while pleading in the Courts. It is to these that the lawyers appeal again and again to impress their point and to draw strength for proving their contentions before the bench in the day-to-day pursuit of their professional practice. It is therefore, logical that they criticise executive encroachment on *convention* of recruiting judges by seniority. In criticising government's measure of superseding judges, what they are safeguarding really is the principle of convention or tradition rather than the right of judiciary."[9]

"Besides their professional orientation to defend 'tradition' and 'convention', the lawyers also stand to serve their professional cause in upholding the time-honoured criteria of appointment-by-seniority in case of Supreme Court Judges. In conceiving that a lawyer will be able to persuade a judge on a particular case to his viewpoint, he must first feel sure that such a possibility is potentially there, which means that a judge must be seen as completely autonomous in his functioning and free from any political or other influences. To the extent, therefore, that a lawyer sees such a possibility being compromised, he will feel professionally insecure and unsafe. We maintain therefore, that the protest-response of the lawyers at convention under discussion, to the supersession of judges, was more a security-guarding effort on their part than their concern for 'constitutionality', 'democracy' or even 'professional autonomy'..."[10]

The Inference and Theory

The evidence presented in the paper is of a highly limited and restricted variety and does not provide any room for a categorical argument. But this is obviously to suggest that we need more data to state anything with a sense of finality and not to say that the meaning of data is not clear.

The heavy dependence of professional self-image and of its social orientations on the structure and conditions of its own *performance* signified clearly that its essence flows from its *existence* and not from any *theoretical-canonical* stipulations. That is to say, that there are no nuclei generating through their immanent force, the attributes of collectivity-orientation or professional autonomy in an automatic manner ; instead, conditions of professional performance structure or re-structure its attributes. And, to say this is not to utter a profundity, but to articulate a common sociological truth, which in the context of the sociology of the professions, has been woefully disregarded so far that, social entities as well as their cognitions are caused by their existential framework. With this realization, the mystique of *professionality* vested uncritically in certain occupations vanishes and attributes that are assumed to have gone into the making and socialization of professionals, can now be seen to have emerged from the manner of their functioning.

The plea is not being made here against the use of ideal types, which indeed have done a yeoman's service to sociology, but only that these be rooted in the sociological sensitivity instead of being constructed out of prevalent cultural perceptions and even shibboleths. Professions should, therefore, be viewed not after pristine cognitive model inherited by sociologists from professions themselves which were the undisputed intellectual leaders in the early twentieth century. Instead, these must be appreciated within the framework of contemporary conditions—both cultural and economic, which can both perpetuate and destroy traditionally inherited professional sensitivities and ideations.

The merit of such a theoretical departure can hardly be adequately appreciated in a country like India where professions like law, medicine and higher education continue to enjoy an aura of intellectual and moral supremacy and participate massively in the tasks of social re-construction. A sociological realism on their functioning would lead to a realism on their role in the contemporary society and polity—which would indeed be a substantial gain not for men of theory alone but also for those who expcct the fruit of social action.

NOTES AND REFERENCES

1 Durkheim, Emile, *Professional Ethics and Civic Morals*, Free Press of Glencoe, New York, 1985 ; Carr-Saunders, A.M., and P.A. Wilson, *The Professions*, The Clarendon Press, Oxford, 1933.
2. Madan, T.N., *Doctors and Society : Three Asian Case Studies*, Vikas, New Delhi, 1980 ; Oommen, T.K., *Doctors and Nurses : A Study in Occupational Role Structure*, Macmillan, Delhi, 1978; Venkataratnam, R., *Medical Sociology in Indian Setting*, Macmillan, Bombay, 1979.
3. Rowe, Peter, "Indian Lawyers and Political Modernisation : Observations in Four District Towns," *Law and Society Review*, vol. 3, No. 21, (November 1968-February 1969), pp. 219-250; Gandhi, J.S., "Lawyers and Social Change : A Test Case", *Punjab University Law Review*, vols. 26-27, nos. 1-2, 1974-75, pp. 46-56 ; *Lawyers and Touts : A Study in the Sociology of the Profession*, Hindustan Publication, New, Delhi, 1982; Sharma, K.L., *Sociology of Law and Legal Profession : A Study of Relations Between Lawyers and Their Clients*, Rawat Publications, Jaipur, 1984.
4. Madan, *op. cit.*
5. Oommen, *op. cit.*, p. 61
6. Oommen, *op. cit.*, p. 62.
7. Gandhi, 1974-75, *op. cit.*
8. Gandhi, 1974-75, *op. cit.*
9. Gandhi, 1974-75, *op. cit.*, p. 55.
10. Gandhi, 1974-75, *op. cit.*

6

PATTERNS OF PROFESSIONAL PROCESSES

MOHAN ADVANI

Professionals Profess. They profess to know better than others the nature of certain methods and to know better than their clients what ails them or their affairs.[1] The professionals command authority to the extent that they sometimes refuse to act unless the clients agree to follow their advice. Perhaps, that is why each professional group is bound by self-imposed ethical codes of conduct which its members are obliged to follow. The actions of professionals, in most cases cannot be judged by their clients and hence they rely on the professionals' advice without knowing the merits of it.

Blau and Scott have indicated four aspects of professional's behaviour. (1) The professionals are bound by a norm of service and code of ethics to represent the welfare and interests of their clients. (2) Their authority is rooted in their acknowledged technical expertness. (3) They like to be governed by their internalized professional standards rather than comply with external directions. (4) When a professional is questioned, the right of reviewing its correctness is reserved to his professional colleague group.[2] These aspects of autonomy result in extremely limited social accountability of the professionals.

There are four general attributes of professional behaviour (1) generalised knowledge, (2) primary orientation to community interest, (3) internalised code of ethics, and (4) rewards which primarily symbolise work achievement.[3] The study of professions should focus on these as well as on pertinent sociological questions.

SOCIOLOGICAL QUESTIONS

The study of the structure and substance of professional behaviour is of great significane in the investigation of several problems of society. Professional processes are part of social processes, and the situation of professions at any period of time is built-up from several rational acts in which the active conscious will of the professionals is manifested.

If the professional processes are investigated by traditional methods, people's conscious activity remains unstudied. The professionals are linked with their environment through a system of wants. In certain sense, professionals' reaction to social reality is manifested through this system. The professional behaviour actualises the linkage between conscious needs and the environment.

The professional behaviour is directed towards the maximum satisfaction of social and intellectual needs possible in any given conditions of the social environment. The behaviour is directed at co-ordinating the aims of the collective, social group or other social community of some sort to which they belong. The professionals are also bound to adjust their behaviour to the moral standards, customs, traditions and values that exist in a society. Their behaviour may be alte ed in accordance with the professions broadening need and with the changes taking place in social environment.

The inner organic link in a concrete socio-economic formulation and with the system of specific laws determine the qualitative peculiarities of a profession. This, of course, would include the patterns that are characteristics of the whole period of human history and these would affect the specific acts of the operation of the professions.

There are no grounds for saying that all the features of the professions could be discovered. Apart from certain ones that have been explored, the others have only been intuitively presented.

The economic laws of the relationship of professions and capitalism could be analysed in the framework of Marxian ideology. These, as in socialist countries, could be considered, as the laws of rational utilization of professional services with emphasis on maximum state facilities for the society. The economic laws are in fact the subject matter of political economy whereas the study of the patterns of professional relationships, as affected by these laws could be included in the domain of the sociology of professions.

There are several difficulties in analysing the professional relationships as these are not confined to a particularistic mode of service in any societal system. These relationships are affected by factors like education, culture, technology or special training. The patterns of the functioning of the professions, it must be recognised, operate as trends or tendencies. How far these objective tendencies are converted into objective patterns, depends upon the social and economic conditions of societal development and on the concrete historical inheritance.

The patterns of professional behaviour operate independently whether or not they are cognised. Their mutual conditioning makes themselves objectively felt in professional processes, irrespective of elucidation of the scale of their inter-connections and the degree of their impact upon society.

The society lays great emphasis on the role of the professionals and also places them in an ideal type of role. With prevailing anomalous conditions and lack of motivation among the professionals, the professionals cannot fulfil the expectations of society. The logical structure of the studies on professions could be related to the analysis of evolutionary growth and social processes. The method of course would have ascent from abstract to concrete, but the analyses would throw light on relations of social conditions of life with the dimensions of professions.

EVOLUTIONARY GROWTH

The evolutionary growth of the professions, is irrevocably linked with all nature around it. The chain of evolution, as it affects history, also affects the professions and is the result of transition in society. Morgan distinguished three stages of cultural advance : savagery, barbarism and civilization and linked transition with major technological innovations like pottery-making, domestication of animals and the technology of melting iron.[4] Each of these stages of technical evolution was correlated with characteristic developments in religion, the family, political organization, and property arrangements. In the process of transition of society, the professions began to emerge and broaden primitive men's horizons. The professions encouraged their cohesion, gave rise to their needs and led to the development of brain. Thus, the professions conditioned the needs of man and gave rise to the human "civilized" society.

In the earliest period of human history, biological laws were decisive in determining the conditions of society. The development of modern professions has been a result of very long-drawn out process, and natural selection played a major role in it. An important relative feature of the initial process of the professions was its extreme unevenness in time and place. In the stages of development, the primitive society began mastering over various arts. These arts (early professions) began to serve the society. The seeds of professions in fact lie in the triumph of primitive society over the nature around it and in the concern for the welfare of humanity. At the same time circumstances began to develop where society needed professional services to solve their multi-dimensional problems.

Every civiliz ation, according to Danilevsky, develops its particular style, which is especially evident at the age of maturity.[5] More precisely each civilization excels in one or few realms of activity. Thus, the Greeks accented beauty, the Romans specialised in law and political organization ; Semitic civilization emphasised religion. In more recent times, Germano-Romanic societies excel in the political, technological, and esthetic fields, while Slavic civilization shows greater promise in all fields.

The professions during the feudal period were largely aimed at rendering service to the feudal lords. The professionals not only served them but acquired a feudal character within the professions. The professions, in this period, acquired a number of qualitative features. With continuing systematic support, the professions progressed and started scientifically exploring the problems faced by the society. The way the professions were linked with particular periods of human history could also be understood in Marxian framework.

MARXIAN FRAMEWORK

Marx showed that, during the accumulation of capital, there was a growth of wealth at one pole and of poverty and lack of rights at the other. Following Marxian doctrine it would be said that capital accumulation, by virtue of the very nature of the capitalist mode of production, will not allow the fruits of professional knowledge reach the proletarian substratum of society. The bourgeois would conceive variations in capital accumulation and would attempt to exploit the cause of professional service. They would have us believe that with the accelerated growth of professional knowledge variations would occur in the quality of service rendered—there would be pressure on the services—best services would be provided to those who could afford to contribute more. In excess of the needs of capital for self-expansion, in pace and scale of capitalist accumulation, a relatively surplus population is constantly deprived of better quality professional services.

Lenin emphasised, in his work on the position of working class and its struggle that the order existing in the capitalist world always and inevitably inflicted countless sacrifices on the working class.[6] Thousand upon thousands of people toiled all their lives to create wealth for others and died of starvation or chronic malnutritions and diseases brought on by abnominable working condition and terrible housing. How could the professions contribute to providing relief to such a state of affairs ?

With the increase in mass surplus value appropriation by capitalists, one can see the rise in the degree of exploitation of professionals and by the professionals.

From the analysis of the nature of professions in capitalist world one can conclude that under capitalism the productive forces undoubtedly support the development of professions for safeguarding the interests of the capitalists. This explains the exceptional interest of bourgeois ideologist in the development of the professions and their endeavours to use the professionals as their tools.

PROFESSIONS : SOCIO-ECONOMIC CATEGORY

By posing the problem of the development of professions into its social and historical contexts means studying the status of professions in each historical system of economy separately, and studying its inter-relation with the given system. When profession is analysed in its inter-connection with social and economic system, it must be taken as a socio-economic category.

Continuous technical advance is a necessary element in the socio-economic process as well as in the growth of professions : "The planned socialist system of economy combines accelerated technical progress with the full employment of able-bodied citizens."[7] The planned character of socialist economy provides opportunities for a greater control on the process of professionalization which ultimately ensures benefit of the services to the community. The services in such a situation are rationally related to the needs of the society. The professional manpower is linked with the degree of economic efficiency. This results in a maximum correspondence between economic effect and rational levels of use of all resources of various types.

In connection with the need to maintain a certain ratio between the amount of professional manpower and of the professional services, a change in former must go hand in hand with a corresponding change in the latter. A progressive change in the form of the distribution of services of the professionals necessitates and ever greater improvement in such services.

SOCIAL NEEDS

The profession must satisfy the requirements of providing continuous maximum satisfaction of the needs of the members of the society and of ensuring the necessary growth of the professions. Thus, the profession as one of supporting factors of society affects the welfare of society. The profession, therefore necessitates a certain amount of connection with the needs of society for greater satisfaction of the wants of the society.

The consequences of the extent of the professional services received is largely dependent on one's ability to pay have already been noticed. In terms of the capacity of the professional systems to serve the community, one of the most important effects is the tendency of professionals to work in more affluent areas of a country. As a result urban and rural poor suffer because of inadequate services. The simple financial access model of utilization could be applied on professions, especially the medical profession.

RATIONALITY : CASE OF MEDICAL PROFESSION

A key term which appears frequently in discussions of professional service is "rationality." In general, the term is used to describe the process of formulating policies for the health care delivery system by constantly keeping in mind the goals with which these policies are intended to achieve.[8] Sometimes the lack of rationality has been attributed to "professional dominance."[9]

The medical profession is often held to represent the professional ideal in modern society. It ranks high in social prestige and financial remuneration and it performs essential services within the community backed by specialised knowledge and expertise.[10]

The role of a doctor is quite in proportion to the continuum of increasingly high levels of technical competence required for the performance. Parsons, indicating the collectivity orientation of the doctor, mentions : "The 'ideology' of the profession lays great emphasis on the obligation of the physicians to put 'welfare of the patient' above his personal interest, as regards 'commercialism' as the most serious and insidious evil which it has contended".[11] According to him : "Affective-neutrality is also involved in the physician's role. As an applied scientist: the physician is expected to treat an objective problem in objective scientifically justifiable terms."[12] He further stresses, "The primary definition of the physician's responsibility is to do everything possible to forward competence, early painless recovery of his patient."[13]

Mechanic observes that the average general practitioner has found himself with a workload, too large to fulfil the enthusiastic and idealistic expectations concerning his role in dealing with social and psychological implications of medical problems, nor is he equipped to do by training.[14] Loomis emphasizing the collectivity-orientation of doctor, states that the profit motive is excluded and also his nature of duties cannot be encompassed with the office hours.[15] He further states, if the privileges of business were permitted in the sense of "caveat emptor" they would be dysfunctional to the collectivity and to the "community of fate" of doctor and patient.

Merton stresses the need of preventing the disease and not only to curing illness, though the society largely rewards medical men for the therapy.[16] The values, governing the physicians self-image relate to his self-education, medical responsibilities, self-critical attitude, sense of autonomy, specialised education, moral character, and advancing medical knowledge.

Medical chapter and verse could easily be cited to show that the great physicians in every age have recognised that patient must be seen as a whole, including that is to say, his interpersonal relations and his social environment.[17] Although the conception of "the patient" as a person is long established and generally acknowledged in medical circles, it is also said to be a conception more honoured in breach than observance. Many physicians it is said, continue to regard the patient as a case of sickness rather than a person.[18]

The doctors occupy a higher status in the society not only because of high professionalization but also because they deal with health and life of human beings. The risk of patients' life forces them to do what doctors say. This, therefore, becomes a necessity that doctors possess high moral character and maintain high professional ethics. If the societal system gives way for the fulfilment of their self-interests, the patients are likely to suffer more.[19]

It has been observed that in several cases, the doctors enter into malpractices, vested interests, and bargaining. This prevents the patient from proper medical care. Though the society invests a lot on their training and education, many a time they forget their main goal i.e. service to the society. The poor patients who do not have enough means of support, suffer most in this process.[20]

Even most developed country like the U.S.A. has experienced that access to health care and the quality of care is largely dependent upon one's ability to pay. One of the most effects of this is the tendency of physicians to work in more affluent areas of the country. As a result whole communities, such as composed of the urban poor, receive inadequate medical care.[21] The solutions such as Medicare and Medicade have been tried. There have been efforts for implementing comprehensive health care insurance plans which insures all of the people all of the time for all of the care. Still it is felt that there are some stubborn social structural factors that keep blocking the development of more rational, better integrated approaches.

The British National Health Service could be regarded as one way of coping with the issues of health care delivery, and, like any other, a result of circumstances peculiar to that society at given points in time. The National Health Service has strengths and weaknesses within the British contexts as a device for accomplishing agreed social ends, and has strengths and weaknesses compared to other systems of health-care delivery in terms of the types of output it generates.[22]

In the health care field, the British have been able to move and so have the Canadians although we have remained far short of the health care achievements. Access to services has expanded in Communist countries : in Bismark's Germany, in the Soviet Union, in the Scandinavian countries, and most recently in China.

The Chinese system which incorporates the concept of barefoot doctors has attracted the attention of several countries. Important aspects of Chinese system include (1) deprofessionalization of medical care through use of barefoot doctors, worker doctors and Red medical worker with short periods of formal training ; (2) the bringing of services directly to the people at every level of rural and urban organization ; and (3) mass participation on the part of the people in preventive medicine and public health campaigns.[23]

DYSFUNCTIONS OF PROFESSIONALIZATION

The process of professionalization is greatly tuned to the modern scientific society. Its inevitable nature and necessity has prevented the fuller elicitation of the dysfunctions of excessive professionalization, yet, some attempts have thrown light on the deviations occurring in the ideal professional roles. The criticism has been frequently pronounced more by the press than by the sociologists. A pertinent observation has been made by Bay who has compared the situation of professionals with that of bureaucrats. He has pointed out that the sociologists tend to use the words "professional" and "bureaucrat" as neutral terms and it appears that dysfunctions of bureaucratic institutions and behaviour have received more critical attention than the dysfunctions of professional behaviour.[24] This kind of perspective is further supported by the Slater's observation, who has asserted that the principle behind every professional organization is (a) to restrict membership, and (b) to provide minimum service at the maximum cost.[25] The second principle is particularly striking in the case of privately practicing professionals. This also reflects upon the tendency of professionals towards exploitation of their clients. Though the number of professional organization is increasing, this sort of critical perspective is missing in the literature of organizational analysis, yet surely this is an important part of the truth. Indeed, it would be difficult to explain the struggle towards professionalism in so many occupations without recognizing the advantages that professional recognition brings to practitioners. In our deeply unequal society, this is the road to relative status, riches, security and freedom.[26]

POST-PROFESSIONAL ERA

Professions are in a state of transition. This transition is marked by a growing number of studies and critical appraisals of the existing professions and technological innovations. The changes which may take place in professions will have greater emphasis on team work, decentralization, deprofessionalization, mass participation, continuity with past and motivation. The problems of professions will also be associated with some of the social problems brought on by new technologies. We could also predict the emergence of a "Post-Professional Era" where most of the professional functions will be taken over by the computers. This would necessitate a total restructuring of the professional organizations. The problem of this new era would involve maintaining the humanistic values of professional systems. This would further change the character of professions in society with newer type of professions emerging to gain importance at the place of present ones.

Perhaps social changes in the form of movements or revolutions like that of Jacksonian wave of populism in the U.S.A. and Maoist Cultural Revolution in China are needed to deprofessionalize our professionals to the extent that they can work together in friendship and mutual respect to serve the society in general and the downtrodden in particular.

NOTES AND REFERENCES

1. Hughes, E.C., "Profession," *Daedalus*, Vol. 94, no. 4, 1963, p. 657.
2. Blau, P.M., and R. Scott, *Formal Organizations*, Routledge and Kegan Paul, London, 1970.
3. Barber, B., "Some Problems in Sociology of Professions," *Daedalus*, Vol. 92, no. 43, 1963, p. 426.
4. Morgan, L.H., *Ancient Society*, World, Cleveland, 1963.
5. Danilevsky, Nicholas, *Russia and Europe*, 1969. His work has been summarised in Timmsheff, N.S. and Theodorson, G.A., *Sociological Theory*, Random House, New York, 1976, p. 94.
6. Lenin, V.I., "A Characterization of Economic Romanticism," *Collected Works*, Vol. 2, Progress Publishers, Moscow 1976, p. 179.
7. *The Road to Communism*, Progress Publishers, Moscow, 1962, p. 513.
8. Schwartz, H.D., and C.S. Kart, *Dominant Issues in Medical Sociology*, Addison-Wisely, California, 1978.
9. Bay, J.E., and C. Bay, "Professionalism and the Erosion of Rationality in Health Care Field", *American Journal of Orthopsychiat*, Vol. 43 no. 1, pp. 55-64 ; Schwartz, and Kart (ed.), *op. cit.*, pp. 469-476. The theory of professional dominance asserts that if any one profession tends to enjoy pre-eminent recognition in a particular field, then paradigms and practices of that particular profession will tend to be rather uncritically imitated by all other relevant professions.

10. Elliot. P., *The Sociology of the Professions*, Macmillan, London 1972, p. 83.
11. Parsons, T., *The Social System*, Free Press, New York, 1951.
12. *Ibid.*
13. *Ibld.*
14. Mechanic, C.D., *Medical Sociology*, Free Press, New York, 1968.
15. Loomis, C.P., *Social System*, D. Von Nostrand, New Jersey, 1960, p. 351.
16. Merton, R.K., "Some Preliminaries to a Sociology of Medical Education", R.K., Merton, (ed.), *Student-Physician*, Harvard University Press, Cambridge, 1957, pp. 73-75.
17. *Ibid.*, p. 25.
18. *Ibid.*
19. Advani, M., *Doctor-Patient Relationship in Indian Hospitals*, Sanghi Prakashan, Jaipur, 1980, p. 21.
20. *Ibid.*, p. 22.
21. Schwartz, *op. cit.*, p. 424.
22. Draper, Peter, Gary, Grenholm, and Gordon Best, "The Organization of Health Care : A Critical View of the Reorganization of National Heath Service," 1974; David, Tuckett, *An Introduction to Medical Sociology*, Tavistock Publication London, 1976, p. 254.
23. Sidel, V.W., "Medical Care in Peoples Republic of China: An Example of Rationality," Schwartz and Kart (eds.), *op. cit.*, pp. 477-499.
24. Bay, J.E., *op. cit.*, p. 63.
25. Slater, P., *The Pursuit of Loneliness: American Culture at the Breaking Point*, Beacon Press, Boston, 1970, p. 136.
26. Bay, *op. cit.*, p. 473.

7

A RETHINKING ON THE THEORY OF SOCIOLOGY OF PROFESSION

SHEOBAHAL SINGH

Profession is not a new concept, yet the sociology of profession as a distinct sub-field has come into prominence only recently. Derived at a high level of abstraction and endowed with a mystic character, profession has been treated by sociologists almost as a sacred category. In view of the crumbling code of ethics in contemporary society that gives profession a status far superior to that of a tradesman or as a result of the growing confusion of roles which the society at present is finding difficult to set right the conventional theories of the sociology of profession are losing their relevance. It is, therefore, necessary to have a new perspective for the analysis of profession in relation to the social structure.

Parsons who is the pioneer of the structuralist approach to the study of profession defines that "a profession is a cluster of 'occupational' roles, that is roles in which the incumbents perform certain functions valued in the society in general and by these activities typically 'earn a living' at a 'full time job.' Among the occupational role types, the professional is distinguished largely by the independent trusteeship held and exercised by the incumbent of a class of such roles of an important part of the cultural tradition, usually, by a formally organized educational 'socialisation', so that only those with the proper training are considered qualified to practise the profession. Furthermore, only members of the professions are treated as qualified to interpret tradition authoritatively and if it admits of this to develop and to improve it. Finally, though, there usually is considerable division of labour within such a group, a sizeable majority of the professional will be concerned largely with the 'practical application' of tradition to a variety of situations where it can be useful to others. The professional man is thus a 'technical expert' of some order by virtue of his mastery of the traditions and the skills of its use.[1] Profession thus, includes expertise in relation to a cultural tradition as a criterion of a professional role.

The prevailing major approaches of the sociology of profession are the interactionist and the structuralist ones. The interactionists look at a profession as a set of role relationships between the professional and the client. The professional as an expert provides skill in service to a client who in turn gives trust and payment of fee to the former. A profession according to Hughes, "is a social role defined by the nature of relationship between the professional and his client."[2] Hughes perceives autonomy and authority of the professional to be maintained by the fact that on the one hand the client is ignorant or incompetent to understand what has been mastered by the professional[3] and has no option but to trust him. The professional on the other hand keeps his knowledge secret and mystifies his practice. Mystique building and secrecy maintenance are, however, the common practices more often associated with the applied than the academic professionals. It is because the former's interest is to improve practice whereas improvement of knowledge is the interest of the latter.[4] The profession if viewed from the interactionist's point of view appears to be free from any objective control mechanism. The only control which may work on them is the fear of probable demystification of their professional competence by way of successive dissatisfaction to the client. Profession being a part of the social structure must be objectively under control of a defined social mechanism. In the absence of social control, autonomy and authority (said to be the main characteristics of a profession) will give much scope for deception and exploitation of the client by the professional. Interactionists, however, perceive occupational culture arising from role performance and the role relationships.[5] The professional's syndrom of authority and autonomy remains infact only in the traditional occupational culture. In the wake, of modern technological sophistications and rationalization, the autonomy of a profession is the worst to be threatened.[6] The loss of professional authority and autonomy resulting from rationalization has been observed by Crozier.[7]

The structuralist approach looks upon profession as highly abstracted and theoretical functional units fulfilling a particular need of society in accordance with the prevailing social values and goals. In contrast to the interactionist, view structuralists' emphasize social structure as the determinant of the degree of professionalization and not the mystique associated with it. Parsons, the greatest exponent of the structuralist model spells out certain important attributes of profession and attempts to associate them with the normative pattern of social structure. Rationality, according to him, is the one attribute, the importance of which in modern professions generally, but particularly in those important ones concerned with the development and application of science serves to emphasise its role in the society at large.[8]

Authority, another significant attribute associated with the profession is a peculiar sociological category. It is based on the 'technical competence' of the professional man. The scope of authority is very much contextual and limited. About professional authority Parsons writes: There is a very important sense in which the professional practitioner in our society exercises authority. We speak of the doctor as issuing 'orders' even though we know that the only penalty for not obeying them is possible injury to the patient's own health. A lawyer generally gives 'advice' but if the client knew just as well what to do it would be unnecessary for him to consult a lawyer. This professional authority has a peculiar character, it is not as such based on a generally superior status as is the authority, a southern while man tends to assume over any Negro, nor is it a manifestation of superior 'wisdom' in general or of higher moral character. It is rather based on the superior 'technical competence' of the professional man...Professional authority like other elements of the professional pattern is characterised by 'specificity of function'...A Professional man (therefore) is held to be 'an authority only in his own field.'[9] Yet another important characteristic of a profession is universalism. A profession is universal in so far as the professional role is related to technical competence. Science is essentially universalistic...who states a proposition is as such irrelevant to the question of its scientific value.[10]

Profession has been usually distinguished from business on the basis of the nature of motive orientation. Business is characterized by self-interest and the profession by disinterestedness. Even though Parsons, emphasizes rationality, functional specificity and universalism as common characteristics between profession and business yet, he does not negate the fact that self-interest distinguished business from profession which according to him is ethical and sacrificing. We would like to argue that in the modern world which is becoming predominantly materialistic and profit-oriented, the sanctimonious character of profession as highlighted in sociological literature is not free from doubt. It is, however, not disputed that the loss of inviolability of a profession is largely a result of changing social values, but its probability and current eventuation has been almost ignored by professional sociologists. The doctor for instance is supposed to be candidly devoted to the service of the patient and not be guided by the motive of self-interest. But do we not find at least some of them completely engaged in making money even at the cost of the patients' health. We would seldom find a doctor or a lawyer doing service to the patient or the client who is unable to make the payment in return. If it is true how can a profession be given an honour of social service. What we would like to emphasize here is that in a developed society no possible distinction between profession and a non-profession can be categorically made. The idea of self-interest or disinterestedness is non-rational in the context of modern occupational structure which is characterized by a complex division of labour and the so-called professions form just one element in the whole of the social system governed by the same institutionalized normative patterns. Specification of professional categories is merely a futile exercise.

The theories of sociology of profession have wrongfully circumscribed the list of profession unjustifiably ignoring the possible diversifications of occupational roles. The professional behaviour which has been delineated in the theories of profession corresponds more appropriately with the normative patterns of a traditional society. It does not represent the occupational roles of civilized and advance societies which are more formal, contractual, self-oriented, and largely free from emotional moorings. It is, therefore, deciderated that in the event of emerging dimensions of various professions, the concept of profession should be re-defined and more coherent and contextual methodology should be evolved for the study of profession in a changing situation. There is for instance, growing loss of professional autonomy in academic profession. The state bureaucracy is practically tightening its grip over the universities. The teacher's autonomy has been minimized and his authority impaired. Bureaucratization of profession is yet another dimension of change which deserves attention. Professions, now have been reduced to money grubbing trades. Doctors are interested not in the patient's pulse but his purse, educational institutions have become entrepreneurial teaching shops, where the ruling deity is not Saraswati but Laxmi. Your lawyer can not be trusted because he may have been paid off by his counterpart on the other side.[11]

Modern society from the Weberian point of view advance towards increasing rationalization. Heydebrand and Noell rely on this assumption of future iron cage of bureaucracy.[12] Mannheim too looks forward to a perfect society based on functional rationality.[13] Rationality of the planned society as envisaged by Mannheim has recently been observed by Bell also.[14] In the modern society professional knowledge is not only extensively rationalized and consequently aliented from its traditional autonomous character. It is also increasingly pervaded by highly organized bureaucratic structure. The society is facing a situation or ambivalence in so far as bureaucratic organization changes into professionalization and professions undergo a process of bureaucratization. At this juncture the traditional concept of profession as formulated in sociology becomes irrelevant and therefore a new perspective for the study of profession has to be evolved. It is now more appropriate and imperative as well to understand the changing values associated with different kinds of occupations, occupational mobility and the level of commitment.

NOTES AND REFERENCES

1. Parsons, T., *Essays in Sociological Theory*, Light and Life Publishers, New Delhi, 1954, p. 372.
2. Hughes, Everett C., *Twenty Thousand Nurses Tell Their Story*, J.B. Lippincott, Philadelphia, 1958, p. 236.
3. Hughes Everett C., *Men and Their Work*, The Free Press, New York, 1958, pp. 46-55.
4. ——, "Professions" *Daedalus*, vol. 92, Fall 1963 p. 657.
5. Montague, Paul D., *Occupations and Society : Toward a Sociology of the Labour Market*, John Wiley and Sons, New York, 1973, p. 204.
6. Montague, Paul D., *Certified Public Accounting : A Sociological View of Profession in Charge*, Scholars Book Co. Lawrence, Ka, 1974.
7. Crozier, Michel, *The Bureaucratic Phenomenon*, University of Chicago Press, Chicago, 1964, pp. 100-107
8. Parsons, *op. cit.*, p. 36.
9. Parsons, *op. cit.*, p. 38.
10. Parsons, *op. cit.*, p. 42.
11. *India Today*, July 13, 1984, p. 7.
12. Heydebrand V. and James J., Noell, "Task Structure and Innovation in professional organizations" in Heydebrand, V. (ed.) *Comparative Organizations : The Results of Empirical Research* : Prentice Hall Englewood Cliff, N.J., 1973, p. 295.
13. Mannheim, Karl, *Man and Society in an Age of Reconstruction*, Harcourt, Brace, New York, 1940.
14. Bell, Daniel, *The Coming of Post Industrial Society*, Basic Books, (New York, 1973) p. 78.

PART II

TEACHING PROFESSION

8

SOCIOLOGY OF THE PROFESSIONS : AN OVERVIEW WITH ANALYTICAL NOTE ON UNIVERSITY TEACHING AS A PROFESSION

R.N. Srivastava

Institutionalization, specialization and professionalization seem to go together and perhaps coincided with the emergence of sociology as an independent discipline. Institutionalization standardizes a set of social relations and fixes social roles while professionalization implies a peculiar kind of institutionalization characterized by the extensive self-determination of the activity by its own members. When the conditions of work, standards of performance, and standing of members are determined by some outside agency, we would not call it a profession. Sociology got *institutionalized* once it became a recognised department in the leading universities of the world and began to be taught by specially trained teachers holding degrees in the subject. Sociology became *professionalized* together with the establishment of recognised scientific societies. Sociology took to many a channel of *specialisation* when it branched itself off into specific areas for deeper analysis and insights, say analysing an "analytic structure" piece-meal and yet understanding it "all of a piece", the "Verstehen" of totality of structure in togetherness with all of its functioning aspects, say keeping the locus always in full view and yet changing the focus as relevant to demand of the situation by placing accent on one aspect or the other at one moment of time whichever matches finest with the given social context and fits into the intellectual atmosphere around. Above are the surest signs of the social crystallization processes rolled-into-one, and operating all at once all of a time on sociology and now turning it into a successful professional discipline.

Now let us take a look at the Indian social scene moving around. We find ourselves pre-occupied with development planning tending to lead to economic growth with distributive justice. In the meanwhile, we have ceased to be critics of economic primacy. We do not live now by the values that we once cherished and upheld. The modes of economic and social organisation and specially the meanings, uses and goals to which productive activities were traditionally directed, now appear to be passing. We feel compelled to put greater reliance on the Instrumental goals. Evidences of a New Materialism are not wanting. There is lot of mind-blindness when we try to evade the pervasive aspects of human relationships, notwithstanding the organizational professionalization, or the lack of it. It goes without saying that all patterned relationships involve all kinds of aspects and problems, those of power and responsibility, of transmission of relevant knowledge and attitudes and of allocation of scarce goods and services. Thus, even where formal organizations, economy-based, reign supreme, however, the fact remains that the economy or bureaucracy is to be properly treated as an analytic structure or category rather than a concrete one.[1] One may properly ask to which family an individual belongs, which town or region, which caste or community, perhaps which social "class"? But one cannot ask if he is a member of the economy. If he is alive, he is. He is first and last, a human being, a social being, a cultural being. He cannot exist merely as an economic being, professional in that strict sense. The earlier decades were dominated, no doubt, by the physical and dismal sciences; 1980's must be devoted to sociology for dispelling the gloom and bringing back the bloom in budding humanity. Humanities seem to be taking a turn in the direction of getting synthesised into sociology and with monistic interpretations of human phenomena becoming absolute, it is highly probable that sociology may emerge as the architectonic science and sociologist as the great social engineer, the real architect of society.

Turning to theme proper, sociology of the professions is an intellectual endeavour of analysing the complex intersection of economic and non-economic elements in the supply and distribution of very specialized services. The scope is as wide as the orbit and problematics of professional practice. Within professional institutions, business dealings clash with normative elements that specify positive duties and restricted action.

Defining the Professions

The literature on criteria of professionalism is indeed large, and definitions are by no means uniform. The definitions alone, given by leading scholars in the field, would fill many pages but with small gains in achieving uniformity or standardizing the criteria. Parsons writes differently[2] from what Hughes says,[3] and still different view is presented by Barber.[4] If we talk of "learned" professions alone, we stand to gain both in terms of understanding and analysis; and possession of technical qualifications, belonging to formal organization and enjoyment of autonomy, restrained by responsibility, constitute clearly condensed characteristics of learned professions. One may add with profit two more criteria, namely service-orientation and commitment to a calling which although normative in character get closely-meshed in a pragmatic manner, and find their fulfilment in thorough make-up of professionalism. The demands on the professions are *specialized services* and the essence of professional service is the provision of solutions or at least attempted solutions to life's problems that lie beyond the pale of a common man. The professionals constituted a fast swelling occupational category both in modernized and modernizing societies. The range of professional occupations is widening day by day and newer and still newer professions are springing up due to increased specialization and increasing number of subject matter specialists. The explosive expansion of science and technology, multiplication of social ills and evils and extension of the notion of secular rationality seem to be responsible for professional growth and continual spread of occupational range and roles.

Role Conflict in Professions

The universe of professionals is characterized by unity in diversities. The established professions of law and medicine may be considered as a case in point of professional-client relations whereas university professors and the clergy are the salaried class and have superordinates/subordinates different from their clients contrasting to the situation where the client is the employer. In private practice, the individual client comes up with a complaint, problem, or challenge before the professional demanding technical advice or competent service which is generally beyond his own capabilities and here we find that the economic nexus is indeed a curious one in as much as there is an inter-section of clashing principles rather than meshing interests and amicably settled, meeting grounds. Fee-setting principle varies for considerations from the quantity and quality of service rendered to the clients ability to pay, ranging from the "charity case" to the "man of wealth." However, individual practice is on the decline. We are having more and more of medical clinics, law firms, or firms of engineering consultants. "Commercialism" is being held under check in established professions. The "authority" of the professional depends solely on the client's faith. For this faith entrusted to the professional, he is circumscribed by many a personal commitment and orientation, say that of competent service, efficient discharge of duties and protection of and loyalty to the client's best interests over and above personal judgement to the best of ability and knowledge. Then, there is the prevailing concept of "privileged communication" usually in vogue in the professional practice. In spite of all of these restraints and constraints, certain abuses may exist here or there. In dealing with a salaried professional, the position of the client is still weaker. The client takes such services as "fringe benefits" and more a matter of courtesy than of right. And in certain situations, the salaried professional's authority may exceed advice and might even constitute orders.

The Professional and His Colleagues

The colleagues stay high in the role-set of the professionals. Inter-colleague relations are many-sided and largely governed by the codes of conduct, competence and ethical performance adopted by professional bodies, associations, societies and congresses. Such bodies do not only settle the problems of jurisdiction and disputed competence among specialists but as well insure "responsibility" in return for the "trust" of the client. In terms of role relationships. the innocent client simply cannot judge the details of the professional's performance; he can, however, look to consequences, being interested only in end-results. Further, there is no denying that superior skill does carry power, the client must be saved from the peril of the asymmetrical power distribution. Both, the client and the professional need to be protected, the client against the unqualified and unscrupulous practitioner, and the trained professional against unhealthy and unfair competition. Monopoly of skill might result as one side effect of this set of self-controls but that outgrowth can be taken good care of by the state machinery, in an easier way in a democracy that we are wedded to.

Teaching Professions and University Services

We cannot close the foregoing discussion without making a mention of the university, considered by one and all as the sacred "mother" of professions. Indian universities are so rife with professional specializations and consequent rivalries that nominal colleagues in the same department or discipline find nothing interesting to say to one another, even though each can identify real friends on other campuses. It is, by no means, clear in the university that there is an equivalent of the internist, say a research fellow or teacher fellow who considers the student-client in somewhat more integrated terms. These are only some of the tragic reflections of existing societal conditions, only rendered more vivid by the more limited framework of the university.

Unlike Marx's concept of alienation, which referred to man's feelings of estrangement from work, its products, self, and others, Durkheim's concept of anomie was directed to a condition of the social system in which the rules of the group no longer provide limits to individual's impulses. Merton's rendering of anomie is more effective when he focusses on the deregulation of means while stressing Durkheim's suggestion that the deregulation of goals is not the only condition of anomie. More specifically, the undue emphasis placed on "success" in our society and the lack of corresponding emphasis placed on legitimate means for its attainment lead to a "demoralization" of the means. Lesser is the access to legitimate channels or means, greater is the spread of normlessness. This kind of analysis suggests that our contemporary society, in general, and university system, in particular, happen to be suffering from the combined effects of both, alienation and anomie ; the teaching class hit hardest perhaps, with the kinds of values or goals integrally bound up with its peculiar nature of work and its peculiar condition that seem to encourage unrealistic aspirations. Furthermore, there is the suggestion that the university teacher's self-esteem is closely bound up with his work and repute which again allude to alienation from self and others. The shift from achievement-values to success-values in the university educational system strongly suggests coming in of the hiatus between the teacher force and their assigned work roles. Indications are there that the professional ethics of university teaching with its emphasis upon work as an end in itself is on the decline as a normative system. This leads also to weakening of the supportive base of motivation in our social system constituting a big threat to system maintenance understood in functional terms. In simpler terms, if the will to work is threatened, the social system is likewise threatened. This is how the university teacher's general apathy is both a social cause and a psychological consequence. In a word, university seems impaired today by too many conflict situations, for example, culture-conflict, value-conflict, ideological-conflict, role-conflict and what not ? The teacher force is dissatisfied for lack of facilities for work, job-involvement, norm-orientedness, adequate incentives and motivating factors, purposefulness of teaching and research activity, self-acknowledgement in a world of economic and social determinism and popular secularized commercialized culture. Knowledge is suffering from the pangs of powerlessness and meaninglessness.

University teacher is becoming more and more alienated from his professional role since he is finding it difficult to identify with it. Why would a worker fall to identify with his role ? Why the lack of responsibility ? The lack of responsibility toward his role is due to his frustration that he meets with at various social counters. Pushing the analysis likewise. Feuer has gone so far as to identify alienation with frustrations.[5] And the worst of it, the Indian university teacher is labouring under "relative deprivation" and constant "threat to his personality". Another aspect of divergency emerges in the conflict between his manifest and the latent roles. For example, if the professional standards, dictated by the latent role, happen to be in conflict with the organizational and the bureaucratic standards, we may speak of the university teacher as being alienated from his professional role. That is, he is forced to pursue an activity with which he does not identify.

In turn, this opens channels for non-conformity. From the viewpoint of the individual, this means he distrusts the motives of those around him. He regards others as determined to use him for their own ends. In short, he lives in a "context of mutual distrust." To describe this condition Merton uses the term pseudo-gemeinschaft.[6] In this way, the role-strain afflicting the teachers may lead to the breakdown of reciprocal trust and might even damage the normative-pattern of our university, holding it yet under perpetual threat and in ultimate analysis, might prove dangerously disruptive to the stability of our society.

Reiterating the whole thing, now in brief and general terms, we touched upon two important dimensions of role relationships, both involving problems of role-conflict. The first is the question of the primary identification of the salaried university teacher as between his university authorities and his colleagues, both junior and senior ; the second, closely linked, is the conflict between loyalty to the employer (Chancellor, Vice-Chancellor, Syndicate, Senate, etc.) and to clients (students who are not the paymasters) where the two parties are not one and the same.

The problem of organizational loyalty as compared with professional loyalty is endemic wherever professionals are employed in bureaucracies or administrative organizations.[7] This problem is acute in colleges and universities where the preponderance of the staff is professional. The professor's status-stature together with his market price is linked up with his name and fame (earned through sheer work), in the professional academics across the country and perhaps, in winning over world-wide recognition rather than it goes by the favourable judgement of his departmental colleagues, students, opinion and/or the goodwill of the university administrative officers. Some professors may, however, choose a limited local acceptability but that would surely make them for more reliant on the Campus ballot than if they are pre-eminently marketable intellectual commodities. No doubt, these cases present clear-cut ambivalence in role-responsibilities and loyalty-senses, yet, all of these, in no uncertain terms, bring on the mind lot of role-strain. Many a time and on many occasions, the role relationships appear to be ambiguous and role-confusion following as an unintended consequence.

An added load of headship turns the professor into an administrative authority and he is further clouded by the circumstances while "going over to the enemy" in some degree, at least, in as much as he begins siding the organizational interests, which at times may run counter to strictly academic and professional interests. Further on, he suffers from the double loss. In face of the fast revolving world of knowledge, the administrative professor gradually loses his professional authentication. His calibre and competence begin stultifying. And since he is paid a little more than specialists engaged in the same department but as subordinates to him, he is treated with feelings of contempt and envy. He is often criticised as a chooser of an alternative path to success that perhaps he was not going to achieve on strictly professional grounds.

To conclude, the noble, peace-loving, truth-seeking, teaching-preaching-researching, intellectual-services-oriented life of the university teacher, a "learned" professional, all of which, incidentally is mostly genuine is still not free from role ambivalence and conflicting ideologies.

NOTES AND REFERENCES

1. Levy, M.J. Jr., *The Structure of Society*, Princeton University Press, Princeton, New Jersey, 1952, pp. 88-100.
2. Parsons, T., "The Professions and Social Structure," *Social Forces*, vol. 17, 1949, pp. 457-467.
3. Hughes, E.C., "Professions," Kenneth S. Lynn (ed.), *The Professions in America*, Houghton Mifflin, 1965, pp. 1-14.
4. Barber, Bernard, "Some Problems in the Sociology of the Professions," Lynn (ed.), *Ibid.*
5. Feuer, L.S., "What is Alienation ?" *New Politics*, Spring 1962, p. 132.
6. Merton, R.K., *Social Theory and Social Structure*, Free Press, New York, 1957, p. 138.
7. Korn Hauser, W., *Scientists in Industry : Conflict and Accommodation*, University of California Press, Berkeley, 1962.

9

TEACHING IN UNIVERSITY SYSTEM : NEEDED AREA OF RESEARCH

UMED RAJ NAHAR

The forces that transformed religious *calling* into academic *profession* through the university system of the West were cultural as well as social structural. Culturally, the rise of protestantism and puritanism in the continent coincided with the growth of scientific profession and reinforced its development.[1] The pursuit of teaching and scientific discoveries was liberated from the traditional values of the Church ; faith now incorporated more of reason, and calling more of commitment. This is how the cultural pre-requisites of science and scientific profession, such as universalism. disinterestedness and organised skepticism as mentioned by Merton emerged. This led to secularisation of the academic pursuits and societalisation of the academic role-structure. A profession as different from the religious calling derives its norms by consensus and not revelation ; its source of authority is rational-legal and not traditional-charismatic, and its selectivity is open and not closed. The academic profession, once an organic part of the church for these cultural reasons became its main rival and adversary. This cultural transition also embodied the forces of change that academic profession released in the social system of the West.

The social structural factors entered into and influenced this process of change. First, there was change in the system of social stratification. The "estates" disintegrated, and the feudal social organisation gave way to liberal democracy or its variant forms. Industrialisation and urbanisation accelerated this process and offered institutional and financial support which helped in the growth of universities as new centres for creation and communication of values and knowledge. The role of the urban middle classes, industrialists and of the enlightened aristocracy in this endeavour was crucial, although its pattern may differ if we move from the case of the USA to U.K., France and Germany. It may differ in respect of private versus public financing to the universities, institutionalisation of norms for recruitment to the profession, dispersal of authority and definition of responsibility within the faculty or the department. But everywhere the universities do share the basic cultural and social structural attributes of the academic profession that is, universalism, secularism, rational organisation, and allocation of roles was possible because of the typical nature of the growth pattern and its historical concomitants in the Western society. Today the maladaptations in the same university system are contrarywise generating social tensions and conflicts.[2] The reason for this too is cultural and sociological.

In India, the academic profession and the university system emerged as a result of historical contact with Britain, and this contact too was selective. The model of the London university was followed and the universities of Madras, Calcutta and Bombay were established around the middle of the nineteenth century, but these universities did not have a corporate existence like the Universities of Oxford and Cambridge. Only in the early twentieth century, a beginning was made towards establishment of residential type of the universities.

Being a part of an alien institutional innovation, Indian universities could not establish an organic relationship with the social and cultural system of the country. As agencies of social change and modernization, universities in India gave birth to a new sub-culture largely dissociated from the main currents of social system at large. The university educated elite used to become a class apart. Within the educational system too the universities created dissociation and hierarchy since the mode and content of education at the levels of varnacular school, high school, college and university education had many glaring cultural and environmental contradictions which led to contradiction and tension in educational socialisation of our youth.[3]

Since the academic profession in India emerged as a result of historical imposition of the Western university system, the teaching profession from the beginning developed an alienative rather than consensual attitude towards existential, political and socio-cultural life problems of the society. This alienative attitude went along with the colonial setting and the structural constraints under which the academics had to perform their roles. It also harmonised with the overall mode of sub-cultural, sub-structural modernization during this period. The social structure of the academic profession was segmental rather than organic and its emotional psychic complexion was rooted in ambivalance. For historical and existential reasons, the Indian intellectual in the universities and outside got disenchanted from his historical past (tradition) without having struck a deeper organic root in the new (Western university tradition) tradition to which he yearned to belong. No doubt that Westernisation as well as protest against the West resulted from the spread of university education in India.

These contradictions though deep had a localised character during pre-Independence period in India, the academic profession was itself drawn from the upper castes and sections of the society and in most cases it was the traditional literati who entered the role of modern educated elite. So also was the selectivity of students at the university level. Both students and teachers thus formed a culturally, homogeneous group having identical orientation. Following Independence, this equation was radically altered but not the social structure and organisation of the universities. During struggle for Independence, of course, there was a move to discard the Western university system but it was never wholly accepted by Indian leadership or its elites.[4]

We would notice that in the West, growth of universities coincided with basic change in the system of social stratification and economy. In India on the other hand, this system was grafted upon a society which tended to preserve its feudal and hierarchical forms of social stratification and whose indigeneous social base too was depleted by a foreign colonial power to orient it to its political economic needs. Thus, universities in British India had not only a sub-cultural but also an artificial existence. Here was an attempt to introduce an open professional ethics and system of roles in a society which had a closed social structure.

It was following Independence alone that attempt was made to introduce changes in the closed and hierarchical system of Indian social stratification ; abolition of feudalism, agrarian reforms, democratisation of power and growth of technology and science were the new context in which the university system for the first time in India had to interact to develop an organic character. Their process over the years has created many problems and vital issues with which university system and academic profession in India is today confronted with. This change in the nature of university's relationship with society rendered it no longer a sheltered institution dissociated from the social and existential milieu of the society, rather it became increasingly an area of competition and conflict between classes and groups for access to educational resources and power. Higher education ceased to be merely a cultural accomplishment, it became a scare commodity, and a resource for access to status and power.

This is evident from the proliferation of a number of universities after Independence. The selectivity of students to those increasing number of universities has also been broadened in terms of class and caste status and regional affiliations ; higher education is no longer a monopoly of the traditionally upper classes or urban groups. The demand for wide access to university education, after Independence has also mostly come from regional and sub-regional centres of political pressure groups. It is sharpened as education is a state subject under the Constitution. With the increase in the number of universities, the size of the academic profession has also increased and its role is also expected to be more consensual than alienative, especially in the structural sense. Now universities are forced to respond to the immediate demands of the social milieu and economic political pressures of their region more than in the past. The change in the medium of instruction to regional languages only highlights one important aspect of such demands for consensus between the university and society.

But a serious question about the nature of this consensus arises : What kind of consensus is it for which our universities and its academic profession should strive ? Is the professional norm of science and search for truth where the governing values are of universalism, disinterestedness and organised skepticism to be given a predominant emphasis in this consensus or should it be the consensus of a political character where norms relate to sharing of resources and power ? Consensus in a professional community qualitatively differs from that of a political party. Here, emphasis should be given on the principles of legitimation and institutionalisation of the goals and norms of the academic profession. This problem should be deeply understood especially in a regional setting of university structure and its functions. It may be tentatively hypothesised that as the regional character of a university is more dominant the nature of consensus in its value structure is more on lines of the political than academic model. In political model of professional consensus, the university is thought of more as a resource for economic and power gratification rather than as a base for creation, communication and consumption of knowledge and values. Universities may on this basis form a continuum of political academic consensus ; where political consensus is dominant, one may find greater and active interaction of the university system with the outside social and political system, the aspiration of teachers may be such that far surpasses their commitment to pursuit of knowledge, professional status within departments and faculties might be legitimised more on the basis of control over institutional mechanism of the authority (by being Head of the Department, Dean etc.), than by academic quality or performance by incumbents ; the campus politics in liaison with the regional and local politics may be more active among academics in such circumstances than issues of scientific values and validation.[5] Recruitment to the academic profession too under this situation may be favouring partisan interests than academic performance and even vice-chancellors may represent factional interest than values of academic excellence and freedom. The converse may be dominant in universities having academic consensus. The problem of academic consensus and legitimation has thus both inter-systematic (university versus outside social structure) and intra-systematic (within the university) levels of functioning and organisation, and both need to be properly understood.

Connected with the problems of consensus is the issue of social responsibility of the academic profession and the universities. The Report of Education Commission (1964-66) lays down the functions of the universities in free India as :

(1) "to seek and cultivate new knowledge, to engage vigorously and fearlessly in the pursuit of truth and to interpret old knowledge and beliefs in the light of new needs and discoveries ;"

(2) "to provide the right kind of leadership to all walks of life, to identify gifted youth and help them develop their potential to the full by cultivating right interests ; attitudes and moral and intellectual values ;"

(3) "to provide society with competent men and women trained in agriculture, arts, medicine, science, and technology and various other professions, who will also cultivate individuals imbued with sense of social purpose ;"

(4) "to strive to promote equality and social justice and to reduce social and cultural differences through diffusion of education ;" and

(5) "to foster in the society generally, the attitude and values needed for developing the 'good life' in individuals and society."[6]

These functions of the university and its academic profession, visualised for the needs of an independent and growing nation offer a frame-work in which the potentiality of the academic profession to perform these tasks as well as the problem arising therefrom for the profession should be comprehended.

The type of balance between the pursuit of academic values, fundamental to the life of an academic profession and the social responsibility of the academics as laid down by the Education Commission is a matter which can be investigated in terms of the extent of its possibility in our present day university system only after its thorough structural, functional analysis. Its nature may be determined by the forms of consensus prevalent in the university system mentioned above as also by the regional, political, cultural demands with which most often the growth system of universities may be linked. For this, it would be necessary to analyse the system of university in the context of other system outside of it, especially socio-political, economic and cultural. This could be done by a regional study where the structure and function of academic profession and university system within an entire region is studied deeply and in terms of its organic relationship with systems exogenous to it that bear upon the universities' internal system of norms, activities and institutions. Such a study could reveal first, the nature of social structure of the academic profession and the academics, its consensus pattern and system of authority ; its institutionalised principles of role legitimation and their psychic, cultural and existential ingredients ; its form of social stratification and its consequences to the profession as a whole, secondly, it could analyse the areas of conflict, deviation and tension emerging into the structure of the system due to the mode of functioning of the system ; here the extent and possibility of balance between the fundamental values of academics and their social responsibility could be studied in the context of continuity and change in the structure of the profession. Thirdly, study could focus on the major issues, areas and causal elements of change in the university system and academic profession resulting from the internal structural tensions and needs of innovations and new adaptations. Here the role of major groups within the system such as the teachers and their various ranks, students and administration could be analysed.

This analytical enterprise then could be carried into the second stage of study where explanatory formulations of trends and possibilities of change in the profession and university system are arrived at by comparing the structural functional processes within the university system, as mentioned above, with social system outside and its selected structural—functional relationships or spread effects on the university and its profession. It is here that politics, social structure, economy and cultural systems of the region as a whole would be relevant for drawing causal historical inferences on innovation, conflict and change. The process of modernization would constitute an important conceptual referent of this analysis of change.

There is an urgent need for such a study for various reasons. First, because of structural contradictions in which university is involved in India today for reasons mentioned above. The feeling of disenchantment towards this system is growing among academics, students, elites as well as the public. There is need for objective study to set the reality of university life and academic profession in a proper and objective perspective. Secondly, there is need for such study for educational planning and formulation of policies for further expansion and adaptive changes. Thirdly, education being a resource, its rapid politicisation makes it a sensitive instrument for controlling peoples' gratification, deprivation and consequently it performs a dual role as an agency of modernization and change. First, by creating new infra-structure, activities and personnel organization and secondly, by setting a cultural process into motion which lays emphasis on values of equality, social justice, freedom, and high aspirations. At this second level, the educational structure becomes organically involved with the trends of stability and change in the broad social system at large. This process must be studied as it may inhere clues to basic factors of change in our society. Fourthly, educational system at higher level is an important rationally organised institution which seeks to bridge the gap between generations by institutionalised interaction within a role structure and value-system context. The widespread student movements reflect the fact probably that somewhere the basis of this institutionalised mode of interaction which so far was going smoothly has gone amiss and calls for rethinking and re-orientation. This could be done scientifically only when the boundary of the problem is at least roughly defined by set of variables which enter into this phenomena. Finally, a study of this kind is needed in order to rationalise the structure and function of academic profession and universities for seeking through them the social and academic objectives for which they have been devised.

In the light of the above factors, a study of academic profession, university organisation and social change should be planned as a regional study which should, cover the following aspects of the problem :

(*a*) *Structure of Academic Profession* : Recruitment, stratification, role allocation and its structure, system of authority, its principles of legitimation, forms of consensus, academic profession, psychological and motivational correlates of academic roles and activities, historical basis of academic profession, its development and growth, types of universities, its background in relation to the nature of its academic profession.[7]

(*b*) *Academic Profession as a Functioning System* : nature of academic commitment, teaching and research, relationship between structure of profession and commitment, forms of commitment, alienative, consensual and instrumental, variables influencing commitment, social obligation of the profession and function of the profession, response pattern and academic function ; students, teachers, teacher-colleagues and teacher-administration, response pattern.

(*c*) *Conflict* : Deviance and innovation, nature and source of innovation in the profession, conflict and adaptive demands in the system, group structure of the profession and conflict ; psychological, social or cultural bases of conflict ; conflict within and between systems ; students' movements ; conflict and academic professions. Dysfunction of authority, consensus, legitimation and recruitment and resources and its relationship with conflict, and change.

(*d*) *Academic Profession, University Organisation and Outside system* : Political system, state and academic profession, social structure of the region, regional culture and resource and the university profession and organisation, structure of university and outside systems, State,

UGC and other organisations. Impact of outside system on the structure and function of the Academic Profession.

(*e*) *Academic Profession and Social Change* : Analysis of trends.

NOTES AND REFERENCES

1. Merton, R.K., *Social Theory and Social Structure*, Amerind, New Delhi, 1968.
2. Theodore, Rozak, *The Dissenting Academy*, Pantheon Books, New York, 1968 ; Bundy. G., "Where Those the Days ?" *Daedalus*, Summer, 1970.
3. Singh, Yogendra, "Socialisation and Education", M.S. Gore, I. P. Desai and S. Chitnis (eds), *The Sociology of Education in India*, NCERT, New Delhi, 1967, pp. 71-74.
4. Controversy on this point between Gandhi and Tagore.
5. Singh, Yogendra, "Academic Role Structure and Modernisation : A Study of University Teachers", Satish Saberwal (ed.), *Beyond the Village*, Indian Institute of Advanced Study, Simla, 1972.
6. Report of the Education Commission 1964-66, Ministry of Education, Government of India, 1966, pp. 274-275.
7. Singh, *op. cit.*, Khanna, Kirti, *Role Structure of Academics : A Profile of University Teachers*, Jain Brothers, Jodhpur, 1987.

10

CAREER DECISION-MAKING : A CASE OF UNIVERSITY TEACHERS

KIRTI KHANNA

In the sociology of the professions, process to select a career has been an important area of study. According to the existing norms, one is supposed to be free, at least theoretically, to choose a profession. At the same time, there are many instances to show the role of kith and kin to encourage, advise and guide the aspirants to steer along the road to the profession.

Choosing a profession is a special normative phenomenon. It includes, on the one hand, identifiable social values and norms which, mainly through primary group agencies, motivate, direct and condition one's entry to a certain occupation, on the other it includes the discrete stages through which individuals pass and experience a life's walk in occupational area. Hence, the study of career decision-making provides some cogency about underlying factors determining the choice of the career.

There is a series of studies on various aspects of occupational career-pattern. To quote a few, Lazarsfeld was the first to make a systematic analysis of occupational choice as a socio-psychological process, by reviewing the European studies on this aspect.[1]

Ginzberg and his associates systematized the process of occupational choice by classifying them in three stages, namely: Fantasy, Tentative and Realistic.[2] They emphasized the role of educational structures and emotional conditions but failed to take into account the reference-group members of the chooser. Miller and Form are of the view that rational occupational choosing is rare, and, in most cases, chance is a deciding factor.[3] Blau and his associates maintain that lack of information concerning real opportunities restricts choosing an occupation.[4]

Leaving apart the findings and limitations of various studies, let us now turn to the focus of the present paper. This paper is an attempt to bring out the career decision-making aspects of university teachers. It includes the following aspects : (*i*) sources of awareness of teaching as a career ; (*ii*) stages of choosing teaching as a career ; (*iii*) career decision-makers ; and (*iv*) motivating factors in choice of teaching as a career.

METHODOLOGY

The research focus of the present study is the University of Jodhpur, Jodhpur (Rajasthan). For collection of data, attention was paid to all faculty members having teaching experience of at least one academic session in the university. There were four hundred and twenty-two such teachers in the university during the year 1976-77 when the study was planned. Interview schedules were administered to three hundred and eighty-five teachers only as the remaining were either on long leave or refused to be interviewed. Three variables were considered for analysis of data. These variables are :—

(*i*) *Faculty* : All the five faculties of the university have been grouped into two broad categories, namely :
- (*I*) Faculties of Engineering and Science; and
- (*II*) General faculties consisting of the
  - (*a*) Faculty of Arts, Education and Social Sciences,
  - (*b*) Commerce, and
  - (*c*) Law.

(*ii*) *Rank* : Professor, Reader and Lecturer.

(*iii*) *Sex* : Male and Female.

SOCIAL PROFILE OF THE UNIVERSITY TEACHERS

The teaching profession of the University of Jodhpur is male-dominated (eighty-seven per cent). Females constitute only a small proportion of the teaching-staff. The average age of the university teachers indicates that they are generally young (38.5 years). Among them, most of the teachers are Hindus (86.0%), followed by Jains (10.4%), Christians (1.8%), Sikhs (one per cent) and Muslims (0.3%). Although Brahmins do not have the monopoly over the profession, nevertheless 94% of the teachers belong to twiceborn castes. Only three teachers belong to Scheduled Castes (0.8%). The profession is heavily urban dominated as 90.4% of the teachers are brought-up in urban environment.

A persual of inter-generational mobility shows that the teachers are more educated than their previous generations. The percentage of teachers whose grand-fathers were highly educated was only 7.5% which went up to 34.6% in the fathers' generation. In terms of occupation, 42.9% of the teachers' grand-fathers and 68.6% of teachers' fathers were engaged in white-collar occupations. Hence, teachers, by and large, represent advantageously placed segment of society.

SOURCES OF AWARENESS OF TEACHING AS A CAREER

To begin with, teachers were asked to recollect as to how they became aware of this profession. Analysis of multiple responses obtained in this connection revealed that there was considerable diversity in this process. It is clear from Table 1 that one-third of the respondents came to know of this profession from their teachers and another one-third were instinctively-oriented to the profession of teaching. Parents and relatives, who were also teachers, were source of information in the case of 21.8% of them. Data in terms of faculty and rank do not indicate any cognisable difference. Sex-wise, while a higher percentage of males (35.5%) than of female teachers (22%) came to know of this career from their teachers, a higher percentage of females (32%) than that of males (20.3%) came to know of this profession from their parents and relatives. The difference is cognisable.

STAGES OF CHOOSING TEACHING AS A CAREER

Teaching could not have been the only career, the incumbents

TABLE 1

Sources of Awareness of Teaching as a Career*

	Respondents Knew From					
	Parents Relatives	Teachers	Instinct	Friends and other close associates	Chance	No Response
TOTAL	84	130	129	17	61	3
	(21.8)	(33.8)	(33.5)	(4.4)	(15.8)	(0.8)
Faculty						
Engineering and Science	40	59	60	9	38	2
	(20.0)	(29.5)	(30.0)	(4.5)	(19.0)	(1.0)
General	44	71	69	8	23	1
	(23.8)	(38.4)	(37.3)	(4.3)	(12.4)	(0.5)
Rank						
Professor	1	5	7	2	4	1
	(5.5)	(27.8)	(38.9)	(11.1)	(22.2)	(5.5)
Reader	8	16	18	3	8	—
	(15.7)	(31.4)	(35.3)	(5.9)	(15.7)	
Lecturer	75	109	104	12	49	2
	(23.7)	(34.5)	(32.9)	(3.8)	(15.5)	(0.6)

(*Contd.*)

Sex						
Male	68	119	114	14	51	3
	(20.3)	(35.5)	(34.0)	(4.2)	(15.2)	(0.9)
Female	16	11	15	3	10	—
	(32.0)	(22.0)	(30.0)	(6.0)	(20.0)	

*It is a multi-response Table. Figures in parenthesis indicate percentage.

got acquainted with. It is a well-known fact that as a child grows and comes in contact with persons playing different roles, he starts dreaming of his own future-role, imagining himself in the different roles he sees others playing. This process goes on over a number of years till the final career-choice is made. As already noted, Ginzberg has identified three specific stages in the decision-making process involved in career choice, namely fantasy (when a child cannot assess his capacities), tentative (when he weighs various satisfactions) and realistic (when he makes compromises between his individual-wants and the actual opportunity which exists for him).[5]

In the light of Ginzberg's observations, teachers were asked to specify the stages at which they thought of choosing teaching as a career. The stages were :—

(*i*) during childhood ; (*ii*) at school stage ; (*iii*) at college/ university stages ; and (*iv*) after completing education.

These stages, broadly, cover the three stages mentioned by Ginzberg. While stage one of our classification corresponds to the fantasy stage, stage two, to the tentative stage and stages three and four of our classification, taken together, correspond to the realistic stage of Ginzberg's classification.

As is evident from Table 2, while a little more than two-fifths of the teachers (43.4%) first thought of teaching as a career at their college or university stage, almost half of them thought of this career after they had completed their university education (48.3%). This category also includes those respondents who thought of this career at the time of doing or after completing their researchwork or doing other job.

Analysis in terms of faculty shows that while three-fifths of the teachers of the faculties of Engineering and Science thought of this career after completing education, research work or other jobs, a half of the teachers of the General Faculties thought of it at their college or university stage. The difference is cognisable. Data in terms of rank and sex do not show cognisable differences. However, one-tenth of the female teachers (included in "other" category) thought of this career a couple of years after leaving their studies and leading a married life.

TABLE 2

Stages of Choosing Teaching as a Career

	During Childhood	Stages		After Completing Education	Other	Total
		At School Stage	At College/ University Stage			
Total	7	20	167	186	5	385
	(1.8)	(5.2)	(43.4)	(48.3)	(1.3)	(100.0)
Faculty						
Engineering and Science	1	5	73	119	2	200
	(0.5)	(2.5)	(36.5)	(59.5)	(1.0)	(100.0)
General	6	15	94	67	3	185
	(3.2)	(8.1)	(50.8)	(36.2)	(1.6)	(100.0)
Rank						
Professor	2	—	5	11	—	18
	(11.1)		(27.8)	(61.1)		(100.0)
Reader	—	4	21	26	—	51
		(7.8)	(41.2)	(51.0)		(100.0)
Lecturer	5	16	141	149	5	316
	(1.6)	(5.1)	(44.6)	(47.1)	(1.6)	(100.0)

(Contd.)

Sex						
Male	6	18	148	163	—	335
	(1.8)	(5.4)	(44.2)	(48.6)		(100.0)
Female	1	2	19	23	5	50
	(2.0)	(4.0)	(38.0)	(46.0)	(10.0)	(100.0)

Figures in parentheses indicate percentage.

Analysis of data in terms of Ginzberg's classification shows that an overwhelming majority of our respondents considered teaching as a career at the realistic stage (ninety-three percent). Only a small minority of teachers thought of becoming teachers at the fantasy stage (1.8%). It is evident that a majority of teachers did not consider teaching as a career at the age of fifteen or sixteen when, as stipulated by Ginzberg, occupational values usually become significant point of reference.[6] Their choice of teaching career, thus, appears to have been a belated compromise with reality.

CAREER DECISION-MAKERS

It is a generally held view that though every individual is supposed to choose a career on his own, his primary group always plays a major, if not decisive role in deciding about career. To find out whether our respondents chose the teaching career under the influence of others or on their own accord, they were asked to report as to who decided teaching as a career for them. It is revealing to note that as many as eighty-one per cent of the respondents themselves chose this career on their own. The percentage will further increase if we take into account those also in whose cases decision were taken by others alongwith the respondents (3.9%). Parents and others, including teachers and friends seem to have played some role in the decision-making only in the case of a minority. Analysis in terms of faculty, rank and sex shows the same decisive role of self in choice of teaching career (Table 3).

MOTIVATING FACTORS IN CHOICE OF TEACHING AS A CAREER

Choice of a career depends on many factors ranging from socio-cultural to personal and to chance-factor. According to Rosenberg, whenever an individual makes a selection from the given set of alternatives, he is influenced by some values which determine the priority of the choice.[7] Occupational choices are also influenced by certain attitudes which condition the individual's perception of the diverse aspects of the world. Money and security are the two important values which

TABLE 3

Career Decision-Makers

	Decision-Makers				
	Self	Parents	Others	A joint decision	Total
Total	312 (81.0)	28 (7.3)	30 (7.8)	15 (3.9)	385 (100.0)
Faculty					
Engineering and Science	165 (82.5)	15 (7.5)	13 (6.5)	7 (3.5)	200 (100.0)
General	147 (79.5)	13 (7.0)	17 (9.2)	8 (4.3)	185 (100.0)
Rank					
Professor	13 (72.2)	1 (5.5)	2 (11.1)	2 (11.1)	18 (100.0)
Reader	44 (86.3)	2 (3.9)	2 (3.9)	3 (5.9)	51 (100.0)
Lecturer	255 (80.7)	25 (7.9)	26 (8.2)	10 (3.2)	316 (100.0)

(*Contd.*)

Sex					
Male	277	20	26	12	335
	(82.7)	(6.0)	(7.8,	(3.6)	(100.0)
Female	35	8	4	3	50
	(70.0)	(16.0)	(8.0)	(6.0)	(100.0)

Figures in parentheses indicate percentage.

influence the occupational choice in the modern society. About social determinants of occupational choice, Rosenberg writes that the prevailing conditions—both economic and social—and the society determine the range and context of fulfilment of the individuals' expectations and aspirations.[8] Thus, understanding of motivation behind choice of a career provides a basis for a clear perspective about a profession.

In conformity with the dominant social values, it is likely that generally idealistic reasons would be reported for entering a career, such as intrinsic interest in teaching or service-orientation. Salary consideration and strenuous work situation would seldom be reported.

However, when asked to estimate the motivation to enter the teaching profession, an interesting syndrome has emerged from the multiple responses obtained. The central motivation is described as ambition for individual identity, self-discovery, self-expression, personal independence and the like. This has been termed as "self-orientation" which has been reported by 43.4% of the respondents.

The respondents are certainly cognisant of the privileged status of the teaching profession. Success value such as social prestige and economic opportunity are acknowledged as reasons for opting teaching by 37.7% of the respondents. They are those who considered the profession as the admission-ticket into the upper segment of society. This attitude, therefore, has been termed as "utalitarian-orientation."

The third category "humanitarian-orientation" weighed heavily in case of 23.9% of the respondents. Their conscience motivated them to serve the society and this profession, according to them, offered a way to that end.

In respect of some teachers (12.5%), chance played a role and they strayed into this profession without any motivation. Only a microscopic minority (3.6%), categorically mentioned that they entered in this profession with a specific motivation to contribute to the academic life (Table 4).

It is undoubtedly true that "self-orientation" was a major consideration for a large number of teachers of both the faculty groups, but the proportion is higher of the teachers of General faculties than those of the faculties of Engineering

TABLE 4

Motivating Factors in Choice of Teaching as a Career*

	Factors				
	Utilitarian orientation	Humanitarian orientation	Self orientation	To contribute to academic life	No particular orientation
Total	145 (37.7)	92 (23.9)	167 (43.4)	14 (3.6)	48 (12.5)
Faculty					
Engineering and Science	73 (36.5)	43 (21.0)	74 (37.0)	9 (4.5)	34 (17.0)
General	72 (38.9)	50 (27.0)	93 (50.3)	5 (2.7)	14 (7.6)
Rank					
Professor	5 (27.8)	5 (27.8)	10 (55.5)	3 (16.7)	3 (16.7)
Reader	20 (39.2)	13 (25.5)	27 (52.9)	1 (2.0)	3 (5.9)
Lecturer	120 (38.0)	74 (23.4)	130 (41.1)	10 (3.2)	42 (13.3)

Sex					
Male	121	81	145	13	42
	(36.1)	(24.2)	(43.3)	(3.9)	(12.5)
Female	24	11	22	1	6
	(48.0)	(22.0)	(44.0)	(2.0)	(12.0)

*This is a multi-response Table. Figures in parenthesis indicate percentage.

and Science. The difference is cognisable. Irrespective of rank of teachers, self-orientation is the predominant motivation in most of the cases, though the percentage is the highest among the professors (55.5%) and lowest among lecturers (41.1%). Utilitarian orientation seems to dominate more among female teachers (48%) than males (36.1%).

This description makes it obvious that, by and large, teachers are neither motivated to enter the profession to contribute to the academic life which could be the normal expectation from them, nor by the sense of dedication and the missionary-spirit to serve the society, which elevates a calling into a profession. As a matter of fact, other considerations weighed heavily.

CONCLUSIONS

Career decision-making syndrome of the university teachers reveals the role played by the teaching profession itself in awakening incumbents' awareness towards this profession. Those who opted for this profession were almost always inspired by their teachers with whom they remained in constant contact throughout their educational career. It is, therefore, not surprising that as a consequence of this, one-third of the respondents developed interest in teaching profession. Similarly, having relationship in immediate and extended family members of which are themselves teachers, also worked as a source of awareness in the case of one-fifth of the teachers. Obviously, these contacts facilitate identification with them and also the feeling of becoming as one of them.

Further, it seems that fascination for profession's status in society and the desire for higher social prestige, better prospects and chance for self-expression played a role in motivating respondents to choose teaching as a career.

Interestingly, in spite of longer contact with teachers, self-orientation and utilitarian considerations, it took time to choose teaching as a career, by the respondents. Most of them decided to enter this profession either at the stage of getting higher education at college or university level or after completing education. Further, it took more time to the teachers of the faculties of Engineering and Science to choose teaching, as their technical education could have provided them other avenues also. In comparison to them, more teachers of General faculties made up their mind to enter this profession while getting higher education. However, in general, the decision was taken at the realistic stage of life when respondents had become capable of weighing the pros and cons of various job-alternatives. Thus, the pace of selecting this profession is connected with the process of social and emotional maturation.

This may be further supported by the fact that eight out of every ten teachers chose their career on their own. This finding does not conform the prevailing opinion that primary groups play a significant role in deciding the career. On the face of it, this seems to be inflated because most of the teachers have already mentioned that their parents, relatives and teachers were the source of awareness of teaching as a career for them. It may be that teachers have identified themselves with the social environment to the extent that what they called as their own decision was the outcome of sub-conscious influence which their parents, relatives and teachers had exerted on them over the years. This with their social and emotional maturity, took shape in their own choice in realistic stage of life.

NOTES AND REFERENCES

1. Lazaısfeld, P.F., Judges and Beruf, Merton, R.K., *The Student Physician*, Harvard University Press, Cambridge, 1969, p. 110.
2. Ginzberg, *et. al.*, *Occupational Choice : An Approach to General Theory*, Columbia University Press, New York, 1951.
3. Miller, D.C. and W.H. Form, *Industrial Sociology*, Harper and Row, New York, 1951, p. 651.
4. Blau, P., *et. al.*, "Occupational Choice : A Conceptual Framework," *Industrial and Labour Relation Review*, vol. 9, (July 1956), pp. 531-43.
5. Ginzberg, *op. cit.*
6. Ginzberg, *op. cit.*, p. 74.
7. Rosenberg, M., *Occupations and Values*, The Free Press, Glencoe and Illinois, 1957, pp. 4-7.
8. *Ibid.*

11

ACADEMIC PROFESSION AND SOCIAL DEVELOPMENT

UTTAM BHOITE

The role played by the modern professionals like the scientists, engineers, medical practitioners, the teachers of higher education and the like, as agents of modernization, cannot be over-emphasized. All of them work as creators and/or distributors of knowledge, values and skills which have significance for the process of modernization.

It is well recognized that the system of higher education has a crucial role to play in the context of modernization and development of the underdeveloped countries. Upholding this, Shils comments : "The success of the programme of modernization of the new states is, to a large extent dependent on the performance of their university systems."[1] Analysing the role of education in a modernizing society, Shah comments: "In developing societies which attempt to introduce rapid social changes through democratic and peaceful ways, education is considered as the chief activity that can initiate and speed up the mobilization and transformation of human resources that are needed for modernization."[2] Gore has also stressed the significance of education for modernization of society, although with certain reservations.[3] The Education Commission (1964-66) too has acknowledged the strategic significance of education in the programme of national development, while initiating its report by saying that "the destiny of India is now being shaped in her class rooms."[4]

Like other new states, India aspires for modernity, to be among the world's modernized nations. The governments in India both at the state and central levels have adopted various strategies and programmes to effect modernization in the various areas of life. They have given impetus to economic modernization by initiating, implementing, supporting and sponsoring various economic programmes and by creating a network of economic and industrial structures. By adopting legislative measures they have tried to do away with anachronistic elements in the traditional social structure. Realizing the significance of education as means of modernization in the sphere of values, beliefs and attitudes, they have included in their strategy of planning for modernization, spread of education in general, and of higher education in particular, as one of the most important items.

Modernization involves changes in the social, political and economic spheres. However, it can also be understood in terms of changes in values and ideologies since it also involves changes in values and personality dispositions of the individuals. In other words, modernization takes place at the level of social system, cultural system and personality system. Admittedly, modernization at these different levels is interdependent, mutually reinforcing and sustaining. Education assumes considerable significance in the context of modernization at all the levels, particularly at the personality level. Modernization at the personality level envisages changes resulting in the promotion of rationality, individualism, scienticism and secularism, which can be considered as the major components of a modernized personality. While pinpointing the ways in which education can be functional to the programme of modernization, Dube writes : "By enlarging the cognitive map of those who exposed to it, education suggests alternatives to tradition, brings into focus the rewards implicit in them...." As an instrument of socialization, it can project new images and values. Purposely used, it can be of help in obliterating attitudes and behaviour patterns that are disfunctional to programme of modernization.[5] It is mainly in this sense that education has significance for modernization. However, this is not to deny the significance of the education system has for modernization, in other respects.

But efficacy of education as an instrument of modernization depends upon various factors in the situation at the operational level. An important and the one relevant here is the teachers who are entrusted with the job of imparting education with a view to bring about modernization of those who receive it. The teachers would be effective as agents of modernization to the extent, they themselves are properly oriented towards modernization and to the extent they themselves have been influenced by those ideas and values which are components of modernization. Gore raises a very pertinent question in this context. He asks : "Obviously, if the agents of change are themselves not persuaded by about the messages they are supposed to transmit and at any rate are unable to incorporate them in their own lives, how can they carry it to others ?"[6] Education can accomplish a good measure of success as an instrument of modernization, provided the teachers, who are supposed to spread the message of modernization, themselves have modernized personalities, an indomitable faith in the values of modernization.

Theoretically, it is consistent to expect the teachers in the higher education, those working in colleges and universities, to act as modernizing elites. They are the ones who have attained the highest educational qualifications in their respective disciplines. The education, which they had received was at least contentwise, modern, liberal and scientific. They are also believed to be well-acquainted and equipped with modern ideas and values viz., rationality, empirical outlook, secularism and the like. Such persons presumably would work as effective communicators of modern ideas and values. And it is in this context that they can be counted among the India's modernizing elites. As modernizing elites, they can greatly contribute in effecting modernization on ideational and attitudinal levels, not only of their students, but also of the members of wider community around them. Through their communicative activities, they can propagate new ideas and knowledge, instil new belief and values and create new points of views among the people and foster the process of their modernization. It is also possible for them to stimulate and accentuate the people's receptivity for change. Singh rightly asserts : "In so far as university teachers are both creators and communicators of knowledge, engaged in socializing the restive new generations of youth, they clearly occupy a strategic position in the social structure of societies undergoing modernization."[7]

But on the level of actuality, the efficacy of the teacher's role as modernizer, as said earlier, is a function of the commitment to the modernity, his education has generated in him, obliterating his commitment to the tradition.

With these considerations in mind, an effort was made to guage the degree of commitment of 193 college teachers working in forty Arts, Science and Commerce colleges affiliated to Marathwada University, Aurangabad. This study constituted a part of the wider study of intellectual role activities of these teachers. The data for analysis were collected through a questionnaire and also through interviews with a large number of respondents. It must be conceded that the study was not purported to be an exhaustive attempt to understand the level of modernity, the respondents have achieved. The enquiry was directed to know whether and how far the respondents had acquired modernization at certain points viz., involvement in religion and religious practices, belief in occult powers and charismatic holy persons, involvement in the associations of their ethnic group and the like.

RELIGIOSITY OF THE RESPONDENTS

It is generally presumed, not without any reason, that those who have acquired modern scientific education would exhibit a low degree of religiosity and religious involvement. The data collected revealed that 57.51% of respondents worshipped their family-gods daily and 37.31% did not do so. 4.66% respondents said that they did worship the family gods, but occasionally. 75.83% of the respondents said that they worshipped the gods as a family tradition. When data, collected through various other questions were computed, it was revealed that in all, 89.9% respondents were believers. The other sixteen respondents proclaimed themselves as non-believers and nothing conclusively could be said about the remaining four respondents. 39.38% respondents had conceded that they were involved in other such religious practices, as observing fast on certain days in the week, visiting temples and shrines and reading religious scriptures etc.

BELIEF IN OCCULT POWERS

It can be legitimately hoped that highly educated persons like the respondents would not ordinarily have any faith in the occult powers and magical practices. However, surprisingly, 64.25% of respondents indicated their belief in the Occult Powers and magical practices as against 33.16% who did not have faith in them. It was quite striking to note that 46.87% of the respondents belonging to the Science faculty were among those who were believers. Moreover, 59.07% of respondents admitted that they were disciples, followers or devotees of charismatic persons or of men of miracles. On the other hand 38.34% categorically stated that they were not followers or disciples of any of such persons.

TRADITIONALISM

The extent of alienation of an individual from the tradition can be taken as an approximate indicator of the measure of modernization, he has acquired. The individuals' commitment to tradition can be measured at different points. An attempt was made to judge the respondents' commitment to the tradition at a few points. The data collected revealed that 54.93% of the respondents performed their various religious rituals in their traditional details and only 5.70% of them said that they did not celebrate them at all. With a view to ascertain representatively as to what extent the respondent could resist the pressure of tradition, a question inquiring about the way in which his marriage was celebrated, was included in the questionnaire. The replies, received to this question from 189 respondents revealed that in the case of

96.83% of respondents, the marriage was performed in the traditional way while in the case of the remaining six respondents, the marriage was registered civil marriage. The data collected can be taken as signifying the traditionalistic orientation of a large majority of the respondents.

INDIVIDUALISM

A perceptible growth of individualism and autonomy at the personal level can be considered as a characteriological attribute of a modernized personality.

With a view to assess the measure of propensity, the respondent has developed at the personal level to nurture his individual autonomy, a question, "Who arranged your marriage ?", was incorporated in the questionnaire. Information collected through the replies given by 189 married respondents revealed that in the case of 68.25% of respondents, the marriage was arranged by the parents and relatives. 26.46% of respondents had reported that their marriages were arranged by their parents, however their consent was sought. Only 5.29% of respondents arranged their marriages themselves.

INVOLVEMENT IN THE PRIMORDIAL GROUPS

An active involvement in the affairs of his particularistic ethnic group can no way be considered as an attribute of a modernized man. In the context of purpose of the enquiry, it became pertinent to investigate whether and how far the respondents were participating in the working of formal structures of their ethnic groups viz. caste, community and the like. The data collected are presented here : (i) 63.21% of respondents were having knowledge about the existence of the associations of their castes/communities and 35.76% were reported to be unaware about them. (ii) Those who had these associations on their cognitive map were asked to specify the nature of relationship if any, they had with these associations. It can be stated that 87.7% of the respondents had fraternity with these associations as members, sympathizers, office-bearers or as beneficiaries.

A COMPREHENSIVE VIEW

It must again be emphasized that this was an enquiry, modest in its scope and objectives. It was more of denotative nature and less of substantive.

Viewed together, the data collected indicate a low degree of modernization, the respondents had acquired. It highlights a high degree of religious involvement of these academics in terms of their belief in God, and indulgence in religio-magical practices. However, it would be wrong to conclude that the respondents were as much committed to the religion as a common man is. From the discussions with the respondents, it appeared that the orthodoxy and the element of religious rigidity were on decline. Nevertheless, the persistence of religious consciousness at the levels of beliefs and of actions was perceptible. The data substantiate Shil's analysis of the religious involvement of the Indian intellectuals. He observes : "The religious indifference, which is so wide spread in the educated classes of the West has little counter part among Indian intellectuals."[8] He further comments : "Perhaps it is more in their religiosity than in any other sphere that the Indian intellectuals evince their rootedness in what is central in their culture."[9]

The religiosity of the academic is consequential in other spheres, viz. his affiliation with his ethnic groups. To say the least, it blocks his modernization at several other points.

A stronghold of the tradition on a large section of respondents is also perceptible. The spirit of defiance against the tradition which marks the modernized personality, appears to be very incipient among the respondents. Those who prefer to cast their lot with something which is the way of tradition, can not be much different from those who are core-traditionalists.

The hold of tradition-hinders the growth of individualism or individual autonomy which again are characterological traits of the modernized personality. Gore observes : "Individualism means the right of individual to think for himself, to differ from others, not to conform to traditional or customary expectations, to make his own decisions."[10] As the data reveal, the respondents in general were marked by little growth of individualism.

The respondents' deliberate indulgence in the affairs of their ethnic groups is otherwise very striking. The education appears to have made little dent on the primordial loyalty of a large number of these respondents.

During the course of interviews with the respondents, it appeared that though initially they were shy of acknowledging their links with the associations of their castes/communities, soon they become bold enough not only to acknowledge but also to justify the same. The shamefacedness in the case of many respondents appeared to be superficial than real.

The modern education system in India has given rise to a class of "the new intellectuals." The college and university teachers can be considered as a representative of cross-section of this class.[11] Desai, endorsing Shils' views on this point observes : "(thus) the common belief that the new Western education completely destroyed the old intellectual tradition or its influence does not seem to be true."[12] Damle's comments are still more incisive. He says : "It is true that Indian intellectuals are governed on the ideational plane by notion and concepts which they want to adopt from Western societies. But when it comes to the operational use of these concepts and knowledge, the Indian intellectuals find themselves governed by the existing features of the social system."[13]

The academics' persisting commitment to the tradition and its sway over their behaviour become understandable, if viewed in the context of their personal and social life situations. In a society dominated by mass culture, the professions tend to loose their elite character, in terms of broadening of their recruitment base. Even the sophisticatedly organized professions like the medicine and the law have to yield to public pressures to keep their doors open a bit wider. The impact of mass dominance in the Indian academic profession is quite visible. The pre-requisites, one is required to have to gain an admission in the profession, are lowered enough to suit the requirements of the newly educating castes and communities. As an impact of this, there is an influx of people from the traditionally-non-education-taking castes and communities and also from the rural families into the profession. Only 11.46% of respondents came from the families following the white-collar occupations. Only 11.92% of them had fathers educated upto graduation and above. 77.72% of them had illiterate mothers. 50.86% of them belonged to castes/communities other than the Brahmins. More than 71% of them had rural childhood background. In brief, the socio-cultural milieu in which a large number of these academics were born and brought up, can be aptly described as the traditionalistic one. What type of value-orientations the respondents must have developed during their childhood is any body's guess.

The data collected also showed that the respondents have continued interactions with the members of the families of their orientation and other kith and kin. This continued contact with the tradition-bound family milieu keeps on reinforcing the childhood value orientations of these teachers, defying whatever the modernizing impact their education had on them. The teachers also have to experience tradition-dominated situations in their work-life as well as in their daily community life.

About 93% of respondents were working in the colleges situated in mofussil areas in the Marathwada region in Maharashtra which is proverbially known as backward. The colleges in which the teachers were working are run by private organizations in the management of which the caste consideration is highly pronounced. Most of the colleges are dominated by the members of one or two castes/communities. Despite the rules of the university, caste/community considerations play very decisive role in the matters of recruitment and promotions of the teachers, as well as in the distribution of patronage. All these things cannot but have sharpening impact on the traditional value-orientations of the teachers. The towns and villages in which these colleges are situated are small communities which cannot even remotely be categorised as urban. The daily encounters, which the teachers living there have also reinforcing influence on their caste/community consciousness and traditionalistic orientations. This became evident when the respondents were interrogated on the nature of their relationship with the members of the local communities in which they lived.

What emerged through the discussions with the respondents, was quite revealing. Apparently, these teachers are placed in something of dilemma ; the dilemma between what they learnt through education, what they profess in their class-rooms and what they are required to practise in their daily life situations. For example, the teacher condemns the caste system and casteism in his class-room lectures and on public platform, but at the same time he is required to make a use of his caste indentity to get and retain his job ; to get a promotion or to win an election of academic body of the university. He remains committed privately to something which he does not profess publicly. The situational factors, thus mitigate whatever little modernizing impact the education might have on them. How far genuinely and effectively these teachers can carry the message of modernization to the students and the community members is anybody's guess. On the other hand educated as they are, a possibility of their becoming sophisticated and articulate supporters of the tradition or of becoming revivalist cannot be ruled out.

It is not purported here to draw dismal picture of the situation. The university education system in India is understandably playing a very consequential role in modernizing the Indian society at different points. It can be broadly said that the higher education has largely contributed to the growth of technical capabilities and skills of the people. However, there is little which could be said to the credit of the university education for its role in bringing about modernization on the ideational and attitudinal levels. This has happened despite the modern, scientific, secular, liberal, ideological content of the education. Admittedly, the efficacy of the university system in promoting developmental, modernizing and innovative ethos in a society is determined by the socio-cultural milieu in which the system works. However, we can strengthen the university system to overcome the handicaps, set by milieu by bringing about certain structural changes in itself. To put it briefly, it is necessary to create at least work-situations in which meritocracy will be established and the particularistic considerations such as those based on caste and the like will be least effective. That would probably generate consciousness about the values and ideas that constitute modernity in the minds of the academics.

NOTES AND REFERENCES

1. Shils, Edward, "Modernization and Higher Education," Myron Weiner, (ed.), *Modernization : The Dynamics of Growth*, Hegginbothams, Madras 1967, p. 243.
2. Shah, B.V., "Problems of Modernization of Education", A.R. Desai, (ed.), *Essays on Modernization of Underdeveloped Societies*, Thacker and Co., Bombay, 1971, p. 243.
3. Gore, M.S., "Education and Modernization" *ibid*, pp. 228-239.
4. Ministry of Education, Government of India, *Report of the Education Commission* 1964-66, New Delhi, 1966, p. 1.
5. Dube, S.C., "Modernization and Education", Desai, *op. cit.*, p. 507.
6. Gore, *op. cit.*, p. 235.
7. Singh, Yogendra, "Academic Role Structure and Modernization" Satish Saberwal (ed.), *Beyond the Villages*, Indian Institute of Advanced Study, Simla, 1972.
8. Shils, Edward, *The Intellectuals Between Tradition and Modernity : The Indian Situation*, Mouton and Co.. The Hague 1961, p. 64.
9. *Ibid.*, pp. 64-65.
10. Gore, *op. cit*, p. 237.
11. Shils, *op.cit.*, p. 70
12. Desai, I.P., "The New Elites", T.K.N. Unnithan, Indra Deva and Yogendra Singh, (eds.), *Towards a Sociology of Culture in India*, Prentice-Hall of India, New Delhi, 1965, p. 162.
13. Damle, Y.B., "For a Theory of Indian Sociology" *ibid.*, p. 94.

12

A FUNCTIONAL ANALYSIS OF UNIONISM AMONG COLLEGE TEACHERS

C. PRASAD RAO
AND
V. VENKATARAMANA

INTRODUCTION

Trade union movement of teachers is a recent phenomenon of higher education in the country. While its existence and growth on the college and university campuses is quite obvious, the consequences of its spread and power are not empirically investigated. The functionalist perspective accounts for unionism by comprehending its direct and indirect implications for higher education and the society, the two important frames of reference for this kind of analysis. The specific and limited objective of the analysis reported in this paper is to examine, variations in, and consequences of unionism among college teachers with the help of available primary data. For the particular purpose of this paper, unionism is defined as a mental orientation or pre-disposition sanctioning a political approach and/or action on the part of college teachers in meeting their job-related problems arising from within and outside college campuses. Formal organisation, collective expression, continuous appraisal and monitoring of conditions, events and developments threatening common interests of the college teaching community, collective decision-making and corporate action for redressal of grievances are the chief elements of the unionist frame of mind. Therefore, unionisation, the process of emergence of unionism of college teachers in its more extreme expressions signifies action tendencies and choices explicitly and positively endorsing a negotiational and agitational methods of solving problems. In the present study, however, unionism was not measured so comprehensively as the above broad statement implies. Instead, as will be explained later, a cruder proxy was made use of.

The term "function" in the context of this paper signifies a direct or indirect, manifest or latent consequence of an institutionalised behaviour pattern. Unionism is the only problematic, independent variable of this analysis concerned with establishing the degree of prevalence of unionism among college teachers, and some of its attendant empirical functions.

BACKGROUND OF TEACHER UNIONISM

Value emphasis and standardised role definitions would not change as rapidly as the objective conditions that once played a part in their coming into being. In the march of social change, lags and discrepancies intervene between normative expectancies, ideational postures and existential conditions. Broadly stated, this characterises more or less the context of the origin of trade unionism among college teachers. Teaching was, and perhaps is, considered a noble and responsible profession, dealing as it is with the moulding of the minds and characters of the pupils, and with the preservation and communication of vital social values, apart from its subject-matter instructional obligations. The natural derivative expectation, therefore, is that the teacher as a professional should develop and maintain a culture of his own and, strive to insulate himself from the false, foul and corruptive influences prevailing in the society at large, at present. As Parsons observes, professionalisation involves such behaviour modes and norms as objectivity, affective-neutrality, universalism, etc.[1] Among all the professions, teaching belongs to a very special professional category. For instance, in the case of professionals like doctors and lawyers, their professional concern ceases once for all with the desired "cure effected" or with the "winning of the contest" in the court of law. But the professional impact of a teacher does not end merely with the "examination passed" by the student. The professional role of a teacher is not analogous to that of a lawyer or doctor because the former's influence endures and is reflected in minds sharpened (or not sharpened), personalities shaped (or not shaped) and characters moulded (or not moulded).[2] At the same time that such valuations and normative expectations tend to persist, there are existential forces at work which obstruct, or render difficult the realisation of those normative expectancies and role obligations. In the past, when both colleges and college teachers were fewer in number, conditions probably were ideal to professionalise college teachers easily and adequately or to recruit professionalised teachers into colleges. College education being organised on small scale, the chances then were higher for finding well qualified and professionally committed recruits into college teaching jobs. The post-Independence rapid and massive expansion of college education could not generate and sustain the conditions facilitative of the emergence of professionalism on the campuses. On the contrary, deprofessionalisation and commercialisation made in-roads into college education. This expansion in more numbers has resulted not only in a steady dilution in the recruitment criteria and practices but also in a greater openness form the social structural and demographic standpoint. A greater multiplicity of personalities of wide-ranging aptitudes, values and cultural and social backgrounds entered colleges as teachers.[3] The dearth of government resources to meet the over-increasing demand for new colleges lay the field open to private initiative, investment and management in college education. Parochial, pecuniary and political motives have led to the starting and running of colleges on communal, caste and commercial lines. Higher education ceased to be the pursuit of excellence any longer. It is to this context of operational realities that one has to trace the emergence and growth of trade unionism among college teachers.[4]

Creation and fostering of trade unions may be justified by the teachers by the structural realities of their working lives.[5] But what concerns a social scientist most are the latent and manifest dysfunctions of such union-like developments in the field of higher education. For instance, it may be asked whether trade unionism is compatible, at the academic and pragmatic levels, with professionalism among teachers, and whether the two can co-exist as a harmonious team ? Will not unions of college teachers weaken college administration, foul the academic climate, and over-protect the college teaching community from their faults and defaults ? Will not unionism alienate the teachers and the managements from each other ? Will it promote or weaken commitment to college ? Some of these functional contingencies of trade unionism among college teachers are empirically explored in this paper, since trade unions of teachers emerge as powerful forums and have the potential to acquire great political and bargaining power,[6] for either the benefit or detriment of higher education, and the society at large.

FOCUS OF THE STUDY

As already mentioned unionism is the independent analytic variable.[7] The dependant variables functionally related to unionism in the present study are : (1) two alternative measures of professionalism and professional orientation ; (2) a single measure of occupational values of college teachers ; (3) an index of college commitment-cum-involvement ; and (4) two separate measures of powerlessness (alienation). The variables and their measurement are discussed in the following sections. The strategy adopted was first to examine the incidence, variation, and distribution of unionism among college teachers and then correlate it with the various dependant variables taken as its direct functions. Positive endorsement of unionism was measured by membership in a teacher union,[8] and rejection of unionism was operationalised as non-membership in any teachers' union. Among union members, distinction was made in terms of active and passive participation, and in terms of position-holding and non-position holding. Thus, several nominal categories of teachers representing different action choices were distinguished : (a) non-members, (b) passive members, (c) active members, and finally (d) position holders. The functional profiles of each of these categories of college teachers were then comparatively analysed to determine whether there is a definite gradation of variation in the functional correlates of unionism along the continuum formed by non-members, at one end and position holders, at the other end.

Since the continuum in unionism is best measured not as a series of nominal categories but as an interval scale, unionism was sought to be measured as a continuous variable as discussed in following section.

DATA, SAMPLE AND MEASUREMENT

The sample for this study consisted of 727 degree college teachers working in the affiliated colleges of Andhra University. A fifty per cent sample from a total number of eighty-three affiliated colleges was taken depending upon (a) the age of the colleges, and (b) the type of management (Private or Government). In designing the sample of this study it appeared desirable to give particular attention to these two selection criteria, as they were assumed importance in determining the college composition, and the attitudes and experiences of teachers. All the eighty-three colleges were first listed according to their age *i.e.*, year of starting. They were categorised as very old, old and recent colleges and each category was subdivided on the basis of management. Thus the stratified sampling procedure resulted in the entire list of colleges breaking up into six groups. From each of the six groups, colleges were selected at random to have in the sample at least fifty per cent of the colleges from each group. In this way forty-two colleges were selected, a fifty per cent sample of the colleges. From each of the selected colleges a fifty per cent sample of the teachers on pay roll was selected for the final study. This selection was made from the department-wise faculty lists prepared on the spot on the basis of seniority of appointment at each college. The teachers in a department were first listed according to the seniority of their appointment and every alternate name was picked up as respondents for the sample. About 2,900 college teachers were working in all the eighty-three colleges at the time of the study, *i.e.*, 1981, and out of this total universe, 727 teachers (one-fourth approximately) were selected.

UNIONISM

Using three simple questions eliciting the membership status of the teacher respondents in teacher unions, the respondents were first classified nominally as Members (480) and Non-Members (247) ; Passive Members (255) and Active Members (225), and Position Holders (124) and Non-Position Holders (356). Treating union membership as an operational indicator of unionism as explained early, it is found that a fair majority of the respondents in the sample (480) have accepted unionism by registering themselves as members of one or the other association. The percentage of respondents joining the teachers union is sixty-six, thus accounting for two-thirds of the sample. If finer distinction than simple membership status is to be reckoned as empirical measures of unionism the data show that almost half of the members (225) have reported themselves as active members in their respective unions, and one-fourth of the members (124) have reported active position holding. These distributions throw some light on unionism among college teachers.

In order to facilitate correlation analysis of the data, an interval measure of unionism was also constructed taking the entire sample into account. This consisted of converting a respondent's responses into scores as follows :

(*i*) Each respondent was given a score of two, if he/she frequently expressed his/her grievances relating to his/her work in college with his/her colleagues. The assigned score was one, if the reported response was "no".

(*ii*) A score of two was given if he/she would regularly read any official magazine of the teacher's association, like *College View*. The score assigned was one, if the respondent did not report reading.

(*iii*) A score of two was given if he/she was a member of any teachers' association; if not, his/her score was one. Thus, a respondent's unionism score would range on the above three items from three to six depending upon his/her "yes" or "no" responses. A respondent was given additional scores if he/she reported that he/she was holding a formal position in a teacher's association and depending upon his/her self-rating as an active or passive participant. The total unionism score was, thus, stretched to vary between three to ten. The higher the score, the higher is respondent's unionism. The average unionism score for the entire sample (727) was 6.53 within an observed range of three and ten, which indicates a moderate incidence of unionism when even non-members were pooled with members into a single sample. It should be mentioned that what was used here is a simplistic and crude measure of unionism.

SCALE OF OCCUPATIONAL VALUES AND ROLE PERCEPTIONS

This scale was operationalised as a composite scale of several sub-dimensions. The various components of this scale are : (1) work-related perceptions and values, (2) perceptions about desirability of teacher training ; (3) perceptions about teacher's personality, character and behaviour ; and (4) attitudes towards the college, students and fellow teachers. These sub-dimensions are discussed below in brief :

The first component, work-related perception and values, measured by ten statements elicits a teacher's valuation of the role of college teaching, the teacher's part in subject matter learning by students, imparting training to students in independent and critical thinking, perceptions of general knowledge requirement of teacher, and attitudes towards private tution, politics and trade unionism of teachers. This component is correlated positively and significantly (r=0.93) with the overall summated scale of occupational values. Two statements designed to measure this dimension are given below as illustrations : "One should opt for the job of a teacher only as the last resort," "The teacher should not tutor students for pay."

The second sub-scale of perceptions about desirability of teacher training was measured by three statements. The items refer to innate versus acquired abilities of teaching, and desirability of formal training. This sub-scale, intercorrelates positively and significantly with the overall scale (r=0.71). Two statements of this sub-scale are given below for illustration. "A teacher is made ; not born," "college teachers also must get teacher training as school teachers."

The third component, namely perceptions about teacher's personality, character and behaviour consisting of seven attitudinal statements, elicits a teacher's feelings about character and moral conduct, moral lapses, habitual weaknesses, personal responsibility for the reputation of their college and their own professional community and his objectivity, trustworthiness and freedom from prejudices. This personological and characterological dimension correlates positively and significantly with the overall scale of occupational values ($r=0.86$). Two of the seven statements used are "character deficiencies and moral lapses of teachers are as tolerable as they are in other individuals," "the person of a teacher is more important than his role."

The last dimension reveals a teacher's attitudes towards his fellow teachers, his institution and students measured by eight attitudinal statements, which cover such elements as concern and regard for his own fellow teachers, extra-academic duties of teachers, an honest interest in college administration and student teacher rapport. This "Teacher Involvement" dimension also correlates positively and significantly with the overall scale of occupational values ($r = 0.87$). For illustration, two statements of this sub-scale are "A real teacher takes active interest in the general welfare of his students", "a teacher should defend any member of the profession who is unjustly attacked".

Thus, the scale of occupational values and role perceptions consisting of twenty-eight statements split into four sub-scales, is an internally consistent and unitary scale revealing a teacher's over all image of his self, his role and role relationships.

In the construction of this and other scales, Likert's Summated Rating Technique was used. Accordingly, each scale item consisted of five response categories : strongly agree, agree, undecided, disagree, and strongly disagree. The responses were scored five to one or one to five depending upon the positive or negative tone of the content of the statement. In the first instance, a set of fifty-four statements were designed and pretested on an independent sample of 160 respondents. The total scores of the respondents pre-tested were rank-ordered from the highest to the lowest total score obtained by summing over all the fifty-four statements used for pretesting. The top twenty-five per cent of the high scorers and the bottom twenty-five per cent of the low scorers (forty) were used as the criterion groups for determining the discriminative power of each of the fifty-four statements. For each statement a Critical Ratio (C.R.) of the mean difference between the high-score and the low-score criterion groups was computed. A total of twenty-eight items with high C.R. values were selected to constitute the final scale. As a cross check, Internal Consistency test was also performed. The items were rank-ordered on the basis of both the test values separately, and Rank Order Correlation was done. The Rank Order Correlation between the C.R. values and the values of the Internal Consistency Test for the selected twenty-eight items is 0.95, which is statistically significant at 0.01 level.

The score on occupational values and role-perceptions ranges for any respondent in the sample from twenty-eight to 140; a high score indicating a high acceptance of occupational values and role-perceptions. The split-half reliability coefficient for this scale is 0.71. And as for the validity of the scale, it is based on the logical and construct validity. As an instance of construct validity, the scale was correlated with a number of other variables of known relationship to occupational values, and in almost all the cases the correlations obtained were as predicted and statistically significant.

ALIENATION : POWERLESSNESS

Alienation was measured in terms of powerlessness. The procedure of constructing and pre-testing the powerlessness scale was the same as described for the scale of occupational values and role-perceptions. Out of a total of thirty-four attitudinal statements in the pre-test questionnaire, a set of seventeen statements were selected to constitute the scale of powerlessness dimension of alienation, on the basis of the C.Rs. computed for each statement. The C.R. values were compared with the Internal Consistency test values by means of the Spearman's Rank Order Correlation, and the coefficient obtained was 0.84, which is significant at the one per cent level. The correlated split-half reliability coefficient of this scale is 0.89. In this case too, as in the case of the first scale of occupational values and Role-Perceptions the validity of the scale was based on its logical and construct validity. The scale was correlated with a number of other variables of known relationship to powerlessness, and it is found that in almost all the cases the correlations obtained were statistically very significant and as predicted.

The seventeen statements that constituted the powerlessness scale were designed to measure powerlessness in both college and general contexts. For the purpose of this paper these two measures of powerlessness were used separately. There are seven statements measuring powerlessness in the college context. The score, thus, for any respondent on this sub-scale ranges from seven to thirty-five. A high score within this range shows high powerlessness in the college context. In the entire sample of the study the average powerlessness in college context is 20.31, which may be considered a high score. Two of the seven statements of this sub-scale are listed below as an illustration : "People like me cannot do anything to eradicate the malpractices of the students in the examinations." "As far as the working conditions are concerned people like me have to accept what the management gives us." The remaining ten statements measure powerlessness in the general context with the score ranging form ten to fifty for any respondent, a high score showing high powerlessness in the general context. The average score of powerlessness in the general context in the entire sample of the study is 32.79. This average may be considered as fairly high within the range of ten and fifty. As an illustration of the statements designed for measuring powerlessness in the general context, two are given: "I generally have confidence that when I make plans I will be able to carry them out", "We cannot avoid being used by others for purposes other than our own." The two sub-dimensions of the scale were inter correlated positively and significantly (r = 0.82). But the two dimensions were used here as separate functional correlates of unionism, because powerlessness in college context is a more appropriate functional correlate of unionism in this study.

PROFESSIONALISM

Professionalism was measured in terms of (i) subscription to professional journals, (ii) length of time devoted to reading these journals, (iii) active or passive participation in professional associations, and (iv) participation in seminars, workshops, etc., during the year immediately preceding the survey. The details of the scoring are given hereunder :—

(*i*) If the respondent reported that he/she was subscribing to subject matter journals, he/she was given a score of two, but only a score of one if not subscribing. The score of two was multiplied by the number of journals subscribed. Thus a respondent could get on these two items a minimum score of one and an indefinite maximum score.

(*ii*) The next was a score based on the reported average time per week actually spent in reading subject matter journals.

(*iii*) Similarly, a score of one was given if the respondent was not a member of any subject related professional association and two if he/she was a member. The score of two as multiplied by the number of such associations in which he/she was a member. Again the obtained score ranges from a minimum of one to an indefinite maximum for each respondent.

(*iv*) The participation of the respondent in professional associations was quantified as follows. He/she was given a score of two if he/she was an office bearer and a score of one if he/she was merely a member.

(*v*) He/she was also given a score of two separately if he/she ever contested for an official position of the association and one if he/she did not.

(*vi*) Similarly, the number of professional association meetings he/she attended was simply recorded.

(*vii*) Lastly, the number of times he/she participated in seminars, workshops, summer schools, symposia and conferences in the year immediately preceding the survey was recorded.

A pooled score was obtained as an arithmetic sum of all the above mentioned seven items. This pooling of the values on apparently disparate items may be questioned on mathematical grounds. We, however, feel that it is justified to pool all the values together into a single summary score because the values reflect separate aspects of professionalism of teachers, such as interest in reading professional literature, and participation in professional associations, seminars and workshops etc. Therefore, this summated score was used as the measures of professionalism of the respondent. A high score indicates high professionalism. The score for professionalism ranged in the actual sample between four and sixty-six, the average being 7.21, a rather poor record for the sample.

PROFESSIONAL ORIENTATION

An alternative measure called professional orientation was also designed. This was measured by four statements, which elicit information on the respondent's academic or professional orientation. The score for any respondent will vary from four to ten in the actual sample the range is from four to twenty. The average score for the entire sample is 13.83, which may be considered a high score. The four statements designed to elicit information for this dimension are : (i) College teachers now-a-days are more political minded than academic minded. (ii) The good teacher keeps himself aloof from politics. (iii) Teachers in the academic professions should present themselves as individuals and not as members of a labour union. (iv) Teachers should not develop trade union mentality towards their institution. As can be seen from these statements, thus measure of professional orientation is logically and diametrically opposite to the unionism measure; therefore, unionism is expected to be associated negatively with professional orientation. The coefficient of correlation between the two measures of professionalism is 0.14 significant at one per cent level. It shall be recalled that the respondents on average scored moderately high on professional orientation, but very low on the professionalism measure. This result will be discussed later.

COLLEGE COMMUNITY-CUM-INVOLVEMENT

This is a summated score of two sub-scales constructed using the same procedures of item designing, item selection, item analysis and validation as in the case of occupational values, role-perceptions and powerlessness scales.

The first sub-scale, labeled "college commitment" consists of six items with respondent's score ranging from six to thirty. A high score indicates a high commitment to college. The items making up this dimension relate to satisfaction over (a) subject; matter teaching assignments; (b) appreciation and recognition for good teaching; (c) freedom and facilities for teaching; and (d) dis-satisfaction over work which is unrelated to teaching. As an illustration, two of the six statements are given : "I am not satisfied in teaching in this college because I cannot teach the way I want to", "the Principal/Head has proper appreciation of what good teaching is". The second sub-scale, named "college involvement" consists of four items indicating teacher's identification with and loyalty to his college. The score on the summated items ranges from four to twenty and the highest score shows the highest degree of college involvement. Two out of the four statements used are described below for illustration : "there is a feeling that teachers in other colleges are more satisfied than teachers in this college", "our college does not believe or practice participative management". The scores of the two sub-scales were correlated positively and significantly ($r = 0.73$) and, therefore a summated college commitment-cum-involvement score was used in the study. The score based on the total of ten statements ranges for any respondent from ten to fifty. The average score for the entire sample is 32.53, which may be considered a moderately high involvement and commitment.

RESULTS AND DISCUSSIONS

As mentioned in the preceding measurement section, the frequency distribution data on membership status provides good and generalisable evidence of the prevalence of unionism among college teachers. Two-thirds of the respondents in the sample (sixty-six per cent) have enrolled as members of some or other teacher's union and half of these members (forty-seven per cent) rated themselves as active participants and one-fourth of the members (twenty-six per cent) have reported themselves holding some position in the unions. We have not probed the reasons for respondents becoming members or remaining as non-members. The causes of unionisation of college teachers were briefly discussed in the introductory section. The average unionism score for the whole sample of respondents is 6.53 ranging empirically in the data from three to ten. This may be considered as an adequate indicator of the unionist pre-dispositions of the college teachers.

Variation in unionism by college type, sex and caste was examined and the findings are as reported below. There were in the sample 206 respondents from government colleges and 521 respondents from private colleges. The mean unionism score of government college teachers is 6.31 (standard deviation = 2.33) and the average unionism score of private college teachers is 6.61 (S.D. = 2.42). The difference between the two means was found to be statistically significant (t = 2.4). By inference, teachers in private colleges are more unionist than teachers in government colleges. The main reason for this variation is that teacher-management conflicts and feelings of security seem to be more among teachers in private colleges than in colleges managed by the government. Teachers working under private managements have to contend with different college managements all of which are not interested in the cause of higher education. Some research documentation attests to this fact. For instance, during the past five years, more than fifteen colleges in Andhra Pradesh were declared as problematic by the private college teachers' associations, and the ACTA (Affiliated College Teachers' Association—Andhra) called on all the teachers in the state to rally to protect the interests of the teachers working in these colleges. In some private colleges it was reported that teachers were abused and treated badly on the college campuses by goondas hired by the management.

The average unionism score of the 590 male teachers in the sample is 6.52 (S.D. 2.38). The 137 female teachers is 6.61 (S.D. = 2.43) and the mean difference is not statistically significant (t = 0.67). Sex is not a discriminator of unionism.

Out of 727 respondents (94.36%), were Hindus. The average unionism score of the Hindu respondents is 6.44%. Of the remaining respondents 3.99% were Christians. Their average unionism score is 6.92. There were 1.19% Muslim respondents in the total sample. Four respondents did not report their religion.

Variation in unionism was observed on the basis of caste, too. Out of the 686 Hindu respondents thirty persons did not prefer to report their caste. The remaining 656 respondents belonged to twenty-seven caste groups. However, the caste-wise analysis of unionism was restricted to only eleven caste groups because the representation of the other sixteen castes in the sample is in negligible numbers. The eleven castes together comprise of 623 out of 656 respondents. In percentage terms, they cover ninety-seven per cent of the caste Hindu respondents of the sample. The simple criterion for selecting the eleven castes is that the caste group selected must consist of at least ten members as respondents for conducting the analysis of variance rest for determining significant inter-caste differences in unionism.

Table 1 presents the average unionism scores of the eleven caste groups with their respective ordinal rank positions, and 'F' value. Economic status of the caste groups was also measured in this study in terms of earning member ratio, per capita family income and level of living index. These data were also presented in the table for enabling comparisons of unionism ranks with the ranks on the economic status dimensions of the caste groups.

From the table it will be noted that Patnaiks have taken the highest rank, their average unionism score being 8.08 followed by Reddys (7.85), Kapus (7.47), and Kammas (7.37) in that

TABLE 1

Caste, Average Unionism Scores, and Economic Position of College Teachers : Analysis of Variance Test

Serial No.	Caste	No. of respondents for 11 major caste groups (N=623)	Economic Measures						Unionism Scores	
			Earning Member Ratio		Per capita family income		Level of living index		Average	Ordinal Rank
			Average	Ordinal Rank	Average (in Rs.)	Ordinal Rank	Average	Ordinal Rank		
1	2	3	4	5	6	7	8	9	10	11
1.	Brahmin	237	0.358	4	441.337	6	11.190	5	6.131	9
2.	Kumma	85	0.389	2	466.970	2	11.529	3	7.365	4
3.	Kapu	58	0.360	3	454.467	4	10.948	7	7.466	3
4.	Vaisya	57	0.312	8	372.851	8	10.982	6	6.193	8
5.	Kshatriya	45	0.310	9	366.506	9	11.556	2	5.178	11
6.	Reddy	41	0.342	6	511.129	1	10.732	9	7.854	2
7.	Scheduled Castes	34	0.436	1	455.878	3	10.588	10	6.794	7

8	Velama	24	0.346	5	442.708	5	11.750	1	7.125	5
9	Telaga	19	0.301	10	363.178	10	10.895	8	5.947	10
10	Patnaik	13	0.338	7	417.058	7	11.462	4	8.077	1
11	Devangula	10	0.249	11	284.875	11	10.000	11	7.000	6
	Whole sample average (N=727)		0.37		454.55		11.200		6.534	
	F-Value :		—		—		—		6.714 (Sig. at 0.001 level for 10,612 d.f.)	

order. The Scheduled Castes have taken the ordinal position of seven (6.79). It is interesting to note that the three twice-born castes, viz., Brahmins (6.13), Kshatriyas (5.18) and Vaisyas (6.19) have obtained the 9th, 11th and 8th ranks respectively on unionism. For the entire cluster of the eleven castes an analysis of variance test was run which yield 'F' value 6.53, significant at the 0.001 level. The test conclusively demonstrates evidence of caste being a significant source of variation in unionism among college teachers. In order to find out whether ritual or economic ranks of the caste was the cause of variation in unionism, Spearman's Rank Order correlations were computed and the correlations obtained between the ranks on unionism and the ranks on all the three economic status dimensions were not found significant. Nevertheless, a positive though weak association was found between the unionism ranks and the economic status ranks of the various caste groups. When product moment correlations were computed between unionism on the one hand and the three economic measures on the other, the results found are not significant statistically (the zero order correlation of unionism with earning member ratio is—0.033 ; with per capita family income is 0.002 ; and with level of living index is 0.069). As an extension of this analysis all the 727 respondents were purposively rearranged into six groups. The results were presented in Table 2. The first group consisted of the three twice born castes of the Hindu society. Their average unionism score is 5.834, and their ordinal rank position is six. The second group consisted of the four dominant upper sudra castes of Andhra Pradesh viz., Kamma, Reddy, Kapu and Patnaik. Their average unionism score is 7.691 with an ordinal rank of one. The middle and lower sudra castes formed the third (average=6.545 ; rank=three). The Telagas were excluded from this group because their score on unionism is abnormally low in comparison with the other nineteen castes in this group. The Telagas were, therefore, treated as a separate group viz., the fourth (average=5.947 ; rank=five). The fifth group consisted of Muslims and Christians (average=6.973 ; rank=two). And respondents who did not like to mention their religion and/or caste were grouped as a last

TABLE 2

Average Unionism Scores of Re-grouped Sample Respondents

Group	Composition	No. of Respondents	Average Unionism Score	Rank
Group I	Twice-Born castes (Brahmins, Kshatriyas and Vaisyas)	339	5.834	6
Group II	Upper Sudras (Kamma, Reddy, Kapu and Patnaiks)	197	7.691	1
Group III	Middle and lower sudras (excluding Telagas) (19 Hindu castes including Scheduled Castes)	100	6.545	3
Group IV	Telagas	19	5.947	5
Group V	Christians and Muslims	37	6.973	2
Group VI	Others (Who did not like to mention either their religion (4) or caste (31)	35	6.299	4
Whole Sample :		727	6.530	33

residual category (average=6.299 and rank=four). The results in Table 2 shows that the twice-born castes still rank lowest on unionism in comparison with the other five rearranged groups. The group consisting of the four upper sudras scored the highest on unionism ; followed by the group consisting of the religious minorities of the Indian society. The score of the middle and lower Sudras on unionism is very close to the over all average of the entire sample (6.530).

To sum up the results so far discussed, unionism seems well established among college teachers with significant variation occurring between private and government colleges ; and between atleast some castes and the major groupings of castes. Upper Sudra castes have reported the highest unionism scores whereas the three twice-born castes have registered the lowest unionism scores in the sample. These results cannot be attributed to differences in the economic position of the respondents, since the correlations with the various economic measures were small and insignificant.

UNIONISM AND OTHER PREDICTORS

Unionism was correlated with a few other variables such as age, educational score, family size, etc. In general, these factors did not make any impact on unionism of college teachers. Only family size was correlated negatively with unionism (r= —0.135).

FUNCTIONAL CORRELATES OF UNIONISM

Using the nominally distinguished categories of membership status, average scores for the six functional correlates of unionism have been computed. The six functional correlates are: (1) occupational values and role perceptions, (2) professionalism, (3) professional orientation, (4) college commitment-cum-involvement, (5) powerlessness in the college context, and (6) powerlessness in the general context. The nominal categories of membership status of the respondents together with the respective average scores for the six functional correlates have been presented in Table 3.

The original hypothesis of the analysis was that the various nominal membership categories should display gradations of

TABLE 3

Profile of Unionism With Other Six Functional Correlates of the Study Among College Teachers

PROFILE	Union Member or not (N=727)		Nature of Membership (N=480)		Position holders and Non-Position Holders (N=480)	
	Members in Union (N=480) $\bar{X}$ (S.D.)	Non-Members in Union (N=247) $\bar{X}$ (S.D.)	Active Members (N=255) $\bar{X}$ (S.D.)	Positive Members (N=225) $\bar{X}$ (S.D.)	Position Holders among Members (N=124) $\bar{X}$(S.D.)	Non-position holders among Members (N=356) $\bar{X}$ (S.D.)
Occupational Values and Role Perceptions	92.31 (23.27) (t=32.87)	103.32 (15.70)	87.79 (25.35) (t=19.57)	96.38 (20.52)	87.59 (26.65) (t=12.23)	94.01 (21.78)
Processionalism	7.13 (5.39) (t=1.28)	7.35 (4.54)	7.46 (6.52) (t=2.86)	6.85 (4.15)	7.40 (5.40) (t=1.44)	7.05 (5.38)
Processional Orientation	12.80 (3.74) (t=16.24)	14.96 (2.39)	12.04 (3.93) (t=8.33)	13.49 (3.42)	12.36 (4.34) (t=2.83)	12.96 (3.51)
College commitment-cum-involvement Score	34.10 (8.39) (t=19.05)	29.49 (10.24)	36.15 (7.25) (t=14.60)	32.37 (8 88)	36.07 (7.97) (t=8.92)	33.42 (8.44)
Powerlessness (in college context)	19.26 (6.45) (t=15.90)	22.36 (6.16)	17.78 (6.25) (t=12.01)	20.53 (6.25)	17.57 (6.43) (t=8.45)	19.80 (6.28)
Powerlessness (in general context)	31.15 (9.56) (t=21.67)	35.96 (7.29)	28.87 (9.74) (t=15.14)	33.11 (8.98)	28.88 (10.35) (t=9.27)	31.95 (9.17)

variations in occupational values, professionalism, professional orientation, college commitment-cum-involvement and powerlessness in college and general contexts. The results summarised in Table 3 may, therefore, be discussed as follows.

The average score on the scale of occupational values and role perceptions for non-members is 103.32, for members 92.31 for passive members, 96.38 for active members 87.79, for non-position holders 94.01 and for position-holders 87.59. Tracing the continuum from non-members to position-holders through passive and active members, the gradation in average is 103.32, 96.38, 87.79 and 87.59, indicating that occupational values and role perceptions show a declining trend from non-members to position-holders. The table also presents the values of "t" test of statistical significance of mean differences between categories. We thus note that non-members ($\overline{X}$= 103.32) differed significantly from members ($\overline{X}$=92.31) in respect of occupational values and role perceptions (t=32.67). Similarly, the active members differed ($\overline{X}$=96.38) significantly from passive members ($\overline{X}$=96.38) ; and the t—value is 19.57 for this functional correlate of unionism.

As for professionalism, there was no evidence of a gradient of variation from the non-member category to the position-holder category. The inter-category mean differences in professionalism were also not statistically significant as shown by the 't'—values, except in the case of average differences between active ($\overline{X}$=7.46) and passive members ($\overline{X}$=6.85 ; t values=2.86, significant at the five per cent level).

As regards the functional correlate of professional orientation, there was a weak gradation in variation from the non-member category ($\overline{X}$=14.96) to the position-holder category ($\overline{X}$=12.36). The inter-category "t" —values for the mean differences were all statistically significant.

A reverse gradient of variation has appeared in the case of college commitment from the position holder category ($\overline{X}$=36.07) to the non-member category ($\overline{X}$=29.49) and the "t"—values for inter-category mean differences were all statistically significant.

A gradient of variation in the expected fashion was seen for powerlessness in the college context from the non-member category ($\bar{X}=22.36$) to the position-holder category ($\bar{X}=17.57$) and the inter-category mean differences were all statistically significant.

A similar gradation of variation was found in the expected manner for the functional correlate of powerlessness in the general context from the non-member category ($\bar{X}=35.96$) to the position-holder category ($\bar{X}=28.88$) and all the inter-category mean differences were found to be statistically significant.

To pronounce a more definitive verdict on the effects of unionism, a simple correlation analysis was undertaken, correlating unionism with each of its six functional correlates. The results are summarised in Table 4.

The correlation coefficients presented in the column no. 1 bear out almost all our apriori assumptions concerning the manifest functions of teacher unionism, which was found to be associated negatively and significantly with occupational values of teachers. In other words, the active unionists and position-holders among the college teachers felt quite confident about their power and control over situations and events occurring on the campuses in particular, and in the society, in general. In contrast to this, their professional orientations, occupational values and role perceptions were adversely affected by their unionist postures and involvements. The implications of these trends for higher education, college administration and campus environments can easily be imagined when it is recalled that about two-thirds of the college teaching community were unionised, about one-fourth of them being active unionists. The implications become more obviously serious if it is remembered that a teacher as a professional is not comparable to other professionals like lawyers, engineers and doctors, who do not have a durable impact on their clientele. The dysfunctions of teacher unionism need not be elaborated further.

There is a positive and statistically significant correlation between unionism and college commitment. This implies that active unionists were more committed and involved in the college than non-unionists or poor unionists. This result is probably because of their high sense of powerfulness in the

TABLE 4

Unionism and its Six Functional Correlates : Matrix of Correlation Coefficients (727)

Serial Number	Attitude or value dimension	1	2	3	4	5	6	7
1.	Unionism	1.00						
2.	Occupational values	−0.33**	1.00					
3.	Professionalism	−0.05	0.25	1.00				
4.	Professional orientation	−0.38**	0.50**	0.14**	1.00			
5.	College commitment-cum-involvement	0.39**	−0.47**	−0.19**	−0.44**	1.00		
6.	Powerlessness in college context	−0.35**	0.61**	0.18**	0.67**	−0.44**	−1.00	
7.	Powerlessness in general context	−0.37**	0.65**	0.06**	0.65**	−0.70**	0.82**	1.00

**Significant at the 0.01 level.

college context, whereas the poor unionists and the non-unionists, suffering as they are from high feelings of powerlessness in the college context, were reporting correspondingly low commitment and involvement in the college. The results in Table 4 show that occupational values would not necessarily or automatically lead to a high sense of professionalism as measured in terms of membership in professional associations, exposure to professional literature and participation in seminars, workshops and symposia, etc., the respondents have registered a very poor average score. But, when professionalism was measured in terms of opposition to unionism, the mean score recorded was high. The intercorrelation between the two alternative measures of professionalism was 0.14, significant at one per cent level of probability. This rather weak, though statistically significant and positive correlation between the two alternatively measures of professionalism is probably due to the relatively low scores on one of the measures. An implication of this pattern of results on professionalism measures is that there is scope for increasing the respondent's professional commitment, orientation and involvement, and for reducing their unionism, if only opportunities, incentives, facilities and encouragement are not lacking on the college campuses for the teacher's participation in seminars, workshops and symposia, and other profession related and professionalising activities. Their very absence or infrequency on the campuses accounts mostly for the poor, average professionalism score of the respondents. The U.G.C. as well as the college managements should be persuaded to provide more and frequent professionalising activities and opportunities on the college campuses.

NOTES AND REFERENCES

1. Parson T., "The Professions and Social Structures," *Essays in Sociological Theory*, The Free Press, Glencoe, 1953, p. 49. An ideal-typical view of a profession is that it involves such attributes as prolonged socialization, collective identity, control and regulation of the behaviour of the professional by the professional body,

professional fraternity, etc., Gandhi, J.S. "Sociology of Professions in India, *Sociological Bulletin*, vol. 32, no. 1, March 1983, pp. 13-34.

2. Wilson Bryan, R., "The Teacher's Role : A Sociological Analysis", *The British Journal of Sociology*, pp. 15-32.
3. Rao, C.R. Prasad, "Educational Malaise : A Diagnosis", *Educational India*, vol. 37, no. 4, October, 1970, pp. 111-115.
4. Ramesam, G.P. "The Role of Teachers Associations in the Colleges", *College View*, vol. 5, no. 3, 1980, p. 1; Rao, M.J., Manikya, "For and Against Tcachers' Trade Unions" *The Hindu*, January 5, 1982, p. 28.
5. The Unions project an image that managements, particularly private managements, are not for teachers for higher education, *College View*, vol, 5, no. 9, 1980, pp. 1 and 7 ; Nirmal Singh, "A Perspective on Higher Education in India : The Case of Private Control", *Journal of Higher Education*, vol. 5, no. 1, Monsoon 1979, pp. 8-28.
6. Rao, M.V. Krishna, "Education : My Views and Experiences", *Education in Andhra Pradesh : 1956-1976*, Telugu Akademi, Hyderabad, 1977.
7. In the state of Andhra Pradesh, the unions of college teachers operating area Affiliated College Teachers' Association, Andhra (ACTA), Telangana Affiliated College Teachers' Association (TACTA), Government College Teachers' Association (recently formed rival union of ACTA), All India Federation of University and College Teachers' Organisation (AIEUCTO).
8. Drawing upon our own experience, observations and the available literature, a preliminary pre-test questionnaire was drafted. This questionnaire consisted of a large number of statements to be sorted out and seleted as final scale items to be used in this study. The entire pre-test questionnaire consisted of items forming different scales of the study. The pre-test questionnaire was administered on 160 respondents selected from six degree colleges which were already selected for the final study. Two colleges each were selected from the three groups stratified on the basis of college age. Private and Government Colleges were included on the basis of 2 : 1 ratio. Both men and women were covered in the pre-test.

13

PROFESSIONAL COMMITMENT OF SCHOOL TEACHERS

SURENDRA K. GUPTA
AND
ANITA RANI

In primitive societies family and clan are the main agents of socialization and education. But in modern societies, the primary agents of socialization and education are supplemented by the secondary agents such as school, and college. In modern societies, though the foundation of "Basic Personality Structure" is laid in the family, the formal education in schools and colleges is considered as necessary for overall development of individual and society. Education is expected to promote the attainment of social goals "...such as development of personality, individuality, freedom, equality, social justice, human welfare, etc."[1] Other functions performed by education can be (*i*) transmission of values and skills, (*ii*) to promote the capacity to devise and accept new bases of social stratification, (*iii*) to promote rationality and scientific spirit, (*iv*) to promote efficiency as well as new sets of values, and (*v*) to promote autonomy in the individual members as well as the society as a whole.[2]

In a developing society like India, where majority of the parents are not equipped adequately to socialize their young ones according to the changed values and skills. the role of formal education in school becomes all the more important. In such societies "...education is looked upon to promote efficiency as well as a new set of values which would be dynamic enough to take cognizance of the changing situation."[3] Since in school, everything depends on the teachers, their role is very crucial for the attainment of the goals of education. The professionally committed teachers will enhance the process of attainment of goals, whereas the non-committed teachers may perform negative or indifferent role. In this paper an attempt has been made to analyze the professional commitment of school teachers in the Punjab. The specific questions to be investigated are :

(*i*) What is the level of professional commitment of school teachers ?

(*ii*) Is there any difference in their commitment according to their sex, age, education, rural/urban background and length of service ?

METHODOLOGY

The teachers selected for the study belonged to three higher secondary schools of a small town Samana in Punjab inhabited by 30509 people[4] and six high schools from the nearby villages within a radius of fifteen kilometers of the town. In all 183 teachers, ninety-five from the town and eighty-eight from the villages have been included in the study. Out of ninety-five town teachers, thirty-four are males and sixty-one females, whereas among village teachers fifty-four are males and thirty-four females. 126 teachers (sixty from town and sixty-six from villages) are teaching higher level classes and the remaining fifty-seven (thirty-five from town and twenty-two from villages) are teaching primary level classes. Out of ninety-five town teachers, five are living in villages and from the remaining eighty-two reside in Samana and eight in Patiala. Among village teachers sixty-two stay in villages and remaining twenty-six commute from nearby towns (seventeen from Samana and nine from Patiala). The average age of urban and rural teachers is 35.5 years and 30.6 years respectively. Their combined average age is 33.1 years.

PROFESSIONAL COMMITMENT

It is not necessary that all the persons who have joined the teaching profession are highly committed to the profession. Some of them might have joined the profession under compulsion as they could not get any other job. In this section we have attempted to analyze the professional commitment of the teachers. Their commitment to profession has been measured in terms of their professional training, earlier occupation, future plans, responsibility they feel towards students, and membership of teacher's organizations.

(i) PROFESSIONAL TRAINING

Professional training is a necessary qualification for a teaching assignment, especially at the school level. In our sample there are only seven teachers (3.8%) who have joined the profession without any professional training. Six of them are teaching in town and only one is serving in a village. Of these seven teachers, five are in the teaching profession for the last two and a half years, and two are in the profession for more than six years. The rest of the teachers have joined the profession after having some professional training. The distribution of rural-urban teachers according to their professional degree is given in Table 1.

TABLE 1
Professional Degree of the Teachers

Professional Degree	Urban	Rural	Total
B. Ed.	38	45	83
J. B. T.	39	29	68
O.T.	6	4	10
Diploma in Arts and Craft	4	6	10
Diploma in Physical Education	2	3	5
No Training	6	1	7
Total	95	88	183

Of the eighty-three teachers who have done B.Ed., forty-two joined this course after obtaining their Master's Degree whereas the remaining forty-one did it after graduation. The teachers who join JBT and OT courses, can do it after matriculation. Generally, the teachers with B.Ed. degree teach higher level classes (eight, ninth and tenth), whereas the teachers with JBT and OT courses are preferred for lower classes.

(ii) EARLIER OCCUPATIONS

More than seventy per cent of the teachers accepted teaching assignment as their first job. Of these 52.6% come from Samana and the remaining 47.4% are teaching in rural areas. There are only twenty-five teachers in the study who tried to get some job but did not succeed (13.6%). There are other twenty-five teachers who joined the teaching profession after serving in some other occupations. Seventeen teachers joined this profession after working as clerk, four were petty shop-keepers, and of the remaining four, one worked in agriculture, one in military, one as a labourer and one as a bhangra coach.

There are twenty-four teachers in the school who have completed more than twenty years in the profession. About thirty-nine per cent of the teachers have not yet completed their five years in the profession. The rest of the teachers have gained the experience of more than five years but less than twenty years.

132 teachers have taught in more than one school. There are only fifty-one teachers in the study who have not yet shifted their school. Of these, five have not even completed one year in the profession. Twelve have 2-5 years experience, thirteen have 6-9 years experience and the remaining nine are teaching in the same school for more than ten years.

(iii) FUTURE PLANS

114 teachers out of 183, would like to continue in the same profession (73.2%). This was stated when they were asked to tell about their future plans. Of those teachers who would like to continue in the same profession, about fifty-two per cent belong to Samana and rest forty-eight per cent are teaching in

villages. About thirty per cent of the teachers want to leave the present job. Of these, eighteen would leave only if they get a better government job, five want to join bank service, two gave preference to business. The other jobs preferred by one each teacher are to practice as a lawyer, work in language department, to join P.C.S., to be bhangra coach (the same person who left the job of bhangra coach to join teaching), scientific research and defence service. There were another twenty-four teachers who said that they would go for another job only if remuneration is better.

Of those who want to leave the present job, forty have put less than ten years of service, and the rest have more than ten years experience.

(iv) RESPONSIBILITY TOWARDS STUDENTS

A hypothetical case was put to teachers to find out their commitment to the profession. The case is as follows :

"Two boys started fighting while returning home from the school. Two teachers of the same school were also passing through the same route. One teacher wanted to stop the fight. The second teacher was of the opinion that the boys were outside the school premises and it was none of their business to interfere." The respondents were asked "which of the two teachers comes close to your way of thinking ?"

175 teachers favoured the first teacher (95.5%). Two teachers from the town did not agree with both the teachers, whereas one teacher did not respond to the question. There are only five teachers who favoured the second teacher.

Of those teachers who wanted to stop the fight, 134 considered it as a part of their duty. Seventeen teachers wanted to stop the fight because the students belonged to their school. Five teachers wanted to interfere because they considered that teachers are responsible for all round development of students. There were five more teachers who said that quarrelling is not good. Fourteen teachers did not give any reason.

Of those who did not want to stop the fight, three said that since the students are disobedient, so it is not necessary to interfere. The remaining two teachers did not give any reason to support their answer. Teacher who mentioned that both are wrong also did not give any reason.

(v) MEMBERSHIP OF TEACHERS' ORGANIZATION

Only sixty-four teachers are members of various teachers' organizations (thirty-five per cent). Of these, thirty-seven belong to the town and twenty-seven are teaching in villages. One person is holding the post of President, two are Secretaries while the remaining are ordinary members.

When asked about their participation in activities of these organizations, twenty-nine said that they have never participated in any activity. Among the rest, nine are regular participants and twenty-six are casual participants.

PROFSSIONAL COMMITMENT INDEX

On the basis of these five questions a professional commitment index was prepared. The scores given in Table 2.

TABLE 2
Scoring Scheme

1.	Professional training ?	Yes	1
		No	0
2.	Have you done any other work before teaching ?	Yes	0
		No	1
3.	Would you like to continue in the same profession ?	Yes	1
		No	0
4.	Responsibility teachers feel towards students ?	Yes	1
		No	0
5.	Membership of teachers' organization	Yes	1
		No	0

The total score varies between 0-5. The teachers scoring 4-5 are ranked as high, between 2-3 as medium and one as low. A person with zero score has been identified as a person with no professional commitment. The distribution of teachers according to their scores is given in Table 3.

TABLE 3

Professional Commitment Index

Index	Range	Weightage	Urban M	Urban F	Urban T	Rural M	Rural F	Rural T	Total M	Total F	Total T
High	4-5	3	15	20	35	24	3	27	39	23	62
Medium	2-3	2	18	37	55	28	30	58	46	67	113
Low	1	1	1	4	5	2	1	3	3	5	3
Total			34	61	95	54	34	88	88	95	183
Mean Score			2.41	2.26	2.31	2.40	2.05	2.27	2.40	2.18	2.29

A majority of the teachers in the study fall in the medium category of professional commitment (Sixty-one per cent). The urban teachers have scored slightly more on professional commitment in comparison to their rural counter-parts.

Sex-wise, there is no difference in the mean scores of males from rural and urban areas. The professional commitment of urban females is slightly higher than rural females. On the whole the professional commitment of males is higher than the females.

Now, in the following pages we will analyse the relationship between professional commitment and a few independent variables such as age, education, and length of service.

AGE AND PROFESSIONAL COMMITMENT

The relationship between age and professional commitment is shown in Table 4.

The urban teachers irrespective of their age exhibit more or less same level of professional commitment. Among rural teachers, the teachers above forty-five years of age have scored the highest on professional commitment followed by younger teachers. The middle aged rural teachers have scored minimum. On the whole, the older teachers have shown more professional commitment than other two groups.

EDUCATION AND PROFESSIONAL COMMITMENT

The relationship between education and professional commitment is shown in Table 5.

The distribution shows that the untrained teachers, both from rural and urban areas are least committed to the profession. The trained teachers from urban areas have scored more on professional commitment as compared to their counterparts from rural areas. On the whole, all the trained teachers are more committed to the profession as compared to untrained teachers.

TABLE 4

Age and Professional Commitment

Age	Urban					Rural					Total				
	H	M	L	T	Mean	H	M	L	T	Mean	H	M	L	T	Mean
20-34	16	23	3	42	2.30	20	44	2	66	2.27	36	67	5	108	2.28
35-44	12	21	1	34	2.32	4	11	1	16	2.18	16	32	2	50	2.28
45 and above	7	11	1	19	2.31	3	3	—	6	2.50	10	14	1	25	2.36
All ages	35	55	5	95	2.31	27	58	3	88	2.27	62	113	8	183	2.29

TABLE 5

Education and Professional Commitment

Education	Urban					Rural					Total				
	H	M	L	T	Mean	H	M	L	T	Mean	H	M	L	T	Mean
M.A., B.A. with B. Ed.	15	23	0	38	2.39	15	29	1	45	2.31	30	52	1	83	2.34
Matric with training	20	30	1	51	2.37	12	29	1	42	2.26	32	59	2	93	2.32
Untrained	0	2	4	6	1.33	0	0	1	1	1.0	0	2	5	7	1.28
Total	35	55	5	95	2.31	27	58	3	88	2.27	62	113	8	183	2.29

LENGTH OF SERVICE AND PROFESSIONAL COMMITMENT

Table 6 shows the distribution of teachers according to their length of service and professional commitment.

The data indicate that the length of service affects the professional commitment of school teachers. Higher the length of service, more is the professional commitment. This trend has been indicated both by rural as well as urban teachers.

CONCLUSIONS

Growth and Development of a profession depends on its members. The more committed members can play positive role not only in the development of profession but also in the overall development of the nation. To have more committed members in any profession, it is necessary that the profession provides opportunity for the growth and development of an individual and at the same time it has to be quite remunerative and attractive. The study shows that the teaching profession in India especially at the school level does have very committed persons. The study reveals that only those persons who crossed forty years of age are more committed than the younger teachers. It appears that to join another profession after forty years of age might be quite risky in a country like India. Persons who have crossed this age find no other alternative. Besides age, the place of work also affects the commitment of teachers. The study reveals that the teachers teaching in rural areas are less committed as compared to urban teachers. This must be due to poor facilities in rural areas which inspires them either to seek transfer to urban areas or to try for other jobs.

Other factor which affects the commitment of school teachers is their sex. The male teachers from rural and urban areas are more committed than female teachers. Among females, urban teachers are more committed. It must be due to the fact that in urban areas, the female teachers supplement the income of their family (husband or father) without cost. But the female teachers teaching in rural areas may find it

TABLE 6

Length of Service and Professional Commitment

Length of Service	Urban					Rural					Total				
	H	M	L	T	Mean	H	M	L	T	Mean	H	M	L	T	Mean
Less than 10 years	15	28	4	47	2.23	20	44	2	66	2.27	35	72	6	113	2.25
10-19 years	12	18	1	31	2.35	3	11	1	15	2.13	15	29	24	46	2.28
20 years and above	8	9	0	17	2.47	4	3	0	7	2.57	12	12	0	24	2.50
Total	35	55	5	95	2.31	27	58	3	88	2.27	62	113	8	183	2.29

difficult to live there all alone, or even to commute daily may pose problems which in turn affects their commitment to the profession.

NOTES AND REFERENCES

1. Damle, Y.B., "The Role of the Teacher in a Developing Society," S. P. Ruhela (ed.), *Sociology of the Teaching Professions*, NCERT, New Delhi, 1970.
2. *Ibid.*, pp. 171-72.
3. *Ibid.*, p. 172.
4. *Census of India, 1981*, Government of India, New Delhi.

14

PROFESSIONALIZATION OF SCHOOL TEACHERS IN INDIA

SATYA PAL RUHELA

I

INTRODUCTION

How ironical is it that while Illich, the author of the extremely controversial yet celebrated work *Deschooling Society* decries the professionalization of teachers as being the root cause of the decay and dysfunctionality of education, we in India are today decrying the fact that school teaching has not yet become a profession and so education in our country is ineffective.

Next to the army of soldiers in India is the army of school teachers estimated to be about six lakhs. Conventional thinking demands that unless this huge body of Indian school teachers qualifies to be called a professional body, it is really difficult to cure the imperfections and ills of our school education which they are expected to deliver. A comprehensive set of criteria to judge whether a calling is a profession or not comprises of the following : (*i*) requirement of a general education, (*ii*) specialized preparation based on esoteric knowledge and official certification, (*iii*) inservice training, (*iv*) emphasis on service rather than on personal gain, (*v*) a broad range of autonomy for both the individual practitioners and for the occupational group as a whole, (*vi*) reasonable financial rewards, (*vii*) a code of professional ethics, (*viii*) dedication of the professionals, (*ix*) professional organization and leadership, and (*x*) recognition by the public. Let us see how our school teachers as members of their calling fulfil these criteria.

OBSERVATIONAL DATA

A lot of observational data, mostly impressionistic in nature, lies scattered in the innumerable articles, papers, speeches, and research report. They tell us different things about different teachers of different regions/areas or state. While urban teachers are painted as professional, rural teachers are branded as unprofessional. In the same manner, while men teachers are said to be professional, female teachers, being more timid and homely, are decried as "hopeless unprofessionals." While older teachers are generally said to be calculative and unprofessional, and younger teachers are also painted as unprofessionals, being inexperienced, timid and disinterested, the middle-aged teachers are portrayed as the real professional ones. In some regions while primary school teachers are more vocal as a professional body, in others secondary teachers dominate the scene. So in a very big country like India, it is really difficult to understand what exactly are the valid conclusions one can draw from this plethora of diverse impressionistic observations.

FINDING OF AN EMPIRICAL WORK

Wadhawan's work on school teachers of Delhi is very revealing.[1] Based on 375 teachers—278 males and eighty-seven females, 135 rural teachers and 240 urban teachers, 147 Post-graduate teachers and 228 Trained Graduate teachers, the study pursued the following hypotheses :

1. The higher the socio-economic background of the teachers, the greater will be the degree of professionalization.

2. The social class background of women teachers is generally better than those of men teachers.
3. The more a teacher is exposed to the teacher training programme, the more his attitudes and behaviour are likely to be those of the professionals.
4. The women teachers tend to be less professional in their outlook than the men teachers.
5. The more professional a teacher is, the more he/she is likely to be satisfied with teaching as his/her career.
6. The more professional the general environment of the school is, the greater will be the degree of job-satisfaction in teachers.

The data collected and analysed revealed that :

The first hypothesis was supported on the variables like "choice of teaching as a career as the first preference" and "willingness to stay in it for life." A significant relationship between the teaching profession and lower middle class background of the teachers has been established on the variables of family income, family facilities and family immovable property. It was found that 46.4% teachers belonged to the income group of Rs. 3000-7200 per annum. A meaningful relationship between urban family background and teaching profession has been established as measured on the occupational background variable. About forty-one per cent men teachers and sixty-four per cent women teachers have urban background.

The second hypothesis that the social background of women teachers is generally better than men teachers stands proved. Women have an edge over men in participation in various associations.

The third hypothesis was not fully accepted. The respondents rated their teacher-educators good, but the training college atmosphere and facilities were rated as average, and the practical utility of training in actual classroom teaching in schools was rated "as just average" or "so-so". Although more than half the teachers (fifty-three per cent) attended inservice workshops, yet they did not seem to understand and appreciate the significance or utility of these programmes. Mostly the teachers were found to be indifferent to publication work.

The fourth hypothesis stood proved. Men were found to be more professional than women teachers. While teachers advise their daughters to be teachers, they do not want their sons to follow their footsteps. On the three variables namely Reading Index, Attending Parent—Teacher Association Meetings and Attending Meetings of Professional Associations, most of the teachers did not emerge as good professionals.

Only twenty-five per cent men and twenty-four per cent women teachers spent some time (twenty-one to thirty hours a month) in reading books relating to the school subjects taught by them. About forty-five per cent teachers say that older teachers help younger teachers in their work by way of guidance, but their willingness was rated as "average". The general ability of teachers was also rated as average. Most of the teachers (sixty-three per cent men and fifty-nine per cent women) were professional in the sense that they did not bother or hesitate in giving the score "Fail" to a student if he deserved that.

It was found that about fifty-five per cent teachers did involve themselves in the co-curricular and extra-curricular activities of the school. About sixty-three per cent teachers (both men and women) kept school records willingly and properly, and eighty-three per cent teachers considered making "Report Card" of their class students an important part of their duties. Two-thirds of teachers did not mind teaching subject which may not be their speciality. About eighty-six per cent teachers assured the researcher that they enjoyed their teaching assignments, but their ratings about school facilities was average. As many as forty-six per cent teachers liked their students most. Most of the teachers have expressed satisfaction that they have a voice in running their school administration.

A majority of teachers expressed frustration with their profession due to uncordial, strict and insensitive principals whose behaviour was termed as "unprofessional." Almost half of the teachers opined that parents did not help their wards in their home-work and thus the teachers felt displeasure in teaching and dealing with their pupils.

Accommodation in the schools, academic reputation of the schools, school discipline, social background of the students and encouragement given to innovative teachers were rated as "average" by majority of men and women teachers.

More women than men teachers expressed satisfaction with their salaries, and more men teachers than women teachers reported that they were not getting grades according to their qualifications. Most of the men teachers were worried about their financial problems, and so resorted to tution work which they themselves admitted was unprofessional but essential for their survival.

The fifth hypothesis was tested on nine variables : evaluation of principals, evaluation of colleagues, colleague group-orientation and teacher autonomy, general ability of teachers, evaluation of students, evaluation of parents attitude, teaching assignment, professional aspirations, and job-satisfaction. As many as ninety-nine per cent teachers gave poor evaluation of their principals. The majority of teachers rated their colleague-group orientation as "just so-so". As many as forty per cent respondents (thirty-seven per cent men and forty-seven per cent women) gave average rating to teacher's autonomy. As many as forty-eight per cent teachers (forty-six per cent men and fifty-three per cent women) gave "average" rating to the general ability of teachers. About fifty-one per cent teachers rated the respect of teachers in the community as "average" or "fairly or tolerably good". The majority of teachers, i.e. eighty-six per cent enjoyed teaching assignments, and forty-nine per cent wanted a life-long career in teaching. Only seventeen per cent men and fourteen per cent women teachers aspired to be educational administrators. The overall assessment of these data reveal that the teachers included in the sample turned out to be less professional and less satisfied with teaching as their career.

The sixth hypothesis stood proved on the two variables, environment of school, and job-satisfaction.

In the light of these findings, it was inferred that mostly the school teachers in Delhi are not highly professional people and school teaching is not yet a highly professional occupation. This naturally leads to the question : if school teachers of even Delhi, who are well paid and exposed to better training, school amenities and professional perks, dignities etc., are less professional and do not pride themselves as professional members of a dignified profession, then how can the professional image of the calling of school teachers in other parts of India be better than them ?

YET ANOTHER SCAR ON THE FACE OF SCHOOL TEACHING

The above-mentioned research findings apart, there are yet many more ugly scars on the face of the calling of school teachers in India which, it seems, would not be possibly removed even in the next twenty years.

A sizeable percentage of school teachers continues to be untrained. The Annamalai University Correspondence Course for B. Ed. enrols about 600 to 800 students from Delhi itself every year, not to speak of the numbers of candidates from other parts of the country. The so-called Public Schools unabashedly appoint any "bright" untrained teacher, and now even university departments of B.Ed./Education care a fig for the professional qualifications and appoint untrained persons as lecturers, readers and even professors of education. The pressure politics of educational institutions works more in favour of untrained than trained teachers and teacher educators these days.

The exploitation of teachers, and more so of women teachers, goes on unchecked as a roaring business in almost all private schools, aided and unaided teacher training colleges of Rajasthan and other states. It is a common place knowledge to all that teachers are asked to sign for double or forty per cent more the salaries they are actually given in private schools throughout the country. And yet no voices of protest are raised, and even if raised they are not supported by professional bodies and unions of teachers, and they are the least bothersome to the education ministers and educational administrators. It is widely known that private institutions are opened, recognised, granted land and other amenities in states like Haryana, M.P., Rajasthan, U.P. and elsewhere by giving bribes, and yet the professional body of teachers witnesses all this dream of anomie as helpless and may be also consenting collaborators and spectators.

The attitudes of principals and educational inspectors, deputy directors of education in almost all states in India are unprofessional by and large ; they conveniently forget the ordeals of their days when they were also teachers in schools. They consider it to be their duty to oppose the moves of professional bodies of teachers, and to be generally unsympathetic to teachers' grievances. The trend to appoint raw I.A.S. officers in certain states like Rajasthan, Delhi as Directors of School Education, and the lack of any protest from the cadres of school teaching profession reveals how week, meek and sick is this professional body which tolerates this.

The professional organizations of teachers in India are nowhere in comparison to National Union of Teachers in England, or professional bodies of teachers in USSR and USA in regard to the unity, efficiency, range of activities and services, and impact on society. Mostly they lack resources, dedicated workers, co-operation of members and due support from public and state. Mutual jealousies and agitations on small matters in parochial and self-seeking perspectives are their two most pinching weaknesses.

In Willard Waller's days school teaching in England, America and elsewhere was considered to be a profession of "unsaleable men and unmarriagable women."[3] Certainly, this is no more true for the calling of school teachers in India, for we definitely find pretty, intelligent, talented girls and also quite good boy students joining our B.Ed. training courses. However, on closer scrutiny, we do find that while better stuff from the womens' side is joining this profession, men teachers are mostly coming from inferior social strata, mostly Scheduled Castes, Scheduled Tribes, backward classes and rural lower socio-economic levels. In not too far a future, may be in just 10-15 years, school teaching in India will wholly become the professional activity of women teachers only, and men will be completely thrown out of it, if the ever increasing numbers of women entrants in the training courses are any indication.

It is too much to expect that the professional equipments and climate of Indian schools will improve in the coming years, in view of the rising inflation, population growth and eroding moral of society in general. Unrealistic salaries of teachers shall continue to force village teachers doing their side business of dairy farming, agriculture, shop-keeping and the like, and the urban school teachers engaged in private tutions, and side business of shop-keeping etc. Overworked and role-tensioned lady teachers also cannot ever find time and motivation to prepare for their classes thoroughly. What inducements are there for school teachers to cultivate professional excellence and strengthen professional commitment. At a time in the Indian social history when corruption, nepotism, anomie, and decay of human and social values are at their great heights what hope can be there for the school teaching to become a powerful and effective profession ?

NOTES AND REFERENCES

1. Wadhawan, C.L., *School Teachers in Delhi* : *Relationship Between Their Social Background and Professionalization*, Doctoral Thesis in Education, Jamia Millia Islamia, New Delhi, 1980 (unpublished).
2. Ruhela S.P., (Ed.), *Sociology of Teaching Profession in India*, New Delhi, NCERT, 1970.
3. Wallard, Walker, *Sociology of Teaching*, Basic Books, New York, 1935.

[illegible]

[illegible] Thus [illegible] to become a powerful [illegible] possession.

[illegible]

[illegible] New York, 1935.

PART III

SCIENTISTS

15

INDIAN SCIENTISTS AND SOCIAL SYSTEM

SRI CHANDRA

"The comparative historical evidence about societies shows clearly that the status of professions, particularly of scientists in our society is unique."[1] This statement of Parsons holds good in the case of our country also. It is a curious paradox that scientists who are the primary spear-heads of the development of the country have not been taken notice of by the social thinkers of our country. Many studies of this skey group have been done in the West.[2] These works inspired to undertake study of Indian scientists. Some findings are presented here.

THE WORK CLIMATE

In regard to the attitude of Indian scientists toward conditions conducive to scientific research, it is found that, in most cases, the scientist feels that his job matches his equipment and training and it holds out better prospects for him. By and large, the scientists studied reflect an attitude of dissatisfaction as far as their emoluments, financial resources are concerned. The interview records show that majority of scientists express the view that they are not provided with proper equipment and adequate funds. Bureaucratism or "through the proper channel" method is considered to be a definite hindrance in their work and achievement. Feeling of insecurity and lack of appreciation of their work are, in many cases, reported as definite hindrances particularly in the case of junior scientists. They also express the view that emoluments are low and promotions are not always made on fair basis.

The Indian scientists are found to make a number of suggestions regarding the factors that may provide impetus to research work. Majority of them feel that there should be greater autonomy in research organisations. Some scientists think that red-tapism should be minimized. Others feel the need for more efficient administration (sixteen per cent). Some suggest complete reorganisation of the institutes and laboratories with a view to freeing them of the control of non-technical persons. Decentralization of authority is another suggestion made by twelve per cent of scientists; while nationalisation of all research Laboratories and proper co-ordination of research wings of research institutes is also recommended. Some scientists express the view that encouragement of young scientists, training of scientists abroad and complete impartiality in matters of appointments and promotions would greatly improve matters.

Prompt supply of necessary and latest equipment is recommended by most of the scientists, and some of them suggest that more funds and more foreign exchange would provide the necessary impetus to scientific research.

Besides the above suggestions, some of the scientists recommend longer duration for seminars, workshops and symposia and more facilities for cultural and recreational activities.

Coming to the question of interference by authorities or government appointments and promotions, efficiency of authorities/subordinates, organizing and administrative ability of the boss and degree of co-operation that obtains between subordinates/authorities, it is found that practically as many scientists allege too much interference on the part of government or authorities as those who deny it. Strangely enough, the feeling in regard to too much interference is also shared by some senior scientists. Scientists, on the whole, however, regard the colleagues to be fairly efficient in their research work and feel that their bosses possess the ability for organisation and administration. By and large, colleagues are looked upon as co-operative in their research work.

INTER-PERSONAL RELATIONSHIPS

In regard to the question of pattern of inter-personal relationships and its impact on research achievement of scientists, it is found that friends and colleagues, in most cases, have been co-operative and helpful. Their inspiration has been one among other factors which has encouraged many scientists in their career. Most of the junior scientists have expressed the view that authorities have not shown enough co-operation. The interview records, by and large, also reflect an attitude of dissatisfaction on their part in regard to too much interference by the boss and authorities in their research work. In many cases, they feel that there is inefficiency in the administration, and that the spirit of co-operation among various categories of scientists is lacking.

Another significant finding focuses on the fact that majority of scientists express the view that discussion of research problems with colleagues is rewarding. The relationships with colleagues are thus professionally intimate and often result in mutual benefit. The questionnaire findings as well as interview records, on the whole, bring out that bureaucratic temper and attitude on the part of seniors is distasteful. But, even in the face of poor co-operation from authorities, scientists are able to make satisfactory adjustments and their research achievement does not seem to suffer seriously.

LIFE STYLE OF SCIENTISTS

Scientists' style of life appears to be peculiar to them. For them, family interests are secondary to their research work. But, they do enjoy family-life and spend sometime regularly with their wife and children. On the whole, they lead contented, peaceful and happy home life. Family obligations are given due consideration but not at the cost of their professional and research responsibilities. The interview data make it obvious that the scientists' sense of identity comes from their professional role; that is why their roles at home hold relatively little interest for them. Their role as scientists remain distinct from their roles as fathers or husbands. They do devote time to family-duties and obligations but it is true that the scientist's style of living is work-oriented. For some scientists research-centredness may be looked upon as an escape from the daily botherations of family life; for others it accounts for the neglect of the family which results in tension.

Married life, as revealed by the interview data, has had no adverse effect on their research work and academic pursuits. There does not appear to be any clash between their roles as husband and scientist. Rather, they feel that their wives relieve them of domestic responsibilities which leave them free to devote most of their time to their research and studies. The same consensus is not found among the scientists in regard to the role of their friends. The roles attributed to them show a good deal of variation. Some scientists report that their friends are inspiring, while a much larger number of them look upon their friends as indifferent. Only in some cases their role has been regarded as discouraging. The specialized nature of the work of the scientist coupled with the capabilities and interests of friends may account for this situation.

The findings of the present study undoubtedly reveal that most of the scientists give priority to their research and academic pursuits over their family obligations or participation in community life. Usually their social group is restricted to academic persons and they love to talk about their research work. They also enjoy participation in parties, dinners and other social functions but never at the cost of their professional work. On the whole, they do not have adequate time to participate in the general life of the community. This finding is also borne out by the results of correlational analysis. A negative and significant correlation was found between years of research and social value, indicating that the longer the scientist has been engaged in research, the more he is likely to get divorced from interest in community and social life.

Some of the scientists do not admire colleagues who attempt to become public-figures or take part in politics. They have generally a distaste for attempt at exhibitionism. Some of them appear to be ambitious to become administrators or bosses. For these persons, indulgence in politics appears to be a "must". The higher they climb on the administrative ladder, the less time they are able to give to academic and creative work. These very persons become the target of attack by the public as well as their colleagues. Persons with conflicting loyalties and motivation are generally not approved by the scientists who are devoted to their vocation.

Turning to the pattern of recreation of scientists, it is found that, like anybody else, they enjoy leisure and spend sometime in recreational activities. But there is no compulsiveness about it. Leisure time is spent mostly in playing indoor games, seeing movies, reading, listening to radio or watching T.V. and pursuing hobbies like photography, painting, music and gardening or going out for a picnic party with their family and friends. Some of the scientists are not in favour of long vacations as these interfere with their research work; others prefer to keep the work and recreation apart. Most of the scientists welcome some kind of recreation and younger scientists, in particular, feel the need for diversion to break the monotony of their work. Some important theories of play get demonstrated in their recreational activities. The type of activity in which scientists spend their leisure time reflects the aspiration, longings and attempts at partial gratification of childhood-wishes which still linger with them. Recreation helps to release the pent-up emotions of the scientists. It is refreshing and helps the scientists to return to their work with renewed vigour.

The experience balance (erlebnistyp) in the Rorschach shows how an individual experiences life and not necessarily the way he lives. The ambiequal pattern that characterizes our scientists reveals the way they approach the world and the way they could live. Our scientists reflect a style of life that is marked by this trend. They are as much prompted by the inner resources as they are responsive to stimulations from without. They seem to have a good capacity to experience and enjoy life.

CONCLUSIONS

In conclusion I would like to point out that my attempt has been to ascertain the social, familial and organizational climate in which the Indian scientist functions, and the nature and character of their influence on research productivity. The scientist is no doubt part and parcel of a larger social system, and spends quite a sizeable amount of time outside the laboratory with other men in other walks of life as also his family. In this process of interaction with the organization, undue interference and red-tapism stand out as the crucial factors which impede research achievement. In his book entitled *The Organization Man*, Whyte puts forward the thesis that the emphasis of the Social Ethic (i.e., increasing power of the society over the individual) is wrong for the organization man.[3] He must fight the organization. The acceptance of bureaucratization in scientific research or for that matter in any organization has brought about its ills and must be fought by the worker.

NOTES AND REFERENCES

1. Parsons, T., *Essays in Sociological Theory*, Free Press, Glencoe Collier, 1959.

2. Roe, A., "Artist and Their Work", *Journal of Personality*, vol. 15, 1946; "Analysis of Group Rorschach of Biologists", *Rorschach Research Enchange*, vol. 13, 1949, pp. 25-43; "Psychological Examination of Eminent Biologists", *Journal of Consultive Psychology*, vol. 18, 1949, pp. 225-246; "Analysis of Group Rorschach of Physical Scientists", *Journal of Projective Technique*, vol. 14, 1950, pp. 89-395; "A Psychological Study of Eminent Biologists," *Psychological Monograph*, vol. LXV, no. 14, 1951, p. 68; "A Psychological Study of Physical Scientists," *Genetics Psychological Monograph*, vol. 43, 1951, pp. 121 and 235; "A Study of Imagery in Research Scientists", *Journal of Personality*, vol. 19, 1961, pp. 459-470; *The Making of a Scientist*, Dodd, Mead, New York, 1952, p. 244; "A Psychological Study of Eminent Psychologists and Anthropologists and a Comparison with Biological and Physical Scientists", *Psychological Monograph*, vol. LXVII, no. 2, 1953, p. 55; "*The Psychology of Occupations*, Wiley, New York, 1956; "The Psychology of Scientists", *Science*, vol. 134, 1961, pp. 456-459; Eiduson, B.T., "Artist and Research Scientists: A Comparative Study", *Proceedings of American Psychological Association*, Washington, D.C., (September 1958); "The Changing Self Image of Scientists", *Proceedings of American Psychological Association*,

Cincinatti, (September 1958); *Scientists : Their Psychological World*, Basic Books, New York, 1962, p. 299 ; "Scientists as Advisors and Consultants in Washington", Presented as Lecture at *Interdisciplinary Symposium*, The RAND Corporation, Santa Monica, Mimeographed, July 28, 1965.

3. Whyte, W.H.Jr., *The Organisation Man*, Simon and Schuster, Inc, 1956.

16

SOCIAL STRUCTURE AND PROFESSION OF SCIENTISTS

A. Ramanamma
and
Usha Bambawale

Sociology has been attracted to the study of professionals and has come a long way in the last fifty years since the time, Carr-Saunders and Wilson completed their comprehensive work on British professions.[1] Greenwood attempted to identify and describe essential elements in the ideal-type profession setting out five distinguishable factors.[2] Wilensky while examining in detail the differences between the professional and non-professional speaks of professional competence which comes from a systematic body of skill and knowledge acquired through long prescribed training.[3] The social structure of a profession is governed by certain norms and has its own culture. Therefore, there are recognizable differences between the culture of each profession. Danielson from his study concludes that there are recognizable differences between the scientists and other groups of workers such as managerial, clerical and manual workers in an organization, particularly with regard to their goals, needs and personality traits.[4] They possess natural as well as trained scepticism and objectivity which are expressed by their non-acceptance of things at face value. Danielson goes further and points out that the error of over-simplification may be committed by a direct, straightforward comparison between professionals like scientists and engineers and other professionals such as doctors, lawyers and so on.[5]

PROFESSION AND PROFESSIONAL

In a study of professionalization process, a distinction must be made between the profession and the professional. The profession refers to a special type of occupation where as the professional refers to a special type of person. "The term professional has many connotations. There is little agreement as to which dimension it encompasses and few of the several dimensions usually identified are very precisely defined. To the extent that the term has any common meaning, however, it refers to a person who by virtue of long training is qualified to perform specialized activities autonomously, relatively free from external supervision or regulation."[6]

Professionals are expected to have higher levels of education and occupations. So, those desiring to have a professional status can strive for higher education levels. A code of ethics may indicate too the public, good intensions and confidentiality of the members of the profession, namely their alleged service-orientation. Licensing of professionals shows the community that the professional has met certain skill requirements, has been examined in some fashion and has been found fit to serve the community. The presence of professional association implies an organised body that is working to upgrade standards to control its own members, to standardize licensing and so on. Some mechanism of peer control within the occupation either formally in the association or informally on a local level, will give an appearance of professional self-control and orientation to service. Denton thinks that these five factors may also be used as a basis for arguing for greater autonomy.[7] It is believed that a professional tries to retain his standard of excellence by protecting his autonomy. Autonomy, means (i) that a qualified practitioner is best able to determine how a function ought to be performed and that he must be free to exercise his own judgment in the specific case, (ii) the desire of the expert is not only to have a free hand in merely determining the line of action towards a specific end, but may also like to define a problem in precise terms, (iii) the scientists yearning to follow his own inclination of scientific pursuits at least during such periods when organizational pressures are not making too great a demand on his time for quick solutions to produce problems. According to Wilensky, a modernized complex society places a strong value on autonomy which is conducive to isolation in all spheres of life including that of professionalism.[8] The rewards of a professional-lie provide an impetus, to the professional's craving for independence. One has to take cognisance of the fact that professional people are not supposed to be concerned with money. Professional norms emphasise the values of service to society rather than pecuniary gain.

SCIENTISTS ARE PROFESSIONALS

For the making of a professional, there are certain requirements. Scientists are recruited on the basis of :

(*i*) *Higher academic orientation*—one major factor of importance is that the class of degree appears to be a key variable: "It is those who get or expect to get good honours, who are most likely to choose an academic career."[9] Currie for example, has shown in one inquiry that students had a distinct image of the university professor and that those who contemplated an academic career closely conformed to this image.[10] Students would be aware of the qualities demanded by their chosen careers and attach different degrees of importance to those attributes which are most relevant. "Universities attempt to adapt their organizational structure to the needs of the professional staff-members rather than requiring professional staff-members to adapt to pre-existing bureaucratic requirements of the employing organization."[11] Clark points out that the university structure better be described as a form of federated professionalism along with segmentation and individualization.[12]

(*ii*) *Training*—Storv starts from the hypothesis that the characteristics of a scientist above all is his desire to be creative.[13] But confirmation of his creativity can only be achieved through recognition by the scientific community. Only his peers are competent to judge the worth of his contribution. And only by conformity to the norms can the individual scientists earn the recognition of his peers. Behavioural conformity to the norms of science is part of the training. The notion of *role* and concept of identity enable the scientist to perform his duties. "Identity refers to what a man is, as to how he sees himself; role refers to how he is expected to behave."[14] While a scientist is in training during his academic education as well as when he is a junior scientist he is trained in the standards of technically and morally allowable patterns of behaviour, indicating what is prescribed, preferred, or permitted. The culture of science refers, then, to more than habitual behaviour; its norms codify the values judged appropriate for the people engaged in doing science.

(*iii*) *Selection*—there is a strong association between expected class of degree, commitment to science and preference for an academic career. We know that a good honours degree in science is the pre-requisite for academic work. "We also know that a high proportion of those with good honours in fact choose a university post in preference to industry."[15] Cotgrove and Box make it a point to mention that the nature of the Ph.D. degree in the present form influence graduate students away from an industrial employment towards an academic career. Thus, students who select science and become scientists are well aware of the norms. At the same time those scientists who select to be in a particular setting for scientific work are aware of the sets of task and rules that govern the institution to blend these imposed inconsistencies into reasonably consistent action.

GOALS OF SCIENTISTS

Science above all is a social activity. Scientists typically communicate their findings to other members of the scientific community. The emphasis on the imperative to publish, to share findings is one of the most distinctive features of science. Science is above all "public knowledge."[16] The goal of science is public knowledge and the scientific community pursues this goal. To look at science as an organised social system, it is desirous to identify the major norms of science :

(*i*) The first norm is *communality* which underlines the imperative to publish. It directs scientists to regard their discoveries as something they should share with others and not as their own private property. "Secrecy would fatally hinder the consensual process.[17]

(*ii*) If the goal is consensus on public knowledge then each scientist must look critically at the contributions of his colleagues. Cotgrove and Box opine that only those contributions which can withstand the scrutiny which follows from such *organized scepticism* become part of the consensus. Further, the criterion for assessing a contribution must be confined to those relevant for science, and must exclude for example, the nationality of the scientist, or the geographical location of the work. It is this norm of *universalism* together with the norm of *communality* which gives science its international character.

(*iii*) The norm of *disinterestedness* exhorts the scientist to seek only the rewards of science—the recognition which follows from the acceptance of his contribution. As Haggstrom argues, we may usefully think of the social system of science as a system in which free gifts of knowledge to the scientific community are exchanged for recognition.[18] Such rewards form an important element in the social organisation of science in the form of eponymy fellowship, and a variety of honours. The norms of dis-interestedness is important because it limits the rewards for which the scientist may legitimately strive and ensures that the research which he undertakes is determined by scientific criteria. In short, the value of contribution to knowledge can only be determined by other scholars not by its market value or by the confirment of political honours. We can further say that the length of socialization at school and university produces persons who become strongly committed to the values and norms of science. Merton argues that the norms are accepted as binding simply because they are seen to be functionally necessary.[19] Storv and Haggstrom have explored this aspect of the problem and feel that breaches of norms will lead to the withholding or withdrawal of recognition for the gifts of knowledge.[20]

SCIENTIFIC RESEARCH AND SOCIAL NEEDS

The understanding of natural phenomena through scientific methods and controlled experiment leads us inevitably to have some control over the nature. Even in the course of science's history we had first a body of empirical knowledge which arose directly from the efforts to satisfy the immediate needs, such as the manufacture of tools, the handling of metals, and the techniques of agriculture. Later it was innate curiosity which led man to investigate his environment as a purely intellectual pursuit. Science as we know is a systematic exercise at unravelling nature on the one hand and a means for enriching our living conditions on the other, with a close interplay between the two aspects. Electricity, telephone, radio, aeroplane, penicillin, nylon amongst a host of others, came into the world as a result of application of scientific principles.

Today an increasing proportion of graduates in science are employed in industry, government, research institute and teaching.

Changes in the social needs have also brought changes in the scientific community. The age old tradition of a laboratory in the home with research for research sake, like that carried out by Newton, Faraday or Graham Bell is no more. Scientists have dispersed in three directions.

ROLE AND LOCATION OF SCIENTISTS

Scientists as a class are of two types—those involved in basic and applied research. These scientists are located in National

Laboratories and Universities are a privileged class of intellectuals who consider themselves a cut above the vast majority of scientists. The second category of scientists are those involved in applied research and are located in the R and D units of public and private sector industries. These scientists occupy roles in distinct sub-system of society, each with specific goals and norms. The primary function of the industrial research laboratory is not the advancement of knowledge as such, but rather the application of scientific knowledge and skills to the development of marketable products. "This may involve discovering new knowledge. But the objective is not to contribute such knowledge to the current store."[21] Cotgrove and Box make it clear that on the contrary, the general industrial practice is to control production by delaying unit covered by patents.[22] The scientists in an industry are useful only to the firms' products, to the audience in his colleagues, managers in the firm, and not the scientific community. The scientist is working in the economic sub-system, therefore, the goals are marketable products, and the criteria and rewards are economic. Though the norms of science are not completely irrelevant but the norm of communality is clearly inappropriate. An industrial scientist may be called upon to play a role in production management and technical sales or purchase. A knowledge of science may be essential for effective performance even though the job does not involve carrying out any of the normal functions of a scientist.

There are three main types of scientific roles—(*i*) academic (*ii*) professional, and (*iii*) organisational. The pursuit of knowledge is the major function of academics. It is professionals who are concerned with the application of expertise, in the form of knowledge and skills. The organisational role is essentially that of an employee.

We can thus see that the scientists employed in universities, more or less fall in the first role category, those in National Laboratories in the second, and the industry based scientists in the third category.

In the case of university and National Laboratory Scientist, they pursue academics for the sake of research, they teach and guide. They can publish their work and share it with the scientific community.

On the other hand the R and D scientists in industry find that their success as a professional depends upon the degree to which they can successfully sell their services to a client who wants to buy them. Professional activities include the risk of individual failure in obtaining clients' support and also in the sense, the true professional must typically assume individual responsibility for seeking out client support. Scientists have moved out of academic departments and obtained employment in governmental institutions and industry. There are indications that scientists have simultaneously developed more concern with professionalization and entrepreneurship. In so far as scientists can seek out and establish a clientele to support their individual research interest, it appears that they can thereby pressurise their professional autonomy and capabilities whether they are employed in a university, industry, government or independent research organisation. Today private and public sector industry is the greatest employer of scientists. With different areas of changes and different role-expectations among all the three groups of scientists, we find that there is considerable role-conflict.

ROLE-CONFLICT

The characteristics of scientists give rise to certain types of conflict when such professionals associate themselves with rigid bureaucratic organisations. For instance, the management of industrial organizations seem to place a high value on profits, loyalty to company, hierarchical authority, growth of business and financial soundness. Some writers have argued that initial conflict can at least be moderated by modification in the attitudes of the professional scientist ; by a measure of re-socialisation or by changes in the education of undergraduates. Abrahamson suggests that the initial conflict between professionals and administrators centres around the different expectations, each has about the appropriate level of authority a researcher should be granted.[23] Whyte in his polemic against anti-individualism of the modern corporation sees the process rather as one of the deliberate company indoctrination of "eccentric" scientists through an emphasis on team planning, group research, harmonious inter-personal relations, and insistence on company loyalty.[24] Mareson described the practice of a large electronics company which sent scouts to universities a full year before graduates' studies were programmed to be completed.[25] These scouts attempted to select scientists with interets in projects that higher management had already decided to have investigated. Once employed, the scientists' research aspirations were continuously redefined by supervisors, using the criteria of what was technically and personally feasible, and what was financially supportable. Shepard has argued that those companies which employ scientists in more basic and applied research, should develop a dual system of status hierarchies with less formal and informal links between the research sections and higher management via research-directors and group leaders.[26] Laporte found in his study of an aerospace industrial complex, that accommodation between scientists and managers was arrived at, by a process of structural separation of scientists, managers and administrators.[27] Kaplan in a study of scientific productivity argued that laboratories will and tend to be more effective, the more they *satisfy five requisite conditions*.[28] Firstly, by showing enthusiasm for new ideas and by being receptive to innovation. Secondly, by removing the typically high level of pressure on employees that characterises other type of production. Thirdly, by tolerating "odd-balls" researchers who do not fit in with the strictness of organisational conformity. Fourthly, by giving researchers more freedom to choose problems and by allowing them to change research direction. Lastly, by devising suitable professional incentives and rewards, such as more freedom to attend scientific meetings, both nationally and internationally. Kornhauser expresses that in the case of professional scientists in industry the straining between autonomy versus integration causes role-conflict and stress.[29] Associated with functional autonomy is the emphasis on free inquiry, scientific standards, research creativity and responsibility to the scientific community.

We have looked at the scientist from every angle and find

that his role as a scientist and his culture as a scientist clashes at some juncture because of the social structural constraints due to the organisations where they are located. Therefore, we find an evidence of role-conflict which leads to ambivalence. We shall take up this issue later in the light of our data and discuss the implications.

METHODOLOGY

This study was conducted in two major industrial cities, Bombay and Pune in Maharashtra.

We have chosen only one type of scientists that is a chemist to enable us to keep one variable constant. These scientists are in the R and D establishments of public and private sectors as also in the Chemistry Departments of Universities. The sample comprised of personnel in the Chemistry Departments from :

(1) Universities—Five campuses namely :
   (*a*) University of Bombay,
   (*b*) University of Poona,
   (*c*) I.I.T. Bombay,
   (*d*) B.U.T.C. Bombay, and
   (*e*) Institute of Science, Bombay,

(2) Public Sector Undertakings such as :
   (*a*) BARC—Trombay,
   (*b*) NCL—Pune,
   (*c*) SASMIRA—Worli,
   (*d*) TIFR—Colaba,
   (*e*) Haffkine Institute Parel.

(3) R and D Division (Chemistry) Private Sector Establishments, they are :
   (*a*) Six large-scale organisations,
   (*b*) Twelve medium-scale organisations,
   (*c*) Twenty-four small laboratories where applied and developmental research activity was conducted.

The total sample consisted of eighty scientists from academics. 323 from the public sector and 377 from the private sector establishments.

Questionnaire/schedule and indepth interview techniques were used for data collection. The organisations were stratified on the basis of large, medium and small scale of R and D establishments based on their annual turnover. The collected data were computed to give actual numbers and percentages.

DATA AND DISCUSSION

In this work we are going to study the scientists in various organisations. Fundamentally, the problem arises as a result of transformation of research work from an activity conducted primarily by separate individuals on a relatively small scale to an activity increasingly carried out by professional groups in a large organisation. Scientists of yester years (mentioned earlier—Faraday—Newton, etc.) did not have facilities but conducted their research in their home with improvised equipment, with complete autonomy adhering to scientific norms.

In the twentieth century, research is conducted within the organisation with modern technological equipment. Earlier science and research used to be mainly an academic activity carried on in universities. Today the scientific profession is persued in the national laboratories wherein the greater emphasis is on research and development to be applied in industry for the betterment of production.

The scientists invariably, are subjected to ambivalence, often due to constraints of the social structure and often due to role-conflict. This state of ambivalence is rather overwhelming but cannot be avoided. The structure is difficult to remould, therefore ambivalence must be understood as part of the system.

AMBIVALENCE

"The bureaucratisation of Science, it is argued, is now facing scientists with threats to their autonomy, loss of control over the goals and methods of research, and loss of control over the products of their intellectual activity...[30] Moore and Renck believe that a fundamental conflict exists between the expectations and values of professional employees and the opportunities which they need to realise their ambitions.[31] Burns and Stalker suggest that political and status struggle between professionals and non-professionals exists because scientists compared with other longer-established employees, claimed more recognition, higher status, more control, and more independence of the authority or management.[32]

We have observed that science appears as one of the great social institutions. Science has its corpus of shared and transmitted ideas, values, and standards designed to govern the behaviour of those connected with the institution.

"As is well known, scientists typically experience multiple independent discoveries as one of their occupational hazards. These create occasions for acute stress. Few scientists indeed react with equanimity when they learn that one of their own best contributions to science—what they know to be the result of long hard work is 'only' (as the telling phrase has it) a rediscovery of what was found some time before or 'just' another discovery of what others have found at about the same time."[33] Many a times this also causes behaviour, ambivalent to the culture of science for scientists show marked deviant behaviour by being secretive during early stages of inquiry lest they be fore-stalled. Violent conflicts over priority causes a flow of premature publications designed to establish later claims to have been first. "The ambivalence towards claims of priority means that scientists are contemptuous of the very attitudes they have acquired from the institutions to which they subscribe. The sentiments they have derived from the institution of science with its great premium upon originality, makes it difficult to give up a claim to a new idea or a new finding. Yet the same institution emphasizes the selfless dedication to the advancement of knowledge for its own sake. Concern with priority and ambivalence towards that concern together register in the individual what is generated by the value system of science."[34] Merton further elucidates : "as a result, their deep interest in having their priorities recognised by peers is seen as training their nobility of purpose. This assumption has a germ of psychological truth ; any reward, fame, money position, is morally ambiguous and potentially subversive of culturally esteemed motives..."[35] The observed ambivalence of scientists towards their own interest in having their own priority recognised—an ambivalence we have seen registered even by that most astute of psychologists. Freud shows them to assume that such an ancillary motive somehow tarnishes the purity of their interest in scientific inquiry. Yet it need not be that scientists seek only to win the applause of their peers but rather, that they are comforted and gratified by it when it does ring out.[36]

Analysing the data with the help of Tables reveal many facts of a scientist's work. We begin by checking out areas of ambivalence through the salary, job satisfaction, publication, attendence at conferences, adequacy of assistants, degree of supervision and job mobility. The pattern of recruitment will help us to identify great or lesser ambivalence of these chemists in their chosen arena of work—the university, private sector industry and laboratories.

Table 1 shows us the academic qualifications of scientists. This table is self explanatory but one must take cognisance of the fact that academics draw Ph. D's in greater number (100 per cent). This shows the requirement of high academic degrees in the university setting. Besides, that public sector undertakings have more Ph. D's than the private sectors. This also highlights the recruitment pattern.

Logically, it seems that private sector is engaged in developmental and applied research hence they appoint scientists with lesser qualifications so that they can be trained according to the needs of the organization. Public sector and academics are interested in basic research and awarding higher degrees, hence these sectors have more Ph.D's.

Table 2 gives us an overview of the teacher's perception of their job. Teachers, in majority viewed their salary scales as not satisfactory ; while nearly fifty percent felt that the freedom to choose work-colleagues and career-ladder are satisfactory.

Regarding freedom to publish, and freedom to choose research-subjects, overwhelming majority felt them to be excellent or satisfactory. This proves that they are not money-minded and try to be true to the norms and culture of science to some extent. Yet, ambivalence is due to the salary and also due to the junior scientists inability to choose their own projects, career-ladder and work-colleagues.

TABLE 1

Qualification of Scientists

Qualification	Private Sector	Public Sector	Academician
B.Sc.	77 (20.4)	56 (17.3)	
M.Sc.	219 (58.1)	166 (51.4)	
Ph.D.	42 (11.1)	77 (23.8)	80 (100.0)
Ph.D. (foreign)	4 (1.1)	8 (2.5)	
Double M.Sc.	4 (1.1)	—	
Diploma of B.Sc.	15 (4.0)	12 (3.7)	
Diploma after M.Sc.	10 (2.6)	1 (0.3)	
Diploma after Ph.D.	3 (0.8)	2 (0.6)	
Foreign diploma	3 (0.8)	1 (0.3)	
	377	323	80

Table 3 shows that a greater number of scientists in public sector felt that their capabilities are utilized by the organization. Moderately satisfied with the job are 58.3% and with the degree of supervision are 47.4%. But a greater number seem to be silent on many issues. This shows a very great degree of ambivalence. Since a majority are either dissatisfied or choose not to reply or express inability to reply. This

TABLE 2

Teachers Perception of Their Job

	Excellent	Satisfactory	So So	Not satisfactory	No reply	Total
Salary Scales	2 (2.50)	20 (25.0)	48 (48.0)	6 (7.50)	4 (5.0)	80
Freedom to publish	24 (30.0)	46 (57.50)	6 (7.50)	3 (3.75)	1 (1.25)	80
Freedom to choose	30 (37.50)	35 (43.75)	8 (10.0)	3 (3.75)	4 (5.0)	80
Technical equipment	3 (3.75)	21 (26.25)	11 (13.75)	25 (31.25)	20 (25.0)	80
Freedom to choose work-colleagues	15 (18.75)	26 (32.5)	25 (31.25)	12 (15.0)	2 (2.50)	80
Career-ladder for scientists	8 (10.0)	33 (41.25)	24 (30.0)	11 (13.75)	4 (5.0)	80

TABLE 3

Job Perception by Public Sector Scientists

	Satisfaction	Dissatisfaction	Can't say	No reply	Total
Satisfaction with salary	127 (39.3)	153 (47.4)	43 (13.3)	—	323
Satisfaction with job	188 (58.3)	77 (23.8)	58 (17.9)	—	323
Adequacy of research-assistants	104 (32.2)	71 (22.0)	123 (38.1)	25 (7.7)	323
Prospects of promotion	73 (22.6)	80 (24.8)	162 (50.2)	8 (20.4)	323
Degree of supervision	153 (47.4)	86 (26.6)	69 (21.4)	15 (4.6)	323
The extent, your capabilities are used	265 (82.0)	50 (15.5)	8 (2.4)	—	323

attitude is due to ambivalence and structural constraints. This happens because they are in government organizations where bureaucracy and high expectations go hand in hand. The scientist's comment on the proper utilization of their capacities and skills yet they feel dissatisfied with prospects of promotion, degree of supervision etc. This shows that they are victims of sociological ambivalence.

Table 4 shows that nearly forty-five per cent of scientists in the private sector are satisfied with salary, fifty-four per cent with the job and seventy-seven per cent felt that their talent and capabilities are properly utilized. However, sixty-one per cent expressed inability to comment about prospect of promotion. This shows that private sector evaluations are different from the value of science. The ambivalence in their case is shown in spite of (1) better salaries, (2) proper utilization of services. Even then, if dissatisfaction emerges then it might be because of their lack of dedication to science and research. They fail to a degree in keeping alive the normative culture of science in (i) disinterestedness (ii) openness in research (iii) reward system etc. This is borne out by the factor of liberty to publish, attending the conferences etc.

Table 5 is self-explanatory and shows that academicians publish papers because of the scientific culture while only seventeen per cent scientists from the private sector could do so. From the public sector, in spite of opportunities and possibilities to publish their scientific findings fifty-one per cent have not done so. The reasons for non-publishing and non-attendance at conference are given in Tables 6 and 7.

We find that organizational structures come in the way of scientists from publishing and also from attending conferences.

CONCLUSIONS

We have defined the role of scientists in the structural framework. We have dealt in detail professionalism and proved that scientists are professionals. This profession is based on high academic performance, training, selection and communality of science based on organized scepticism. We have further

TABLE 4

Perception of Their Job by Scientists in the Private Sector

	Satisfied	Dissatisfied	Can't say	No reply	Total
Satisfaction with salary	170 (45.1)	107 (28.4)	100 (26.5)	—	377
Satisfaction with job	207 (54.9)	97 (25.7)	73 (19.4)	—	377
Adequacy of research-assistants	132 (35.0)	85 (22.5)	82 (21.80)	78 (20.7)	377
Prospects of promotion	56 (14.6)	72 (19.2)	231 (61.3)	18 (4.8)	377
Degree of supervision	166 (44.0)	136 (36.2)	54 (14.3)	20 (5.4)	377
The extent to which talent and capabilities are utilised	291 (77.1)	70 (18.6)	13 (3.3)	4 (1.0)	377

TABLE 5

Papers Published by Scientists in Scientific Journals

No. of papers published	Academicians		Private sector		Public sector	
	Foreign	Indian	Foreign	Indian	Foreign	Indian
1–3	30	25	14	41	58	97
	(37.5)	(31.3)	(3.9)	(10.9)	(18.0)	(30.0)
4–6	5	10	16	22	27	34
	(6.3)	(12.5)	(4.2)	(5.8)	(8.4)	(19.5)
7–10	2	10	14	18	6	13
	(2.5)	(12.5)	(3.9)	(4.8)	(1.8)	(4.0)
11–15	5	15	9	6	6	6
	(6.3)	(18.8)	(2.4)	(1.6)	(1.8)	(1.8)
16–20	4	9	6	2	6	10
	(5.0)	(8.8)	(1.6)	(0.5)	(1.8)	(3.1)
21–30	5	8	5	7	2	3
	(6.3)	(10.0)	(1.3)	(1.9)	(0.6)	(0.9)
None	29	5		1	4	1
	(36.3)	(6.3)		(0.3)	(1.2)	(0.3)
No reply/ No publication	—	—	313	280	214	159
			(83.0)	(74.3)	(66.3)	(49.2)
	80	80	377	377	323	323

TABLE 6

Factors which may come in the way of Publication of Papers

Factors	Private sector	Public sector
(1) The organization for which I work does not allow every research finding to be published.	150 (39.8)	58 (18.0)
(2) I write more than I publish. I am afraid papers of junior persons are not accepted.	13 (3.4)	44 (13.6)
(3) Would you consider migration from your present organization in case this freedom is curtailed or modified.	27 (7.2)	31 (9.6)
(4) After a project is finished to the satisfaction of the organization, more work would be necessary to make it adequate to publish in an Academic Journal, I don't find time.	48 (12.7)	69 (21.4)
(5) Most of the important findings are patented and therefore there is no need to publish.	25 (6.6)	20 (6.2)
(6) I am busy with my personal problems after my duty is over. I need more free time if I were to increase my publications.	14 (3.7)	32 (9.9)
(7) My company insists on complete coverage by patents before publication, by this time I am no longer interested.	6 (1.6)	3 (0.9)
(8) My task in the industry does not warrant any paper to be published.	93 (24.7)	58 (18.0)
(9) Any other.	1 (0.3)	8 (2.4)
	377	323

TABLE 7

Reasons for Attending/not Attending Scientific Meetings

Reasons	Private sector	Public sector
(1) I do not want to attend any meetings than I attend now	23 (6.1)	35 (10.8)
(2) Though I would like to attend more meetings I could not, because :		
(a) Of the time and distance factor	79 (21.0)	51 (15.8)
(b) The Organisation for which I work does not encourage R and D staff to attend many meetings	125 (33.1)	53 (16.4)
(c) I did not have any original papers to contribute	81 (21.5)	105 (32.5)
(d) Only one person from the organisation could attend, so I was not deputed	69 (18.3)	77 (23.8)
(e) No Reply	—	2 (0.6)
TOTAL	377	323

found that the scientists role is based on universalism, disinterestedness and non-craving for monetary gains. On this theoretical background we have tried to find out the structural location of the scientist. The structural location and the organisational set-up produces ambivalence and role-conflict. Reviewing the situation from the empirical data we find :

(*i*) Location of scientists vary and they are in academics, public and private sector, R and D organisations. These organisations have special goals. Academics attract elite among the students because of the reference-group, identity with faculty.

(*ii*) The immediate monetary incentives along with the prestige and final achievement of a higher degree seem very rewarding.

(*iii*) They seem to be fulfilling the culture of scientists through contribution to scientific knowledge, sharing it with the peers and showing disinterestedness for monetary gains.

(*iv*) They have a chance to attend scientific conferences, present papers, published articles and books.

(*v*) They are able to be true to science through teaching which dissiminates knowledge and carry on research in their chosen area.

Academicians' Role-Conflict and Ambivalence

This arises because :

(*i*) Research funds are limited.

(*ii*) Funding is not uniform and in majority of cases is dependent on seniority, publication, rank of the scholar and the influence, one has in the scientific community.

(*iii*) Junior scholars are frustrated due to pecuniary strains in the personal life and in the research activity.

(*iv*) The pressure of seniors for joint authorship causes rivalry.

(*v*) We found due to values and reward system of science,

with its pathogenic emphasis on originality produced deviant behaviour like secretiveness during the early stages of inquiry, conflicts over priority, premature publication, which are against the spirit of profession of science.

We can then surmise that in academics, juniors, who are capable of carrying out constructive research are denied the facility and when they do get at a later stage because of their rank, their productive years are passed and role conflict ambivalence have taken their toll because of the structure.

Scientists in Public Sector, R and D

These organisations built by the government are plagued by bureaucracy, nepotism, corruption, short-sighted policies and priorities.

(*i*) Scientists in this setting have to adhere to hierarchical norms instead of scientific norms.

(*ii*) Scientific creativity is dictated by organisational norms and priorities. Government or the head of the section determines the funding, projects to be undertaken and their termination.

(*iii*) Monetary rewards are limited personally and also in the laboratory. Many a times sophisticated research is impossible.

(*iv*) Whatever empirical work is carried out, is for a purpose which may have no social relevance as it is often not acceptable to the industries.

(*v*) Lack of communality and social acceptance of their research, causes unhappiness.

Role-Conflict and Ambivalence

(1) Allotment of projects based on hierarchy and not on ability.

(2) Dictated creativity cramps up discovery.

(3) In spite of openness of publication, there is role-conflict because of pressures from seniors, classified information and restrictions on attending conferences and presenting papers.

Scientist in Private Sector R and D

R and D units are established because it is a prestigious one in private sector. It is all concerned with the economic planning of the company, for R and D units give them tax relief. R and D units are intended to develop the products of the company. Basic research is given a secondary importance and only if it has some future potential for the growth of the company.

(*i*) Scientists, in private sector are like secondary citizens who are outside the promotional channels of the line organisation.
(*ii*) Scientific ladder is only three or four tiered.
(*iii*) Funds are plentiful for the research in which the organisation is interested.
(*iv*) The salary and perks of a R and D scientist in private sector is much more than in academics or public sector organisation.

Ambivalence and Role-Conflict

(*i*) Scientists in R and D units of private sector believe that other scientists view them as merceneries and lackeys of the units.
(*ii*) The spirit and culture of the science is lacking because private sector does not allow the findings to be published or presented for universal consumption.
(*iii*) The basic goal of communality and universality of science as well as disinterestedness are obstructed by the social structure of the organisation. Even though the scientists did good work, no recognition is given to them by the scientific community because of secrecy.
(*iv*) If the organizational need is satisfied regarding particular project, the organisation will not allow the scientist to pursue it to his satisfaction, so this leads to ambivalence and job-dissatisfaction.

Finally, we can conclude, that the profession of scientists in R and D units produce job dissatisfaction and ambivalence because of structural factors of the organisation.

NOTES AND REFERENCES

1. Carr-Saunders, A.M. and P.A. Wilson, "Metropolitan Conditions and Traditional Professional Relationships", Robert M. Fisher (ed.), *Metropolis in Modern Life*, Double Day, Garden City, New York, 1955, pp. 279-87.
2. Greenwood, E., "Attributes of a Profession," *Social Work*, vol. 2, 1957.
3. Wilensky, Harold L., *Intellectuals in Labour Union*, The Free Press, Glencoe, Ill., 1956.
4. Danielson, Lee E., *Characteristics of Engineers and Scientists*, University of Michigan, Ann Arbor, 1960.
5. *Ibid.*
6. Scott, Richard W., "Professional Employees in a Bureaucratic Structure : Social Work", Amitai Etzoni (ed.), *The Semi-Professions and Their Organisations*, The Free Press, New York, 1929, p. 82.
7. Denton, J.A., *Medical Sociology*, Hongton Muffin Co., New York, 1978.
8. Wilensky, *op. cit.*
9. Cotgrove and Box, *Science, Industry and Society*, George Allen and Unwin, London, 1970, p. 42.
10. Currie, I.D. *et. al.*, "Image of the Professor and Interest in the Academic Profession," *Sociology of Education*, vol. 39, 1966, pp. 301-323.
11. Vollmer, H., "Professional Adaptation in Organisation," H.M. Vollmer and D.L. Mills (eds.), *Professionalisation*, Prentice-Hall, Englewood Cliffs, New Jersey, 1966, p. 276.
12. Clark, Burton, "The Colling out Function in Higher Education", *American Journal of Sociology*, vol. 15, 1956, pp. 559-76.
13. Story, Norman, *The Sociology of Science : Theoretical and Empirical Investigation.*
14. Cotgrove and Box, *op. cit.*
15. Cotgrove and Box, *op. cit.*
16. Cotgrove and Box, *op. cit.*
17. Benal, J.D., "The Social Functions of Science", C.K. Zoleschan and Witturch (eds.), *Explorations in Social Change*, 1964, p. 170.
18. Hagstrom, W.O., *The Scientific Community*, Basic Books, New York, 1965.
19. Merton, R.K., *Sociological Ambivalence and Other Essays*, Free Press, New York, 1976, p. 36.
20. Storv, *op. cit.* ; Hagstrom, *op. cit.*
21. Cotgrove and Box, *op. cit.*
22. Cotgrove and Box, *op. cit.*
23. Abrahamson, M., "The Integration of Industrial Scientists", *A S.G.*, vol. 9, 1964, pp. 208-18.
24. Whyte, W.H., *The Organisation Man*, Simon and Schuster, New York, 1956.

25. Mareson, Simon. *The Scientists in American Industry*, Princeton University, 1922.
26. Shepard, Herbert A., "Nine Dilemmas in Industrial Research," *Administrative Science Quarterly*, vol. I, 1956.
27. Laporte, R.T., "Conditions of Strain and Accommodation in Industrial Research Organisation," *Administrative Science Quarterly*, vol. 10, 1965, pp. 21-38.
28. Kaplan, N., "Some Organisation Factors Affecting Creativity", *IRF Transaction on Engineering Management*, vol. 7, 1960, pp. 24-29.
29. Kronhauser, W., *Scientists in Industry*, University of California Press, Berkeley, 1963.
30. Cotgrove and Box, *op. cit.*, p. 4.
31. Moore, D.G., and R. Renck, "The Professional Employees in Industry", *Journal of Business*, vol. 38.
32. Burns, Barry and Staker, *Sociology of Science*, Penguin Books, Harmondsworth, 1972.
33. Merton, *op. cit.*, p. 36.
34. Merton, *op. cit.*, p. 402.
35 Merton, *op. cit.*
36. Merton, *op. cit.*, p. 43.

17

PROFESSIONAL OBSOLESCENCE : A NEEDED AREA OF RESEARCH

A. L. SRIVASTAVA
AND
M. TOHA

The expansion of knowledge in the field of science, engineering and technology is taking place at a very rapid pace. Each day new facts, new theories and new models are being discovered. This has created a lag in the knowledge and skills among those who are engaged in science and technology-based professions. The usefulness of the scientists and engineers becomes less important after a few years of entering into the job because the knowledge which they have gained before, becomes obsolete after a few years in the service. This can be explained through the use of a concept used in nuclear physics which is known as the "*Concept of Half Life*". Occupational "half life" is based on the assumption that enough new developments, techniques and knowledge evolve in short period of time, say five--fifteen years, so that a person becomes roughly half as competent to the job for which his initial training was intended. Consequently, an incumbent frequently must turn to learning activities just to maintain or regain competence. Therefore, there is need for relearning of professional updating. Dr. James Killian, former President of the Massachusets Institute of Technology has pegged the half life of an engineer's usefulness at about seven and one and a half years. He interprets this to mean that the engineer is only half as valuable technically to a firm, seven and one and half years after graduation as he was the day he received his degree. In sociological parlance, this phenomena has been called professional obsolescence. It is difficult to define obsolescence because the research in this field is relatively new and the literature is not extensive.

Siefert has defined obsolescence in the context of engineering profession as (the measurement at some point of time) "the difference between the knowledge and skills possessed by a new graduate of modern engineering curriculum and the knowledge and skills actually possessed by the practising engineer, who may have completed his formal education, a number of years ago."[1]

Shumacher defined obsolescence as a "reduction in technical effectiveness resulting from a lack of knowledge of the new techniques and what is more, perhaps entirely new technologies that have developed since the acquisition of the education by the individual."[2]

Dubin emphasising the motivational aspect of obsolescence has observed the reverse of the activity is the condition of obsolescence. Obsolescence is a developmental process comprising the loss of acquired knowledge and the non-acquisition of new learning which occurs unless effort is constantly made to repair the erosion of knowledge and to stimulate growth and innovation.[3]

Thus it is clear that professional obsolescence is a state in which the role incumbent slowly ossifies and drifts into obsolescence because of the rapid change of knowledge and skill in his specialised field.

TYPES OF PROFESSIONAL OBSOLESCENCY

Ferdinand has described three types of obsolescence for the purpose of identifying the nature and causes of obsolescence among engineers and scientists.[4] These are as follows :

(*i*) *Professional obsolescence* exists in those persons whose technical competence does not embrace the farthest reaches of knowledge and technique in their profession.

(*ii*) *Areal obsolescence* refers to a lack of knowledge in the technical speciality of a person who has allowed himself to settle complacently into a narrow specialized area.

Obsolete individual tend to be afflicted with a complescency which prevents their anticipating or participating in radical developments about to unfold in their speciality.

(*iii*) *Ex-Officio obsolescence* is a form, prevalent in scientists or technical persons assigned to administrative work. Such persons find their technical capabilities declining and out-dated once, they are assigned supervisory and administrative work.

Malmros has divided obsolescence into two categories ;

(*i*) rustiness which results from the lack of proper use, and

(*ii*) failure to grow and keep up with changes.[5] He has associated the failure to grow and keep abreast of new developments with persistence of repetitive patterns of behaviour and lack of sensitivity to change. He has further identified five signs of obsolescence in engineers :

(*a*) engineer became less and less inclined to apply rigorous mathematical techniques to obtain solutions to his problems,

(*b*) he encountered increasing difficulty in reading new technical papers and felt frustrated because he could not follow the mathematics,

(*c*) new technical concepts were confusing to him,

(*d*) new task and assignments began to look too difficult to be practical, and

(*e*) contemporaries did not seek his advice.

Norgren has identified two major types of skills obsolescence :

(*a*) technology-based obsolescence, and

(*b*) product-based obsolescence.[6]

THE REVIEW OF THE LITERATURE

There is a dearth of literature on professional obsolescence. In

U.S.A. where increasing attention is being paid on this area, there too, the research in this field is scanty. In 1963, the Organization for Economic Corporation and Development published a study which reported a number of highly qualified scientists and engineers available in O.E.C.D., the extent of their employment in industries, teaching and administration and the need and the demand for qualified man power for the purpose of maintenance or accelerating the rate of economic growth.[7] A subsequent conference examined policies required for updating the educational system to provide training for economic needs and means by which industry and government could optimise the use of highly qualified personnel by career-training.[8]

In 1963, research was initiated at the Pennsylvania State University to determine what new areas of knowledge were needed by engineers who had been out of school for a number of years. A series of studies were published, based on a sample of 2090 engineers by various specialities (electrical, aeronautical, mechanical etc.) and by various industrial categories and sizes of organizations in the state of Pennsylvania.[9] The results provided data on the self-perceived educational needs of engineers who had been out of college for at least five years in subject-areas in which they needed re-tooling. This study also constituted a rationale for offering new forces in the skills and knowledge which engineers reported, they needed most. Almost forty changes were made in the curriculum of the Pennsylvania State University college of engineering, new courses in probability and statistics and computer technology were introduced and modifications were made in many of the existing courses.

The investigation concerning engineers was followed by studies of other professional groups ; hospital supervisors,[10] managers,[11] municipal managers[12] and natural resource managers and scientists.[13] In these studies the aim was to determine the self-perceived educational needs of the respondents, their subordinates and superiors in scientific subject areas, the extent of their participation in continuing education, methods of updating preferred motivation for updating, attitude of supervisors towards development of subordinates, the availability of financial assistance and reasons for not updating. In some of these studies an additional section dealt with self-development planning, projected over a period of five years.

A division of American Society of Engineering Education known as the Engineering College Achievement Council and the Relation within Industry—Feed Back Committee (ECAC-RWI), surveyed engineers to determine the subject in which additional training was necessary.[14] In both the Pennsylvania state and ECAC-RWI studies the most frequently mentioned topics were management, communication skills, probability, statistics, computer applications and mathematics.

The Goals Study Committee of the American Society of Engineering Education put-forth a major statement of the new professional goal for the whole organization.[15] In the next year, the National Science Foundation in the United States published "Continuing Education for Research and Development Careers,[16] a study which reported on the motivation of research and development scientists in maintaining their scientific competence and the views of top management on continuing education, research and development personnel see themselves as being on the foremost frontier of science and according to this study, they regard continuing education as a necessity for professional obligation to keep up to date, not as a remedial process. They do not see themselves as their colleagues as obsolete or not obsolete. The study also discloses that top management recognize its responsibility to provide opportunities for continuing education but expected the individual scientists or engineers to be self-motivated. The authors recommended that management should provide a supportive educational environment, allowing attendance at professional meeting arranging and sponsoring in lab lectures and seminars and granting sabbatical leave. Margulies and Rala carried on interviews with scientists and engineers in advanced technology laboratory in Aero-Space at nuclear fields from which they evolve categories of activities for professional growth.[17]

MOTIVATIONAL AND ORGANISATIONAL CONTEXT OF PROFESSIONAL OBSOLESCENCE

The literature on professional obsolescence has highlighted two aspects—motivational and organizational. Motivational determinants of professional obsolescence are anchored mainly in achievement motivation. In fact, obsolescence is a problem of personal initiative and aspiration to rise higher in the profession. The high level of achievement motivation leads to a high degree of personal responsibility, comprehensive plans to attain goal and to raise the standard of performance. This naturally leads to a drive or urge on the part of the professionals to innovate, to complete and to keep abreast with the changes in the field of his speciality. Such persons are highly motivated to update their knowledge. In service training programmes, continuing education, refresher courses etc. have been devised to raise the knowledge and skills of the professionals. But these skills of professional updating are not effective in themselves unless the professionals themselves, wish to increase their knowledge, skills and performance.

One of the situational factor which comes in the way of professional updating is associated with the real life situation of the individual. Age, health and family circumstances sometimes inhibit the learning capabilities of individual, though he may be highly motivated.

Another important constraint in the professional updating is the organizational context. Professionals employed in private organizations are largely dependent upon the facilities and resources of the organization for professional updating. If the organization has paucity of funds and resources, then the professionals within the organization have to live within the existing level of competence and knowledge. Those organizations which are resourceful and whose products are not valued in the market, they always provide in-service facilities for improving the level of knowledge and skills.

The institutionalised means of updating and innovation for professional members within organization are many. Some of the most important are : offering a bonus and promotion to members who take part in advanced courses ; paying professional members to participate in seminars and conferences ; building information review and retrieval systems within an organization ; designing career patterns with regular intermittent courses and seminars adopted to various types and age-categories of professionals, leave facilities for particularly successful professionals in the form of educational travelling or of special missions.

When organizations support the professional updating programme, then not only the competence level of the professionals is raised but also the demand for the product of the organization also increases.

SOME EMPIRICAL EVIDENCES

In India there is no empirical research in the field of professional obsolescence, more particularly in professions connected with engineering, computer science, electronics etc. The knowledge gap in India is too wide because most of the fundamental researches and advancement in science and technology are being carried out in the West. India, like other developing countries, is on the recipient end. The new technology which India gets is often second or third generation old. By the time, the same technology is adopted in India much advancement has taken place in the West. At the ideational level, the schism between the Western countries and India is still much wider.

In our exploration of the problem of professional obsolescence among mechanical engineering staff of Institute of Technology, Banaras Hindu University, certain significant facts have come to surface, some of them are mentioned here on the basis of case studies made :

It has been found that though reward in terms of promotions is important but undue promotion to non-deserving persons creates negative motivation in sincere workers. Red-tapism has been mentioned as a great handicap in professional updating. Lack of fund has been reported as one of the major difficulties.

NOTES AND REFERENCES

1. Siefert W.W., *The Prevention and Cure of Obsolescence in Scientific and Technical Personnel*, Industrial Research Institute, Philadelphia, October, 1963.
2. Shumacher, Clifford H., "Reducing Obsolescence of Engineering Skills," Paper Presented at Midwest Conference on Reducing Obsolescence of Engineering Skills, Illinois, Institute of Technology, Chicago, 1963.
3. Dubin S.S., and, Cohen, D., "Motivation to Update From a System Approach," *Journal of Engineering Education*, January, 1970, pp. 366-363.
4. Ferdinand, Theodore N., "On the Obsolescence of Scientists and Engineers," *American Scientists*, vol. 54, 1966, pp. 46-56.
5. Malmros, A., "Obsolescence of Engineering and Scientific Personnel in Industry," Paper Presented at Midwest Conference on Reducing Obsolescence of Engineering Skills, Illinois, Institute of Technology, Chicago, 1963.
6. Norgren, Paul, *Pilot Study of Obsolescence of Scientific and Engineering Skills*, Columbia University, New York, 1965.
7. Organisation for Economic Co-operation and Development. Third International Survey on the Demand for and the Supply of Scientific and Technical Personnel, Paris, 1963.
8. Organisation for Economic Corporation and Development, Policy Conference on Highly Qualified Personnel, Paris, 1967.
9. Dubin, Samuel S., Marlow, H. Le Roy, *A Survey of Continuing Professional Education for Engineers in Pennsylvania*, University Park, Pennsylvania Continuing Education, The Pennsylvania State University, 1965.
10. ——, *The Determination and Measurement of Supervisory Training Needs of Hospital Personnel*, University Park, Pennsylvania Continuing Education, The Pennsylvania State University, 1965.
11. Dubin, Samuel S., Alderman, Everett, and Marlow, H. Le Roy, *Managerial and Supervisory Educational Needs of Business and Industry in Pennsylvania*, University Park, Pennsylvania Continuing Education, The Pennsylvania State University, 1967.
12. ——, *Educational Needs of Managers and Supervisors in Cities, Boroughs and Townships in Pennsylvania*, University Park, Pennsylvania Continuing Education, The Pennsylvania State University, 1968.
13. George, John L., and Dubin, Samuel S., *The Continuing Professional Education Needs of Natural Resource, Managers and Scientists*, University Park, Pennsylvania Continuing Education, The Pennsylvania State University, 1971.

14. "Engineering College Achievement Council and the Relations within Industry Feedback Committee, Education in Industry", *Journal of Engineering Education*, May 1965, pp. 254-256.
15. "American Society of Engineering Education : Goals of Engineering Education", *Journal of Engineering Education*, January 1968, vol. 58, no. 5, pp. 373-443.
16. National Science Foundation, Continuing Education for R and D Careers", N. S. E., 1969.
17. Margulies, Newton and Anthony Rala, P., "Scientists, Engineers and Technological Obsolescence, California", *Management Review*, vol. 10 no. 2, Winter 1967, pp. 43-48.

PART IV

MEDICAL PROFESSION

18

TOWARD A PROFESSION OF HEALTH AND PROFESSIONALIZATION OF HEALTH PERSONNEL

S.R. MEHTA

Profession, Professional and Professionalization

Professionals profess of what they know. The knowledge and skills acquired by them as a part of their long-drawn training stand them in good stead in providing care to the ailments or affairs of their clients. Occupational competence, in that sense, may become an important attribute of a profession. However, over the years, a lot of literature has flown from the Social science disciplines, making attempts to conceptualise and define a profession. But despite that, "no broad acceptance of any authoritative definition has been observed."[1]

A number of other attributes have become significant in conceiving a profession. Flexner, for example, has considered professions as morally superior to other occupations and according to him, a profession would involve intellectual activities based on science and learning for tackling or solving problems. These activities can be taught or learnt. Further, a profession is organized internally and is altruistic.[2] The distinction often made between a "professional" and an "amateur", on the basis of receiving payment of services, further add to the confusion, associated with defining "profession".

Notwithstanding the significance of a number of attributes such as service-orientation, body of theoretical knowledge and autonomy of the work-group,[3] monopoly of judgment[4] and several other factors such as the rise of "consumerism", a more knowledgeable public, and increasing governmental intervention which affect the concepts of profession and professional, it is clear that professions have by and large, emerged in response to the varying societal needs. Irrespective of the fact whether one follows the functional perspective of the profession which views it as a relatively homogenous group or community whose members share identity, values, definitions of role and interests or the processual approach which speaks of many identities, values and interests within the professions, but making progress towards the attainment of attributes of a profession, and in that sense, becoming a corollary of the functional perspective, one has to take into consideration the changing socio-economic and political milieu of most of the developing nations for understanding the development of profession.

As a consequence of socio-economic and technological changes in the developing societies, the human service professions, of which medicine is one, have undergone dramatic changes. Specialization and Super-specializations have brought in segmentation and internal dissensions within the profession. Further, due to division of labour, differentiation process has brought in a large battery of semi-professionals and para-professionals striving hard to attain autonomy in their professions and has affected the prestige and power of some professions.

It is but natural for any occupational group to improve and secure a better position for itself in the occupational division of labour. Professionalization, in that sense, may be defined as a process by which an occupational group secures a sphere of activity against encroachment from other workers. This is made possible through the imposition of entrance criteria, special training programmes, codes of ethics to secure domain of work which in due course of time gets institutionalized after the state recognition and issue of licensure.[5]

Conceptual Framework in the Construction of Illness for Organization of Health Care

Developing countries followed the developed world in organizing health care services. They have over-emphasized secondary and tertiary sophisticated hospital-based care whereas preventive health programmes and primary or basic care to individuals and families in the community at places convenient to them have often been neglected. The health manpower structure is presented by doctors at the top, indigenous medicine practitioners and folk-medicine men at the bottom and a few others in between, unlike the developed countries where a few physicians are supported by a large number of nurses and auxiliary workers in the health set-up. Nearly, two-thirds of the health budget in many countries is devoted to medical education and related teaching hospitals.[6] This over-emphasis on Western medicine is mainly due to advances made in biological sciences. "Germ theory" provided an impetus to discoveries and inventions of wonder drugs responsible for the use and control of many deadly and severe diseases.

In modern Western societies "illness" is viewed as unmotivated deviance, remediable by the application of rational knowledge owned by a special class of persons.[7] In the assumption of the sick-role, the sufferer is not to be held responsible for his deviance. He is exempted from his normal obligations provided he seeks competent help and co-operates with the treatment to acquire normalcy as a functional actor in the social system.

This functional perspective on illness behaviour or the "patient—role" has been critically examined by Freidson who argues that certain aspects of the "Sick role" such as absolution from responsibility for one's condition, are relevant to a wide range of cultures other than the Western societies. But insofaras exemption from normal obligations is concerned, it is variable in degree and depends upon the perceived seriousness of the condition.[8] He develops a typology of deviance in his processual analysis of illness career by adding the dimension of legitimacy to that of imputed responsibility and imputed seriousness.

However, the functionalists have been criticized for presenting a monolithic and homogenous social structure whose participants acted under the influence of exterior, rectified values. Though Freidson, following the labelling theorists or interactionists recognize the relevance of cultural pluralism in his analysis to the American white middle-class, yet he seems to fall in the trap of functionalist framework as his plural groups remain subservient of their values. Further, Freidson tends to treat Western scientific knowledge as more valid than other kinds of knowledge including folk-medical knowledge which may not be true in all situations.

In view of limitations of functionalist and interactionist perspective in the construction to concept of illness, Dingwall argues that people draw on common sense, knowledge of social structure, that is, on ideas about the nature of the society in which they are living, about the typical sorts of people and situations they are likely to meet and the ways of conducting themselves that are appropriate and also on the social world that competent members of the society have to show each other that they are living in if they are to be recognized as normal, rational, and reasonable human beings.[9]

Within this ethno-sociology framework, Dingwall advocates ethno-medicine approach in understanding the concept of illness. Illness in that context has to be viewed as a form of failure at everyday life, a disruption in the "familiar and taken for granted" state of affairs between subjective experience of one's own body and one's knowledge, determined by a competent member of some collectivity, of what is normal experience or conduct. Thus ethno-medicine considers medical knowledge invoked by the physician to interpret a patient's behaviour identical to the knowledge invoked by lay person to any other person's behaviour or conduct. This provides a wider perspective to the understanding of concepts of health and illness, being based on the knowledge that members of some collectivity draw on to make sense in their social and natural world and on the content and organisation of that knowledge.

A brief account of the conceptual frameworks in the construction of illness as a concept is important in view of the medical intervention to be provided by professionals, semi-professionals or para-professionals in the organization and management of health care services to the community.

We do know that there is no single pattern of organization of health care and its structure is largely determined by the structure of other societal institutions of which it forms a part. However, while organizing health care, one has to bear in mind that every society views health problems from the perspective of its own culture and makes efforts to provide coping responses to them according to the understanding, knowledge, values, attitudes and beliefs of people comprising it. As such, the involvement of people in the organisation of health care can become a facilitating factor for promotion of health, and prevention or cure of disease. This pluralistic approach in health care rather than monolithic model of functionalist, provides a better perspective in terms of management and organisation of health services by including in its purview the folk and indigenous medicine practitioners and self-medication practices of the lay persons.

Primary Health Care Team-Work and Professionalization of Health Personnel

In view of a large majority of population in the developing countries residing in rural areas, where health resources are scarce, it is imperative to provide them with low-cost, accessible and relevant health care through their involvement and participation. This fact was recognized and supported at the Alma Ata Conference on Primary Health Care in September, 1978. As a strategy for providing health care to their respective populations, Health for All by the year 2,000 was suggested for developing nations.[10]

It is observed that as the scope of human services and health care are redefined, it is not just possible for any one person to adequately monitor that care.[11] Team work, therefore, has been considered as a method and process for the delivery of Primary Health Care. This care includes education concerning prevailing health problems and the methods of preventing and controlling them; promotion of food supply and proper nutrition, and adequate supply of safe water and basic sanitation; maternal and child health care including family planning immunization against the major infectious diseases and injuries; prevention and control of locally endemic diseases; appropriate treatment of common diseases and injuries; and provision of essential drugs through community participation. As a method, its activities have to be time-bound and target-oriented whereas as a process, it is to be considered and visualized as a continuous process.[12] This approach would need deprofessionalization of physicians and reprofessionalization of health-personnel involved in the health-care team.

While professionalism denotes occupational differentiation and a more complex division of labour, team work denotes sharing, working together, mutual respect and trust, free communications and so forth.[13] In that sense, professionalism and team work tend to move in opposite direction. Team work in a health delivery system would expect a free collaboration among professional peers and between professional and technical or administrative assistants engaged in providing health care to a large population. But the collobora-tive effort can become effective only if it minimizes the formal status of partners in the accomplishment of the common goal of providing health care. In traditional or quasi-traditional social structure which permeates the developing nations, status or rank position is an important barrier in collaborative efforts.[14]

Team work approach has, however, fostered the "professio-nalization of everyone" and there are efforts on the part of health workers to professionalize themselves. For example, a large number of para-professionals and technicians are emerging in the health field as a result of economic development and technological change, consequently affecting the status or rank position of members in the health team as a result of mobility opportunities but this progression of occupations toward profession of health by non-professionals is again based on "attributes" identified as ideal for "professions". This competitive progression sets limit to teamwork approach and creates managerial problems of health care.

Though team work is a desirable method, yet it is difficult to accomplish in health services as a result of economic and socio-cultural gaps between professionals, semi-professionals and para-professionals in the context of Primary Health Care. The author, on the bases of analysis done of country case studies identfiied Job Allocation-roles and responsibilities of Health Personel, Training, Supervision, Co-ordination, Communication and Community Participation as some of the important factors influencing team work in the delivery of health service.[15]

We do know that in many of the countries of Africa, Asia and Latin America, more than fifty per cent of the population has no contact with modern health care, and in some instances, the proportion exceeds eighty and even ninety per cent. This shows that the distribution of health care is extremely uneven especially so in the less developed countries. Even the health manpower is limited in number and seriously mal-distributed, ratios of population to physicians in rural areas of developing countries commonly range from 25,000 to 500,000.[16]

In case of India, it is also observed that the ratio of physicians in urban to rural areas is twenty-five to one, though the population to be catered for is more (seventy-eight per cent) in rural than in urban areas.[17] Besides, there are a large number of medical graduates (18499 as on 31-12-1982) on the live register of employment exchanges, the higher being in Andhra Pradesh (5004) and the next highest in Delhi (1938). Further, despite a turnover of 13,000 medical doctors every year, the number of doctors serving the rural areas is not more than 16303[18] as most of the doctors do not want to serve the rural areas. This skewed distribution and reorganisation of health care services with a focus on delivery of Primary Health Care would necessitate restricting the opening of new medical schools in developing countries and instead increasing the number of training institutions for para-professionals with new curricula and emphasis on team work approach. Even the semi-professional such as Indigenous Medicine Practitioners and Homeopaths and health volunteers inducted in Primary Health care programme will also have to be provided in service training, on a continued basis as they can ensure better community participation, essential in organising health care relevent to the needs of the people.

However, the tendencies on the part of the para-professionals or semi-professionals to imbibe the behaviour pattern of some of their more professional colleagues need to be discouraged. Even the administrative approach to supervise health workers would necessitate a change in the bureaucratic framework of rules ; partial rather than strict enforcement of rules may act as a reward for the subordinates and they may show greater propensities to reciprocate their supervisor's actions.[19] The administrative leadership to be provided by the physicians will also have to be based on human relation approach, rather than on authority structure of the "rational" bureaucratic model. Team work approach would also necessitate a re-structuring of medical education and reorientation of physicians to the concept and method of community health. This would be part of deprofessionalisation of physicians and reprofessionalisation of health personnel involved in Primary Health Care. Basic training of health personnel including professionals, para-professionals will further have to be strengthened by the in service training programmes especially based on the concept of team training. The major thrust will have to be on the profession of health than on profession of medicine which has acquired an elite character.

Community participation is one of the main elements of organising Primary Health care at the local level but this may be a major hurdle in the professionalization of health personnel involved in the team work. Stratification systems in most societies do not ensure fuller participation of community members from all strata and this poses a problem of equitable distribution of health care to all. Besides, there are vested interests of individuals and groups in the community which do not encourage a greater participation of people.[20] As such, the professionalization of health personnel involved in primary health care and the deprofessionalization of physicians because of certain built in contradictions and complexities in the health service delivery systems and community social system in which these processes get legitimized, would necessitate a change in the authority structure of the health services and a different socio-political structure at the community level.

A basic question remains: will the medical elites at the helm of affairs in the organization of health care services and the political masters, accept the decentralized planning and organization of primary health care services ? These fundamental structural constraints will restrict the development of profession of health and professionalization of health personnel. We will have to find ways and means of tackling these more basic challenges.

NOTES AND REFERENCES

1. Cogan, M.L., "Towards a Definition of a Profession," *Harvard Educational Review*, vol. 23, 1953, pp. 33-50.
2. Flexner, A., "Is Social Work a Profession ?" *Proceedings of the National Conference on Charities and Corrections*, Hildeman Printing Co., Chicago, 1915.
3. Sussman, M.B., "Occupational Sociology and Rehabilitation," M.B. Sussman, (ed.), *Sociology and Rehabilitation*, American Sociological Association, Washington, D.C., 1966,
4. Greenwood, E., "Attributes of a Profession," *Social Work*, vol. 2, no. 3, 1957, pp. 44-55.
5. World Health Organisation, Report of WHO (SEARO) EXPERT GROUP, *Team Work for Primary Health Care*, SEARO, New Delhi, October, 27-31, 1980.
6. The World Bank, *Health Sector Policy Paper*, Washington, D.C. 1980.
7. Parsons, T., *The Social System*, Free Press, Glencoe Ilinois, 1951.
8. Freidson, E., *Profession of Medicine*, Dodd and Mead, New York, 1971.
9. Dingwall, Robert, *Aspects of Illness*, Mortin Robertson and Co., London, 1976.
10. World Health Organisation, *Strategies for Health For All by the Year 2000 A.D., SEARO*, New Delhi, December, 1980.
11. Ducans, Alex, *et al.*, *The Interdisciplinary Health Care Team : A Hand Book*, Aspen System Corporation, London, 1979.
12. Mehta, S.R., "Team work in Primary Health Care : An Analysis of Country Case Study," Discussion Paper for *Consultation Meeting on Review of Country Studies on Team Work*, World Health Organization, SEARO, New Delhi July 30-August 3, 1984 ; *Rural Develop-*

ment Policies and Programmes : *A Sociological Perspective*, Sage Publication, New Delhi, 1984.
13, WHO, 1980, *op. cit.*
14. Mehta, 1984, *op. cit.*
15. Mehta, *op. cit.*
16. Bryant, J.H., "Principles, of Justice as a Basis for Conceptualising a Health Care System," *International Journal of Health Services*, vol. 7, no. 4, 1977.
17. Mehta, *op. cit.*
18. Government of India, *Health Statistics of India*, Central Health Intelligence Bureau, Directorate General of Health Services, New Delhi, 1983.
19. Schwartz, Michael, The Reciprocities Multiplier : An Empirical Evaluation," *Administrative Science Quarterly* vol, 9. no. 3, 1984.
20. Mehta, *op. cit.*

19

DOCTORS AND DOCTRINF

AMBIKA CHANDANI

THE ideological expectation from the medical profession is that of altruism. They are expected to contribute to the well-being of society over and above the return for their own gratification. This expectation is a reality or myth needs to be properly comprehended for a better understanding of the existing situation. It is proposed here to investigate this in terms of three aspects : (1) we would try to know the major area of interest of the doctors *i.e.* whether their major concern is service to the society or to earn money or such other things, (2) further the attitude of the doctors towards private practice *i.e.* whether or not they are willing to undertake private practice, and (3) whether doctors are willing or not to go to villages to serve the sick people. The data and the analysis would be able to indicate the prevailing concern of the doctors. It would show if they are true to their doctrine to serve the sick. The present paper focuses on these aspects.

RESEARCH SITE AND METHODOLOGY

The study has been conducted among the practitioners of modern medicine located in the city of Jodhpur, the capital of erstwhile Marwar Estate and now the Head Quarters of Jodhpur Division. There were 179 registered doctors at the time of the survey. The study is based on the interview with 152 doctors of whom 119 are institutional and thirty-three are private practitioners. Interview-schedule was used as tool of data collection. Data have been analysed in terms of two variables, namely (1) private practitioners and institutional doctors, and (2) sex. There are 125 male and twenty-seven female doctors.[1]

It is appropriate to present in brief the social background of the respondents.

SOCIAL BACKGROUND

The doctors are generally male (82.2 %). The average age of the respondents is 38.3 years. Numerically, Hindu doctors are in pre-ponderant position (79.9 %), mostly belonging to clean middle castes (53.3 %). Nine out of every ten doctors have been brought up in cities. In regional terms, most of the respondents belong to Rajasthan (Seventy-three per cent). Hindi is the mother-tongue of 59.9% of the doctors and all the doctors are at least bilingual. As many as 92.9% of the respondents are married. A majority of the respondents live in joint family (54.9%) and on an average they have 4.7 members in their family. The average income of the doctors is Rs. 957.6 per month and ninety per cent of the doctors belong to middle class. Only thirty-two doctors have visited foreign countries.

The study commences with assessing the doctors, major area of interest.

DOCTORS, MAJOR AREA OF INTEREST

Doctors may evince more interest in one area than the other. To examine this they were asked : please rank the following in terms of the interest you have in them : (1) serving patient (2) earning, (3) teaching, (4) research and (5) administration.

To understand the relative importance the doctors attach to these items, 5, 4, 3, 2, and 1 scores were assigned to first through fifth rank respectively. Table 1 shows the major area of interest of the doctors.

It is clear from the table that the doctors were more interested in serving the sick than in any other thing. Serving the sick was their ideal. Earning came next. It had been given second rank. Teaching and research had been given third and fourth rank respectively. The availability of medical college had not inspired the doctors to be interested in teaching or research. Administration was the last and it was given the fifth rank. Both private and institutional doctors gave first rank to "serving the sick." Second rank was given to earning by private practitioners but this was given third rank by institutional doctors. They gave second rank to teaching. There was perfect agreement between male and female doctors in their ranking. Both of them assigned first rank to serve the sick Table 1.

TABLE 1

Doctor's Major Area of Interest

Items	Total	Ranking			
		Private	Institutional	Male	Female
Serving patients	1	1	1	1	1
Earning	2	2	3	2	2
Teaching	3	3.5	2	3	3
Research	4	3.5	4	4	4
Administration	5	5	5	5	5

This makes it amply clear that doctors, by and large, maintain that they are mainly to serve the sick people. It is at this stage essential to ascertain if they are more interested in private practice or serving the sick in real sense. It is with this purpose, that we now examine the attitude of doctors towards private practice.

PRIVATE PRACTICE AND THE DOCTORS

The in service doctors of Government hospitals do private practice and receive the fee from patients after their official duty hours. It is maintained that the private practice by hospital doctors severally affects their official duty in the hospital as private practice becomes the major concern of the doctors and such private patients if admitted in the hospital get better care than other patients. It results in malpractice and the poor patients are the worst sufferers. It is in this context that doctors were asked to state whether or not they approve of private practice by in service doctors.

APPROVAL OF PRIVATE PRACTICE

From the responses of the doctors, it is clear that two-thirds of them approve of private practice by in service doctors. There does not exist a significant difference between private and in stitutional doctors as far as opinion regarding private practice by inservice doctors is concerned and same is the situation in terms of sex-distribution of the doctors (Table 2).

TABLE 2

Approval of Private Practice

Doctors	Approval			
	Approve	Disapprove	No comment	Total
Private	22(66.7%)	11(33.3%)	—	33
Institutional	79(66.4%)	37(27.7%)	3(5.9%)	119
Male	82(65.5%)	40(32.0%)	3(2.5%)	125
Female	19(70.4%)	8(29.6%)	—	27
Total	101	48	3	152

PRIVATE PRACTICE AND IMPARTIAL ATTITUDE TOWARDS PATIENTS

After ascertaining the views about the advisability of private practice, doctors' opinion was also sought on the question whether private practice affected their attitude towards other patients or not and if it did so, to what extent ?

Except a microscopic minority, a vast majority of the doctors felt that private practice by hospital doctors affected their impartial attitude towards the patients. Three-tenths of the doctors felt that impartial attitude was affected to a great extent while 57.9% thought that it was affected at least to some extent. Eight doctors did not know anything about it. There was no difference between private practitioners and institutional doctors in regard to their opinion about the effect of private practice on other patients. A higher proportion of female doctors (92.6 %) than male doctors (87.2 %) accepted that the private practice did affect the impartial attitude of the doctors towards the patients. Chisquare test did not show any significant difference in the opinion of male and female doctors in this respect (Table 3).

TABLE 3

Effect of Private Practice on Impartial Attitude Towards Patients

Doctors	To a great extent	To some extent	Not at all	Do not know	Total
Private	11(33.3%)	18(54.5%)	2(6.1%)	2(6.1%)	33
Institutional	35(29.4%)	70(58.5%)	8(6.7%)	6(5.4%)	119
Male	35(28.0%)	74(59.2%)	8(6.4%)	8(6.4%)	125
Femle	11(40.7%)	14(51.9%)	2(7.4%)	—	27
Total	46	88	10	8	152

Since two-thirds of the doctors approved of the private practice by in service doctors and at the same time 98.2% of the doctors felt that private practice affected doctors' attitude towards patients, it is of interest to understand the reaction of doctors on ban on the private practice.

By and large, a large number of doctors are against abolition of private practice. Only a small number of them favours the ban. While non-clinical doctors are against the ban as it affected adversely their income, the clinical doctors were in favour of it as they did not have any private practice. Similarly, those doctors who did not have much private practice want ban as against those who have roaring private practice. There is hardly any difference among doctors on this issue in terms of variables. A large proportion of each is against the ban (Table 4).

TABLE 4

Reaction of Doctors on Ban of Private Practice

Doctors	Reaction					
	Favourable	Against	Indifferent	Others	No response	Total
Private	1(3.0%)	22(66.7%)	1(3.0%)	3(9.1%)	6(18.2%)	33
Institutional	4(3.4%)	87(23.1%)	6(5.0%)	7(5.9%)	15(12.6%)	119
Male	4(3.2%)	88(70.4%)	7(5.6%)	8(6.4%)	18(14.4%)	125
Female	1(3.7%)	21(77.8%)	—	2(7.4%)	3(11.1%)	27
Total	5	109	7	10	21	152

Stating the reason for their opinion those who are against the ban on private practice, argued that there has been severe financial implication of the ban for the practitioners. It has severely affected their income. The profession demands round the clock duty by the doctors and the salary in comparison to duty is meagre. The non-practising allowance does not adequately compensate the loss. According to them, ban caused great inconvenience to the patients also. The patients could not and did not get the services of the doctors they wanted at the time, they needed. The non-availability of such a doctor was a very serious problem to the serious and emergency cases. It was dangerous and disastrous to their life. The patients did not get the proper care and attention by the doctors as they used to, when they paid for their visits to them and called them more than once at home. There was a general dissatisfaction among patients. In pay clinics, they had to pay more. At the same time, the illiterate patients were ignorant about the details of the ban, and therefore, they were greater sufferers.

The ban on private practice adversely affected the interest of doctors in patients. The general attitude of doctors was that of indifference, the incentive which was money, was not there. This indifference caused serious implications and complications in doctor-patient relationship. A comment by a respondent illustrates this point. Earlier, enquiring about the patient, the doctor used to call him by name but after the ban, he called him in terms of bed number. The oral response was stated thus. Earlier the doctor enquired : "How is Mani Ram ?" Now he asks : "How is Bed No. 30 ?" It indicates the personalised attitude of the doctors. To them patients were now objects. They did not deny, that it was human psychology that one took interest in something provided he got benefit out of it. They believed in the assertion that money goads the man. The ban on private practice could not succeed. It had its own loopholes. Pay-clinics were for private consultation. Doctors managed to get patients there, to get money. Such patients naturally got more attention than other patients. Therefore, the basic idea that the ban on private practice would lead to uniform and impartial attention to the patients was defeated. Besides, the doctors were not seen devoting more time for teaching and research. They complained against the heavy rush in the hospital and the non-availability of time. No money, no academic work seemed to be their motto. Academic work for its own sake did not appeal to them.

The supporters of the ban had their own arguments. They held that it eliminated the professional cut-throat competition in the race of money ; it lessened the feeling of jealousy and rivalry among doctors. It helped in doctors working-efficiency.

We would now turn to examine the interest of doctors to serve the village people.

PLACE OF WORK : RURAL-URBAN

The vast majority of Indian people live in villages. There is great need to provide medical service to rural folk. But the irony of situation is that though resources of the community are utilised to train doctors, they generally do not like to go to the villages to serve the sick and the suffering. This is confirmed by the statements of the doctors who were asked : "Where do you think doctors generally like to work in ?"

According to 86.8% of the reespondents, doctors would like to work in the city. Only three respondents (1.9% thought that the doctors would work wherever they were placed, in village or city. Four doctors (2.6 per cent) did not make any comments. A vast majority of both private and institutional doctors would like to work in the city. Similar is the result if we examine the distribution of doctors in terms of sex (Table 5). The findings of this study is in comformity with Banerji's comment on the marked reluctance of Indian doctors to serve in the country-side which continues to lack elementary medical cover.[2]

TABLE 5

Doctors' Desired Place of Work

Doctors	City	Village	City or village	No comment	Total
Private	30(90.9%)	1(3.0%)	2(6.1%)	—	33
Institutional	102(85.7%)	2(1.7%)	11(9.2%)	4(3.4%)	119
Male	109(87.2%)	3(2.4%)	9(7.2%)	4(3.2%)	125
Female	23(85.2%)	—	4(14.8%)	—	27
Total	132	3	13	4	152

Stating reasons of doctors' preference to work in the city, the respondents said that they were city-born, accustomed to urban life. They find all kinds of modern facilities of work, living and education in cities. Good social life, best chances for utilisation of talent and expertise were available in the urban areas. Specialists could find job-satisfaction only in urban environment. Hence, they preferred to work in cities, rather than in villages. There were some doctors who opted the city as the field of their work for personal and family reasons. Old age, illness, non-availability of male members in the family and old parents, create situation in which they preferred to live in city.

The doctors who preferred to work in villages were attracted by simple and quiet life of the rural folk. They wanted to serve the rural people and so they preferred the village to the town. Moreover, they felt that villages needed them more than the cities.

Some of the doctors who had shown no perference either for city or village stated that their aim was to serve humanity and so they could go anywhere and everywhere. There were others who would prefer to work only at one place where modern facilities were available. Some of the medical practitioners would prefer the place where money could be earned easily. may be a city or the village. Their wish was not place-bound but money-bound. A few of the institutional practitioners of medicine submitted themselves to fate and to chance in government service. They would work wherever they are posted by government. They seemed to believe in the dictum "beggars can't be choosers."

CONCLUSIONS

Serving the patient was given the first rank by the doctors as preferred range of their activities. Doctors, whether private or institutional, male or female, expressed the same view. But still, private practice by hospital doctors have been approved by two-thirds of the doctors, though most of them knew that it affected adversely the hospital patients. And more than seventy per cent of the medical practitioners were against the ban on private practice. Most of them were of the opinion that this would affect their efficiency. In most of the cases, they would prefer to work in cities than villages. Taking into account the social background of the doctors, it is not surprising that most of them would be reluctant to go to rural areas. As a matter of fact, they are not adequately trained to deal with the health problem in rural areas. Due to their urban-orientation, many of them have strong distaste for rural life. This reflects on one of the cruelest ironies of the prevailing system of medical education in India that the resources of the community are utilised to train such doctors who are not suitable to provide service to rural areas where the vast majority of the people live and where the need is so desperate.

By identifying itself with this highly expensive and urban-oriented system of medicine, the Indian system of modern medicine actively and very deliberately encourages the doctors who look down on the facilities that are available in the rural areas. In the light of doctors' response that their major concern was to serve the sick, seems almost platitudinous and vague.[3] A much more driving force seems to be the glamour of being a doctor which also carries high prestige and status in the society and which also provides an opportunity for making a lot of money. This is further corroborated by their attitude against ban on private practice even though they feel that private practice, by hospital doctors affects their impartial attitude towards patients. This may drive one to think that : doctors are pretending to be professional and rendering service to the society whereas in fact they are a variety of businessmen under local conditions ; that under the exigencies of the backwardness of the country, the professed goals of the profession have given way to the actual goals. Here in, is the problem of deviation of theory from practice. As a group phenomenon this goes beyond the mere distinction between normative and actual role. Hence, the doctors' doctrine to serve the sick is more a myth than a reality.

NOTES AND REFERENCES

1. Chandani, Ambika. *The Medical Profession* : A Sociological Exploration, Jainsons, New Delhi, 1985.
2. Banerjee, D. *Medical Alienation in India*," *Hindustan Times*, March 3, 1974, p. 19.
3. *Ibid.*

20

PROFESSIONALS AND THEIR CLIENTS : A STUDY OF DOCTOR-PATIENT RELATIONSHIP

MADHU NAGLA

INTRODUCTION

A PROFESSION is neither a structure nor it is a state of mind, it is a social object. It is not the rules, but the activity that gives the professions its social reality. Hughes defines "profession (as a type of occupation), as a social role defined by the nature of the relationship between the professionals and their clients. Client delivers himself into the hands of the professional who presumably is the sole decision-maker regarding the nature of the services to be delivered.[1] But in the Indian context, it is defined directly as compared to United States of America where direct system of payment is involved. This can perhaps be found in the case of private practitioners in our country. In case of general hospitals, the treatment is mostly free of cost or the payment is made by the patient on the basis of his income. When the treatment is free, they do not directly hire the services of the professionals. The payment is made to the professional by the State. But the patients are clients, in the sense, that some agency is paying for the professionals and it becomes the responsibility of the professionals to provide proper medical care to their clients. The patients are dependants on the professional and are not the customers who have the free choice of bargaining.[2]

The patron-recipient relationship must be distinguished from the patron-client relationship. The latter can be a mechanism for the development whereas the former could hardly be such. The patron-client relationship did serve in some ways to politicize constituents. The patron-recipient relationship also articulates the same purpose but these are critical differences that must be taken into account and that are manifest when one examines relationship.[3]

Scott has provided a definition that is cited most frequently. "The patron-client relationship—an exchange relationship between roles—may be defined as special case of dyadic (two-persons) ties involving a largely instrumental friendship in which an individual of higher socio-economic status (patron) uses his own influence and resources to provide protection or benefits, or both, for a person of lower status (clients). The client, on his part, reciprocates by offering general support and assistance, including personal services to the patron." The patron-recipient concept refers that situation (whereby goods and services benefits) are supplied by one party (patron) to another (recipient) under circumstances that do not require the recipient to reciprocate in any sustained and systematic way. The patron does not depend on the support or loyalty of the recipient to maintain the patron's role. The only requirement of the recipient is that he or she be in need of the services offered by the patron.[4]

The recipient receives from the patron and asked to do nothing but receives the benefits (reciprocity is absent). Unlike the political patron-client relationship where the client clearly has to give continuing support *e.g.*, vote, the recipient is not called upon politically to support the patron. The client becomes a political actor ; the recipient remains a political non-actor. Theoretically the patron-client relationship is based on the premise that after a certain point individual recipient will no longer need the benefits offered by the patron. Thus, the relationship is terminal. This, of course, is not a characteristic of the patron-client relationship. Therefore, it is not expected that a permanent or even long-term relationship be developed between the patron and the recipient. Again, unlike the patron-client association, it is hoped that the particular patron-recipient relationship will be ephemeral and transitory. It is difficult, therefore, to perceive a viable and sustained political foundation built upon such orientation. One of the phenomena which seems increasingly to characterize relationship between professional and their clients in the United States is an unwillingness on the part of the client to accept, without question, the authority of the professional. The 'revolt of the client' and the demand for accountability signify a growing public suspicion that neither the expertise nor the goodwill of the professional are to be taken on trust or at face value. There is much evidence of what many have seen as a consumer movement among health care clients. As Reader points, the term *professional* and *clients* are giving way to a distinction between *health providers* and *health consumers*[5] are suing physicians for malpractice in increasing numbers. We may thus consider it to be a relationship in which there is a joint participation of two persons involved, it is neither a structure, nor a function (such as the "personality" of physician or patients). It is rather, an abstraction embodying the activities of the two interacting systems.

Thus, we examine the medical profession with its important aspect of practice (i.e.), the client. The bulk of a consulting practitioner's work relationship involve clients, not colleagues. Clients, unlike colleagues are not usually in the same social world as the professional ; that is, they are frequently not in the same class, ethnic group, or of the same educational level. And of course, they have not undergone the same training and socialization as the professionals. Clients, therefore, do not "speak the same language" as the professionals, they do not share the same phenomenological meanings, assumptions or concepts. Illness never means the same things to the client and to the professional alike. Hughes put his finger on the most obvious difference between professional and client perspectives when he said that what was routine to the professional was an emergency to the client.[6] The client, however, can ignore or handle his emergency himself if he so wishes. The professional on the other hand, needs clients to carry out his work, to apply his knowledge, to practise his calling. He must persuade clients to accept his ministrations or be able to place them in a position where they have nothing to say about the matter. Professional practice cannot exist without clients. But the influence of the client over the professional does not end with that simple dependence. Freidson describes, that the power of the client makes different demands on the practitioners, and the way he meets these demands significantly shapes his routine of work.[7] Secondly, different types of clients force the practitioner to do different kinds of work not all of which carry the same prestige in his colleaguial world. The every day work life and the social identity of the professional are thus intimately related to his clientele. In modern times, the expectations of patients have also been rising due to the urbanizing and industrializing influences and moreover, the politicization of masses. Furthermore, exposure to mass media, better access to town and cities due to improved means of transport and communication, rail and road links with their villages, brought this awareness. As a consequence, there might be greater pressure on the professionals due to heavy load of patients, politicization of health-delivery system and raised expectations of the patients and their relations.

Design of the Study

The present study is an attempt to examine empirically the phenomenon of medical profession and medical practice. It has been carried out at the Medical College Hospital, Rohtak (MCHR) in the State of Haryana. Most of the studies on doctors in India have been done on social background of doctors,[8] and their routine role practices rather than professional orientation, in particular, client-orientation and professional commitment. None of the studies gives a complete picture of medical professional as well as professional-client relationship. Most studies by and large, with the exception of a few, have analyzed the professionalization of doctors without giving due importance to the attitudes of the patients and their evaluation of doctors' role. Their orientation towards patients in terms of expectation, satisfaction and recovery are some of the other dimensions that need to be analysed for a proper perspective of the medical professionals. The behaviour of physicians is largely influenced by the nature and pattern of medical care practised. It is envisaged that the primary care to a patient depends upon the physician's knowledge, attitude, assumption and availability of information regarding a particular patient, and on the manner in which he evaluates the patient's complaint. His evaluation and understanding of the patient, in turn, will depend upon his training, family background and the location of his working place. His commitment to work further depends upon the rewards he receives in terms of remuneration, prestige, satisfaction of patients, and on the satisfaction derived from doing service to others.

On the other hand, a patient's expectation of the doctor is in terms of proper diagnosis, co-operative and sociable behaviour, communicating the cause or symptoms of disease, good treatment and interest taken in patient's recovery. His satisfaction level is generally marked by early relief from sickness or disease and comfortable stay in the hospital. In this study, our main objective is to analyze the functioning of medical practice and profession in its processual form to understand doctor-patient relationship. The medical professional tries to translate his learning into practice or enacts his role vis-a-vis the patient. He himself is not only a healing agent but also a social personality belonging to a particular profession, enjoying a particular socio-economic status, a member of a particular kinship and religious group. It is in the doctor-patient relationship that social milieu of the patient and the doctor, intersect. It will therefore, be relevant to ask how the doctor is likely to be influenced by the patient's social background in performing his role, and how his own social background tends to influence the doctor-patient interaction. What sort of a role-conflict does he experience while interacting with the patient ? As such, it becomes imperative to look into the doctor-patient relationship for the proper understanding of the perspectives of the medical professional.

Methodology : Keeping in view the time constraint and resources available to carry out this study, it was thought best to have two stage sampling. In the first stage, it was decided to select three wards from important departments like Medicine, Surgery and Orthopaedics. The main factors kept in view in choosing these specialities were their relative importance, better ratio of male/female doctors and patients and considerable length of patient's stay. In the second stage, doctors and patients were selected from these departments for interview purpose. All the sixty—two doctors of these departments were interviewed with the help of an interview schedule.

In regard to interview of the patients, it was thought desirable to interview only, fifteen per cent sample of the in-patients from each of the selected departments due to constraint of time. The patients were selected through random selection of beds. Out of three internal wards, namely : Surgery having 255 beds, Medicine having 210 and Orthopaedic having ninty-three beds, a sample of thirty-eight was chosen. Hence in all, eighty-two patients were administered another interview schedule designed for them.

The interview schedule was pretested in the selected wards. These were suitably modified in the light of observation made and finally administered to the respective category of respondents over a period of three months (from November 1981 to January, 1982). To supplement the data collected with the help of interview schedule, the hospital records were also consulted from relevant wards. During the course of carrying out the study, certain situations reflecting doctor-patient interaction were also observed. The data were analysed in the form of simple and cross—tables. The statistical methods were also used wherever considered necessary.

Doctor-Patient Relationship in the Hospital Setting

The focus of the study has been to analyse the doctor-patient relationship as it existed in a hospital setting with a view to understand the sick—role. It has been said that Parsons' conceptualization of the sick—role is the single most important contribution to the sociology of health because it offers the most systematic and consistent framework for analyzing the socially necessary behaviour of sick individuals in Western and other societies, though this has not been adequately examined in India.[9] Thus, to be sure, most theoretical concepts and frameworks in the sociology of health have emerged as a result of attempts to refute or to extend Parsons' sick-role concept. Basically, the sick-role concept is the type of behaviour which is expected from and associated with the sick person. The literature criticizing Parsons' concept of the sick role continues to grow and Wolinsky and Wolinsky in their paper on "Expecting Sick-Role Legitimation and getting It" have expressed their opinions.[10] However, there is general agreement that Parsons's contributions have been both profound and of enormous benefit to the sociologically informed understanding of health and illness in contemporary society. However, we have tried to examine the doctor-patient expectations and satisfactions to understand their relationship for and receipt of sick-role ligitimation. Therefore, the analysis has been made by taking into account both the doctors' and patients' point of view to find out the factors which influence the doctor-patient interaction. Attempts have been made also to analyse in what way and extent the doctor-patient interaction affects the role performance of the doctors in a hospital organisation. This paper is divided into three major sections. The first two sections deal with the view-points of doctors and patients respectively. In the third section, the doctor-patient relationship has been discussed in terms of their interaction.

When the patient enters into the hospital, he starts playing the role of a sick man. He comes into contact with the doctors whose role belongs to the general class of 'professional' roles. By the institutional definition of the sick-role, the patient is helpless and, therefore, is in need of help. Thus, the sick person is in a state where he is suffering or disabled or both, and possibly facing risks of worsening, which is socially defined as 'not his fault'. Thus, suffering, helplessness, disablement and the sick or death, constitute fundamental disturbances of the expectations by which the sick men live. Thus, he is in a situation where he will like to interact in a most intimate manner with a man, who can feel his sufferings and at the same time convince him of the chances of a quick and complete recovery. When he approaches a doctor, he thinks that only he is suffering and the rest of the world around is happy. On the other hand, the role of physician centres around his responsibility for the welfare of the patient, in the sense of facilitating the patient to recover from illness, to the best of his ability. His primary responsibility is to do everything possible to effect the complete, early and painless recovery of the patient. So far as the successful performance of his role is concerned, the doctor is expected to play a universalistic, functionally specific and affectively neutral role.

To study the interpersonal relations between the doctor and the patient, we have examined the patient's feeling about the physicians and doctors expectations of the sick-role from the patient. In this context, Parsons' sick-role concept[11] would provide a good context to study the doctor-patient relationship which has been analyzed both from the doctor and the patient point of views.

Doctors' Point of View

The initial attitudes of doctors towards patients depict not only diagnosis and prognosis of the disease but also reflects doctor's feelings towards the patient as a professional, as a human-being and as a service-oriented person. As revealed by collected data, as many as 83.87% respondents had opined that it was necessary first to make patient comfortable for his satisfaction (humanistic-orientation). 61.29% wanted to seek information from patients about symptoms for proper diagnosis and 20.96% wanted to keep patient under observation (professional ethics), and 40.32% viewed to start immediate treatment (service-orientation or duty-bound). All these perspectives depend upon the nature of doctor and his training. All doctors were in favour of taking case history of patients. In this regard, 45.16% doctors took interest in case history only when it was most necessary for providing any treatment of disease. Similiar observations have been made by Srivastava.[12] Invariably, all the doctors consulted the last revisit report of patients and nurses as the majority of them i.e. 69.35% doctors went through the last reports and only 30.65% i.e. is, slightly less than one—third, the reports when it was necessary. In both the situations, junior doctors were consulting the last reports as well as interested in knowing the life history of the patients than the senior doctors.

treatment. They should change the treatment if it is not giving relief to the patient. They should also use the treatment of therapeutic methods in their treatment.

(2) *Humanistic* : Doctors should talk to the patients and their relation with affection having sympathetic and honest attitude towards them. They should understand the difficulties from patient's point of view, for this can help them to present a good image of themselves.

(3) *Services* : They should go to rural areas to serve the people. They should be restricted for going abroad and private practice by providing them more financial facilities, reducing the work-load of doctors by the recruitment of more doctors and also fixing a limited number of patients for treatment under each doctor :

(4) *Facilities* : Doctors should enquire from the patients whether they were getting medicine, diet or other facilities or not. They should also improve the hygienic conditions of wards and they should regulate the visitors.

(5) *Advice* : They should allocate approximate time and advice patients about expenditure for the treatment and precautionary measures.

Patients' Expectation and Satisfaction

Client satisfaction is an important outcome of health care delivery. In terms of the interests of medical profession, the patient may be characterized as a consumer of a product-health care. Client satisfaction leads to continued use of services necessary for the economic viability of the practice and the health of its patients.[14] Satisfied clients are also less likely to sue for malpractice, a growing economic burden on physicians and the organization in which they work. And satisfied clients are more likely to co-operate and comply with the physicians' directions.[15] This not only makes the doctors' job easier, but is necessary for the health of patient since a physician can do little to improve health without the patient's co-operation. From the patient's perspective, health is not the only desired outcome of medical care. Satisfaction, in itseif may be considered as an important function of care.[16]

The study revealed the expectation of the patients from the care provided to them in the hospital. They gave the following multiple responses in terms of their expectations. It is pointed out that higher the quality of technical aid, illness care led easily and obviously to higher satisfaction. As many as 54.87% patients desired that they should get medical care from competent and senior doctors for effective diagnosis and proper treatment. They also expected that the physicians should be more responsive to his clients or to colleagues, and show friendly attitudes. That is why, 52.43% patients expected sympathetic attitudes from doctors towards them and expect that they should be taking soft way and behave as if they had friendly relations with them. Doctors should attend whenever patients call at them and doctors should give assurance to patients that they would soon get well. Thirteen patients (15.85%) wanted immediate relief from their diseases whereas 36.53% desired less expensive treatment and they demanded free medicine and free tests and even all other sorts of comforts from the hospital. In searching for the factors that contribute to client satisfaction, Ross, Wheaton and Duff considered two broad categories, "experience" and "expectations".[17] Experience with care include the quality of technical management of illness, the quality of the caring, psychological aspects of the doctor-patient interaction. Expectations, on the other hand, are culturally determined ideas and stereotyped that a client holds on entrance to the medical care system. Both expectations and experience may affect patient satisfaction. Expectations may be confirmed by experience, or expectations that are contradicted by experience may be modified overtime. The quality of doctor-patient relationship depends upon, both the participants, and the views of patients clearly affect their relationship with their doctors. It is, therefore, imperative to analyse directly the patients' satisfaction and discontent. When patients were asked whether they had satisfaction or dissatisfaction with the treatment, the most frequent answer given by the majority (69.52%) showed satisfaction on their part whereas 30.48%

patients complained about the treatment. Moreover, 70.18% who had rural background, had satisfaction as compared to 29.82% who had urban background, conversely, slightly more than seventy per cent who had urban background patients were dissatisfied as compared to slightly less than thirty per cent who had rural background. Moreover, patients from the lower income-group were comparatively highly satisfied with their treatment than those coming from higher income-group and vice-versa. Furthermore, the satisfaction and dissatisfaction level of the respondents have also been correlated with the education of the patients. The Chi-square test $x^2=3.55$; $p=5.99$, $df=2$ shows that there is some association between the income level of the respondents and their satisfaction and dissatisfaction. The data show that a large number of them, illiterate and lower educated patients were more satisfied (85.96%) whereas on the contrary forty per cent patients who had graduate, post-graduate degree or diploma courses were comparatively dissatisfied with the present treatment. Thus, it shows that patients from urban background, higher income-group and higher educational level had less satisfaction level than other.

On further probing in regard to the reasons they gave in favour of or against the satisfaction and dissatisfaction, some of the patients gave the following reasons in support of satisfaction with present treatment :

(1) *Proper Treatment* : Full diagnosis, relief in terms of caring, improving or recouping, medicine were provided by the hospital.

(2) *Regular Visits* : Doctors were doing check-ups from time to time and examined their patients whenever they were asked.

(3) *Behaviour* : Sympathetic attitude of doctors who showed love for their patients, they always asked about the progress and gave them useful advice, and also discussed their problems while on rounds.

On the other hand, the following reasons were given against their satisfaction with treatment.

(1) *No Proper Treatment* : Delay in treatment, no proper

diagnosis or investigation, that is why, no improvement and condition further deteriorated. They provide less medicine and other facilities. Post-operative care is also not proper and they do not take precautionary measures.

(2) *Communication Gap* : No talk between the patient and his doctor, for example, they do not tell time, date and expenditure for the operation and evade them all the time. Doctors often turn deaf ear to complaints, they also do not bother for diet and other facilities.

(3) *Lack of Commitment* : Senior doctors do not visit, and send their students and many times they were not available when patients were in serious conditions.

(4) *Over busy* : The much rush in wards, non-availability of beds, and lack of proper attention as such, they were not satisfied since the service becomes impersonal.

Attitudes of Patients Towards Doctor

The behaviour of doctors build up their good or bad images upon the patients. 14.63% patients had love for doctors out of whom 83.33% were having urban background and 16.66% were having rural background. Besides, out of 66.68%, 16.66%, and 16.66% patients were in the income group of Rs. 100-600, Rs. 600-1200, and Rs. 1200-3000 respectively. On the other hand 34.14% patients had mentioned fear from doctors and they were mostly from rural background and belonged to the lower income group i.e. Rs. 100-600. Besides, there was a group of respondents 51.23% who had stated respect for doctors. There was insignificant difference in regard to this opinion among respondents so far as their rural-urban background was concerned, but mostly they were in the lower income group. It may be viewed that urban patients had expressed affection for doctors in the form of love and respect whereas an insignificant number of patients in the higher income group i.e. Rs. 1200-3000 who had fear from doctors.

Nevertheless, about ninety per cent rated medical profession as a whole to be very high, whereas 13.41% rated it average and except one there was no other patient who rated it to be low. Thus, it is evident that the majority of the respondents rated profession of doctors to be very high as they deal with the life of human-being. Out of these there were 57.15% patients from rural background and 42.85% having urban background. Moreover, 71.43% and 28.57% patients were in income group of Rs. 300-600 and Rs. 600-1200 respectively. Furthermore, it was found that there was almost an equal number of respondents (slightly more than forty per cent) who were illiterate or educated upto middle or matric level except nine patients 12.85% who were highly educated. Thus, the patients who rated the profession of doctors to be very high, mostly had rural background, were illiterates or had lower education and were from lower income-groups.

DOCTOR-PATIENT INTERACTION

Communication

Communication forms the bases for all social interaction; it enables the transmission of cumulative knowledge and makes possible the existence of empathetic understanding among individuals. Communication is an essential aspect for doctor-patient relations within the hospital. This study reveals that 76.83% patients had no problem of communication with doctors whereas 23.17% had problems to do so. The difficulties in communication felt by patients were as follows. Out of nineteen patients, 47.39% felt that doctors are big persons and they may rebuke us, whereas 26.32% patients had language problem. 21.03% patients felt that doctors do not look towards us because we are poor and not known to them and 21.04% said that they never got a chance to speak. By and large it is due to status gap that communication is not effective between the patient and the doctor. On the other hand, doctors also viewed their difficulties in communication with patients. As many as 74.20% doctors did not have any difficulty but 25.80% doctors had some difficulties while communicating with the patients. We found that doctor's major difficulty was because of lack of education in 43.75% cases. This was followed by lack of time (twenty-five per cent), lack of trust 18.75%, ignorance (twenty-five per cent), fear (twenty-five per cent) due to veneral disease or certain diseases which carry social stigma 12.25%, and lack of attendants 6.25%.

Co-operation

Adequate communication is effective for the co-operation between doctors and patients. 64.52% doctors stated to receive full co-operation from patients, 4.83% mentioned as usually whereas 30.65% doctors had difficulties in seeking co-operation from patients. The most important reason for lack of co-operation was lack of understanding and adequate communication. On the part of patients, the main reasons were : ignorance, illiteracy, poverty, traditional belief, misapprehensions and misgivings. For example, for the donation of blood etc. it was observed that those doctors who had difficulty in communication would not get co-operation of a patient by narrating an incident as follows : "One lady came to me for consultation of her problem. She belonged to a very rich family. I told her to get the operation immediately done for her relief. I admitted her for some investigations and suggested her complete rest. She was not found when I went on a round. Somebody told me that she had gone to attend her 'Kitti' party. Next day, we examined her in the operation theatre and found her unfit for operation as she did not take rest etc." That showed lack of co-operation on the part of patients.

Accessibility and Acquaintance to Seek Treatment

Generally, people believe in accessibility and acquaintance to get care and proper treatment. The ethnic feeling of same caste and class dominates in this matter e.g. a patient comes to the hospital and starts thinking immediately as to who is known to him and to whom he can approach to get treatment in the hospital. Out of total sample 86.59% patients did not have any special favour from doctors, but as many as 13.41% patients were benefitted out of such favours. These special favours were viewed in the following ways:

Doctor allowed a patient to stay for more days even after he was discharged, in getting medicine, in getting more diet, in having good linen bed etc. (27.27%). Doctors and nurses gave extra attention to patients (54.54%) and they admitted them on first day itself and gave private rooms and also the operation was performed soon without delaying procedures. Access of the patients to the doctors may suggest "feeling of personal relationship". We have found that the majority of patients (78.05%) felt that doctors were easily accessible to them as compared to 21.95% who had difficulty in meeting them. Patients who had negative feelings replied that they did not find doctors whenever they needed them (11.11%), they were only available for six days and only during fixed hours in routine (66.66%). Doctors kept themselves so busy and there was too much rush to approach them (11.11%), juniors were there but they were not experts (16.66%). Conversely, we have gathered the views of patients who had no problems of accessibility to the doctors. Their responses were as follows : 68.75% patients felt that doctors were bound by duty and they came on rotation in the day or night and twice or thrice they were also available in the duty-rooms of their respective wards. For example mostly the house surgeons remained in the wards and kept all the records, and other came immediately on making an emergency call. Another 97.81% viewed accessibility to doctors as they knew some of them personally, 9.37% had recommendation from other sources ; 3.12% felt that home emergency call was used for having access to particular doctors. Thus, most of the patients felt that their relationship with their doctors was 'business-like' rather than friendly whether they had access to the doctors or not. The 'business-like' relationship is the product of complex modern societies. To know this, we asked the patients whether money was more important than acquaintance with doctor to get treatment, 70.75% patients felt that acquaintance with doctor was more important to get good treatment. Only one ignored the importance of "money" and "approach" for good treatment.

Our data reveal that 84.15% patients had never given money to clerks and other functionaries as compared with 15.85% who admitted to have paid to get things done in the hospital. About fifty-eight per cent patients in medicine had to spend money to have an access whereas an insignificant number (7.89%) in surgery used this method. However, none of the patients had any such experience in the orthopaedics ward. The data show that one-fourth patients had been satisfied with their doctors because they did not pay anything whereas three-fourth patients were discontended as they had to spend some money on doctors as fee etc. particularly in the surgery department. It is interesting to observe that a higher number of papers among patients to para-medical staff were found in medicine ward and to doctors in surgery ward. How money and acquaintance work as an instrument of accessibility? We will cite an example. One of the patients was talking to a junior doctor who came to see him. They had conversation as follows :

Doctor : Did you arrange your private room or not ?

Patient : I could not get private room as there was no vacant room.

Doctor : Any how by giving money and finding acquaintance you have to arrange a room on the private ward otherwise you will have difficulty in your treatment and you would not be able to get proper diagnosis by the specialist who is treating you.

In this way junior doctors bring clients to senior doctors.

One of the 'measures of a doctor' accessibility used in this study was whether the doctor, attending on patient, has ever talked to him about anything other than his illness. The data present that 91.47% doctors had to talk with the patients other than illness as compared to 8.53% who had talks with their patients about their personal problems. Generally, doctors had talked about their marriage, family-members, occupation, economic problem, general health and other physical and mental tensions in order to encourage them to keep their morale high. Moreover, this type of build-up confidence in the patients during the treatment process. Doctors were also asked to state as to what type of talk doctors would prefer to have with their patients. It was found that 19.35% doctors talked about the disease of the patients, 61.29% had talked about the socio-economic conditions of the family and 74.19% discussed about the personal life of the patients besides medical problems. Thus, a major proportion of the senior doctors rather than junior doctors appear to be having appropriate talks to patients. This probably indicates that they have gained enough experience in handling patients and building up their confidence rather than the junior doctors. This might work well as a therapeutic process in the course of treatment.

To analyse doctors, 'agreement' and 'disagreement' about disclosure of diseases to patient, we asked them as to under what conditions did they prefer to disclose the nature of disease and treatment. The multiple responses reflect that 59.67% doctors would disclose the nature of disease and treatment when their diseases were acute, 38.70% stated that only when they were extremely eager to know, 12.9% stated that only to those who were poor and it was difficult for them to bear medical expenses : whereas 22.58%, doctors were in favour to tell about diseases as compared to 4.83% who were not at all in favour of disclosing the nature of problems.

Patients' own socio-economic status and its influence over doctor's role-performance in the process of interaction was also observed. It is closely related with the nature of doctors to develop their relations with the patients. Doctors were asked to indicate whether they agree or disagree on a given set of Statements : Most of the doctors (62.90%) stated that they would give equal attention to all irrespective of their socio-economic status, whereas 37.10% thought otherwise. A majority of doctors (82.25%)

agreed to the statement as compared to 17.75% who disagreed with it. Generally those who had higher status and influence received greater attention from the doctors than others ; 38.70% doctors agreed and 61.30% of them disagreed with the statement that irrespective of the status of patients, doctors examine on those who can provide them more money.

Another question which throws some light on the personal nature of the doctor-patient relationship was to ask from the patients in order to know their reaction towards doctors on action-pattern variables. These have developed to understand the professional-client relationship for our analysis in the frame-work of action pattern-variable given by Parsons.[17] Each action pattern variable provides two mutually exclusive alterna-tives. The patients were asked to give their choice from one of each pairs. We have analysed four basic pattern-variables, each representing polar opposites. On universalism and particularism, 40.24% patients perceived the behaviour of doctors as universally accepted precept as compared to remaining who perceived that factors behaved in terms of particular qualities of the persons towards with whom they had oriented their action. To identify the typical choices made, another set is termed rational and non-rational for our analysis. Seventy five patients (91.47%) perceived rational behaviour of doctors as compared to others who thought doctors behaviour was non-rational. Not a single patient, however, could point out the irrational behaviour of doctors in orthopaedic department. The rational behaviour is justified by the relations found among doctors and patients. Davis and Eichhorn found greater degree of 'compliance' with the doctor's advice when patients felt their relationship was business-like rather than friendly.[18]

The third action of pattern-variable is termed affectively neutral and affective which also represents the difference in choice of doctors. Slightly more than ninety per cent patients found that the doctor remains 'objective and affectively neutral' as Parsons also subscribed to this view.[19] Only 8.53% patients in our study observed affective or affectionate behaviour of doctors. This supports

Bynder's theory that "in those doctor-patient relationship which exists over a long period of time, the doctor becomes much more emotionally involved with at least some of his patients than would otherwise be the case". The last set of action variable is that of specificity and diffuseness in terms of choice made by taking into account, limited and specific factors. 73.18% patients felt that doctors were interested in patients for very specific reasons as compared to the remaining who mentioned diffuseness on the part of doctors in terms of their relationship with patients.

The doctors were asked to rank a set of factors which they consider while interacting with the patients. They ranked the condition and behaviour of patients in terms of (1) poverty stricken, (2) humble, (3) ignorant, and (4) cunning.

Similarly, patients also perceived the behaviour of doctors differently. As many as 31.71% patients felt that the doctor behaved nicely. It was found that there was almost an equal number of patient from each category of educational background who expressed nice behaviour of the doctors ; 52.44% replied that their doctor's behaviour was satisfactory. Of these forty-three, the majority of the patients (51.16%) had education between primary and matric. On the other hand 15.85% patients were more critical of the doctors who behaved in rude manner. Of these thirteen, a maximum number of patients (76.92%) were illiterate. Furthermore, the doctors evaluated the behaviour of patients as follows : Thirty-nine (62.90%) doctors viewed that their patients were sympathetic towards them as compared to 9.06% who expressed unsympathetic attitudes of patients towards them and 18 (29.04%) were of the opinion that their patients' behaviour was indifferent. The indifferent attitude of patients appears to be stated more by junior than senior doctors.

Besides, patients also evaluated the behaviour of other auxiliary staff, particularly nurses and para-medical staff. As para-medical staff is an important link between the doctor and the patient and its influence on doctor-patient interaction is very significant, the patients were asked about their attitude towards the behaviour of the para-medical staff. The data revealed that 52.45% patients were of the opinion that para-medical staff took keen interest in the care of the patients, 40.25% stated that para-medical staff did not take proper care of them. One patient replied that they were greedy and the rest stated that they were indifferent and rude in their behaviour. Furthermore, how accessible patients felt that their doctors were, was reflected by the number of complaints listened, complaints made by patients directly against their professional colleagues, 91.94% stated that doctors listened complaints against administrative staff, 96.78% against other workers as compared to rest of those who didn't give attention to the problems. The data give a clear picture that urban patient had higher number of complaints made against the doctors than other staff members as compared to rural patients.

Patients' Care : Suggestion for Improvement

The doctor-patient relationship is not only marked by interaction between the doctor and the patient but also by understanding the opinion of the doctor about his patients and the quality of medical care given to them and suggestions for improvement. Except seven, a majority of doctors (88.71%) were not satisfied with medical facilities provided to the patients. Doctors encounter many problems, in providing care to the sick person in the hospital. These are mainly :

(1) *Political Interferences and Administrative Problems* : More bureaucratic procedures which cause delay in treatment: over-crowding of patients due to less number of beds and doctors, more burden, lack of time and non-co-operation from colleagues, interference of senior doctors, inter-departmental problems, inefficient and non-co-operative para-medical staff, patient-nursing problem, less number of nurses and class four employees.

(2) *Lack of Amenities* : Medicines, equipments.

(3) *Patients-Problem* : Illiteracy, ignorance, orthodoxy of patient and their attendants, non-co-operation of patients and

their attendants such as giving their blood, poverty of the patients depicting the poor hygienic condition.

(4) Moreover, there is a growing tendency among the patients to suggest and demand what they feel should be rather than listening to the doctor for proper treatment.

Doctors have given the following suggestions for the solution of some of these problems while providing medical facilities to the patients :

(1) *Improvement in management and administration* : There is a need for inter-departmental co-ordination, every category should be represented on decision-making bodies for hospital-working. There is also a need for trained staff for utilization of the sophisticated equipments. There should be more scope for development of super-specialities and more so, more number of doctors and sophisticated equipments so that investigation may be done in the hospital in time to avoid delays. There is also a need of more number of beds, operation theatres, better and service-oriented staff. There should be proper care of wards for the improvement of hygienic conditions.

(2) There should be no political interference in the hospital.

(3) There should be availability of funds for the purchase of good quality and brand of medicines and equipments.

(4). *Facilities to the Patients* : Investigations should be free of cost or some method to charge fee according to economic status and life-saving drugs should be available free of cost.

(5) *Suggestion for Doctors* : Private practice should be after duty hours. There is also a need of suitable referral and better follow-up service.

On the other hand, patients mentioned the following difficulties experienced by them during their stay in the hospital. These were :

(1) *Medical Treatment* : Twenty three patients (28.40%), had problems for medical treatment as opposed to 71.96%.

They had problems for getting blood, medicine, glucose bottle, proper diagnosis, regular dressing and "no fixed date" for operation. Doctors also delayed treatment and investigations.

(2) *Linen and Bed* : Thirty-eight (46.34%) patients faced the difficulty for linen and beds as compared to 53.68% e.g., shifting of beds, change of bed-sheet, and non-availability of bed-sheet, pillow, stretcher etc.

(3) *Cleanliness in Toilets* : Except 19.51%, 80.49% patients were disturbed because of uncleaned conditions of toilets. They felt unhygienic conditions in wards and as lack of ventillation. Besides, there was no proper light arrangement and there was over-crowding in the wards.

(4) *Diet* : A majority of patients (83.57%) reacted that their diet like, milk, eggs etc. were taken by the staff-members.

(5) *Behaviour of Doctors* : Out of eighty-two patients, only 21.95% had either communication problem with their doctors or were not happy because of distinction made between general and private patients.

(6) *Behaviour of Nurses and Other Para-medical Staff* : Similarly, 43.90% and 52.44% patients respectively were not happy with the nurses and other auxiliary staff because of their rude behaviour and non-co-operation to them, for example, to collect urine-pan etc. Besides some patients also faced difficulty in getting admission or private room as they had no access to doctors or approach to any other staff member in the hospital, Some patients also had economic problems and felt that medical treatment was a costly affair. Moreover, one patient viewed that there was no security in the wards.

NOTES AND REFERENCES

1. Hughes, E.C., *Men and Their Work*, Free Press, New York, 1951.
2. Advani, M., *Doctor-Patient Relationship in Indian Hospitals*, Sanghi

Prakashan, Jaipur, 1980.

3. Hamilton, Charles, V., "The Patron-Recipient Relationship and Minority Politics", *Political Science Quarterly*, no. 2, 1979, pp. 211-227.

4. *Ibid.*

5. Reader, Leo, G., "The Patient-client as a Consumer : Some Observations on Changing Professional-client Relationship," *Journal of Health and Social Behaviour*, vol. 13, no. 4, 1972, pp. 406-412.

6. Hughes, *op. cit.*

7. Freidson, E., *Profession of Medicine : A Study of Sociology of Applied Knowledge*, Mead and Dodd, New York, 1972.

8. Chandani, Ambika, *The Medical Profession : A Sociological Exploration*, Jainsons, New Delhi, 1985; Madan, T.N., *Doctors and Society*, Vikas, New Delhi, 1980; Oommen, T.K., *Doctors and Nurses*, Macmillan, Delhi, 1978. Ramanamma, A., and Usha Bambawale, "Occupational Attitudes of Physicians", *Sociological Bulletin*, vol. 27, no. 2, (September) 1978, pp. 109-207; Venkatratnam, R., *Medical Sociology in an Indian Setting*, Mecmillan, Madras, 1979.

9. Parsons, T., *The Social System*, Free Press, Glencoe, Ill., 1951.

10. Wolinsky, F.D., *et al.*, "Expecting Sick-Role Legislation and Getting it," *Journal of Health and Social Behaviour*, vol. 22, September, 1981, pp. 229-242.

11. Callaghar, E.B., "Lines of Reconstruction and Extension in Parsonian Sociology of Illness", *Social Science and Medicine*, vol. 10 1976, pp. 207-18.

12. Srivastava, A.L., *Human Relations in Social Organisation.* Chug Publications, Allahabad, 1979.

13. *Ibid.*

14. Mechanic, David, *The Growth of Bureaucratic Medicine*, John Wiley and Sons, New York, 1976.

15. Korgich, B. E. Cozzi and V. Francis, "Gaps in Doctor-Patient Communication : Doctor-Patient Interaction and Patient Satisfaction", *Pediatrics*, vol. 42, 1968, pp. 855-71.

16. Ross, Catherine E., Blair Wheaton, and Raymond S. Duff, "Client Satisfaction and the Organisation of Medical Practices", *Journal*

of Health and Social Behaviour, vol. 22, September 1981, pp. 243-255.

17. Parsons, *op. cit.*

18. Davis, M.S. and Eichhorn, R.L., "Compliance with Medical Requirements : A Panel Study", *Journal of Health and Social Behaviour*, vol. 4, 1963, p. 240.

19. Parsons, *op. cit.*

21

THE DETERMINANTS OF ROLE PERFORMANCE OF STAFF-NURSES IN A HOSPITAL

E. SURYAMANI
AND
K. RADHAKRISHNA MURTY

INTRODUCTION

MODERN complex society requires organizations since they are instrumental in fulfilling the goals of the society effectively and efficiently. One of the important consequences of the large scale formal organizations is the rise of professions and semi-professions. It is understood that if the functions of any role-set relating to the professional or semi-professional in the organization are inadequately performed, then the functioning of the organization tends to fall short of expectations. For instance, the major goal of any hospital organization is to provide best and immediate treatment to the patient. Modern medicine, unlike traditional medicine gives importance to the social and psychological factors in the treatment of the patient. The health team providing treatment to the patients in modern hospital consists of doctors (professionals) and nurses (semi-professionals). While the focus of the doctor is on the curative aspects, that of the nurse is on the care process which is mainly expressive in nature.

The nature of nursing profession, originally, is patient care which includes personal care, motherly affection, counselling, comforting, servicing and feeding the patients. Nurse is the "mother-surrogate" and "bed-side psychologist" to the patients.[1] But, over a period of time, several other non-nursing functions like co-ordination, management, administration and system integration were added to the patient-care function. This has resulted in role-ambiguity, role-confusion and role-strain for the staff-nurse. The doctor, administrator, and patient—all started defining nurse role in ways convenient to their own roles. Such role-confusion of staff nurses leads to incompatible expectations of her role-set members. But the attainment of goals of the organization depends on the adequate role performance of each role occupant. If the role performance of the staff nurse who is solely responsible for providing comprehensive nursing care is not adequate, the hospital organization tends to fall short of its services in providing comprehensive nursing care to the patients.

The conflicting conceptions of the role of nurse, thus, have become an interesting and fascination area for study in recent times for the social and behavioural scientists.[2] These studies have not only attempted to investigate the causes and factors that determine the role-performance of the nurses, but also studied the discrepancy between the ideal and actual role of the nurses in the hospitals. But, these studies were more or less unintegrated and unsynthesized in the sense that several individual factors of role-performance were considered in isolation. The possible inter-connections among all or at least some of them have not been considered. As such, the various evidences were not easily amenable to cummulative synthesis. Further, no attempt has been made to sort out the important independent factors into an internally meaningful, logical, and causal order, placing each factor in valid theoretical relationship with other factors. The present study precisely focuses attention in this direction by exploring and analysing the role-performance of the staff nurse who is the key-functionary in the care process of the hospital and isolates the real determinants of her role performance.

THE PRESENT STUDY

King George Hospital, one of the biggest teaching-cum-general hospitals in the state of Andhra Pradesh located in Visakhapatnam, is selected for the present study. Being the oldest in the State (established in the year 1845), the hospital has well established traditions and culture as a teaching, research and care and cure institution. In terms of its size, structure and organization, King George Hospital is a large scale formal organization in every sense of the term. It has about 1200 bed strength for in-patients manned by about 110 doctors and 165 staff nurses working in and operating various specialized departments and wards. The hospital has two lines of authority and supervision. One is the professional authority and the other is the administrative authority. The medical staff comprising Civil Surgeons, Civil Assistant, Surgeons, House Surgeones and nurses come under professional authority. The Superintendent, Medical Officer, Lay Secretary and Nursing Superintendent come under the administrative authority. Since a nurse is considered a semi-professional, her professional authority is very limited but she is supervised and controlled by the administrators of the hospital. The rationale for selecting the staff nurse as a unit of the present study is that she is the key figure to articulate with the therapeutic process sharing the major responsibility in acting as a mediator between the patients and the doctors. She interprets the patients' problems to the doctors and in turn explains the doctors' instructions to the patients. She infuses confidence in the doctor and in the treatment process. By virtue of playing complex and delicate roles, the nurse has become indispensable in the modern rapeutic system.

The study was conducted in 1977. Since the hospital consists of only 165 staff-nurses, it was decided to study all of them. However, fifteen staff-nurses either refused to provide information or were not available in the hospital due to long leave or being on deputation elsewhere. Therefore, the sample size was restricted to 150 only. Interview schedule was used as the instrument for data collection. Basic organizational and personnel data were collected from the authorities and direct observations were also made of the activities carried out in the different departments and wards of the hospital.

OPERATIONALIZATION OF VARIABLES

Dependent Variable

Role-performance is the focus or dependant variable of analysis in our study. It denotes the actual work turned out by the role performer in his or her job during the work in the organization. In other words, the specific manner in which the individuals enact and perform their role can be identified as the role-performance and it may be influenced by several factors. In our study, we have analysed and measured role performance of the nurse with the help of the response categories of respondents to a set of questions relating to the functions and duties of the nurses.

Independent Variables

Our study has utilised a number of simple and composite independent variables assumed to have some direct or indirect bearing on the role-performance. Some of the simple variables are respondents' age, duration of service, monthly income, family property, family size, earning members in the family, monthly family income, etc. The measurement of these variables is simple and needs no explanation. But there are other independent variables which are composite in nature and which have been used in the study. Significant among them are explained below.

Role-Commitment

Role-commitment is the individual's intensity and quality of participation in an activity on a relatively permanent basis. In other words, commitment refers to the consistent lines of activity of the role performer. In our study, role-commitment was focused on three dimensions, namely; respondents' pre-entry motivation, present consistency in action and anticipated consistency in action.

Role-Perception

It is the individual's definition of his situation with reference to his and others' social positions. It has three dimensions, namely; self-perception of his own role, self-perception of others' roles and role-set members' perceptions of role occupant. The role-perception of a nurse is assessed and measured in our study by asking a set of questions on these dimensions.

Interaction with Role-Set

It is difficult to conceive of a role without role-set or role-others. The occupational role-others of a nurse working in a hospital are : doctors, fellow-nurses, patients and menial staff. The manner in which the professional nurse interacts with other role-set members gives rise to certain role-relations. In the ultimate analysis, the type of interactions and inter-relationships between the role-set members determines their role performance. Hence we have included this as one of the independent variables of the study.

Role-Expectations from Role-Set

In an organization, different role-set members may have different levels of expectations from the role-performer. The manner in which the role-set members expect from a role-performer determines his or her role-performance. Sometimes in meeting the several demands and expectations of different role-set members, the role performer may feel incompatibility in his/her role resulting in role ambiguity and role tension. Such feeling of ambiguity and tension in the role influences the quality and level of role-performance. Hence, our study has included role expectations from role-set members as a critical independent variable.

Role Relations with Role-Set

In a complex organization such as modern hospital, team-work between professionals as well as between role-set members is essential for its smooth functioning. The nurse working in a hospital involves in three basic types of role-relations, namely, professional client (nurse-patient) relations, colleagual (nurse-nurse) relations, and inter-professional (doctor-nurse) relations. The existence of such relations at the work-spot goes a long way in shaping and determining the individual's role-commitment and role-performance. Therefore, the present study has included role-relations as an independent variable.

Basic Facts about the Sample

The respondents' ages ranged from twenty-two to fifty-one years, the mean age being thirty-two years. Almost seventy per cent of the respondents are in the age group of twenty-six to thirty-five years which reveals that the sample is composed mostly of young or middle aged persons. Majority of the respondents are Christians (fifty-four per cent). Hindus constitute fourty-three per cent of the sample and of them 58.5% belong to forward castes, twenty-three per cent to backward and service castes and the rest 10.5 % to Scheduled Castes. While eigthy-one per cent of the respondents were married and living with their husbands, only seventeen per cent were unmarried at the time of investigation. Almost seventy-five per cent of the married respondents had a prolonged duration of married life of five years and above. With regard to the respondents' residential background, sixty-nine per cent were born and brought up in either towns or cities as against only thirty per cent who had rural background. Most of the nurses (66.7%) hailed from Visakhapatnam and its neighbouring districts. The data further revealed that eighty-six per cent of the respondents studied upto the tenth class or Matriculation which is the minimum qualification prescribed for recruitment to nursing profession. Very few nurses have either improved their qualifications after their entry into the profession or entered the profession with higher qualifications. Since promotions are based entirely on seniority, most of the respondents revealed that they were not interested in improving their academic qualifications. However, twenty-eight per cent of the respondents underwent specialised training in different branches of medical case. The monthly income of the respondents varied from Rs. 352 to 800, the average being Rs. 558. The duration of service ranged between one to thirty years, the average being eleven years. Contrary to our expectations, a majority of the respondents were living in extended families. This is obviously, because they need assistance from somebody to look after their children and home as both spouses are employed. The respondents' family size varied between one to eleven with an average of five members. The average family income of the respondents was Rs. 1085 a month within the range of Rs. 352 to Rs. 3867.

To a question "Why did you choose nursing?" sixty-one per cent said categorically that since nursing was a noble profession, their inherent desire to render service to the sick was responsible for their option. About seventy-seven per cent further informed that they joined the profession on their own and that the initiative and decision came from them only. Regarding their own subjective perception and evaluation of their current socio-economic status in society, an overwhelming majority (61.3%) felt that they belong to the middle class. However, most of them really felt that they are not getting due respect and regard from the larger community. But eighty-two per cent of the respondents ranked themselves second in the hospital hierarchy next to doctors, which shows that nurses have a high self-esteem. They perceive and feel that professional expertise is an important basis for hierarchy rather than power and prestige.

Findings of the Study

Selecting role performance of the nurse as the dependant variable, a simple correlation analysis was run with sixteen independent variables. These sixteen explanatory variables were logically derived from the theory related to role-analysis. Of the sixteen variables, only eleven emerged significant for their relation with the role-performance (Table 1). Of these eleven significant variables, three namely, respondent's family-size, role, commitment and role-perception were positively correlated with the role performance. The remaining eight independent variables, namely, respondents' age, duration of service, monthly income, family property, interaction with role-set members, super-ordinate-subordinate relationships, role-expectations from role-set members and communication and discussion with role-set members were significantly and negatively correlated with respondents' role-performance.

Thus, the correlation analysis reveals certain interesting insights. For instance, respondents' role-performance has

TABLE 1

Zero-Order Correlation between the Independent Variables and the Dependant Variable

S. No.	Independent variables	Role Performance
1.	Respondents' age	—0.18
2.	Duration of service	—0.15
3.	Respondents' monthly income	—0.16
4.	Family property	—0.22
5.	Family size	0.13
6.	Number of earning members	0.00
7.	Parental perception and attitude	0.07
8.	Husbands' attitude and perception	0.07
9.	Interaction with role-set members	—0.17
10.	Role-commitment	0.12
11.	Superordinate-subordinate relationships	—0.12
12.	Role relations with role-set	—0.01
13.	Role-expectations from Role-Set	—0.14
14.	Communication and discussion with role-set members	—0.10
15.	Communication and Discussion with patients	—0.01
16.	Role-perception	—0.42

decreased along with an increase in their age which means that those who are young are more committed to their profession, and their performance is also better since their prospects depend on it. Hence, the same is reflected in the significant negative correlation between their duration of service and role-performance. This is quite contrary to our expectations, but nevertheless conforms to Oommen's observation that "by the time nurses reach the fifteenth year of their career, the patient orientation comes down, bureaucratic orientation goes up and professional orientation gets stabilized."[3] The same trend is visible when we take the significant and inverse relationships between respondents' role-performance and their economic position in terms of regular income and assets. Another interesting finding that emerged from the simple correlation analysis is that an increase in the levels of respondents' interaction with role-set members, their superordinate-subordinate relationships and their communication and discussion with role-set members were followed by a corresponding decrease in their role-performance. On the contrary, when the nurses' role-perception increased, their role-performance has also increased which is in line with the finding of Rajagopalan, that "as a rule correct perception of the attributes of role must lead to right role-performance and conversely incorrect role perception is an important factor responsible for improper and unsatisfactory role-performance."[4] The same is true in the case of the significant and positive relationship between role commitment and role-performance.

The results of the above correlation analysis provided us only a proximate indications suggesting broad trends. No firm conclusions could therefore be drawn on the basis of such simple correlation analysis. For this reason, multiple regression analysis was conducted to find out the independent contribution of each of the variables shown to be significant in the correlation analysis, controlling the effects of others in each case. It is to be noted here that of the eleven significant independent variables, we have selected only eight variables for the multiple regression analysis. They are: respondents' duration of service, respondents' monthly income, family size, interaction with role-set members, role-commitment, superordinate-subordinate relationships, role-expectations with role-set members and role perception. The other three variables were eliminated because they were redundant. As shown in Table 2, the selected eight variables taken together explain sixty-one per cent of the variance in role performance yielding an F-value of 32.2. The analysis also revealed that only three variables, namely, respondents' duration of service, respondents' role-commitment and respondents' role perception had a significant effect on the role-performance when the effects of the other five variables were controlled. The rest had no independent contribution of their own to the variation in the role-performance, even though they have very high zero-order correlation co-efficients. They were dropped out as insignificant predictors of role-performance.

TABLE 2

Regression Values for the Eight Predictor Variables

S. No.	Variable	Zero-Order Correlation Co-efficient	Beta Co-efficient	T. Value
1.	Duration of service	—0.15	—0.89	2.162*
2.	Monthly income	—0.16	—0.10	0.530
3.	Family size	0.13	0.02	0.645
4.	Interaction with role-Set members	—0.17	0.12	0.033
5.	Role-commitment	0.12	—0.08	1.982*
6.	Superordinate-subordinate relationships	−0.12	0.15	0.012
7.	Role expectations from role-set members	—0.14	0.12	0.296
8.	Role perception	0.42	0.18	1.254**

R^2 = 0.61 (Sixty-one per cent) ; Standard Error = 1.15;
F=Value = 32.2

*Significant at five per cent level.
**Significant at ten per cent level.

DISCUSSION

The results of our study show that respondents' duration of service was significantly and positively correlated with interaction with role-set members and super-ordinate and sub-ordinate relationships (Table 3). It means that those respondents who are seniors by profession interact freely and frequently with their role-set members. This has resulted in better super-ordinate-subordinate relationships. Interestingly, the impact of all this has resulted in lack of commitment to the job and poor levels of communication and interaction with the patients among the seniors as revealed by the significant negative correlations at Zero-order level. Similarly, the significant null-correlation between duration of service and role relations with role-set members indicates that seniors by virtue of their service and experience never involve in or maintain

TABLE 3

Zero-Order Correlations between Role-Related Variables and the Significantly Emerged Determinant Variables of Role-Performance

S. No.	Role-Related Variables	Duration of Service	Role Commitment	Role Perception
1.	Duration of service	—	—0.25	−0.00
2.	Parental Perception and attitude	0.00	0.12	0.03
3.	Husbands' attitude and perception	−0.02	0.19	0.10
4,	Interaction with role-set members	0.27	0.30	—0.10
5.	Role commitment	0.25	—	0.02
6.	Superordinate and subordinate relationships	0.00	—0.01	0.11
7.	Role relations with Role-set members	—0.13	—0.10	0.11
8.	Role expectations from Role-Set	0,02	0.23	0.03
9.	Communication and Discussion with role-set	0.08	0.10	0.07
10.	Communication and Discussion with patients	0.13	0.03	0.10
11.	Role-perception	0.00	0.02	—

better role-relations with doctors and other role-set members. A cummulative effect of all this has resulted in the emergence of duration of service as a crucial and significant determinant of role-performance in our study.

Favourable parental attitude and perception coupled with their husbands' favourable attitudes and perception towards their profession and career generated in the respondents confidence and commitment to their job, as revealed by the significant and positive correlations between them. The significant null correlation between respondents' role-commitment and their interactions with role-set members further explains the fact that those who are really committed to their job interact less with the role-set members thereby concentrating more on patient care. They are the persons who maintain good and cordial role-relations with doctors and other role-set members, hence, the significant positive correlation between role-commitment and role relations with role-set members. Even though the value of the correlation co-efficient between role-commitment and communication and discussion with patients was very weak and insignificant, since the direction is positive, we can reasonably argue that those who are highly committed to their profession would more and more involve in the communication and discussion with the patients. Hence, role commitment was found to have a significant independent effect on respondents' role-performance.

Those respondents whose perception of their role is very clear have definitely better communication with patients, maintained less non-professional relations with role-set members and thereby showed better role-performance, Hence, role perception has emerged significantly in the regression analysis showing its independent effect on role-performance. In the ultimate analysis, respondent's role performance is determined, conditioned and influenced by their service, role-perception and commitment. Even though some of the economic factors such as respondents' monthly income, family property, family size have emerged significant in the correlation analysis, they failed to have any significance in the regression analysis and hence they have no independent effect on the role-performance of the respondents in this study.

Nursing profession stresses more comprehensive nursing care for the patient. This consists of both direct nursing care functions (like meeting physical, social, psychological, spriritual economic and educational needs of the patients) and indirect nursing care functions (like maintaining supplies and equipments, carrying out clerical and house-keeping functions).[5] Besides learning the techniques relating to these functions, the student nurse is trained in the skills of rendering expressive patient care as an important part of comprehensive nursing care. In the hospital situation the expressive function of a professional nurse involves devotion of time to the patients by acquiring knowledge of the socio-economic background of the patient, reducing the tensions, fears and anxieties of the patient regarding the illness and the course of treatment, extending selfless service and affectionate behaviour and providing physical and psychological comfort to the patient with appropriate care. This expressive care function of a nurse is more important in the treatment of a patient, because doctors' instrumental activities like examining, diagnosing, prescribing and treating are often felt by the patient to be embarrassing, painful and anxiety-provoking and tend to produce high levels of emotional tension in the patient. But, nurse by her explanations, reassurance and comforting ministration can seek to reduce them and prepare the patient for accepting the treatment.

The student nurse joins the profession with such "pre-entry motivation" with a lot of commitment to patient care.[6] After she completes her training, she joins the hospital as a professional employee and in that capacity she is supposed to take the responsibility of the ward to look after the patients and act as a mediator between doctors and patients. But in reality this does not happen. The doctor and the nurse work apart under different organizational conditions. While the doctor is looked upon as the real authority, the nurse is unfortunately treated as a subordinate and assistant to the doctor (instead of a team-mate). She takes orders from the doctors on the therapeutic side and from the Resident Medical Officer on the administrative side. Added to that, the functions prescribed in the Manual of Nurses mostly relate to the administrative and doctor's assistant functions and only a few relate to the physical care of the patient. Significantly, the expressive care-functions of the nurse do not find a place in the Manual. Thus, we find the nurse placed in a very precarious situation. She is socialized and re-socialized in such a manner that during the course of her training, she is made to believe that the performance of expressive functions are important and as she moves forward stage by stage during the period of her service, she is re-socialized as to behave in such a way as to perform only such of those functions as are delegated to her by the doctor in the ward and the administrators of the organization.

A perusal of her routine work would reveal the fact that she is left with no time to perform the expressive functions. Her occupational and organizational conditions produce a new set of expectations and motivations. Her "on-going socialization" further strengthens, modifies or changes her motivation to work and her expectations from the job. In such circumstances, the staff nurse works in the hospital as a "captive of organization", but continues her job with an "indifference-response type", giving importance to "off-the-job pursuits" with only lip-sympathy to the patient and patient-care functions.[7] This is what Merton called "trained in-capacity" and "goal displacement.[8] Consequently, the staff nurse never feels any job satisfaction.

In the work situation, the nurse experiences a series of problems like "work-overload" high nurse-patient ratio, indiscipline and non-co-operation of her subordinates, especially the class iv employees, inconvenient and prolonged working hours and accountability for each and everything that happens in the ward including theft, breakage or loss of the instruments and equipment. All this makes her take more care of supervision and watching than nursing, Thus, the cumulative effect of the conditions existing in the hospital, the semi-professional nature of her occupation and the kinds of interactions with and expectations from her role-set members in the work-situation make the nurse drift away from her professional functions of rendering expressive nursing care to the patients.

What is therefore required for efficient patient care is a change in the organizational set-up of the hospital giving more recognition and time to the nurse to perform her avowed roles efficiently by perceiving her role in a proper perspective, enabling her to get more and more committed to her professional role as the period of her service increases.

It is suggested that policies and programmes aimed at increasing motivation and commitment to work among the staff nurses and reducing work over-load and tension in their job are necessary for improving their role-performance in the hospital.

NOTES AND REFERENCES

1. Rushing, William. "The Hospital Nurse as Mother Surrogate and Bed Side Psychologist," *Mental Hygiene*, vol. 50, no. I 1966.
2. Malone, et al., "The Paradox in Nursing", *American Journal of Nursing*, vol. 61, no. 9, 1961 ; Brodt, D.E., "The Neophyte Nurse : A Role Expectation Study," *Nursing Research*, vol. 13, nos. 1-2, 1964 ; Rajagopalan, C., "Role-Perception and Role-Performance," *Indian Journal of Social Work*, vol. 26, no. I, 1965, Barnes, R.G., "The Role of Hospital Staff Nurse as Ascribed by Nurses : Hospital Administration and Doctors," *Dissertation Abstract*, vol. 32, no: 1-2. 1971, pp. 1-2; Oommen, T.K., *Doctors and Nurses : Study in Occupational Role-Structure*, Macmillan, New Delhi, 1978 ; Venkataratnam, R. *Medical Sociology in an Indian Setting*, Macmillan, Bombay, 1979; Chatterjee, Sukumara, "The Changing Roles of the Indian Nurses", *Nursing Journal of India*, vol. 71, no. 8, 1980 ; Jayalakshmi, D., "Nurses Role-Performance : A Research Study", *The Nursing Journal of India*, vol. 71, no. 3, 1980.
3. Oommen, *Ibid*, p. 111.
4. Rajagopalan, *op. cit.*, pp. 31-37.
5. Jayalakshmi, *op. cit.*, p. 65.
6. Oommen, *op. cit.*
7. Presthus, R., *The Organisational Society*, Alfred A. Knoff Inc., New York, 1962.
8. Merton, R.K., "The Role-set : Problems in Sociological Theory", *British Journal of Sociology*, vol. 8, 1957, pp. 106-120.

PART V

LEGAL PROFESSION

22

ORIGIN AND GROWTH OF THE LAWYERS' PROFESSION IN INDIA

SATYA VRAT PANDE

THE centrality of occupations in determination of individual's status in society has always been well understood, accepted and institutionalised. The process of increasing specialisation of the traditional occupations has been at work in India as elsewhere; it is this process which gives the occupations the character of 'professions.' It is accelerated by increasing education and the demands of an industrialising, modern society. One of such professions, namely, the legal profession has been looked upon here from the standpoint of its origin and growth in India.

Lawyers have been defined as "advocates" in the Advocates Act (1961) of India. They are the ones entered in any roll under the provisions of this Act. The State Bar Council admits persons as advocates on its roll after examining their eligibility for such admission. There are two classes of advocates, namely; senior advocates and other advocates. An advocate may, with his consent, be designated as senior advocate if the Supreme Court is of opinion that by virtue of his ability, experience and standing at the Bar, he is deserving of such distinction. Any citizen of India, having completed the age of twenty-one years and having obtained a degree in law from a recognised university, can be admitted as an advocate on the roll, if he has paid the enrolment fee to the State Bar Council.

The Advocates' Act makes it clear that there shall be only

one class of persons entitled to practise the profession of law, namely, the advocates. Every advocate whose name is entered on the common roll shall be entitled to practise law throughout the territories to which this Act extends. On receipt of complaint or otherwise if the State Bar Council has reason to believe that any advocate on its roll has been guilty of professional or other misconduct, it shall refer the case for disposal to its disciplinary committee (1961).

From this discussion the professional character of legal practice becomes evident. Historically, the profession appears to have been in vogue in the ancient as also in the medieval period in India though its concept was quite different from what it is today. The profession being inseparably related to the system of dispensation of justice, it has undergone various shifts in its orientation and development in our society too. As the king was regarded as the fountain head of justice in the ancient times[1] his court was the highest court of appeal as also the original court in cases of vital importance to the State.[2] The king was advised by learned Brahmins, the chief justice and other judges, ministers, elders and representatives of the trading community.

Next to the King was the Court of the Chief Justice (pradvivaka) which consisted, apart from the Chief Justice, of a board of judges to assist him. All the judges were from the three upper castes. Brihaspati has stated that there were three kinds of tribunals, viz., stationary, movable courts held under the royal signet in the Kings absence, and commissions under the King's presidency.[3] In villages, the local village councils or *kulani*, similar to modern *panchayats* had been in existence, consisting of a board of five or more members.[4] However, from all available, accounts it does not appear that the organisation of lawyers as we know it today existed during the ancient period though the elaborateness of the judicial procedure was such as to warrant it. Though the Smritis, says Kane, do not refer to the existence of any separate institution of lawyers, yet "this does not preclude the idea that persons well-versed in the law of the Smritis and the procedure of the courts were appointed to represent a party and place, his case before the court. The procedure prescribed by Narada-

Smriti, Brihaspati-Smriti and Katyayana-Smriti reaches a very high level of technicalities, and skilled help must often have been required in litigation."[5]

In the medieval period, i.e. during the Muslim period, the Sultan being the head of State, was the supreme authority to administer justice in his kingdom. The three courts of the Sultan—Diwani-Qaze, Diwani-Mazalim and Diwani-Siyasat having separate jurisdictions—were created by Muhammad Tughlaq.[6] The Chief Justice (Qazi-ul-Quzat) was the highest judicial officer next to the Sultan. In 1248, Sultan Nasiruddin, being dissatisfied with the then Chief Justice, created a superior post of Sadre Jahan who became defacto head of the judiciary. The changes and reforms that followed were many till the year of ascension on the throne of Sher Shah Suri who overhauled the entire system in order to render more effective, speedy and clean justice. The great Mughal King Akbar improved upon the system introduced by Sher Shah.[7]

In so far as the profession of lawyers is concerned, it had come into existence in order to represent the litigants before the courts. Popularly known as *vakils* they used to be professional legal experts. Though there was no institution of lawyers like the Bar Association as it exists today, yet the lawyers played an important role in the administration of justice. Two Muslim Indian codes, viz., Fique-Firoz-Shahi and Fatwae-Alamgiri, clearly state the duties of a vakil. Mawardi stated that "specialised knowledge of law was necessary both for acting as a Quazi and for the legal practice."[8]

Government advocates were for the first time appointed during the reign of Shah Jahan to defend civil suits against the State. During Aurangzeb's reign, wholetime lawyers were appointed in every district, who were known as vakile-sarkar. The lawyers as professionals had a right of audience in the Court. It was expected that they would maintain a high standard of legal learning and behaviour.

Nevertheless, the modern legal profession properly speaking had its beginnings in the first years of the British rule. The Hindu Pandits, the Muslim Muftis and the Portuguese lawyers who served under earlier regimes had little effect upon the system of law and legal practice that evolved and developed under the British rule in India. The first real step in the direction of organising the legal profession in India was taken in 1774 when the Supreme Court was established in Calcutta in pursuance of the Regulating Act of 1773. Clause 11 of the Supreme Court Charter empowered the Court to "approve, admit and enrol such and so many advocates and attorneys at law" as the Court "shall seem meet". They were to be attorneys of record and were authorised "to appear and plead and act for the suitors" of the Court. The court could remove the said advocates and attorneys "on reasonable cause". No other persons whatsoever, but such advocates and attorneys so admitted and enrolled were to be "allowed to appear and plead or act" in the Court, for or on bahalf of such suitors.

The "advocates" entitled thus to appear were, "only the English and Irish barristers and members of the Faculty of Advocates in Scotland; and attorneys were the British attorneys and solicitors. The Court was thus an exclusive preserve for members of the British legal profession."[9] An Indian lawyer had no right to appear before the Court. (The same position obtained when Supreme Courts were established in Bombay and Madras later). The Bengal Regulation VII of 1793 created for the first time a regular legal profession for the company's Courts. The Sadar Diwani Adalat was given powers to enrol pleaders from among the Hindus and the Muslims for all such courts. The 1833 legislation, however, modified the provisions of the earlier regulation in that only persons duly qualified, to whatever nationality or religion they might belong, could be enrolled as pleaders of the Sadar Diwani Adalat.

The Legal Practitioners Act of 1846 is a milestone in the way of progress of the profession of law. It made important innovations as follows:—(1) the profession of pleaders was thrown open to all persons of whatever nationality or religion duly certified by the Sadar Courts; (2) the attorneys and barristers of any of Her Majesty's Courts in India were made eligible to plead in any of the Sadar Courts; (3) the pleaders were permitted to enter into agreements with their clients for their fees for professional services. The 1863 Act also confirmed the above provisions and the Act of 1879 attempted to organise the professionals on a more systematic pattern as by this time, quite a few High Courts had been established. Two classes of lawyers were created, namely, the advocates and the vakils. The former were to be barristers of England while the latter were those who obtained their law degree from Indian universities.

It was only natural that, in course of time, the vakils expressed dissatisfaction about the distinction stated above, more so due to the special privileges enjoyed by the barristers and solicitors. There came, therefore, a demand for creating an All-India Bar in the Country. Consequently, the Government of India constituted the Indian Bar Committee under the chairmanship of Sir Edward Chamier in 1923 to look into the matter. Although the Committee did not find it practicable to organise the Bar on an All-India basis at the time, yet it made such recommendations that the dissatisfaction among the vakils was abated by lessening the extent of the discrimination between the two categories of lawyers.

To implement the recommendations of the Chamier Committee, the Central Legislature enacted the Indian Bar Councils Act in 1926 with the express object to provide for the constitution and incorporation of Bar Councils for certain courts. Thus, a Bar Council was to be constituted for every High Court. Each High Court was to prepare and maintain a roll of advocates and the Bar Council was to make rules to regulate the admission of persons to be advocates. Thus, the function of the Bar Council was merely advisory in nature. In course of time, the Calcutta and the Bombay High Courts too liberalised their rules so as to permit non-barrister advocates to practise on their original sides.

The awareness that the Bar was not being allowed to play its rightful role became quite acute by 1950, that is, after Independence of the country. The 1926 Act did not bring the pleaders, mukhtars and revenue agents practising in the mofussil court and revenue officers under its cope and, thus did not set up a unified Indian Bar. "The demand for a unified all-India Bar which arose initially as a protest against the monopoly of the British barristers and the invidious distinctions between barristers and non-barristers received a new orientation with the advent of Independence and became a claim for the fulfilment of a cherished ideal, namely, an autonomous and unified all-India Bar."[10]

It was under these circumstances that the Government of India appointed in 1951, the All India Bar Committee under the chairmanship of Justice S.R. Das of the Supreme Court. The Committee, in its report, made detailed recommendation for the unification of the Bar providing for common roll of advocates who would be entitled to practise in all courts of the country. The committee recommended, *inter alia*, that there should be no further recruitment of non-graduate pleaders or mukhtars. Further, on the recommendations of the Committee an All-India Bar Council and State Bar Councils were also to be set-up. The power of enrolment, suspension and removal of advocates was to be vested in the Bar Councils.

The Law Commission of 1955 considered the wider question of reform of judicial administration and gave its report in 1958 and endorsed all the recommendations of the Bar Committee. The Commission, however, favoured the division of the Bar into Senior Advocates and Junior Advocates, the seniors being by reason of their status, precluded from accepting certain types of work, e.g., that they should neither draft nor settle notices, pleadings, affidavits or other documents nor advise on evidence. The seniors were also not to appear in cases unless briefed with a junior. The autonomy of the Bar was upheld by the Commission, consisting wholly of the members of the profession. The Councils were to elect their own chairman.

The Advocates Act was passed by the Parliament in 1961 in order to amend and consolidate the law relating to legal practitioners and to provide for the constitution of the State Bar Councils and the All India Bar Council, establishing a common roll of advocates who have the right to practise in all courts in India from the highest to the lowest.[11] The Bar has been integrated into a single class of legal practitioners known as advocates. The Bar Councils are vested with the power to entertain and determine cases of misconduct against advocates on its roll as also to safeguard their rights, privileges and interests. The Bar Council of India lays down, *inter alia*, the standards of professional conduct and etiquette for advocates and the procedure to be followed by the disciplinary committee of each State Bar Council.

The 1961 Act also provides that any advocate may, with his consent, be designated as a senior advocate if the Supreme Court or a High Court is of opinion that by virtue of his ability, experience and standing at the Bar, he deserves such distinction. The Act has marked the beginning of a new era in the history of the legal profession by resting largely in the Bar Councils, the power and the jurisdiction which the courts till then exercised. It has fulfilled the aspirations of the advocates demanding for the Council(s) and for creation of a single class of practitioners with powers to practise in all the Courts. They are bound only by the rules made and a code of conduct laid down by their own bodies to which the members could resort to for the protection of their rights and interests.

As is recent history in India, the legal profession has played and can still play a vital role in upholding individual rights, promoting more efficient and widespread justice, and acting as an integrating force in national life. The responsibility of this profession to the Indian society is indeed great.

NOTES AND REFERENCES

1. Kane, P.V., *History of Dharmashastra*, vol. III, Bhandarker Oriental Research Institute, Poona, 1958, pp. 242-316.
2. Dhavan, S.S., "Indian Jurisprudence," *Journal of the National Academy of Administration*, vol. 8, 1963, p. 19.
3. Muller, Max, (ed.), "Brihaspati Smriti," *Sacred Books of the East*, vol. 33, 1906, p. 387.
4. Varadachariar, S., *Hindu Judicial System*, Lucknow University, Lucknow, 1964, p. 88.
5. Kane, *op. cit.* pp. 288-289.
6. Battute, Abu, A. Ibn, *Travels*, George Routledge, London, 1929, p. 194.
7. Ahmad, M.B., *Administration of Justice in Medieval India*, Aligarh Historical Research Institute, Aligarh, 1941, pp. 143-166.
8. Al, Mewardi, "Akhamus Sultanyat", *Journal of the Royal Asiatic Society*, 1916, p. 764.
9. Kulsrestha, V.D., *Land Marks in Indian Legal and Constitutional History*, Eastern Book Co., Lucknow, 1981, p. 430.
10. Ibid, p. 435.
11. The Advocates Act, 1961, Act No. 25 of 1961 (A Government of India Act), Ministry of Information, New Delhi.

23

LAWYERS AND THE LEGAL SYSTEM IN INDIA : A CRITIQUE

SASHEEJ HEGDE

The legal system in modern India, which has almost entirely displaced the system of traditional law, has been a part of the colonial legacy handed out in 1947. Over the years, this system has proliferated and continues to expand in its "mission" to impart justice to the masses. In this paper, an attempt has been made to examine the factors and conditions facilitating the retention and development of the inherited legal system in the country, despite widespread dissatisfaction with its functioning. Further, in the light of the features exhibited by the legal profession in India, the paper questions many of the propositions underlying the theory of professions.

One of the mechanisms for the durability and proliferation of the present legal system in India has been the legal profession. The present legal system continues to be supported by a numerous and influential class of lawyers who are fully committed to the system, have a heavy personal stake in its continuance, and are genuinely convinced of its general virtue.[1] The pre-dominant role of lawyers vis-a-vis the legal system and the wider society in which the system is implicated has been particularly facilitated by the links which the legal profession has fostered with the political system, mainly through membership and active participation. The legal profession occupied, and continues to occupy, a position of strategic significance in our political system.

The rise of the legal profession, both in number and in status, followed a range of administrative and legal developments, especially in the second half of the nineteenth century. The enactment of the codes, the founding of the High Courts, and the grant of the right to employ pleaders in civil and criminal suits alike meant a strengthening of the legal system in India. The growing volume and complexity of legal regulations and the increase in litigation, particularly over land, were chiefly responsible for the rapid growth of the legal profession. In 1866, Sir Henry Maine spoke of "the immense multiplication of legal practitioners" and noted that :

> "the great addition...is due to the numbers and influence of the Native Bar. Practically, a young educated native, pretending to anything above a clerkship, adopts one of the two occupations—either he goes into the service of government or he joins the Native Bar...the Bar is getting more and more preferred to government service by the educated youth of the country, both on the score of its gainfulness and on the score of its independence."[2]

The training of lawyers along Western lines and the knowledge of English gave them the opportunity to win a share in the practice of the High Courts. By 1886, Indians had succeeded in getting a large share of this practice in Bombay, Calcutta and Madras. This essentially meant an increase in the standing of lawyers and a corresponding increase in their income.[3]

Though originally the product of institutional exigency—in that to work the system of law and courts established by the British, there was a need for a class of men, proficient in the art of advocacy or pleading—lawyers gathered their own momentum and developed great power over the orientations of the legal and social order. An important factor contributing to such a development, especially in the latter part of the nineteenth century, was the imposition of more stringent educational standards, both by the High Courts and the government.

As qualifications rose, those lawyers who possessed them, came to view themselves more and more as a group with specialist needs and demanding specialist privileges. The "professionalisation" process underlying the practice of law and the emergence of the legal profession as a distinctive special group can be traced back to the above developments. The increasing bulk and variety of legislative enactments and complexity of court procedure also facilitated the growth of the legal profession, in that only those who know the law and rules of business could be engaged.

The political effects of the growth of the legal profession in India have never been fully explored. The most evident impact occurred at the leadership level : the preponderance of lawyers among top politicians. In regarding lawyers as unrepresentative of the Indian people, the British administrators overlooked the positive effect : "the establishment of a political class habituated to the world of rules and resistant to arbitrary autocracy."[4] Standing as an authority apart from government and able to conduct the constitutional dialogue with their rules, "lawyers marched in the van of politics in later nineteenth century India."

The emergence and growth of the legal profession had a profound impact on the nationalist movement, whose leaders more often than not, were lawyers. The educated were few and most had been absorbed into public service and the professions, particularly law. Of the professions, law attracted the most talented men.[5] Since the government servants were constrained by dependence on the goodwill of their employer, it was the lawyer who became the spokesman for the educated. As Misra notes :

> "The profession of law as a whole exercised a much greater degree of independence. This was...because in India, the chief check on the authority of the executive is to be found in the Courts of Justice, and natives who practice in them rapidly acquire the habit of questioning the acts of authority : and tempted by the security of their professional position, are apt to take a prominent part in movements for their end having attacks upon the government."[6]

The active participation of lawyers in the nationalist movement could be seen at two levels. First, the lawyer, who spoke and understood the language of the colonial master, emerged as a spokesman of nationalist aspirations. In the presidency capitals, it was the successful high court lawyer who was the backbone of politics in the mofussil, it was the pleader at the district bar. An examination of the Congress delegates from 1892 to 1909 indicates that of the 13,837 delegates, 9119 were drawn from the professions. Among these professionals, 5442 were lawyers.[7] The leadership base from which the Congress drew was confined to the class of middle-class professionals, especially lawyers.[8] The two most important leaders spearheading the nationalist movement, Gandhi and Nehru, were lawyers.

At another level, the legal profession appeared as a spokesman of the newly emerging social classes, especially in the urban areas, which evolved in the Indian society during British rule. As the leading representative of a numerous and influential middle-class of professionals, the legal profession strove to maintain the prosperity of the professional classes.

The significance of political power for this purpose was recognized early. This perhaps explains the close association of lawyers, or more generally the professional classes, with the nationalist movement. What from a distance appears as the political strivings of professionals were often on closer examination, their efforts to conserve or improve the position of their own prescriptive group[9]. Such a standpoint is bolstered by the fact that while lawyers spoke of the "un-Britishness of British rule in India," paradoxically enough, they spoke highly of "British justice." Almost without exception the profession viewed the application of English law and procedures as the greatest benefit of the British rule. It was claimed that the riveting of English practice upon India gave to the country a rule of law and ensured for the first time the impartial administration of justice.[10] Though there was some opinion in the nationalist movement in favour of a boycott of the courts, it was never as strong as that opposed to participation in the assemblies.[11] In fact Mahatma Gandhi was highly critical of lawyers for confirming British authority by practising in the colonial courts.[12]

It would not be wrong to assert that a major pre-occupation with the legal profession was to maintain a separate judicial ethos. This was best exemplified by demands for the separation and independence of the judiciary at all levels of the administration and as a bulwark against arbitrary executive action. In fact, the vexstions that accompanied the establishment of a national legal system under British rule, namely, the growing volume and complexity of laws, the rise in litigation, delay in the administration of justice were directly functional to the practice of law[13]. Thus, the legal system implanted by the British only reinforced the vested interest and pecuniary ambitions of lawyers.

In August 1947 British rule came to an end, and power was transferred to two independent dominions, India and Pakistan. The Constituent Assembly confined itself to the task of rebuilding the liberal constitutional and legal order ; it did not question the order itself. An attempt by Gandhians and "traditionalists" to form a polity based on village autonomy and self-sufficiency was rejected by the Assembly, which opted for a federal and parliamentary republic with centralized bureaucratic administration.[14] The existing legal system was retained intact, new powers granted to the judiciary and its independence enhanced by elaborate protections. All in all, the Constitution not only endorsed the prevailing legal system but also necessarily widened the role of law and lawyers.[15]

Such a development was perfectly understandable in the light of the fact that the Constituent Assembly was dominated by lawyers and/or men with law degree. Of the eleven members whom Austin identifies as an "inner circle" consisting of senior persons who guided the work of the Assembly—Rajendra Prasad, Azad, Patel, Nehru, Pant, Sitaramayya, Satya Narayan Sinha, B.R. Ambedkar, A.K. Ayyar, N.G. Ayyangar and K.M. Munshi—eight were lawyers or had taken a law degree.[16] It presented them with an opportunity to draft the judicial system under which they would function. They could not think beyond strengthening the existing legal system. In fact, as Austin observes :

"the subjects that loomed largest in the minds of the

> Assembly members when framing the judicial provisions were, the independence of the courts and two closely related issues, the powers of the Supreme Court and judicial review."[17]

The Constituent Assembly could have meant a break with the past ; yet, the law, legal system and institutions which Britain imposed on India were retained. The retention of the system lends credence to the surmise that in 1947, power was transferred from a British autocracy to the professional monopoly. Such a development rested on the legal professions, judgement of what was practical and desirable. In fact, their wishes and interests were expressed through the political system. When the Constitution was forged, the concept of a quasi-federal policy, nay, the entire constitutional structure, "could only be expressed in foreign cosmopolitan terms, and the lawyers were the only ones who understood it and could explain it."[18]

An attempt was made in the preceding paragraphs to account for the retention of the legal system obtaining under British rule in terms of the efforts and initiatives of the legal profession. Over the years, the legal system has proliferated and exhibits a striking durability, despite becoming virtually pathological.[19] The lack of organized concern by the legal profession, in so far as a restructuring of the legal system is concerned, gives rise to the impression that lawyers have a degree of vested interest in the system.

From time to time, doubts have been expressed in many quarters about the validity and usefulness of existing legal system. Particularly, much attention has been paid to the problem of delay and arrears in the administration of justice which stand as a direct threat to the prevailing legal system.[20] Galanter's observations are quite relevant in this context :

> "Lawyers and judges agreed that the system displayed serious defects—perjury, delay, proliferation of appeals, expenses. But they did nol attribute its shortcomings to its foreignness... While many lawyers called for re-examination or even radical reformation of the legal system, almost none could perceive any advantage in reversion to pre-

> British models. The reform of our legal profession and our legal system does not lie in that way of Village Panchayat Revival. It is a suicidal policy that will lead only to factions an anarchy."[21]

Thus, lawyers insist that there is no alternative to the prevailing system, and accordingly reject any fundamental change of the system which may render them redundant. They focus almost entirely on "procedural law", that is :

> "On court administration (delay, expense, corruption), complexity of procedure, unsuitability of rules of evidence, the adversarial rather than conciliatory character of the proceeding, and (occasionally) the nature of penalties."[22]

There is virtually no critical discussion of "substantive law". This is perhaps because procedural law is almost exclusively the lawyers' domain, and is, therefore, an indirect way of asserting their power and autonomy against control and interference. Indeed, this emphasis on procedural law may be seen as a part of an attempt to bewitch the reality and thus increase the realm of dependency.

Such a conservatism has gone hand in hand with the dominant role and political position of the legal profession in the politics of Independent India. Lawyers have wielded considerable political clout, both in the legislative and executive branches of government. The figures given hereunder indicates the percentage of Lok Sabha members with law degree.[23]

TABLE

Lok Sabha Members with Law Degree

Years	Total number of members	Number with law degree	Percentage with law degree
1952-57	487	148	30 4
1957-62	494	141	28.6
1962-67	494	133	27.0
1967-71	494	123	25.0
1971-77	518	137	26.5
1977-80	542	183	33.8
1980	542	167	31.0

Considering the Council of Ministers as a whole, at no point of time was the percentage of ministers with law degree less than forty-two, and occasionally it went up to fifty-one.[24] In 1982' the representation of lawyers in the Cabinet was an all time high of seventy-four per cent, and forty-eight per cent of the Council of Ministers as a whole were law-graduates.[25] Constituting as they are a crucial part of the political stratum, it islittle wonder that the inherited legal system remains ascendant.

In accounting for the dominant position of lawyers in Indian politics and public life over the last three decades, two possible lines of argument could be given :

The first of these lines of argument centres on the relations between the "class" of legal professionals and the State itself. It is through the courts, of which lawyers are a composite part, that the State establishes its authority. The politicization of the legal profession, in terms of their participation in politics, is a natural outcome in that political functions are involved in their work, namely, to uphold the law enacted by the State. Such a function has gone hand in hand with an abiding concern with maintaining the "autonomy of the legal profession" and the "independence of the judiciary" as the citadels of justice and freedom. This could be seen as an attempt by legal professionals to "de-politicize" the political sphere. That is, to give the domination of the State and law, which is inherently class-domination, the form of an impersonal authority standing outside and above society for public-welfare. Accordingly, the State, as Mahatma Gandhi asserted, has been able to retain its power through the "instrumentality of lawyers".[26]

A second basis for the predominance of lawyers in politics stems from the fact that political participation and activity is directly functional to a lawyer's professional skill, reputation and practice. It not only implies free and legitimate publicity but also contracts. Apart from this, the very intrinsic nature of the legal profession enables lawyers to enter the political arena. As Sharma notes :

> "It is found that lawyers are more active in politics than other professionals partly because of their professional autonomy and partly because of their knowledge about the

> political set-up, constitution, and legislative and legal structures and contacts with wider sections of society."[27]

Thus, to a great extent, the political power wielded by lawyers confers economic privileges on them. The control of office within party and government and the use of political leverage and controls confer wealth and privileges on lawyers. Of course, such a politics of aggrandizement is not unique to lawyers. Alternatively, it would also not be wrong to argue that the economic privileges, that the legal system entails, especially through servicing the economic order—by dealing with property transactions, taxation and commercial litigation—and also contributing to general "law and order", have been retained through political power.

It is said that the participation of lawyers in politics is not in their capacity as professionals but as public-men. Lawyers have been in the fore-front of struggles against the government in upholding civil liberties and human-rights. This is no doubt partly true. But that, as Mahatma Gandhi asserts, "does not undo the mischief that is inherent in the profession".[28] The State has been able to retain its power through the "instrumentality of lawyers" in that they oversee the law's domination over the people. Moreover, the point cannot be set aside that participation in politics is conducive to a lawyers reputation and practice. Considered in this light, there is the substantive question—to what extent can one insulate the two roles, *i.e.* as a career-minded individual or professional and as a "responsible" citizen? An exploration of this question would require independent analysis and is beyond the scope of this paper.

The image of the legal profession as an exclusive body of experts and as disinterested and objective in its dealings with clients and the law is sought to be promoted by the various aspects of professional training and control by a governing body. The All-India Bar and Bar Councils (in States), as also the Advocates' Act, 1961 seek to regulate professional conduct by laying down norms for the practice of law and protection f their rights, interests and privileges. The Bar Council of India and those in the State are responsible for the maintenance of standards in legal education. Such an "instrumental collectivism", typified by the Bar Councils, has essentially meant that the legal profession directs its main efforts towards winning a greater share of resources for its members. This is done not by challenging the existing framework of the legal system but by working within this framework.

The organized nature of the legal profession has meant the increasing strangehold of lawyers on the legal system. The concentration of work in the hands of a few senior lawyers, the substantial influence that lawyers, especially the senior ones, wield over the Bench and the court room bureaucracy, their forensic habits, and the various "unwholesome practices" indulged in during the process of trial, all contribute to the work-load and arrears in our courts.[29] The fact is that, as Baxi comments : "the existing rules of the game seem to allow far greater leverage to lawyers than to judges".[30]

The strangehold of lawyers on the legal system has accentuated the pernicious consequences that stem from the relationship between law and the class-structure of a society. That is to say, although normatively the law is the same for all citizens of India "in practice, the incidence of enforcement of rights and liabilities varies depending on the location of persons involved in the socio-economic structure."[31]

This class system of justice rests very largely on "differences in the availability and quality of legal representation."[32]

It is indeed paradoxical that the legal system requires the services of trained lawyers for its effective use and at the same time prices such services beyond the means of a large number of individuals. Not only is the use of lawyers less prevalent among lower than upper classes, but also lawyers representing persons from the lower class tend to be the least competent, in terms of their technical skill, members of the bar and invariably take advantage of their clients. Further, the competence (legal and otherwise) displayed by a lawyer in handling matters for his client is in direct consequence of the fee. Given this state of affairs, it is difficult to escape the conclusion that it is the values of a limited clientele with characteristic proprietory interests which the legal profession promotes. Of course, other interests (of the indigent and the oppressed) may be articulated on the legal system, but cannot hold away over the rich and the powerful. Such a class system of justice has been evocatively captured by Shourie :

> "Observe how many of these fellows (the powerful and the rich) get the *Hyderabadi goli.* Observe how they get anticipatory bail for the asking. Observe, once the cases start, the innumerable clauses and sub-clauses, these fellows are able to invoke in their favour. And contrast all this with the helplessness of the simple tribal who is dispossessed of his land by *sahukar* from the plains, who retreats in the forest and clears some land to keep himself from starving, and who is then arrested for violating the Forest Act.
>
> Contrast the clauses that come to their aid with the helplessness of those who have been languishing in jails for seven years as under-trial prisoners.
>
> Contrast the way in which the law works for them with the way it works for those who, having been acquitted on the charge of having committed a crime, are now facing trial for conspiring to commit the crime for which they have been acquitted.
>
> And while you are at it, count the numbers of landlords in our vast country who have been sentenced for not paying minimum wages or for exacting a higher-than-legal share of the crop from their tenants.
>
> What does all this tell us about the judiciary, about the legal system ? Is he not right then who tells us that 'Law is nothing but the convenience of the powerful'. (And incidentally the one who said this was not Man nor some roving Naxalite, but Gandhi)."[33]

Contributing significantly to all these obnoxious developments have been the lawyers.

In recent times, there have been definite efforts on the part of both the government and the legal profession to bring "law and lawyers to the people". The objective is to ensure that "the poor" have access to the legal apparatus to the same extent as "the rich". It is in this context that we hear of legal aid, public interest litigation, etc. Essentially these developments have had the effect of compounding the domination of the law over the people. Concomitantly, we have the process pushing us towards a litigious society. This also creates the pressure to abandon extra-legal methods of dispute settlement in favour of legal ones, which only goes to meet the vested interests of lawyers.[34] Under such conditions, professional proliferation is inevitable. A recent estimate places the number of lawyers at 2,28,000 approximately 336 for each million people, a ratio far larger than in other Third World countries.[35] This suggests something of the litigation orientation of our society or, for that matter, the overbearing influence of law over the people, which, to a large extent, is channelized through the lawyer. More importantly, this whole attempt at bringing "law and lawyers to the people" raises a larger substantive issue—even if there is a growth of legal aid schemes and public interest litigation for the benefit of the people, can law really be liberative for the disadvantaged ? This issue, however, is beyond the scope of this paper.

Despite the stratification of lawyers on the basis of income and prestige, lawyers share a common legal culture, which they put into the service of a wide variety of interests.[36] This is clearly manifested not only in the widespread ritualism in legal proceedings, characterized by Gadbois as one of "procedural nitpicking", "hair splitting legalism", "literal interpretation", "narrow, technical and mechanical",[37] expressing "concern for form, not for policy or substance"[38] but also in the strong material incentives and calculative strategies employed by lawyers, the impassivity of clients vis-a-vis their lawyers and the creation of patron-client networks among lawyers and litigants.[39]

It must be maintained that this common legal culture is chiefly shaped by the system of professional-client relations, which involve a high degree of client dependence on lawyers. The complex procedures involved in the legal process, the plethora of legislations as also their ambiguous and technical character and the prescription that only those who are trained are eligible to practise, the profession reinforces an atmosphere of dependency on the lawyers. The pattern of behaviour lawyers exhibit, the decisions they make, the advice they tender—all these critically influence the lives of the people they "process." People are at the mercy who are supposed to know the jargon. In fact, it would not be wrong to assert that what courts do depends largely on the kinds of arguments that lawyers make. Under such conditions, it is understandable that lawyers have come to have a vested "pecuniary" interest in the retention of archaic and formalistic features.

Thus, in the final analysis, the legal profession in India continues to be so organized as to retain its hold over the legal system.

How do these facts of the legal profession in India, reconcile with the larger framework of theoretical knowledge about professions ?

Most scholars in the study of professions, for instance Greenwood, Goode, Barber, Wilensky and others, have relied on two basic ideas to express the essence of a profession.[40] First, a profession is characterised by its autonomy which, it is emphasised, is attained through the establishment of a professional body. The specification of a set recruitment procedure and the norms of professional practice in terms of a code of ethics are considered a part of this process of maintaining "professional" autonomy. Second, it is stressed that a profession incorporates "such values as personal service, a dislike of competition, advertising and profit, a belief in the principle of payment in order to work rather than working for pay and in the superiority of the motive of service."[41] In short a profession is characterized by a "collectivity orientation."

In the context of the analysis made above, the legal profession in India militates against this conception of a profession as a united and autonomous body of experts, maintaining proficiency over their sphere of competence and characterized by a spirit of altruistic service. Neither autonomy nor a collectivity orientation are characteristic of the legal profession in India. Rather than being guardians of the law for the benefit of all, lawyers have increasingly become accomplices in the service of capital. In subjecting itself to the pressure of a powerful clientele, the legal profession has mortgaged its autonomy and self-control. Facilitating such a development has been the colonial legal system, which to a great extent, expresses the hegemony of lawyers and whose expensive and dilatory character has accentuated the sectional bias that the legal profession has fallen a prey to.

Thus, the practice of law as a profession must be seen not in terms of a set of ideal typical attributes, as many have done, but in terms of an assessment of the existential social conditions under which the practice of law is carried on. The deeply functionalist underpinnings of much theorisation in the sociology of professions obfuscates the true role played by professions, in this instance the legal profession in society. As Derrett pithily observes :

> "In so far as they (lawyers) subserve the interests of litigants they are in large part parasitic. In so far as they uphold the machinery of the State (without which they would have little employment), they are servants of the polity."[42]

Such an evaluation divests the professionals of their autonomy and service orientation. In fact, the legal profession could be viewed as "disabling" agents of laymen[43] and "enabling" agents of entrenched vested interests

In conclusion, it may be said that lawyers in India form a collectivity pursuing definite interests, the achievement of which presumes the retention of the existing legal system. The absence and failure of movements to restore systems of community-oriented justice, best described as "Nyaya Panchayats," in post-Independent India in spite of widespread dissatisfaction with the prevailing legal system could be explained in terms of the low level of commitment of lawyers to such a change. To effect a change of the system would mean placing an obstacle in their attempts to define their own ends and means. The legal profession in India, as in other capitalist societies, is marked by a highly "practical" orientation to law. This orientation has been associated with an instrumentalism in the utilization of professional skills and extra-legal tactics to advance specific interests, and thereby secure their own.

In the context of what has been analysed above, it is fit to conclude with the observations of the Krishna Iyer Committee (1973) "the legal profession in India ... enjoys a near monopolistic power"[44] and permits no equalisation of the bargaining power between the consumers of legal services and the closed group of the legal profession." The committee noted that the legal profession is merely an aspect of "the capitalistic society," where the "greatness of lawyer is measured by the amount of the fees, he charges and not by the quantum of social service which he renders as a lawyer."

NOTES AND REFERENCES

1. Galanter, Marc, "The Aborted Restoration of Indigenous Law in India," *Comparative Studies in Society and History*, vol. 14, 1972, pp. 53-70.
2. Seal, Anil, *The Emergence of Indian Nationalism*, Cambridge University Press, Cambridge, 1970.
3. *Ibid*, pp. 123-129.
4. Morris Jones, W.H., *The Government and Politics of India*, Hutchinson and Co., London, 1971, p 43.
5. M. Cully B.T., *English Education and the Origins of Indian Nationalism*, Columbia University Press, 1948, p. 191.
6. Misra, B.B., *The Indian Political Parties*, Oxford University Press, New Delhi, 1976, p. 39.
7. Kochanek, S.A., *The Congress Party of India*, Princeton University Press, New Jersey, 1968, p. 324.
8. *Ibid*, p. 358.
9. Desai, A.R., *Social Background of Indian Nationalism*, Popular Prakashan, Bombay, 1976, pp. 196-200.
10. Galanter, 1972, *op. cit.*
11. Morris-Jones, 1971, op. cit., p. 42.
12. Gandhi, M.K., *The Law, and the Lawyers*, Navajeevan Publishing House, Ahmedabad, 1962.
13. Misra, B.B., *The Indian Middle Classes*, Oxford University Press, New Delhi, 1961; Rudolph, L.I., and Susanns Hoeber, Rudolph, *The Modernity of Tradition: Political Development in India*, University of Chicago Press, Chicago, 1967,

14. Austin, G., *The Indian Constitution: Cornerstone of a Nation*, Clarendon Press, Oxford, 1966.
15. Galanter, *op. cit.* 1972, p. 55.
16. Austin, 1966, *op. cit.*, pp. 18-19.
17. Austin, *op. cit.*, p. 164.
18. Derrett, J.D.M., "Lawyers as Leaders", Pandey, B.N. (ed.), *Leadership in South-Asia*, Vikas, New Delhi, 1977, pp. 55-72.
19. Baxi, Upendra, *The Crisis of Indian Legal System*, Vikas, New Delhi, 1982.
20. *Ibid*, pp. 58-83.
21. Galanter, 1972, *op. cit.*, pp. 56-57.
22. Galanter, 1972, p. 56.
23. Oommen, T.K., "The Legal Profession in India: Some Sociological Perspective", *Indian Bar Review*, vol. 10, no. 1., 1983, p. 5.
24. Aurora, S.K., "Social Backgcound of the Indian Cabinet", *Economic and Political Weekly*, vol. 7, nos. 31-33, 1972, pp. 1523-32.
25. Oommen, *op. cit.*
26. Gandhi, *op. cit.*, pp. 126-127.
27. Sharma, K.L., *Sociology of Law and Legal Profession*, Publications, Rawat, Jaipur, 1984, p. 154.
28. Gandhi, *op. cit*, p. 124.
29. Baxi, *op. cit.*, pp. 70-77.
30. Baxi, *op. cit.*, p. 70.
31. Baxi, *op. cit.*, p. 4.
32. Carlin, J.E., and Howard Jan, "Legal Representation and Class Justice", Aubert, Vilhelm, (ed.). *Sociology of Law*, Penguin, Harmondsworth, 1969, pp. 332-350.
33. Shourie, A., *Symptoms of Fascism*, Vikas, New Delhi, 1978 pp. 210-211.
34. Bankowski Zenon, and Goeff Mungham, *Images of Law*, Routledge and Kegan Paul, London, 1976.
35. Galanter, Marc *Competing Equalities : Law and Backward Classes in India*,Oxford University Press, New Delhi, 1984, p. 514.
36. Oommen, *op. cit.*
37. Gadbois, George, H. Jr., *The Emergency, Mrs. Gandhi, the Judiciary and the Legal Culture*, Mimeographed, 1977.
38. Galanter, 1984, p. 484,
39. Baxi, *op. cit*.; Gandhi, J.S., *Lawyers and Touts : A Study in the Sociology of Legal Profession*, Hindustan Publishing Corporation, 1982 ; Sharma, *op. cit.*

40. Goode, Williaim J., "Community within a Community : The Professions", *American Sociological Review*, vol. 23, no. 1, 1957 ; Greenwood, E. "Attributes of a Profession", *Social Work*, vol. 11, No. 3, 1957 ; Barber, B., "Some Problems in the Sociology of Professions" *Daedulus*, vol. 92, no. 1963 ; Wilensky, Horold L., "The Professionalisation of Everyone ?", *The American Journal of Sociology*, vol. LXX, no. 2, 1964.
41. Elliot, P., *The Sociology of the Professions*, Macmillan, London, 1972 ; Watson, Hony. J., *Sociology, Work and Industry*, Routledge and Kegan Paul, London, 1980.
42. Derrett, *op. cit.*, p. 78.
43. Illich, Ivan, *et al.*, *Disabling Professions*, Marion Boyars, London, 1977.
44. Krishna Iyer Committee, *Processual Justice to People*, 1973.

24

COLONIAL LEGACY AND CLASS NATURE OF THE LEGAL PROFESSION IN INDIA

N. JAYARAM

Professionalization of an occupational category and the consequent appropriation of power, privileges and fortunes by its members do not occur in a socio-historical vacuum. In the west, the development of the legal profession was shaped by the emerging capitalistic socio-economic formation. Over a period of time the practitioners of law acquired a virtual monopoly over knowledge and procedures associated with the administration of justice, which were appropriate to certain social needs. Nurtured by the ideology of liberalism, the profession attained operational autonomy and social exclusivity.

In India the legal profession was implanted through the constitution of courts and legislative enactments by the British. The process which had begun by the time, the East India Company made over to the Crown in 1858 accelerated in the 1880s. Till around the first quarter of this century law was "by far the most important" of the emergent professions. The phenomenal growth of the profession in India, unlike in the West, was associated with "educational, judicial and administrative developments" rather than with "technological and industrial progress."[1] Given socio-economic background from which the lawyers and their clients were drawn, the types of issues that the profession had to deal with and the structure and culture of the legal system within which they had to function, the legal profession essentially developed class-characteristics.

By the time India attained Independence, the anglicization

of the legal profession in the country had been complete. The new values derived from the liberal polity and the capitalist economy of the West were internalized by the minuscule minority of the English-educated Indians in general and the practitioners of the various professions in particular. Not surprisingly, it is the English-educated Indians, and particularly the legal professionals, who become the protogonists, nay, the self-appointed sentinels of the inherited legal system.

That the inherited legal system is confronted by a crisis is now being increasingly acknowledged. Baxi has analysed the nature, dimensions and magnitude of this crisis.[2] Of the several elements identified by him, the legal profession is one. However, no one has so far attempted an in-depth study of the contribution of the legal profession to this crisis.

This paper analyses the colonial legacy and class nature of the legal profession, and from that vantage point, it examines the crisis in the legal system. Part one outlines the origin and development of the legal profession in the colonial era; part two examines the present state of the profession *vis-a-vis* the crisis confronting the legal system ; and, part three ties up the main observations.

The earliest courts were established by the British in India to keep peace among the servants of the East India Company in the presidency towns. Gradually, the territorial jurisdiction of these courts was expanded to include residents of these towns and then of the districts. With a view to reorganize the district administration, which had broken down with the decline of the central authority of the Mughal Empire, the British Government, under the Governor-Generalship of Warren Hastings, replaced the Indian courts administered by the Muslim agents of the Emperor with British courts. Gradually, this British legal system embarked on a phase of expansion and systematization.

At the time of Hastings' reorganization of the district administration, the native 'lawyer' was called vakil (*waqil*).[3] According to Misra, the term vakil did not signify any specific profession, nor was there a separate class of legal practitioners under this name :

"It was a generic term employed in the sense of an

> agent or ambassador who represented his principle for varied purposes. A zamindar, for exmple, would send his vakil to an officer of Government to account for an arrear of revenue or miscellaneous acts of commission and omission. A country Government might likewise appoint a vakil to deputize for it in the court of another ruler or sovereign. The person who represented a party in court was also called a vakil."[4]

Representing clients in a court for a fee, the vakils soon learnt the art of protracting litigation.

The Judicial Code of 1781 drawn up by Elijah Impey, the then Chief Justice of the Supreme Court at Calcutta, brought the district courts under the control and direction of the *S dar Diwani Adalat*—the high court established by Hastings at Calcutta. This involved "defining in some detail their respective duties and powers" and "drawing up precise rules governing the mode of procedure and adjudication, record keeping and process serving."[5] The growing complexity of the legal system rendered it more and more difficult for plaintiffs and defendants to plead their own cause. They were consequently constrained to engage vakils who knew the laws and the rules of justice-administration.

> "Thus, Impey could be said to have laid the foundation for the practice of law to grow into a profession which required a mastery not only of the increasing bulk and variety of legislative enactments, but also of the subtle techniques which courts were called upon to follow under rules."[6]

With the object of making the pleading of causes a distinct profession, the Regulation VII of 1793 "vested the *Sadar Diwani Adalat* with exclusive powers to appoint pleaders, for themselves as well as for the provincial and district courts."[7]

In course of time, the system of registering the practitioners in the Company's courts came into being. Those seeking such registration were required to acquire certain professional qualifications (which among others included a knowledge of Persian, which was the court language, Hindu and Muslim law, and the regulations enacted by the Governor-General in Council). In 1835 the Government under Bentinck accepted in principle the study of law as a separate faculty, and regular courses in law came to be offered from 1855.

The above Regulation introduced the principle of free contract in the pleader-client relationship. The client was free to select a pleader whom he trusted most, by giving him a retaining fee along with a *vakalatnama*. He could change his pleader at any time before the passing of judgement. The fees payable to the pleader after the passing of the judgment were also prescribed.[8] Any breach of such a contract was punishable by the court.

The foregoing developments in the legal profession were essentially the outcome of changes in the administration introduced by the British. But the *primum mobile* for the professionalization of legal practitioners was the importation of the institution of private property in land. In pre-British India, there was no private ownership in land. The new revenue system introduced by the British "superseded the traditional right of the village community over the village land and created two forms of property in land" and a legally protected land-holding class.[9] By introducing the Permanent Land Settlement for Bengal, Bihar and Orissa in 1793, Cornwallis created Zamindari landlordism. By initiating the Ryotwari system for Madras in 1820, Thomas Munro created the individual peasant proprietorship. As a form of private property, land became a commodity with realizable value in the market. It could be sold and purchased or mortgaged or partitioned. This necessitated the proper registration of title, by precise and legally enforceable definitions.

Another addition to the legal system was the "will" through which property could be transferred by choice. Wills became effective in Bengal in 1792, in Bombay since 1860 and in Madras since 1862. A general set of rights and requirements were established by the Hindu Wills Act of 1870. The introduction of wills freed "the individual from the tradition corporate group."[10]

By 1875, creditors and owners respectively were permitted to bring to sale debtors' or their own interest in their families' property. Contract became a legal institution and this meant that private claim of property could be validated only in a court of law through judicial decision.[11]

As a logical corollary of the institution of private property in land, the British also brought about changes in revenue and rent-laws. These in turn revolutionized social relationships and considerably weakened the stability of the traditional society. The Regulation of 1793 authorized authorities to sell the farms and estates of owners who failed to meet the annual revenue demand. Land became "saleable collateral." The unreasonable assessments imposed by utilitarian enthusiasts and the unbending rigour with which revenue laws were enforced compounded the effect of such laws.[12] According to Rudolph, there was an increasing speculation in land and those "with inside knowledge of revenue arrears and low assessment took advantage of forced sales."[13] Turnover in land increased rapidly. They quote Bernard Cohn's study of the Benares region where about forty per cent of the land had changed hands by mid-nineteenth century.

There was another crucial development. "In his anxiety to effect the security of property, Cornwallis "divested revenue authorities of all their judicial functions, and recognized the right of private individuals to sue Government or its officers for any act of infringement."[14] As a consequence there was an enormous increase in litigation. On the one hand, this brightened the prospects in the legal profession and attracted more and more people to join it. On the other, the fact that the Government could be sued, necessitated appointment of government pleaders to conduct public suits. The government pleaders, who were appointed by the Governor-General in Council (*vide* Regulation VII of 1793) "were at liberty to engage in any suit except on behalf of the opposite party in suits against the Government."[15]

If Impey's Code had laid the foundation for the practice of law to grow into a profession, Cornwallis' Code produced a boom in that profession. Its numbers rose steadily. "By the later nineteenth century, there were almost 14,000 persons returned as belonging to the profession in the three Presidencies." In Calcutta alone more than 1,500 law graduates qualified by 1888, and "already by 1882 more than 500 graduates had entered the profession to take up private practice."

The phenomenal growth in the legal profession was due to the growing volume and complexity of laws and regulations as also to the increase in litigations consequent upon changes in laws relating to land ownership, revenue and rent.[17] Between 1856, and 1866 the number of civil suits in India almost trebled from 730,000 to 1,908,869.[18] The number steadily increased until the turn of the century.

Available evidence indicates that the incidence of litigation was more in Zamindari tenure areas, especially in the permanently settled areas as in Bengal, than elsewhere.[19] According to Misra "the Zamindars as a class served to feed the courts, and the rent laws designed to protect tenancy rights brought the tenants to contest cases."[20] Based on Statistical Abstracts from 1879-80 to 1901-02, he observes :

> "the total number of original and appellate civil suits there (i.e., in Bengal) amounted to 0.5 million out of 1.6 million for the whole of British India (in 1881). The total value of the suits was Rs. 16.54 crores for British India, of which Rs. 5.18 crores, or nearly a third again, came from Bengal. The number of civil suits in India increased to 2.2 million in 1901, and their value to Rs. 28.71 crores... Bengal's share was nearly one-third of the number of suits and 38 per cent of their value. Together with the United Provinces, Bengal claimed 1.2 million of the total number of suits."

Along with the proliferation of the profession, its status also enhanced. Many lawyers had obtained English education and legal training :

> "From the 1860s a few Indians had qualified as barristers-at-law of the Inns of Court, and they joined the first generation of graduates from the Indian universities in an assault upon the European monopoly of advocacy in the high courts. By 1886 Indians had succeeded in getting a large share of this practice in Bombay and Calcutta, and to a lesser extent in Madras."

Further, "all seven of the Indians who entered the covenanted service between 1871 and 1876 were barristers-at-law," and all excepting one "made their careers on the judicial side."

> "By 1888 there was at least one Indian judge at each of the high courts ; with hardly an exception, the subordinate judges and magistrates were Indians; nine-tenths of the original civil suits as well as three-quarters of the magisterial business of the courts of India came before Indian judges and magistrates."[21]

With a rise in the status of the legal profession, there was also a rise in the income of the professionals. It is found that during 1888-91, on an average 4,713 legal practitioners were earning incomes between Rs. 500 and Rs. 2,000 per annum and 1,181 Rs. 2,000 and over.[22] What a leading Indian lawyer could earn is revealed by the fact that during 1868-90 Badruddin Tayyabji of Bombay earned on an average Rs. 39,898 per annum.[23] Compared to the pittance earned by their brethren in government service, the income of even the less successful lawyers was handsome.

The phenomenal growth of the profession in due course outstripped the demand for its services. In about the last five decades of the nineteenth century the output of law graduates increased by eight times. This increase was far more than the increase in the number of civil suits. The resulting recession in the profession was contained by raising the qualifications for entry into it. Those who possessed the 'high' qualifications came to view themselves more and more as a distinctive social group. To safeguard their interests and protect their privileges, they organized themselves into professional associations.

The crucial position of the legal profession within the colonial system, the exalted status of its members and the strength of their associations yielded quick returns in terms of political power and popular influence. Not having to be, by and large, dependent on the goodwill of the colonial employer, the legal professionals entered national politics in the later nineteenth century. As a single professional group, lawyers predominated in the provincial legislative councils so much that the British characterized the provincial governments as "vakil raj".[24]

It is not surprising that lawyers came to the fore-front of the national movement. The emerging national bourgeoisie, the Indian National Congress, drew its rank and flle substantively from the legal profession. A confidential report of the Chief Secretary to the Government of Bengal, dated 18th July, 1899, showed that "the principal subscribers of the Congress now are the members of the legal profession and their clients."[25] "Over half the delegates at the first Congress were lawyers, and for decades to come more than a third of the delegates at every Congress belonged to that profession."[26]

It must be noted that the participation of lawyers in the national movement was not in their capacity as professionals. In fact, as far as their professional role was concerned, by practicing in the colonial courts, they confirmed British authority and facilitated British rule. Gandhiji rightly attacked the Indian lawyers for enslaving their countrymen by co-operating with the British legal system.[27] However, the fact that the leaders of the national movement *belonged* to the bourgeoise oriented legal profession cannot be wished away. That the proprietory interests were predominant in the Congress is confirmed by its opposition to tenant-rights and support of indigenous capitalism.[28]

In brief, the growth and development of the legal profession in modern India has been essentially shaped by the institution of private property and the rent and revenue laws enacted by the British It is essentially linked to property-disputes and individual rights rather than social compulsions. The legal system implanted by the British only suited the emerging capitalist economy and bourgeoise syndrome.

In this context, two aspects of the legal system deserve special mention. First, the stamp-duty on the institution of suits. This was partly intended to bring revenue to the public exchequer and partly also to discourage irresponsible litigation. "Unfortunately, by discriminating against the poor, it also discouraged responsible litigation."[29] Second, the practice of determining the jurisdiction of courts in civil cases based on a monetary qualification. These necessitated the services of lawyers, and thus, tilted the scales of justice in favour of the rich. These aspects of the legal system, along with the other developments discussed above, shifted the emphasis from justice *per se* to the administration of justice.

The class nature of the system coalesced with the class nature of the profession with the passing of Act I of 1846 which superseded the old rule of pleader's fees being regulated by law. It declared that the pleaders "shall be at liberty to settle with the parties by private agreement the remuneration to be paid for their professional services, and that it shall not be necessary to specify such agreement in the *vakalatnama*."[30] Thus, the operation of free trade in the practice of law necessarily made the legal system an institution of the rich, by the rich and for the rich.

The dawn of Independene offered an excellent opportunity to break the colonial fetters of the implanted institutions. But the political elite which took over the destiny of the country, characterized as it was by bourgeois interests and colonial hangover, could not fulfil this historical task. Instead of evolving a new legal system suited to the aspirations and aims of a new India, the legal system implanted and developed by the colonial masters was preserved intact and endorsed by the republican constitution of India.[31] In fact, "new powers (were) granted to the judiciary and its independence enhanced by elaborate protections''[32].

With the growth of the inherited legal system its defects got multiplied and magnified, and it is now confronted by a crisis. One important aspect of this crisis has to do with access to law. Access to law, in its broader and socially relevant connotation means "access to law-makers, to dispensers of legal services (legal profession) and to normative and to institutional information concerning the legal system." In all these aspects, the inherited legal system, Baxi observes after a detailed examination, "is based on rather clear violations of democratic legality."[33] The problem of accessibility of law is most grave among the rural people and among the under-privileged and vulnerable sections of society.

The second aspect of the crisis, which may eventually cause a breakdown of the system, is the over-loading of courts, familiarly known as the problems of delay and arrears. It is estimated that in June 1978 there were as many as 600,000 cases pending before the High Courts and the Supreme Court. As on 1st April, 1982, 14,061 cases in High Courts and 2,045 cases in the Supreme Court were pending for over a decade. "If this is the rate of pendency in the appellate courts, it is obvious that millions of cases would be pending before trial courts, in both civil and criminal jurisdiction."[34]

It is not that the lawyers and judges were not aware of the glaring defects of the system that was being inherited. To be sure, there was a lot of discussion on the need for a reform of the legal system. But they felt that these defects were not attributable to the alien nature of the system. As widely acclaimed, fourteenth report of the Law Commission of India put it: "the oft-repeated assertion that the present system is alien to our genius" is unsound. It even hazarded the view that "had the ancient system been allowed to develop normally, it would have assumed a form not very much different from the one that we follow today."[35]

In fact, the inherited system was viewed by the profession as the "most beneficient result of the British connection." In his essay, "Re-organisation of the Legal Profession in India," which was awarded the Gold Medal at the Sixth Session of the Madras State Lawyers' Conference in Coimbatore in 1950, Ramachandran wrote, "if at all we are beholden to anything British, it is their system of justice and jurisprudence, that have taken an abiding and glorious place in the life of our country."[36]

It is not as though the professionals have been powerless to bring about a change in the legal system. Their political clout has been throughout significant. The Constituent Assembly (1947-49) contained many lawyers, all of them of course trained in the British tradition of law. Of the twenty-one "most important figures" in this Assembly identified by Austin (1972 : 337-53, Appendix III) thirteen were members of the legal profession.[37] Sixty-two per cent of the members in Jawaharlal Nehru's cabinet and sixty-five per cent in Lal Bahadur Shastri's cabinet were lawyers. On an average sixty-three per cent of the ministers in the first three cabinets of Indira Gandhi had law degrees. Considering the Council of Ministers as a whole, at no point of time was the percentage of law graduates less than forty-two, and occasionally it went up to fifty-one[38].

In 1977, thirty-five per cent of the cabinet ministers had law degrees and by 1982 their percentage shot up to an all time high, seventy-four per cent. In 1982, forty-eight per cent of the Council of Ministers as a whole were law graduates. "The lawyers seem to have a near monopoly in the central ministry" observes Oommen. Based on *Who is Who in Lok Sabha* published by the Lok Sabha Secretariat, he has worked out the representation of law graduates in the seven Lok Sabhas and found that "at no point it went below twenty-five per cent and in 1977-80 it increased to an all time high with thirty-four per cent."[39]

Apparently this complacence of the profession with the inherited system is due to their confusing what is familiar with what is necessary. Being thoroughly committed to the existing system, it was difficult for the legal profession to visualize any alternative. The shortcomings of the existing system "were seen as remediable defects and blemishes, not as basic flaws which required fundamental change".[40] But it is also true that these professionals have a considerable personal stake in the continuation of the legal system in its present form.

It is not surprising that right from the Constituent Assembly days the professionals have opposed the revival of a quick, cheap and efficient panchayat justice in rural areas.[41] The move to amend Article 226 of the Constitution to limit the writ jurisdiction of High Courts (irrespective of the motive of the Government) during the emergency period (1975-76) had to be modified because of an organized resistence by the profession.

It is officially conceded that the Bar, which is the fount of judicial appointees has shown "noticeable reluctance in supplying its leaders as judges".[27] It is disconcerting to note that the profession has not manifested any organized concern for the delays in judicial appointments. We are yet to hear of a strike, or even a threat of any kind, by lawyers protesting against the unpardonable delay in the appointment of judges.

Lawyers themselves are also held to be responsible for the

delay in the judicial process and the mounting arrears of cases in courts. Concentration of cases in the hands of a few senior or well-known practitioners, their forensic habits, and the wanton holding-up of cases through manipulation all contribute to the over-loading of courts.

The stranglehold of lawyers on the legal system is witnessed in other ways also. The Justice J.C. Shah Committee Report on Arrears in High Courts reveals the mighty influence that the senior Bar exerts on the High Court judges. "The existing rules of the game seem to allow far greater leverage to lawyers than to judges." The domination of the Bar over the Bench subverts both the letter and spirit of law.[43]

Any attempt at making the Bar more amenable to judicial control is sure to be cried down as an affront to its autonomy. The warth incurred by Chief Justice Satish Chandra of the Allahabad High Court in attempting to bring about some changes in court-management is a case in point.[44] In view of all this, Baxi is legitimate in observing that "the conception of lawyer as an 'officer of the court aiding it in impartial dispensation of justice seems...to have more or less disappeared from India."[45]

The "legal services market" in India is "essentially a sellers market" where the demand for services is "backed by purchasing power".[46] That the legal profession enjoys a near monopolistic power in such a market has pernicious implications. Professional services are very costly and consequently the judicial process is hardly accessible to the common man. The pace at which the minimal litigation-oriented legal needs of the indigent are met makes one wonder whether justice will ever be meted out to them ; This problem has not caused as much concern to the Bar as has the surpersession of judges.

In the light of all this, it should not be surprising that the legal profession in India has not evolved a tradition of scholarship as has its counter-part in the West. In India, as the Report of the University Education (Radhakrishnan) Commission, 1948-49 has stated :

> "We have many eminent practitioners and excellent judges. The law has also given us great leaders and men

> consecrated to public service. (But) we have no internationally known expounders of jurisprudence and legal studies. Our colleges of law do not hold a place of high esteem either at home or abroad, nor has law become an area of profound scholarship and enlightened research."[47]

This observation, which is as true today as it was in 1948-49 when it was made, is a sad commentary on the Anglo-American orientation of our legal profession and its intellectual dependence on the West. It is indeed ironical that in their defence of the inherited system, the professionals in India quite often resort to arguments which are similar to those advanced by the British for implanting the system in India.

Before concluding this section, we shall briefly analyse the strength and social background of the legal profession in recent times. India has the "second biggest body of legal practitioners in the world." In 1971, there were 147,662 legal practitioners of which 5,943 were judges and magistrates, 90,906 were lawyers and advisors 5,695 were legal assistants, and 45,118 were jurists and legal technicians (including petition writers). This worked out to an average of 270 practitioners per million population.[48]

An overwhelming majority of lawyers and advisors (89.7%) as also judges and magistrates (eighty-seven %), and a substantial majority of jurists and legal technicians (67.5%) are practicing in urban areas. Moreover, 47.3% of legal assistants are also practising in urban areas. This reveals the pre-dominantly urban base of the legal profession.[49]

Studies on the socio-economic background of the legal professionals, whose significance can hardly be exaggerated, are surprisingly few. The available studies focus only on lawyers practising in district courts. They, however, are unanimous in their finding that the profession is, by and large, monopolized by the male members of the twice-born or locally dominant caste groups and the upper or middle socio-economic status brackets in urban areas.[50]

Of course, the doors of the profession are theoretically open to all, and the fifteen-fold expansion of law colleges in the three decades since Independence has made it increasingly accessible.[51] However, the inadequate professionalization of law education imposes constraints even for those obtaining the law degrees. This is especially so in view of the fact that mostly the professionals have to depend on private practice.

The professional success of a law graduate, as Oommen has observed entails certain pre-requisites. These among others include : (*i*) a prolonged period of apprenticeship during which the novitiate is dependent on his family for economic sustenance, (*ii*) the investment of capital for the setting-up of office, library and so on, and (*iii*) the crucial network resources, i.e., kin, castemen or close acquaintance among practitioners, judges, etc.[52] It is extremely difficult for the economically poor and socially backward sections of society to meet these requirements. The policy of protective discrimination can hardly provide any meaningful succour to them in this regard. In brief, the theoretically open doors of the legal profession remain practically closed for most of the aspirants.

This should not, however, suggest that the legal profession constitutes a homogenous and well-knit group. Till about a decade and a half after Independence, lawyers were categorized into six grades, namely, advocates, attorneys and vakils practising at the high courts, and pleaders, mukhtiars and revenue agents practising at the district courts. Based on the recommendation of the Law Commission (1958), the Advocates Act, 1961, abolished this gradation. The Act provided for the enrolment of law graduates with a Bar Council so as to enable them to practise throughout the country. Notwithstanding the abolition of the formal gradation, the Indian lawyers are substantially stratified informally. They can be arranged in a hierarchy by the level of their practice, the degree of their specialization and the background of their clients.

Such a stratification under conditions of free market in legal service has two consequences. First, a small section of senior and renowned lawyers, corner much of the cake of legal practice, and the vast majority of the practitioners get only crumbs.[53] The minority of "successful" lawyers besides earning a substantial income, are embellished with esteem and are in the ante-chambers of power. The majority of the indigent lawyers are forced to seek their clients and have to depend on touts.[54]

Second, there exists a client-specific differentiation of lawyers.[55] There is the rich man's lawyer who charges exhorbitant fees and the poor man's lawyer who has to accept even paltry sums as fees. The more serious implication of such a situation is a small section of professionals acting as the spokesmen of a small section of clients with characteristic proprietory interests and value-orientations. This is wrought with pernicious consequences in a society which places its members theoretically equal before law but where access to justice is unequal in practice.

The legal system in modern India was implanted by the British as a part of a broader strategy to extend their hegemony over the country. The most fundamental change that the British brought about was the importation of the institution of private property in land. This, together with the changes in revenue and rent laws, led to several changes and set the society on the road to capitalism. The legal system which had to handle the resulting socio-economic situation was chiefly influenced by the liberal ideology of the West.

The legal practitioners who were initially assigned the modest function of representing clients grew into a profession. Their crucial position *vis-a-vis* the system, their exalted socio-economic status and their political power made them singularly influential. In an emerging capitalist system they defended the interests of the proprietory class, on whose interests their own position depended. That is, they developed as a constituent of the emergent capitalist system. At the same time they were also in the forefront of the struggle to free that system from the clutches of the colonial rulers.

After Independence, the political elite, of which the legal professionals have constituted a crucial part, took over and continues to remain in charge of the country's destiny, inheriting the legal system and the attendant profession as colonial legacies. The defects of this system, have, with the passage of time, assumed the proportions of a crisis. The profession, in its attempt to safeguard the system and the class which has a vested interest in the system, which it needs to protect its own interests, has moved away from the ideal type of a profession. The practitioners of law have got entangled in the crisis, in the creation and worsening of which they have played a significant role.

Expecting the profession to clean its foul nest is to ask for impossible. Attempting to reform it without changing the legal system itself is sure to fail. The initiative for effecting a radical change of the system cannot be expected from a ruling class whose interest it primarily serves. One is reminded in this context of the founder of the sociology of law, Ehrlich, who said: "at present as well as any other time the centre of gravity of legal development lies not in legislation, not in juristic science, not in judicial decision, but in society itself."[56]

As long as the present basic contradictions in society remain untackled, the crisis in the legal system would remain untouched. The time may not be far off when the entire edifice comes down. And, if it does, it will not really matter to the poor and the oppressed, who have remained unserved by it. Nay, it may even better for them if "the convenience of the powerful," as Mahatma Gandhi called the legal system, withers. But how will the profession and the proprietory class react ?

NOTES AND REFERENCES

1. Misra, B.B., *The Indian Middle Classes : Their Growth in Modern Times*, Oxford University Press, New Delhi, 1961.
2. Baxi, U., *The Crisis of the Indian Legal System*. Vikas Publishing House, New Delhi, 1982, pp. 1-40.
3. Another category of legal practitioners was the native law officers attached to the new courts established by the British. The *maulvies* (*qazis*, *muftis*) and *pandits* (*shastris*) acted respectively as the expositors of the classical texts and sacred law books of the Muslims and Hindus, and interpreted the law for the judges. With the assumption of full Judicial knowledge of Hindu and Muslim Law by the British Judges, this category was abolished in 1864.
4. Misra, pp. 162-163.
5. Misra, p. 166.
6. *Ibid*.

7. Misra, p. 167.
8. The Act I of 1846 superseded this as is clear from the last paragraph of Section I.
9. Desai, A.R., *Social Background of Indian Nationalism*, Popular Prakashan, Bombay, 1966, p. 38.
10. Rudolph, L.I., and S.H. Rudolph, *The Modernity of Tradition.* The University of Chicago Press, Chicago, 1967, p. 289.
11. Misra, p. 168.
12. Stokes, E., *The English Utilitarians and India*, Clarendon Press, Oxford, 1963, p. 81-139.
13. Rudolph and Rudolph, p. 290.
14. Misra, pp. 167-168.
15. *Ibid.*
16. Seal, A., *The Emergence of Indian Nationalism* : *Competition and Collaboration in the Later Nineteenth* Century, Cambridge University Press, Cambridge, 1968, pp. 123-124.
17. The incentive for the growth of the profession also came from the changes in the administration of criminal justice. Pleaders who were previously employed exclusively in the conduct of civil suits also took to criminal suits with the opening of criminal courts.
18. Seal, p. 124.
19. Naturally, the profession expanded fastest and the number of law graduates increased quickest here, Misra, 1961, p. 325 ; Seal, 1968‘ p. 125.
20. Misra, p. 325.
21. Seal, pp. 125-126.
22. Based on Seal, p. 129, Table 40.
23. Based on details available in Seal, pp. 128, foot note no. 2.
24. O'Malley, L.S.S. (ed.), *Modern India and the West*, Oxford University Press, London, 1941.
25. Quoted in Misra, p. 353.
26. "Of a total of 13,839 delegates who attended the Congress sessions between 1802 and 1909, 5,442 (or over thirty-nine per cent) were lawyers", Seal, 1968, p 278. footnote 1.
27. Gandhi, M.K., *The law and the lawyers*, Navajivan Publishing House, 1962, Ahmedabad.
28. Misra, pp. 355-357.
29. Edwards, M., *British India 1772-1947* : *a Survey of the Nature and Effects of Alien Rule*), Sidgwick and Jackson, London, p. 210.
30. Quoted in Misra, p. 173.

31. Austin, G., *The Indian Constitution : Cornerstone of a Nation.* Oxford University Press, Bombay, 1972.
32. Galanter M., "The Aborted Restoration of 'Indigenous' Law in India", *Comparative Studies in Society and History*, vol. 14, 1972, p. 55.
33. Baxi, p. 48.
34. Baxi, pp. 61-64.
35. Government of India, Ministry of Law : *Law Commission of India, Fourteenth Report* (Reform of Judicial, Administration), 2 volumes. Manager of Publications, New Delhi, 1958, p. 1030.
36. Ramchandran, V.C., Quoted in Galanter, pp. 5-7.
37. Austin, pp. 337-353, Appendix III.
38. Aurora, S.K., "Social Background of the Indian Cabinet," *Economic and Political Weekly*, vol. 7 no. 31-33, 1972, pp. 1523-32.
39. Oommen, T.K., "The Legal Profession in India : Some Sociological Perspectives", *Indian Bar Review*, vol. 10, no. 1, 1983, p. 5.
40. Galanter, p. 63.
41. Galanter, p. 58.
42. Baxi, p. 66.
43. Baxi, p. 70 and p. 75.
44. FN details, Baxi, pp. 70-74.
45. Baxi, p. 70.
46. Government of India, Ministry of Law, Justice and Company Affairs, *Processual Justice to the People*, Report of the Expert Committee on Legal Aid, Manager of Publications, New Delhi, 1973, pp. 183-184.
47. Government of India, Ministry of Education, *The Report of the University Education Commission*, December 1948—August 1949, Manager of Publications, Delhi, 1962;
48. Oommen, pp. 18-19.
49. *Ibid*, pp. 19-20.
50. Morrison, C., "Social Organization at the District Courts : Colleague Relationship among Indian Lawyers", *Law and Society Review*, vol. 3, no. 2, 1968-69, pp. 251-67; Rowe, P., "Indian Lawyers and Political Modernization : Observations in Four District Towns", *Law and* Society Review, vol. 3, no. 2, 1968-69, pp. 219-46; Kidder, R.L., "Formal Litigation and Professional Insecurity : Legal Entrepreneurship in South India, *Law and Society Review*, vol. 9, no. 1, 1974, pp. 11-37; Gandhi, J.S., *Lawyers and Courts : A Study in the Sociology of Legal Profession*, Hindustan Publishing Corporation, Delhi, 1982.
51. In 1951 there were nineteen law colleges with an enrolment of 13,649 students. In 1961 there were forty-four colleges with 32,000 students. And in 1978 there were 270 colleges with 200,000 students.

52. Oommen, p. 20.
53. One of J.S. interviewees has described the situation succinctly : while ten per cent of the top lawyers monopolized ninety per cent of the practice, the remaining ninety per cent lawyers scrambled for ten per cent of cases, Gandhi (1982 : 77).
54. Gandhi, J.S., 1982.
55. Oommen, p. 14-15.
56. Ehrlich, E., *Fundamental Principles of the Sociology of Law*, Harvard University Press, Cambridge, Mass, 1936.
57. M.K. Gandhi, Quoted in A. Shourie *Symptoms of Fascism*, Vikas Publishing House, New Delhi, 1978, p. 5.

25

LEGAL PROFESSION AND SOCIETY : A CASE STUDY OF LAWYERS AND THEIR CLIENTS

K.L. SHARMA

This paper is based on the findings of my research project—"Relations Between Lawyers and Their Clients" which was sponsored by the Indian Council of Social Science Research, New Delhi. The project was completed in 1981. The study was carried out at Jaipur, Capital of Rajasthan, (India). The study was confined to the lawyers of this city and their clients. Information regarding socialization, professionalization, stratification and networks of lawyers as well as clients was gathered initially through an enumeration schedule in case of lawyers and later on through two separate interview guides for lawyers and clients. Sources such as Census Reports, bar council library, legislative enactments, university law school library literature, some reports etc., were also tapped as supportive/base. In all, out of 420 lawyers of Jaipur city, 140 were interviewed and keeping in view the norm of "one client-one-lawyer," 125 clients were interviewed. The norm could not be met as only 125 clients were finally contacted. Depth interviews of some key informants were also conducted.

The questions explored in the study related to stratification within the bar, criteria of ranking, effect of clientele milieu on hierarchy among lawyers and strains affecting solidarity and performance. Recruitment to, the bar and training have been discussed in relation to lawyers' socialization and professional achievement. In fact, our emphasis in this study is basically on the structure and process of lawyers and clients in terms of their placement in society. Lawyers had contributed a lot to the emancipation of Indian masses from the British yoke, yet they have a colonial legacy. They are called "swindlers" and "sharks". Even today lawyers as a "community" are represented more than any other group in Parliament and State Legislatures; lawyers have a great deal of professional autonomy and they have also been guided by primordial and political constraints. Why have law firms not emerged (except in metropolitan centres) in India like the United States of America ? Is the lawyer in India "litigational," "individualistic," and not-so-professionals ?" Why is the lawyers in India not like a "social engineer" as he is in England ? With a view to investigate these and several other questions, role of caste, ruralurban background, parental heritage, family ties, law education etc. have been studied in detail.[1]

It goes without saying that sociology of legal profession is an inseparable part in reality of the sociology of law. Emphasis in sociology of law is on investigation of the operation of interests, passions and prejudices of lawyers, clients, judges, citizens, etc. Sociology of law deals with the relationship between law and society in terms of social background of the members and groups in society, positive functions of law and also law as a tool serving vested interests. Law can be viewed as a field of investigation which comprises decision-making (judicial behaviour), and latent grounds, hidden motives, group interests, and extra-legal sources of hidden judicial decisions in regard to judges, social background of lawyers, para-legal functionaries, clients, etc.[2] I have discussed in somewhat detail approaches to law and the relationship between law and society in my recent book[3] and in one article earlier to this book.[4] Debate on study of law centres around the application of "positivist strategy" versus humanistic/culturological approach. I have discussed in my book the following approaches :- (1) legal positivism; (2) culturological approach; (3) functional approach; (4) process approach; and (5) Marxian approach.[5] Let me concentrate briefly on the nature of legal profession in general and then switch on to the findings of the present study.

Parsons, the architect of structural-functionalism, looks at law as a part of cultural tradition in a given society.[6] According to Parsons law as a profession has at least three characteristics : (1) its dependence and independence with reference to state, (2) it is independent of political authority; and (3) the position of the legal profession in the social structure is an "institutional" one. The legal profession is to an important degree, "integrated with" the social structure of political authority, yet organised around partly independent trusteeship of the legal profession. The profession has most of its dealings with private persons, individual and corporate.[7]

Podgorecki lists the functions of the sociology of law as grasping law in its working, providing expert advice for social engineering, an effort to make its studies useful for practical applications and as a struggle with reality.[8] Thus law is not simply confined to the understanding of analytical-linguistic studies. It formulates hypotheses on how law influences and it is influenced by the wider reality. A similar view is expressed by Selznick. He writes: "The sociology of law may be regarded as an attempt to marshall what we know about the natural elements of social life and to bring that knowledge to bear on a consciously sustained enterprise, government by special objectives and ideas."[9] Three stages of development of sociology of law according to Selznick are: (1) the primitive or missionary stage; (2) the sociological craftsman stage, and (3) the "social engineering stage."[10]

A somewhat different view is expressed by Caplan regarding lawyers and litigants. The profession of law has invented a language and a procedure which are unintelligible to the layman resulting in its monopoly by so-called legal pundits. Even the administration of routine human affairs is in the firm grip of lawyers. Legal assistance has become part of human life much like hospital assistance. Consequent upon such a state of law profession, lawyers tend to preserve the status quo and act as a powerful force against social change, particularly changes in relations of production and property ownership. Thus law becomes a rational, market situation-oriented system rather than being a "service profession."[11]

Thus Caplan's approach exposes the problems of routinization and ritual formalism of legal practices which prevail in modern Western industrial society. Whether law profession has been an agent of status-quo or of social change in India—is a very pertinent question. Political economy of legal profession in the Indian context can be evaluated by analysing role of lawyers in the pre-Independence era in regard to freedom movement and in the post-Independent India in regard to legislative process and restoration of civil liberties and protection of human rights through legal aid schemes.

Another important point is whether or not law can be a theoretical and general discipline—of a positivistic nature explaining particularly social uniformities all over the world. Both positions have emphatically been stressed. "Legal positivism" and "functional-realism" have been given enormous emphasis. However, it would be wrong to accept the view that law is an independent variable as the legal positivist would advocate, and also vice-versa as the functional realist would argue. The Marxian view would insist on the understanding of the class origin of law as a universal phenomenon but at the same time this view also emphasizes on understanding of real given class situations. It is difficult to evolve a general uniform theory and practice of law and legal profession. In general, the legal profession is highly stratified internally and also have external influences. In America, legal or law firms dominate the profession.[12] In England, law profession has greater "service-ideal."[13] Law is considered as a factor of social development in the socialist countries.[14] In the countries of the Third World law profession is culture-specific and familistic in nature.[15] The legal profession is not organised in large law firms; it is mainly dependent upon individual legal practitioners divided into high and not-so-high or low-ranking lawyers.

Baxi focuses upon the problems of research in regard to legal profession.[16] Das has listed a number of points under the rubric of sociology of law in India.[17] Das divides sociology of law into four major fields: (*a*) processes of dispute settlement; (*b*) judicial behaviour: (*c*) the legal profession; and (*d*) law and the wider society. She also suggests a study of legislative acts and their effectiveness, a study of the police, the legal profession and the judiciary.[18] Emphasis in Baxi's analysis seems to be on "functional—realism" as he talks of formal legal system in its social context, role-expectations, and makers, interpreters, brokers, enforcers and compilers of norms of law. State and indigenous norms operate simultaneously and sometimes contradictory to each other. Thus, the situation in India is a complex one. Nevertheless law profession is guided by two sets of values : (*a*) ultimate values of society or societal ethics; and (*b*) central reference values of a profession or the ethics of the legal profession.[19] Also like any other profession, law possesses a monopoly of an esoteric and difficult body of knowledge necessary for the continuing functioning of society. Legal profession is, in fact, a mixture of abstract principles, basic human values and life experiences. Thus legal norms being rooted into life experiences cannot be absolute in nature. In view of the above analytic observations, following points were taken up in my study.[20]

1. Theoretically and legally lawyers do not constitute an internal stratification. Law treats all lawyers at par. But in reality bar is stratified based on income disparities and professional esteem.

2. Internal stratification of the bar can also be explored in terms of the clientele milieu. In other words, the nature of clientele would reflect the position of lawyers. The composition of the lawyer-clientele would partially determine the attitudes and value-orientations of lawyers.

3. Heterogeneity in regard to patterns of internalization of common value-orientations and socialization can be related to social class structure and the internal stratification of the bar. The mechanisms of recruitment to the bar and the structure of the process of socialization of the lawyers can be linked up with the heterogenous social background of the lawyers.

4. A specific social background becomes associated with certain type of profession. Hence, association between legal—culture, and class structure.

Scores of questions based on these broad observations were formulated about lawyers and their clients. The questions were related to professionalization, socialization, networks and stratification.[21] Law profession in India is characterised by the following characteristics:

(*a*) Bar is a self-conscious and highly organized group;

(*b*) Besides coalescence, lawyers provide services of value to diverse segments of society; and

(*c*) Lawyers as independent practitioners could spend a lot of time and energy ameliorating the grievances of the poor.[22]

But fact is that in spite of coalescence lawyers in India are sole practitioners, and also despite the fact that lawyers are not members of corporate law firms, they work more for the rich and the privileged than the poor. Galanter takes a more realistic view about law and society. According to Galanter the legal system should be considered as a body of men : who they are, what they do, how they interact with one another and with other social groups.[23] It has been stated that the lawyer is an intermediary, linking the "higher law" promulgated by the Legislatures with the law applied at the local level. The lawyer is also the bearer of legal culture and disseminator of formal norms. He is a broker linking modern and traditional systems of society.[24] These points by Galanter present a formalistic view of law and lawyers rather than indicating substantive reality of Indian society. For example, some pertinent questions remain unanswered. (1) What mechanisms operate in the legal profession ? (2) What is the formal nature of laws ? (3) What real implications do these laws have for the people ? (4) Who are the lawyers and their clients ?

Legal practitioners in India are the second largest body of professionals in the world. They are prominent in public life and are represented in the Parliament and State Legislatures more than any other professional groups. Galanter observes that the Indian lawyer's orientation is towards litigation rather than in advising, negotiating or planning. They have ability to conceptualise in handling of rules. Further, they have individualism but lack rigorous specialization. The lawyer plays the role of courtroom advocate rather than business advisor or negotiator, much less a social planner. The ties with clients are not enduring but episodic. However, lawyers in India have contributed to the national movement for independence, framing of the Constitution, organization of mass movements and restoration of civil liberties.[25]

Some more questions posed by Galanter are (1) Who uses lawyers ? (2) For what ? (3) And how do they contact them ? (4) How widespread is the use of touts and other intermediaries (5) What does their presence connote about the social organization of legal services ?[26] In fact, these questions refer to lawyer-practitioner, lawyer-scholar or lawyer-politician. Galanter reflects upon several ethical questions related to legal profession. He observes that Indian lawyers are court-centered, individualistic in orientation, lack academic quality, they are not planners and agents of modernization. Legal education in India is of theoretical nature, hence no serious concern with people's problems. Anti-lawyer sentiment in India is found mainly due to negative image about the law-practitioner.[27] However, Gajendragadkar pleads that lawyers should not confine themselves to their professional obligations and litigants, they should provide intellectual leadership to the country.[28] I have discussed evolution of legal profession in India from ancient period upto post-Independence era in my recent study of lawyers and their clients.[29]

Singh observes that the legal system, legitimation and social change are interlinked processes and the historicity of the given society helps in shaping these interlinkages.[30] The legal system itself is a form of legitimation and may extend legitimation to other institutions. Singh here refers to three functions of law: as *indicator* of change, as *initiator* of change, and as *integrator* of change. Thus, according to Singh law also performs an integrative function. Singh makes strong advocacy of the structural approach to the study of legal system, legitimation and social change. He considers that the legal system in India is a historical product. But as I have stated that the history of legal system in India goes much farther back, hence continuity exists of ancient and oral indigenous law along with the modern legal system. Also dualism is part of Constitution of India. The Constitution speaks of equality, social justice, freedom and secularism. But at the same time Constitution by its same provisions create inequality, injustice, particularism, etc. This inner contradiction of India's Constitution has not been debated by law scholars and practitioners. Bilegalism has become the norm today whether it refers to the Constitution or to the people of India.[31] Modern legal system historically as well as contemporaneously is a product of the political system.

There were about 75,000 lawyers in India in 1958 as per fourteenth Report of the Law Commission. However, the number increased to 99,988 in 1961. In 1971 the total of all categories of people in law profession went upto 1,47,662. The maximum lawyers per million inhabitants in India are found in West Bengal, and the minimum in Orissa, 263 and seventy-five respectively. In Rajasthan the number is 121 per million people. According to 1971 Census, there were 3,776 lawyers, 230 judges and magistrates, 170 law assistants and 1,520 jurists in Rajasthan. Jaipur district had 426 legal practitioners and advisors in 1961 out of the total of 2,853. This was the maximum number found in any district in the State. The minimum was eight in Jaisalmer district. Even Jodhpur district had 324 lawyers whereas Jodhpur had High Court.[32] Jaipur is not only the Capital of Rajasthan, it is also the biggest town and largest district in terms of population. Jaipur was also the biggest princely state in the erstwhile Rajputana. Thus, Jaipur town fulfilled the requirements of a fairly representative town for studying relations between lawyers and their clients. The field-work for the study was carried out in 1975-76. Through an enumeration schedule basic background information was gathered for all the 420 lawyers practising in the various courts at Jaipur.

Of the 420 lawyers 112 had rural background, fifty-three came from small towns and the remaining 253 belonged to Jaipur city and some other urban centres. Out of seven categories of lawyers, the lawyers having specialization in taxation, civil and criminal cases were found numerically preponderant. However, several lawyers practiced in more than one area of specialization. There were also lawyers having specialization in revenue, transport and labour problems. A sample of 140 lawyers was drawn ensuring equal, proportionate and comparable representation. Of these 420 lawyers, 243 did not hold any office in professional political and social organizations. 261 lawyers had their law education at the School of Law of Rajasthan University, Jaipur, and nineety-three had their education from the universities of other states. Sixty-six were non-matriculate, and eight were without specialized training. In case of 135 lawyers there were more than one member who had law education. 354 lawyers were Hindus, fifty-two Jains, thirteen Muslims, and one Sikh. Only six belonged to lower castes, and 321 belonged to the upper castes. Eighty-five lawyers had mainly rural clientele, 166 had mainly urban, and the remaining 169 had clients from both rural and urban areas. 265 lawyers had individual litigants as their clients whereas ninety-eight had institutions ; thirty-two served governmental agencies, and the remaining twenty-one had mixed types of clienteles. Of these lawyers 140 were selected based on the criteria of experience, rural-urban background and specialization.[33]

Since the universe of the clients of 420 lawyers could not be mapped out, it was decided to pick up one client per lawyer. However, we succeeded in getting 125 clients, generally one for each lawyer, in some cases more than one client and in some others none. All lawyers picked up had some experience of clientship and litigation. Of the 125 clients, ninety-eight were Hindus, twelve Jains, three Sikhs, and twelve Muslims. Thirty-seven of them were illiterate, twenty-three were below matriculation, thirty-seven were educated upto matriculate and higher secondary, twenty-six were graduates and post-graduates, and no correct information could be ascertained in case of two clients. The clients belonged to various caste groups and were engaged in several occupations. Property and agricultural land were the main sources of discords and disputes.[34]

It was found that most of the lawyers took up the legal profession not as the best alternative available to them but rather by accident, often against their own choice. In most of cases, they had no possibility of employment at the time of passing graduation or post-graduation.[35] It is quite easy to get admission in India to an L.L.B., Course than to other professional courses and social science disciplines. These few who had an established practice of their family members opted deliberately for law education. After having obtained L.L.B. degree a large number of them worked hard to get into legal practice. Some even took clerical jobs, and some entered into politics who were better off economically and also had blessings of political bosses. Certainly some lawyers were impressed and inspired by some well-known illuminaries in legal and administrative arenas.

About fifty per cent of our sample comprised of the lawyers-turned-politicians. They were members of Parliament, Rajasthan Assembly, leaders of political parties and social and cultural organisations.[36] Generally, the politician-lawyers did not do so well in legal profession. The first five top lawyers out of a list of fifteen lawyers were not politically active.[37] Also we have not found significant association between law academics and legal practitioners due to a lack of positive relationship between law education and legal practice. The law-teachers lived in a world of their own and had no grassroot experience in-put in their theoretical and philosophical discourses on law. More than law-teachers, the lawyers of our sample were influenced by their friends, caste, family members, relatives and neighbours. However, most of the lawyers reported that hard work, sincerity, income, amenability, legal expertise and political networks were the main criteria of their success. The number of clients was generally considered to be an accurate indication of the level of success achieved.[38] Lawyers were found more successful as politicians because of their contact with the masses and professional autonomy.

Our data show that more than one-third of the clients had background of litigation as their fathers had fought one or more court cases, and majority of them were of upper castes, particularly Brahmins. Economic matters were the main cause for litigation. Criminal offences such as assault, rape, murder, burglary etc. were the second most important reason. The third set of cases included defamation, negligence and refusal to vacate houses by tenants etc. The opponents included close kins, family and caste members, neighbours, relatives, tenants, state government and business firms.

The clients have a full realisation of the fact that litigation would take a long time. They know that they would have to spend a lot of money and waste time and energy. The people generally go to law courts for humiliating their opponents, and for having a sense of satisfaction by dragging the opponents to the court of law for their misdeeds against them. "Professional litigants" are also found in villages and towns. They, in a way promote inadvertently "culture of litigation".

The clients have a negative image of lawyers, magistrates, court clerks and munshis.[39] However, they do not have a negative image of their own lawyers in particular. One of the complaints against the magistrates is that they are not competent enough and also they come from upper and upper-middle class families and therefore do not do justice to the lower and "untouchable" castes. Both court-clerks and munshis are viewed as corrupt functionaries.

Of the 125 clients, seventy-five approached lawyers directly, and only thirty-three through some contacts, and sixteen approached lawyers after having gathered requisite information about them. There is no uniform pattern or practice for paying fee to the lawyers. The fee is determined by the nature of the case and the professional calibre of the lawyer. Only three lawyers used touts or brokers to get clients. The opponents generally belonged to a lower caste than that of the litigants. Mainly cultivators, businessmen and government servants were entangled in litigation.[40] Both educated and illiterate fought court cases, hence, no one to one tie between education and litigation. Seventy-one clients out of 125 had lawyers who either hailed from their neighbourhood, village area or belonged to their caste/community fifty-eight Brahmin and Bania clients had seventy-four lawyers and law students belonging to them based on above criteria. Clients are generally familiar with court-culture, lawyer's tactics, and the role of munshi.

Law education, bar council and legal practice are the pillars of lawyers professionalization. The Law Commission of India in its fourteenth report observes that the legal profession is no more a distinguished public service. It is no more attractive as it was in the pre-Independence period. The lawyer has lost his leadership in public life. The profession is crowded by young men who are hardly able to make a living.[41] These observations of the Law Commission are only partly true Law education is somewhat open, but entry into law profession and more so the success in legal practice are not so open and easy as one would normally visualize. Who becomes a successful lawyer ? This is a very difficult question to answer. The legal profession as it exists today is the outcome of the prevalent legal system, and the latter is an outgrowth of the British judiciary in India.

Lawyers come to know about legal practice from their family members and other independent sources. Mass media and teachers did not contribute much to their knowledge about the nature of legal profession. However, no direct relationship was found between source of knowledge and choice of legal practice as a career.

Out of 140 lawyers, 107 chose a legal career without the advice of parents or other relatives. Even those who had already some family members in law profession were not necessarily guided by them. Not all the lawyers started with legal practice as their first occupation. Fifty per cent were without any job, but the other fifty per cent switched to legal practice from a variety of jobs. A good number of them obtained their law degree as employed students.

Professional competence, honesty, integrity and amenable personality are the main qualities/attributes necessary for a legal practitioner as viewed by 140 lawyers themselves. Out of 140 lawyers we prepared a rank order of fifteen top lawyers, and found that lawyers having specialization in criminal and civil cases were included with the exception of one taxation lawyer.[42] The rank-order of these fifteen lawyers does not refer to the income they earn from legal practice and political power they possess in the society. This refers to the assessment of the lawyers of their own colleagues.

The lawyers admitted their weaknesses including that of toutism, malpractices, bribery, lack of punctuality, short temper, lack of proper attention to the clients etc. For a young lawyer to be on his own needs some patronage of an established lawyer to come out of the phase of struggling in the profession. Lack of proper law education and professional control have also contributed to "unprofessionalism" in legal profession. The Bar Council does not exercise very effective control over its members. Very often professionally competent members do not occupy the chairmanship of the Bar Council. Bar Council professionally controls its members. The control is not adequate since the council's working is not satisfactory—it is not a very active body, nor it takes bold decision.[43]

In our study we found that most lawyers considered themselves as custodians of their clients' legal interest. They thought this to be their legal as well as moral responsibility. Clients too have expectations of highly idealistic short from their lawyers. Inter-colleaguial relationship among the lawyers was preferred more on professional plane rather than at inter-personal level. Lawyers also considered themselves as custodians and protectors of the legal apparatus of Indian society. Some of them thought that legal assistance to the poor should be their philosophy of life. It is upto lawyers to expose loopholes in legislation. However, the lawyers were in favour of more autonomy for legal profession and reduction of interference in their professional activities by the High Court. Besides the autonomy granted by the State, the other important factors conducive to autonomy are the lawyer's art, craftmanship and ideals. In fact, the legal profession has a unit of its own. Legal standards of models also help to make it a unified system. The lack of autonomy is mainly due to continuity of colonial legal culture.

Law education, apprenticeship and academic work by lawyers constitute the core of legal professionalism. It was reported that law courses were theoretically of a very high standard, but were not substantiated well by practical training, Some lawyers thought that the input of morality and ethics be added to the law courses besides a semblance of theory and practice to make the law courses wholesome and relevant. It was also stated that some courses on Indian society in general and on society in Rajasthan in particular be added to the course-programme.

A large number of lawyers felt that legal apprenticeship was necessary for the new entrants. They learn the "tricks of the trade" and actual court procedures and practices by undergoing the apprenticeship. They also learn how to deal with clients and how to solve their legal problems. Apprenticeship is considered a period of learning and not earning. However, the senior lawyers generally do not give much attention to the new entrants. It was suggested that like the Supreme Court practice the senior lawyers should appear with the junior ones at the district courts. Apprenticeship period should be fixed uniformally. The apprentices should be paid at least some money to survive the period of training. They should be allowed to argue in the courts. However, some lawyers felt that confidence and competence can only be gained through independent practice. Apprenticeship also leads to dependency and exploitation.

Out of 420 lawyers only thirty-five were reported to have written books, commentaries, and articles etc. They wrote mainly on land tenancy, property, money-lending and taxation. However, none of the lawyer-writers have discussed the basic philosophical academic issues related to the evolution of legal profession in India. In a large number of cases, the commentaries were written with a view to earn money. These writings do not reflect the social science skill as in the case of writings by some judges of High Courts and Supreme Court, hence weak academic professionalism among the lawyers of Jaipur.

Indian lawyers were discriminated against the British barristers and citizens. Therefore, they fought not only for their own interests, but also for those of the unprivileged and helpless people. In the pre-Independence period several lawyers attained a high level of professionalism and also equally proved proficient defenders of the human rights of Indian people. Professionalism and nationalist clan coincided. Our study shows that any lawyer who violated a canon of ethics was censured and suspended from carrying out legal practice in spite of the ineffectiveness attributed to the Bar Association.

There are certain contradictions in regard to theory and practice of legal profession. A lawyer, for example, advises his client not to be involved in unjust litigation, and the client may not need to his lawyer's counsel and may insist on initiating litigation. The lawyer is supposed to accept the request of his client for defending him by using legal acumen. Such a situation ensues a conflict between the canons of professional ethics and the actual demands of individual practice. In regard to getting business, dealing with courts and other official agencies and in relations with ciients such a dilemma is often faced. However, professional ethics does not remain a strength if legal advice becomes a market commodity in India and also perhaps in a rich country like America.

We have stated earlier that Indian barristers were considered inferior to their British counter-part. The Indian barristers were considered superior to Indian advocates who had their law-education in India.[44] Besides, there were pleaders of two grades and attorneys, solicitors and mukhtars etc. Even after Independence there were as many as nine types of legal practitioners. Such a legacy of hierarchy within the bar has created obstacles in making the legal profession homo-equitus. Out of 140 lawyers, seventy-five faced problems such as of getting clients, adequate income, books, stationary and proper guidance. Lack of knowledge about court procedures, and cut-throat competition from other lawyers were other serious problems. The first five years were a period of real struggle for them. Sixty-four lawyers did not face such problems because they had someone in the profession to pat them up.

The professional aspects of lawyer's career center chiefly around his commitment to professionalization which includes reading, writing subscription to journals, purchase of books, apprenticeship, joint practice, understanding his profession, job performance and the role of the Bar Council.[45] All lawyers, with the exception of four, regularly read legal publications. Only ten lawyers had published articles in newspapers and magazines. Lawyers subscribed to a large number of legal journals and magazines because of professional necessity. Ten lawyers got most of the law magazines required for their practice. About fifty per cent of the lawyers visited the library of Bar Council. Besides academic professionalization lawyers considered themselves as specialists in specific fields and subfields. And this is how a lawyer is perceived different from a businessman. Legal practice is a profession as it is based on formal law education, apprenticeship, professional ethics and service ideal whereas business lacks such attributes of a profession. More than fifty per cent of the lawyers felt that legal practice was better than medical, engineering, university teaching and state level services. Income and reputation are generally considered as the most important criteria for a successful lawyer. However, the following criteria were given by the lawyers for their success. They are :

1. Establishment of practice in a short period ;
2. Opportunity to fight for people's rights :
3. Honest and noble profession ; and
4. Opportunity to expose scandals of government servants and high-ups.[46]

Both lawyers and clients are stratified. Lawyers are stratified in two ways : (1) they are stratified in terms of their legal competence ; and (2) they belong to various castes and communities. The two bases of social stratification are not unrelated. The clients are stratified in terms of their social background. Ideally, lawyers should serve all segments of society and should also belong to all sections of society. But lawyers serve mostly the upper and middle classes, and do not belong to the lower sections of Indian society. Only economically well off people can avail lawyer's services, particularly of the one who is professionally reputed. Thus, the clientele of lawyers is distributed differentially along with social distinctions and divisions in Indian society.

Contrary to the situation in the pre-Independence period now the legal profession is not confined to the upper caste and upper class alone. Pre-law schooling, and the type and quality of law education are not that important for a legal career while the nature of non-legal jobs and the type and status of legal practice are important. Internal stratification among lawyers is mainly due to the "inheritance" of practice, non-legal support and legal competence.

On ideological basis also stratification within the bar has been reported.[47] But more important fact for us is that the bar was divided in terms of designations such as attorney pleader, malabari, barrister, advocate, vakil, mukhtar etc. Distinctions also existed on the basis of court at which they practised law and whether the law education was received in England or India. Also difference was based on the fact whether one practised on the original side or on the appellate side. Today income and prestige of lawyer are two important bases of stratification within the bar. The term "leading lawyers" is used for those who have a combine of these attributes. Charles Morrison's categorization seems to be somewhat convincing. He refers : top lawyers, below top, average, below average and briefless lawyers (beginners). They are sometimes also referred as : "equals", "juniors" and "seniors."[48]

Our analysis shows that there has been a distinct change in the class background of the legal practitioners. Pre-Independence lawyers had more commitment to legal professionalism, national cause and other altruistic objectives. They belonged to aristocracy by birth, but worked for the uplift of the people. Today, lawyers belong to wider sections of society representing all classes. Changes in law-education and national situation, diversification of law and increased litigation have changed the nature of demands on lawyers [49]

Some lawyers had the privilege of having patronage of influential friends, political leaders, senior lawyers, businessmen and trade union leaders. Besides these networks, co-villagers, fellow caste-men and touts were also used by lawyers at the initial stage of their legal practice. These structural networks were required more at the initial stage of law practice. Father and village background have been found as very effective resources for getting clientele. Intermediaries and touts have generally been not encouraged by lawyers of Jaipur However, about one-third of the lawyers worked for other senior lawyers.[50]

We have found that lawyers generally preferred clients who are nol connected with political parties, and who do not belong to their own caste, community, village and neighbourhood. Very few lawyers expressed a preference for businessmen and poor persons as clients in particular. A large number of lawyers were connected with well-known potitical leaders on the basis of affinal ties, friendship and caste membership. A good number of these leaders were lawyers by training and politicians by profession and practice. Also lawyers sought help from senior lawyers and others for establishing their law practice, but generally did not seek help for winning a case for a client.

More than fifty per cent of lawyers wanted their sons to pursue legal practice, however, about one-third of the lawyers, did not want their sons to get into legal profession. The lawyers of the latter disposition were not as much satisfied with legal profession as much as the former category. Active participation in the affairs of Bar Council and other professional bodies was a source of strength for sixty-three lawyers out of 140. Some lawyers were leaders of various political parties and activists and derived strength from them. Clubs, trade unions, caste associations and welfare societies were other organizational networks for thirty-four lawyers. Twenty-nine lawyers extended free legal advice to various organizations, institutions, political parties and persons.

Lawyers have linkages with their clients through many sided structural channels. Lawyers have referred cases to other lawyers as they thought they did not have requisite competence in particular type of cases. Senior lawyers referred some cases to the junior ones. District lawyers have referred some lawyers at the High Court level. However, in most cases lawyers have been referred by the old clients to the new litigants. Thus, both lawyers and clients become effective networks for each other. The clientele of the lawyers of Jaipur was found to be largely rural. Rural clients selected their lawyers based on legal specialization and caste affinity. The urban clients considered specialization and neighbourhood affinity as the criteria for choosing a lawyer. The urban clients comprise of businessmen, professionals, government servants, land-lords and organizations and agencies. The rural clients have litigation related to land, property, crime, rivalry etc.

CONCLUSIONS

We have discussed in the present paper structure and process of legal profession in India based on our study of relations between lawyers and their clients. How lawyers are identified as "superior" and "inferior" or "equal" within the bar, what criteria are used for making such a distinction, how does a differential clientele milieu affect hierarchy among lawyers, and what are the strains affecting performance of lawyers—are some of the questions attempted in this paper. Socializiation of lawyers prior to their recruitment to law practice and its effect on recruitment, training, law practice etc. have also been discussed. The main source of profession in India is not law education as such, but patronage and legal practice itself are the main source of successful professionalization. Finally, income and prestige become the sole criteria of lawyer's position in the bar. Legal advice seems to a market phenomenon, generally beyond the reach of the poor. There are contradictions in regard to legal ethics and law practice, lawyer-client relationship and Bar Council and legal practice. A lawyer is different today from what he was before Independence. However, lawyers in Jaipur are not for toutism and intermediaries. They take a lot of interest in social, cultural and political activities. Choice of law profession was not clearly made out in many cases.

Thus, we have discussed lawyers in the context of their society as well as in their professional setting.

NOTES AND REFERENCES

1. Sharma, K.L. *Sociology of Law and Legal Profession,* Rawat Publications, Jaipur, 1984.
2. Vilhelm, Aubert (ed.), *Sociology of Law.* Penguin Books, 1969 ; Gurviteh, Georges, *Sociology of Law*, Routledge and Kegal Paul, London, 1973.
3. Sharma, *op. cit.*
4. Sharma, K.L. "Sociology of Law and Legal Perspective", *Journal of the Indian Law Institute*, vol. 24, nos. 2, 3 and 4, Silver Jubilee Number, 1982, pp. 528-47.
5. Sharma, *op. cit.*, 1984, pp. 18-21.
6. Parsons, Talcott, "A Sociologist Looks at the Legal Profession", *Essays on Sociological Theory.* The Free Press, New York, 1964, pp. 37-85, Ehrlich Eugen, *Fundamental Principles of the Sociology of Law*, Cambridge University Press, Cambridge, 1933.
7. *Ibid.*, pp. 374-75.
8. Podgorecki, Adam, *Law and Society*, Routledge Kegan Paul, London, 1974, pp. 7-8.
9. Selznick, Philip, *Law, Society and Industrial Justice*, Russell Sage Foundation, New York, 1961, p. 5 ; "The Sociology of Law", Friedman L, S. Man Canlay (eds.), *Law and the Behavioural Sciences*, Indianapolis, 1969, pp. 2-3.
10. *Ibid.*, p. 3.

11. Caplan Jonathan, "Lawyers and Litigants : A Cult Reviewed", Illich Ivan, and others (eds.), *Disabling Professions*, Morion Boyars Publishers Ltd., London 1277, pp. 93-109.
12. Smigel, Erivin O, *The Wall Street Lawyer : Prosessional Organization Man*, Indiana University Press, Bloomington, 1969 ; Levy, Beryl Harold, *Corporation Lawyer : Saint or Sinner* Chilton, Philadelphia 1961 ; Carlin, Jerome E., *Lawyers on Their Own*, New Rutgers University Press, New Burnswik, 1962.
13. Campbell, C.M., and Paul Wiles, "The Study of Law in Society in Britain", *Law and Society Review*, vol. 10, no. 4, 1976, pp. 553-73.
14. Podgorecki, *op. cit.*, 1974.
15. C.J. Dlas et al. (eds.), *Lawyers in the Third World : Comparative and Developmental Perspective*, Quoted from Upendra Baxis "Foreword", *Sociology of Law and Legal Profession*, Sharma, K.L., *op. cit.*
16. Baxi, Upendra, *Socio-legal Research in Indian : A Program schrift*, Occasional Monographs, Series 12, ICSSR, New Delhi, 1975.
17. Das, Veena "Sociology of Law", *A Survey of Research in Sociology and Social Anthropology*, vol. II, Popular Prakashan, Bombay 1964, pp. 367-400.
18. *Ibid.*, p. 368.
19. Parsons, *op. cit.*
20. Sharma, *op. cit.*, 1984, pp. 30-31.
21. Sharma, *op. cit.* p. 31.
22. Schwartz, Richard D., "Introduction", *Law* and *Society Review*, vol. III, no. 2, 1968-69, pp. 195-200.
23. Galanter, "Introduction : The Study of Indian Legal Profession", *Law* and *Society Review*, vol III, no. 2, 1968-69 p. 202.
24. *Ibid.* p. 202.
25. *Ibid.* pp. 201-18.
26. *Ibid.* p. 209.
27. *Ibid.* p. 209.
28. Gajendragadkar, P.B., *Lawyers and Social Change*, National Forum of Lawyers and Legal Aid, New Delhi, 1976, p. 23.
29. Sharma, *op. cit.*, 1984, pp. 43-54.
30. Singh, Yogendra, "Legal System, Legitimation and Social Change", *Essays on Modernization in India*, Manohar Book Service, Delhi, 1978, pp. 136-37.
31. Jones, W.H. Morris, *The Government and Politics of India*, Hatchinson University Library, London, 1967, pp. 38-43 ; Galanter Marc, "The Aborted Restoration of Indigenous Law in India", *Commarative Studies in Society and History*, vol. 14, no. 1, 1972, pp. 53-70 ; Rudolph, L. I., and S. H. Rudolph, *The Modernity of Tradition*, Orient Longmans Ltd. Bombay, 1967, pp. 251-930 ; Misra, B.B., *The Indian Middle Classes*, Asia Publishing House, Bombay, 1961, pp. 198-67 and 330-32.

32. Shevme *op. cit.*, 1984, Chapters 2 and 3, for all the statistical information.
33. *Ibid.* Chapter 3.
34. *Ibid.*
35. *Ibid.* p. 84.
36. *Ibid.* pp. 85-87.
37. *Ibid.* p. 118.
38. *Ibid.* p. 87.
39. *Ibid.* pp. 93-95.
40. *Ibid.* p. 97.
41. *The Law Commission of India*, 14th Report, pp. 584-85.
42. Sharma, Ice, p. 118,
43. *Ibid.* pp. 120-21.
44. *Ibid.* p. 134.
45. *Ibid.* p. 136.
46. *Ibid.* p. 141.
47. Rowe, Peter, "Indian Lawyers and Political Modernization: Observations in Four District Towns", *Law and Society Review*, Vol. III, No. 2, 1968-69, p. 69, p. 238.
48. Morrison, Charles, "Lawyers and Litigants in a North Indian District : Notes on the Informal Aspects of the Legal System", *Law and Society Review*, vol. III, no. 2, 1968-69, pp. 301-02 ; "Kinship in Professional Relations : A Study of North Indian District Lawyers", *Comparative Studies in Society and History*, vol. 14, no. 1, 1972, pp. 100-25 : Gandhi, J.S., *Lawyers and Touts*, Hindustan Publishing Corporation, Delhi, 1982.
49. Sharma, *op. cit.*, 1984, p. 158.
50. Sharma *op. cit.*, pp. 185-87.

PART VI

MISCELLANEOUS

1. **Social Work**

2. **Dance**

26

THE PROFESSIONAL SOCIAL WORKER IN THE MAKING : THE ROLE-PERCEPTION AND OCCUPATIONAL-COMMITMENT

M.K. Singh

The tradition of social work in India can be traced back from the times immemorial. Its genesis lies embedded in our cultural ideology. Our religious teachings have always advocated that help must be given to the handicapped. The blind, the deaf, the mute, the insane, the poor and the deprived were always looked after. The early structure of our society in its organizational and ideological frame-work catered to the incapacitated. Thus, "Though the concept of social work has been there from the beginning of the history of India, the concept of the social worker was not there. The structure of Hindu society was such that the caste feeling created a strong bond of kinship, and the Hindu joint-family saw that its most helpless members were looked after by the family as a whole. Those who were able to work, worked; those who were ill or incapacitated became the responsibility of the family as a whole."[1] We have numerous examples of selfless and dedicated workers who have worked for the cause of humanity.

The concept of "Professional Social Worker" and the rendering of professional social services to the clientele is a very recent phenomenon. The history of professional social work in India, in fact, can be traced back to 1936-37 when Tata School of Social Work, Bombay, came into being. Since then, there has been a mushroom growth of Social Work

Institutes providing training to the candidates and turning out professional social workers. Whether these institutes have a qualified staff or Director, Library or provision for field work, whether the students are receiving proper training and can deliver the goods or not, is of course a separate issue.[2] However, the employment of duly trained social workers, providing professionalized services to its clientele and adoption of social work as a profession by some, has become an accepted pattern today.

THE CONCEPTS : SOCIAL WORK AND PROFESSIONAL SOCIAL WORKER

The conceptual clarification of the two terms "Social Work" and "Professional Social Worker" is very much required here before we proceed further. This is because of the ambiguity in meaning attached to them. In common parlance "Social Worker" means a man or a woman interested or engaged in a welfare activity which concerns the un-privileged sections of the society. Similarly, any individual who gives something or believes in doing charity shall also be called a social worker. Again "In Gandhian era, the political worker and social worker became inter-changeable terms, and even after that era is over, the aroma continues to confuse individuals and groups, to the advantage of politicians and to the detriment of the Social Worker."[3] Thus the term "social worker" draws many different meanings. Similar is the case with the term "social work." The term "social work" is most of the time considered equivalent to "welfare work" which is carried out through social service activities. It aims at providing aid to the individuals or groups in need or those who are unprivileged sections of the society. Social work activities, most of the time, are synonymous with giving "charity," but in the context of the present paper, we shall define these two terms differently.

Social Worker

A "Social Worker" as understood here, is defined as the one

who has received formal training in the discipline, possesses knowledge and skill, and employs these methods and techniques while operating in the field. He shall treat and perform every activity with a professional's capacity and command, just like any other professional, e.g. like an engineer or a doctor. There may also be many others, working as a part of a team, who also might have received a brief training or an orientation even extended to full-time short courses. But for the purposes of our understanding and present analysis, we shall not include them in the category of "professionals." They may be categorised as "Welfare Workers" or "para-professionals."

Social Work

The concept of "Social Work", as understood here, includes the specialized services, which are to be offered by trained functionaries or professionals to a set of clientele, who claim these services on their own right and while not being considered as an object of mercy or charity of a mission or sacrificing order. The social work activity shall aim at facilitating and strengthening the basic relationship and the mutual adjustment between individuals and their social environment for the good of the individual and the society. No doubt the professionals, most of the time, shall be dealing with the unorganized sections of the society or unprivileged groups, but the services provided shall aim at aiding them in one way or the other and bringing in realization of their capacities.

STATUS OF SOCIAL WORK AS A PROFESSION

Inclusion of social work into the profile of professions, is not a very old phenomenon. May be, partly it is due to this reason that "social work" has not so far been able to acquire its appropriate status in India among the generally acknowledged professions. According to one of the writers, social work, as a profession, has neither become popular, nor is there any likelihood of its going to be so.[4] The reasons for the same can be enumerated here. Firstly, it is the nature of clientele which is of a very special kind; it is that section of the society which is unorganized in one way or another; which is economically, socially, psychologically disabled, and whose very existence one would rather not be reminded of. Secondly, it is in the nature of service which the social worker renders to its clientele. The nature of these services is not such without which the survival of the individual should become uncertain (like medicine) or eliminate the troubles of the clientele (like law). On the other hand, the nature of services are such that even if these are of considerable magnitude and frequency, they do not even bear fruits or come to the surface for quite a long time. Thirdly, social work profession is not a highly professionalized occupation and according to Inkles and Ross, it is only highly professionalized occupations which are invariably ranked high in modern industrial societies and enjoy a reasonable status.[5] Fourthly, social work profession lacks all those factors, which provide prestige to the profession, like "ability to acquire power, control wealth, secure high financial rewards, its utility to clients at times of crisis and ability to contribute more to the societal pursuits of ideal."[6] In the absence of these factors, social work profession shall never be considered a prestigious profession.

Social Work as a profession lacks most, if not all, of the above stated features. Hence, social work as a profession definitely is among the lesser acknowledged and lesser prestigious occupations. It is the profession which is most unlikely to be sought after and hence ranks lower in the hierarchy of professions.[7]

ROLE-PERCEPTION, ROLE-PERFORMANCE AND OCCUPATIONAL-COMMITMENT

Before taking up the "role-perception", "role-performance" and "occupational-commitment" of the professional social worker, it is appropriate to precisely define these terms.

By "role-perception" we mean how the role is conceived by the incumbent and what are the role expectations from him ?

By "role-performance" we mean the "role-behaviour", i.e. how the professional social worker behaves and how he acts and reacts in a particular situation while providing professional services ?

By "role-commitment", we mean, "participation in an activity on a relatively permanent basis...The tendency on the part of the person to stick to an organization...and commitment to the task in terms of operations involved in an organization."[8] In case of social work profession, commitment would also involve equating the profession, more or less, with the mission of life.

Now armed with this definitional clarification, the question posed is how does the social work professional perceive his role ? Broadly speaking, a social work professional can perceive his role in three different ways. Firstly, he can perceive his professional role, as he has been taught during his training in the School of Social Work. Secondly, he can perceive his role as the employing agency wants him to perceive, i.e. role perception in a specific work situation. Thirdly, he perceives his role as the "outsiders" want or expect him to perceive—the ideal type.

The "role-performance" of the professional shall be of different type, since the three categories of role-perceptions are not, and cannot be, in congruence. The conflict in perception and its variation from situation to situation (from training stage to employment stage, and from one employment agency to another employment agency) shall derogately affect the "role-performance" and "occupational-commitment" of the professional.

There are many factors (personal attributes) which impede the "role-perception" affecting the "occupational-commitment" of the professional. This shall be taken up later. Here we shall be concerned with only the structural factors affecting the "role-perception."

Structural Impediments

The concept of social work has been defined and understood differently by different groups and under different situations. The contemporary meaning of social work as broadly accepted today implies providing of social justice to the poor and the deprived, and not giving of charity or giving welfare services.

If the professional social worker is to work in this framework, he has to perceive his role with a clear perspective given above. The question raised is—can the present training institutes, with their existing curriculum, help the professionals in making to perceive the above stated roles ? Do the professionals in the making, grasp the broader and widely accepted perspective of their work ? Numerous doubts crop-up when we consider that "majority of the social work curricula even today are based on social and individual problems of pathology, rather than problems in the context of poverty and development. As a result, social work intervention has been basically residual, remedial and rehabilitative in response to the needs of the poverty groups who are not a part of the main stream of the national life."[9] Thus, the training received at the institutes definitely impedes the requisite role-perception as delineated above, affecting the role-performance in fulfilling the above stated role.

The second structural impediment faced by the professional social worker, is no less serious and hazardous than the first one, and we would say that it is rather more serious. This impediment he faces in the capacity of a functionary when he steps into the field of employment. The professional social worker after training, is likely to work with either a government or a voluntary agency. For a governmental agency, the expected role of a professional social worker is simply of a liaison officer between the government and the clientele. Since the policy of the government has been to provide packages of services, rather than giving it to them as their right, the professional social worker has to perceive his role accordingly, and perform it as the situation demands. Whatever his training may have been, he has to mould himself to those requirements. He must perceive and perform as has been asked to, irrespective of its being right or wrong. Now supposing that the professional social worker is employed in a voluntary agency, the structural situation, i.e. grinding poverty, ignorance, malnutrition, illiteracy and deprivation may force him to perceive his role as merely of a delivery agent or as per the policy of the employing agency. Even if the voluntary agency expects the professional to have a broader perspective, it shall remain unfunctional due to other structural conditions and inadequate training received by him. Thus, the role-perception and role-performance shall remain miles apart from the covetted definitional perception of Social Work.

Personal Attributes of Professionals in the Making

In order to identify the additional factors (personal attributes) which impede or help the "role-perception" and "occupational commitment" of a professional social worker, data have been collected from the Schools of Social Work at Pune, for the years, 1983-84 and 1984-85. A sample from these two batches was selected and a structured questionnaire was circulated to the students to collect the information. In addition to the above, informal discussion with the students and the faculty members was carried out in order to get the feel of the situation. Six major variables have been selected in order to gauge the personal attributes affecting the "role-perception" "role performance" and "occupational-commitment" of the social work professionals in the making. The major variables are : urban versus rural background of the students, income level of the family, occupation of the parents, educational level of the parents, the order of preference for the selection of specialization and the rural versus the urban area of choice for work after completion of the training. In addition to these variables, information on medium of instructions, type of school and college attended, academic background and financial standing to meet the needs during the training period have also been collected. The findings of major variables are given here.

Rural Versus Urban Background

Each student was asked to indicate the place where he had spent most of the first fifteen years of his life. Three choices, as shown in Table 1 were given. It is seen that a vast majority of students, in respect of both the batches, had spent the formative years of their life in the rural areas. This means that social work professionals in the making shall be over represented from the rural areas.

Type of Schools and Colleges Attended

Rural background of the sample is also reflected by the type

TABLE 1

Urban Versus Rural Background

S. No.	Area of Study	1983-84 Batch	1984-85 Batch	Total
1.	Village	23 (76.7)	33 (73.3)	56 (74.7)
2.	Town (less than one lakh population)	1 (3.3)	5 (11.1)	6 (8.0)
3.	City (more than one lakh population)	6 (20.0)	7 (15.6)	13 (17.3)
	Total	30 (100.0) (40.0)	45 (100.0) (60.0)	75 (100.0) (100)

of schools and colleges attended by the students. As can be seen from Table 2 a majority of the students, i.e. sixty per cent attended government schools and colleges and 26.6 % attended others, which are normally managed by the municipal bodies. The percentage of students having studied in missionary or public schools and colleges is very small (5.34%) which confirms that the social work professionals in the making, mostly hail from the rural areas.

TABLE 2

Types of Schools and Colleges Attended

S. No.	Type of School/ College Attended	1983-84 Batch	1984-85 Batch	Total
1.	Government	25 (83.3)	26 (57.8)	51 (68.0)
2.	Missionary	1 (3.3)	1 (2.2)	2 (2.7)
3.	Public	—	2 (4.4)	2 (2.7)
4.	Other (privately managed)	4 (13.3)	16 (35.6)	20 (26.6)
	Total	30 (100.0) (40.0)	45 (100.0) (60.0)	75 (100.0) (100.0)

Education of the Parents

It is seen that in case of 45.3 % of students, fathers are illiterate, while in case of 30.7 % cases, they are below

TABLE 3

Parental Education Level

S. No.	Level of Education	1983-84 Batch		1984-85 Batch		Total	
		Father	Mother	Father	Mother	Father	Mother
1.	Not educated	16 (53.3)	20 (66.7)	18 (40.0)	29 (64.4)	34 (45.3)	49 (65.4)
2.	Below matric	8 (26.7)	7 (23.4)	15 (33.3)	13 (28.9)	23 (30.7)	20 (26.7)
3.	Matric and below degree	2 (6.7)	1 (3.3)	8 (18.7)	3 (6.7)	10 (13.3)	4 (5.3)
4.	Diploma equivalent	1 (3.3)	1 (3.3)	1 (2.2)	—	2 (2.7)	1 (1.3)
5.	Graduate and above	3 (10.0)	1 (3.3)	3 (6.7)	—	6 (8.0)	1 (1.3)
6.	Any other	—	—	—	—	—	—
	Total	30 (100.0)	30 (100.0)	45 (100.0)	45 (100.0)	75 (100.0)	75 (100.0)

Matric. Similarly, in 65.4% cases, the mothers are illiterate, while in 26.7 % cases they are below Matric. The incidence of higher education, i.e. above graduation, is negligible in respect of both parents. This indicates that the social work professionals in the making, largely come from the homes where the level of parental education is markedly low. The details are given in Table 3.

Occupation of Fathers

The low level of educational attainment of the fathers of the students is also reflected in their occupational status as well. It has been reported that only four per cent of the fathers are gazetted officers, while 5.3% are junior government servants. 9.3 % are skilled workers, while 10.7 % are white collar employees. As against this, 53.3 % are agriculturists (small farmers only). This further confirms the rural background of the students. The detailed information are found in Table 4.

TABLE 4

Father's Occupation

S. No.	Occupation	1983-84 Batch	1984-85 Batch	Total
1.	Businessman	2 (6.7)	5 (11.1)	7 (9.4)
2.	Gazetted government Official	2 (6.7)	1 (2.2)	3 (4.0)
3.	Junior government servant	2 (6.7)	2 (4.4)	4 (5.3)
4.	Professionalist	—	1 (2.2)	1 (1.3)
5.	Agriculturist—(i) large	—	—	—
	(ii) small	21 (70.0)	19 (42.2)	40 (53.3)
6.	Skilled worker	2 (6.6)	5 (11.2)	7 (9.3)
7.	White-Collar Employee	1 (3.3)	7 (15.6)	8 (10.7)
8.	Any other	—	5 (11.1)	5 (6.7)
	Total	30 (100.0)	45 (100.0)	75 (100.0)
		(40.0)	(60.0)	(100.0)

Economic Level of the Family

As can be seen from Table 5 that a majority, (46.6%) of

TABLE 5

Family Income

S. No.	Income level per month	1983-84 Batch	1984-85 Batch	Total
1.	Low (less than Rs. 500)	12 (40.0)	23 (51.1)	35 (46.6)
2.	Middle low (Rs. 500-700)	12 (40.0)	6 (13.3)	18 (24.0)
3.	Middle (Rs. 700-1000)	2 (6.7)	9 (20.0)	11 (14.7)
4.	Above middle (above Rs. 1000)	4 (13.3)	7 (15.6)	11 (14.7)
	Total	30 (100.0) (40.0)	45 (100.0) (60.0)	75 (1000.0) (100.0)

the families have income level less than Rs. 500 per month, while twenty-four per cent have income level between Rs. 500 to Rs. 700 per month. As against this, only 14.7% families have income level above Rs. 1000 per month. This clearly implies that social work professionals in the making belong to a poor strata of the society.

Order of Preference for Specialization

While giving their choice of specialization, the majority of the students (61.3 %) considering both batches together, have opted for Labour Welfare as their most popular first choice. Correctional Work as the next popular choice (twenty per cent), Family and Child Welfare as the third (sixteen percent) and Medical and Psychiatric Social Work as the last popular choice (2.7 %). Further it is seen that in case they fail to get their first choice of specialization, i.e. Labour Welfare, Correctional Work has been asked for as the second most popular field of specialization (33.3 %). In this way we find that a majority (38.7 %) have given their fourth and the last choice as Medical and Psychiatric Social Work. These details are reflected in Table 6.

TABLE 6

Order of Preference for Specialization

Batch-wise order of preference	Number indicating various preferences: Family and Child Welfare	Correctional Work	Medical and Psychiatric Social Work	Labour Welfare
1983-84 batch				
I	6 (20.0)	5 (16.7)	—	19 (63.4)
II	9 (30.0)	10 (33.3)	4 (13.4)	3 (10.0)
III	4 (13.3)	6 (20.0)	10 (33.3)	4 (13.3)
IV	5 (16.7)	6 (20.0)	10 (33.3)	3 (10.0)
NG	6 (20.0)	3 (10.0)	6 (20.0)	1 (3.3)
1984-85 batch				
I	6 (13.3)	10 (22.2)	2 (4.5)	27 (60.0)
II	13 (28.9)	15 (33.3)	10 (22.2)	6 (13.3)
III	13 (28.9)	10 (22.2)	13 (28.9)	8 (17.8)
IV	12 (26.7)	9 (20.0)	19 (42.2)	4 (8.6)
NG	1 (2.2)	1 (2.2)	1 (2.2)	—
Total				
I	12 (*16.0*)	15 (*20.0*)	2 (*2.7*)	46 (*61.3*)
II	22 (29.3)	25 (33.3)	14 (18.7)	9 (12.0)
III	17 (22.7)	16 (21.4)	23 (30.7)	12 (16.0)
IV	17 (22.7)	15 (20.0)	29 (38.7)	7 (9.3)
NG	7 (9.3)	4 (5.3)	7 (9.2)	1 (1.4)

NG—Choice not given

TABLE 7

Medium of Instructions.

S. No.	Institution	1983-84 Batch		1984-85 Batch		Total		
		Marathi	English	Marathi	English	Marathi	English	
1.	At the School	27 (90.0)	3 (10.0)	45 (100.0)	—	72 (96.0)	3 (4.0)	75 (100)
2.	At the College	18 (60.0)	12 (40.0)	33 (73.3)	12 (26.7)	51 (68.0)	24 (32.0)	75 (100)

Medium of Instructions

It is seen from Table 7 that during 1983-84, ninety per cent students took Marathi as their medium of instructions at the school level, whereas at the college level only sixty per cent students took up Marathi, i.e. another thirty per cent students who studied in Marathi at the school gave it up at the college level. During 1984-85, 100 % students studied in Marathi at the school level. However, at the college a number of students (26.7 %) switched over to English, reducing the students studying in Marathi to 73.3 %. On the whole, we see that there is a definite trend for the students to shift over to English at the college level though a majority still continues to study in Marathi.

Parental Association with Social Work

As regards the parental association with social work, it is seen from Table 8, that during the 1983-84 batch six students (twenty per cent) came from the families where the parents also had been working in the field of social work. However, during the 1984-85 batch not a single student came from such a background. Generally, it can be said that the present day social worker in the making is taking up this profession for the first time to make a career and family tradition is not inducing or encouraging him to take up this line.

TABLE 8

Members of Family Working in the Field of Social Work

S.No.	Response	1983-84 Batch	1984-85 Batch	Total
1.	Yes	6 (20.0)	—	6 (8.0)
2.	No	24 (80.0)	45 (100.0)	69 (92.0)
	Total	30 (100.0) (40.0)	45 (100 0) (60.0)	75 (100.0) (100.0)

Preference of Area for Work after Training

It is seen that though there is a variation in the trend of their urge to work in rural areas versus urban areas, after the completion of their training, in respect of the two batches of 1983-84 and 1984-85, but on the whole for the entire sample of seventy-five students under consideration, only twenty-six per cent wish to work in the rural areas whereas seventy-two per cent desire to work in the urban areas (Table 9).

TABLE 9

Area of Preference for Work After Training (MSW)

S. No.	Area	1983-84 Batch	1994-85 Batch	Total
1.	Rural	6 (20.0)	15 (33.3)	21 (28.0)
2.	Urban	24 (80.0)	30 (66.7)	54 (72.0)
	Total	30 (100.0) (40.0)	45 (100.0) (60.0)	75 100.0) (100.0)

While comparing this data with the data given earlier in Table 1, it is seen that 82.7% students undergoing training hail from villages or towns with population less than one lakh, and only 17.3% come from cities. It is very obvious that these students do not find the rural set-up lucrative enough in keeping with their rising aspirations and they wish to migrate to urban areas, or may be that they do not find adequate openings for jobs in the rural areas. This trend merits serious consideration by the planners.

Financial Standing

As regards the financial standing of the students, considering both batches of 1983-84 and 1984-85 together, it has been reported by forty-four per cent, including those three students who were already employed and were sponsored by their employers are financially well off; whereas fifty-six per cent are with a poorer background and would require alternative sources of funds or assistance to enable them to sustain themselves during the training. Out of the fifty-six per cent who need financial assistance, 14.7 % are looking forward to some sort of scholarship, 17.3% plan to work part-time to earn some money, and 22.7% plan to take loans from various sources. It can be generally said that the students undertaking Masters in Social Work, by and large, are from poorer families (Table 10).

TABLE 10

Financial Standing to Meet Needs During Training for MSW

S.No.	Placed and How needs met	1983-84 Batch	1984-85 Batch	Total
1.	Well placed	18 (60.0)	15 (33.3)	30+3*(44.0)
2.	Not well placed, need to be met by	12 (40.0)	30 (66.7)	42 (56.0)
	(a) Working part time	3 (10.0)	10 (22.2)	13 (17.3)
	(b) Scholarship	2 (6.7)	9 (20.0)	11 (14.7)
	(c) By taking loan	6 (20.0)	11 (24.5)	17 (22.7)
	(d) Any other method	—	—	—
	(e) Not reported	1 (3.3)	—	1 (1.3)
	Total	30 (100.0)	45 (100.0)	75 (100.0)

*Already employed students, who have now been sponsored by their employers for training.

Academic Background of Students

Considering both the batches of 1983-84 and 1984-85 together as regards their academic background, it is seen that 46.7% are graduates in Commerce, and 50.7% are graduates in other Arts subjects, thus making a total percentage of 97.4 for non-Science subjects. Further, it is seen that only 2.6% are with Science background. Also it will be noticed that only 21.3% had secured first division, and balance of 78.7% had secured second and third division during their graduation indicating that a majority of the students are just mediocre in their level of intelligence (Table 11).

SUMMARY OF THE FINDINGS

A vast majority of the professional social workers in the making had spent their formative years in the rural areas. Most of them have been educated in government schools through Marathi medium of instructions. A large number of students come from the families where both the parents are either uneducated or are marginally educated. Most of the social work professionals come from the poor strata of the society and majority of them have farming (small scale) as their parental occupation. In general, it can be stated that social work as a profession is being patronized by persons from the low socio-economic group. Sharma points out : "Since it is well established that level of occupation is highly correlated with levels of income, prestige and power, it is clear that higher professions in India are largely monopolized by people belonging to the upper and upper-middle classes of urban origin."[10] It is but apparent that social work, with a lower ranking amongst the professions, is bound to be patronized by the people of lower and lower-middle class of rural origin.

Analysis

The data presented in this paper helps us to understand the levels of "role-perception", "role-performance" and "occupational commitment" of the social work professionals in the making. Although most of the professionals have spent their formative years in the rural areas, they neither belong to the class which needs social justice, i.e. a class of landless labourers or the tribals or the segments of the society who are poor

TABLE 11

Academic Background of Students

S. No.	Degree	DIVISION 1983-84 Batch I	II	III	1984-85 Batch I	II	III	Total
1.	B. Com.	4 (28.6)	5 (35.7)	5 (35.7)	3 (14.3)	10 (47.6)	8 (38.1)	35 (46.7)
2.	B.A.	2 (12.5)	9 (56.3)	5 (31.2)	7 (31.8)	5 (22.7)	10 (45.5)	38 (50.7)
3.	B. Sc.	—	—	—	—	—	2 (100.0)	2 (2.6)
4.	Post-Graduate	—	—	—	—	—	—	—
	Total	6 (20.0)	14 (46.7)	10 (33.3)	10 (22.2)	15 (33.3)	20 (44.5)	75 (100.0)

down to the earth. These professionals in the making in a way are alien and have not themselves suffered the problems of want. Since they also do not have the tradition of social work in their families wherein the value of social justice is understood and practised, the professional social workers thus remain ignorant on this score. These social work professionals have opted for this profession merely to gain mobility in their social ladder. It is substantiated by the findings that most of them want to work in the urban industrial setting after the completion of their training. They do not wish to go back to the rural setting to work for the uplift of their own community. Since most of the social work students hail from the low socio-economic background, they aspire to use this profession for their personal and family betterment. Therefore, by no stretch of imagination, social work profession can become a mission of their lives.

Social work profession requires the inculcation of special attributes like leadership qualities, understanding of broad philosophy of life, capacity for scientific analysis, expertise in the art of human relations' management, power of persuasion, ability to act as an agent of change and above all have the element of compassion to understand and share the misery of fellow-beings. The presence of these attributes can only help the proper "role-perception", "role-performance" and "occupational-commitment".

Considering the raw material coming for training, the question raised is : can these attributes be inculcated among the professionals ? It is very difficult to answer this question especially when we consider the means being adopted for doing so. Among these means comes the training provided at the Schools of Social Work. It is pity to observe that the training at the Social Work Schools can hardly help to develop the above attributes, because the curriculum is heavily "Western-oriented", and the contents are obsolete. Hence, means cannot provide for the end.

CONCLUSIONS

The data presented in the paper, though limited in many ways, throw light on the social work professionals in the making regarding their "role perception", "role-performance" and "occupational-commitment". It indirectly indicates the efficiency level of the professionals, their suitability to meet the new challenges and grasp the broader perspective of social work profession. It is seen that the professionals in the making are concerned mainly with seeking job-opportunities in urban areas to improve their personal status, and use this profession as a stepping stone for better prospects later, rather than having the aptitude and commitment to the profession. The lower status of the profession by itself acts as a drain and would force the intellectuals, if any, to step out of this profession at the first available opportunity. The social work then shall only remain the profession of the left-overs, and thus, is bound to affect the occupational role commitment and performance unless some concrete steps are taken in this direction.

NOTES AND REFERENCES

1. Wadia, A.R., "Ethical and Spiritual Values in the Practice of Social Work," Wadia, A.R., *History and Philosophy of Social Work in India*, Allied Publishers, Bombay, 1968, p. 7.
2. Barnabas, John, "Factors Impeding Growth of Social Work and Community Work", Gupta, S.D. (ed.), *Towards a Philosophy of Social Work in India*, Popular Book Service, New Delhi, 1967, p. 75.
3. *Ibid*, p. 74.
4. Thomas, P.T., "Professional Training in Social Work", Gupta (ed.), *op. cit.*, p. 52.
5. Inkeles, Alex, and Peter Rossi, "National Comparison of Occupational Prestige", *American Journal of Sociology*, vol. 16, no. 4., 1956.
6. Oommen, T.K., *Doctors and Nurses*, Macmillan, Delhi, 1978, p. 13.
7. Sopedad, A.F., "The Role of Voluntary Agencies in Social Welfare Programmes in the ECAFE Region", A Report Prepared for the United Nations Economic Commission for Asia and the Far East, 1970. Talking about professions, Earnest Green Wood writes:"... at one end of this continuum are bunched the well recognized and undisputed professions (e.g. physician, attorney, professor and scientist); at the opposite end are bunched the least skilled and least attractive occupations (e.g. watchmen, truck-loaders, farm labourers, scrub women, and bus-boys). The remaining occupations, less skilled

and less prestigious than the former, but more so than the latter, are distributed between those two poles... Thus, in the less developed professions, social work among [them, these attributes appear in a moderate degree." Vollmer, H.M., and Donald M. Mills (eds.), *Professionalization*, Prentice-Hall, Engle Wood Cliffs, New Jersey, 1966, pp. 10-11.

8. Oommen, *op. cit.*, p. 67.
9. D'Souza, Dominic, "Social Conflicts: Implications for Social Work in the Asian Region", *Perspectives in Social Work*, vol. I, no. 1, March 1984, p. 4.
10. Sharma, B.R., "What Makes a Manager: Merit, Motivation or Money", *Economic and Political Weekly*, vol. 7, no. 22, May 27, 1972, p. 7.

27

VOLUNTARY ORGANISATIONS FROM INDIVIDUAL'S WELFARE TO PROFESSIONAL RURAL DEVELOPMENT : AN ANALYSIS OF IDEOLOGICAL CRISES

S.L. Doshi

Very indiscriminate observations are made on voluntary action. It is alleged : Voluntary organisations are extremely dangerous. Their working in contemporary India indicates a clandestine "alliance" with the capitalists on the one hand and the government on the other. These agencies functioning not on the rule-of-thumb but by the rationality of a professional organisation, are giving rise to new consumerism thereby providing a receptive market to the corporate sector. Such a trend of the functioning of voluntary organisations is observable when the monopoly houses such as the Mafat Lal Group, Sara Bhai Chemicals, Hindustan Levers and a host of other multinationals have entered in a massive way in the villages in search of agro-business. Both the government and the corporate sector express ostensibly their concern for the uplift of the weaker sections of the society. If there is progress and development at the village level, the country flourishes. The arguments given by the catalysts and the neo-voluntary organisations seem to be tenable. But the emerging structure at the village level and at the level of the structures of weaker segments require a thorough enquiry. Allegations and observations such as these are made on the working of the voluntary organisations. In fact, it is not the whole truth about the matter. There is a tradition of voluntary work in India which is inspired by religion, morality, charity and above all by the metaphysics of Gandhi and Vinoba Bhave. Opinions are divided on the working of voluntary organisations in our country.

Ideological Issues

In contemporary India voluntary organisations have assumed new roles. During the pre-Independence decades and more especially in the traditional society voluntary action was a built-in device for meeting unmet human needs, mitigating human suffering and helping people with resources. During the period of freedom struggle, voluntary organisations were created as a strategy to prepare people to reform themselves, and create their own self-sufficient and self-reliant community. In order to develop a sound village infra-structure, Gandhi in fact, heralded a movement of constructive—*rachanatmak*—work throughout the country. His target groups were mainly two : the Harijans and the Adivasis, the latter being taken care of by Thakkar Bapa. The voluntary organisations working for these groups took to the programmes of cottage industries, social reforms such as the prohibition of liquor and removal of untouchability, and the educational activities. It must be observed in categorical terms that the movement of voluntary organisations which was started by Gandhi was ideologically committed to politics. Though the immediate concern of our voluntary effort during this period was constructive work, its end achievement had to be the attainment of freedom. Funds for voluntary organisations flowed from the masses including the capitalists. But the flow was never from the government. The voluntary organisations were like pressure groups or social wings of the All India Congress Committee.

We have enough evidence to demonstrate that the functioning of voluntary organisations during the pre-Independence period was praiseworthy. Their contribution to the attainment of freedom was quite significant. After we got Independence, the continuance of voluntary organisations became a point of dispute. It was argued that the constructive programmes of education, health and cottage industry which were run as welfare programmes by these organisations were being taken up in a bigger way with massive funds and skilled personnel by the government. Thus, there was no any more fight against the colonial regime. In such a situation of historical transformation, what factors led to the survival of voluntary organisations?

The debate goes further and arguments are given couched in rational-bureaucratic-secular-national ideology for the continuance of the functioning of voluntary organisations in independent India. We have a pluralistic society against a monolithic culture. The voluntary organisations cater to the needs of our cultural plurality. Let us go with these. It is said that if we have to avoid concentration of power, we must retain this multi-group character of the free society and make full use of it. The voluntary organisations serve as power-breaker.[1] There is need for wide diffusion of power, not only within the government from the national to the state level and then on to the local authorities, but decentralisation in democracy should include sharing power with voluntary organisations. Voluntary action in the national society, partly within the areas of the state, helps achieve this objective of decentralisation and also involves participation by citizens outside politics, in work useful to the society.

It is also argued that the voluntary organisations provide an appropriate forum to those who wish to work for bringing about change in society, not through politics and political or governmental institutions alone. Efforts can be made to prepare people for a new kind of society through voluntary work. One very commonly put forward argument for the usefulness of voluntary organisations in free India is based on "parallel bar theory" and the "extension ladder theory." It is said that voluntary organisations could function on both these lines with varied emphasis in the developed and the developing societies.[2] For instance, education is a responsibility of the state. The government runs educational institutions. But side by side there could be services managed by voluntary organisations also. When the state resources are limited, voluntary action would bring forth additional resources and cover the areas uncovered by the state even in the areas in which the state has accepted responsibility. In view of the flexibility, ability at experimentation, pioneering spirit and other qualities, voluntary organisations can continue to work for better standards, better methods and better forms of organisation of educational services. Voluntary organisations can also go in search of new needs, work in new areas, unveil social evils and give attention to unattended needs.

The voluntary organizations influenced by Gandhian ideology have a clear-cut goal to achieve. Accordingly "the ideal Gandhian rural community is a non-exploitative and non-exploited self-sufficient and self-reliant community. The cardinal principles of Gandhian ideology are non-violence, harmony, and people's participation. It is opposed to both, centralism, as well as capitalism. It aims at restructuring the present society into an ideal one, by working from below on the basis of local or decentralised planning".

The arguments which plead for the existence and continuance of voluntary organisations in free India may further be extended. But there is another side to the debate. It is said that in practice at empirical-existential level the voluntary agencies are nothing but the stooges of the ruling party and the corporate sector. They have lost their Gandhian glory of the past. The missionary zeal and the devotion of the voluntary worker is a rare event to observe. In this new role, the voluntary organisations have created a crisis which needs to be comprehended cognitively. To what extent do the voluntary organisations retain their commitment to the cause of the development of the poor ? Do they set a pattern for the government to emulate ? The reality is altogether different. The government and the multi—national bogy in the form of corporate sector of the country are set in to create a class of people to be exploited for the fulfilment of the vested interests. Is it possible for a voluntary organisation to experiment and create new areas of work without the approval and consent of the funds releasing body which in most of the cases is the government ? Can the voluntary organisations, in other words, make tunes notwithstanding the will of the piper providing body ? In fact, the voluntary organisations are at the receiving end. Ideologically, the voluntary organisations may argue for their political neutrality, but in their day-to-day working they are obliged to toe the strategy, the line of approach given by the government.

The ideological crisis gets further deepened with the entry of multi-nationals among the weaker sections for doing development work. The appearance of corporate sector as a voluntary organisation is unhistorical for our country. The monopoly houses earlier provided financial assistance to the needy persons by way of doles or charity funds. This practice has almost become extinct today. The government has provided an incentive by way of income tax rebates to the monopoly houses for doing welfare work. This has brought out the government and the monopoly houses as partners in development work each fulfilling the other's interest.

Take for instance the case of Mafat Lal Groups doing welfare work among the weaker sections of Madhya Pradesh and Gujarat. The district of Jhabua has been "adopted" by the groups. The groups has diversified from textiles into range of agro-products. It entered into collaboration with the German concern Hoechet in the dealing of PVC. PVC had an urban market. Mafat Lal took PVC to rural communities in the form of PVC pipes, etc. It also manufactured water pumps for irrigating the fields. This has been Mafat Lal's take-over of rural technology. The government as a partner in development provides subsidy to the numbers of weaker segments on some of these items. The monopoly house comes closer to the village community by doing welfare work in the form of village water management, dispensary and surgical camps. The monopoly house, voluntary organisation and the government along with the assurance of loaning by a nationalised bank come closer and the deal is struck. The end product of such a deal is the enhanced consumerism of the weaker sections. Corporate sector at the local level is not the only agency interested in the rural development. Foreign multinationals are also interested to develop the weaker segments for enhanced consumerism. Voluntary organisations working in India receive financial supports from OXFAM of Canada and the United Kingdom, Catholic Relief Services, and most recently, the Ford Foundation.

It is a mischievous make-believe that voluntary organisations are ideology-neutral. They are out only to help the poor, to organise him to achieve a better quality of life. If the organisations—Gandhian, secular or corporate, make efforts to develop the life of the weaker segments of the society, what is wrong in it? If the Mafat Lal makes a bargain in PVC and the government and the socialised bank advance subsidy and loan what does the tribal or a peasant lose ? Obviously he is a gainer. But to us it is clearly not a case of ideological, neutrality. But we have perhaps raised wrong kind of questions. If we ask : who has taken benefits of the wrong done by the voluntary organisation ? This question is right to get a proper response. Our guess is that the beneficiaries of the development work done by the voluntary organisations are the higher strata of the rural community. The voluntary organisations have so far ended-up with the creation of cleavages and structural inequalities in the society.

Professionalism in Voluntary Organisations

To give new dimension to the analysis of voluntary organisations, it is said that these organisations have acquired characteristics of a professional body. And in this context, the voluntary workers are now considered as professionals. Much of the professional character of a voluntary organisation depends on how we define it. If a voluntary organisation is run on compassionate grounds by persons charged with emotions and sentiments, it only becomes more or less a charitable trust. Further, if the role of a voluntary organisation is to provide a safety valve to the agitating deprived groups by throwing a few benefits, it loses all its rationality, and hence denial of professionalism. Perhaps Gore gives a definition to voluntary organisation which brings it closer to a professional body : "voluntary agency has been brought into existence on the initiative of members of community, which has an open membership, and where the membership is able through normal democratic processes to exercise controly over the affairs of the agency."[3] Gore stressing the rational or professional character of a voluntary organisation further observes that the voluntary worker does not bring special qualities of the heart to his work. This is a fallacy. Today voluntary organisations are rarely manned by volunteer workers at the field-level. They depend upon paid staff to render the service to the needy persons. The quality of the servies must, therefore, largely depend upon the qualities and skills of the paid staff members rather than on the qualities of the volunteer leader. The differentiation that we make in government offices and voluntary organisations is more a consequence of the small size of the latter. Where the distance between the policy-makers and the workers is not great and where the number of workers is limited, an organisation can be more flexible and does not have to depend upon written rules calling for rigid conformity.

Most of the contemporary voluntary organisations have acquired a bureaucratic character. Professionalism, therefore, has entered both in the structure and functioning of these organisations. The voluntary agencies focussing their attention on the individuals rather than communities are increasingly diminishing. As technology, agriculture and life itself have all become more complex, voluntary organisations have felt pressures to become involved in community-wide projects and have found that they need a variety of expertise in order to do so. In this context, the fact that a person volunteers to join an organisation does not have much meaning unless that person either has a needed skill or can be trained to acquire one. Indeed the degree of "voluntarism" left in voluntary organisations is frequently only the differential between the salary the professional earns from the voluntary group and the salary, he or she would draw in private business or government. The fact has to be accepted, that if service conditions in voluntary organisations do not satisfy the financial and psychological needs and aspirations of the workers, they are unlikely to give their best to the organisation. They would only do the bare minimum necessary to keep their jobs. Some of them would leave a voluntary organisation if they find better working conditions and more attractive prospects.

Franda who has made an enquiry in the working of voluntary associations and local development in India infers that the voluntary organisations have assumed professionalism in present day India. They are professionalized because "they have built-up a corpus of specialised knowledge and experience about what does not work in bringing about socio-economic change. Such knowledge is only in small measure the preserve of the technicians and scientists—geologists, well-drillers, agronomists, engineers, veterinarians, bankers, doctors and so forth—within these organisations."[4]

Verghese who has considerable experience of working with the voluntary organisations also observes that the traditional trend of individual welfare has today become an affair of bygone days. The voluntary efforts are now directed towards the making of a self-reliant community development. Young people in the age-group 20-35 often taken-up social action as a vacation, until their family responsibilities become too much for their income. They will then drop out and take-up more secure and lucrative job that command better income. "Another pattern is for people in their late 40s or early 50s to turn to social action at points when family responsibilities lessen, or for retirees to turn to it in order to do 'something useful."[5]

The professionals working with the voluntary organisations are generally of two categories : highly specialised such as physicians, engineers, geologists, and agronomists , and personnel with few academic titles and little schooling but with especially valuable skills such as mechanics, typists, drivers, and machine operators. Since this category of personnel comes from the village itself, it is more than often that such people tend to remain with the voluntary organisation, moving up in rank and responsibility whenever possible.[6]

The Objectives at Stake

It will be foolhardy to say that our voluntary organisations have become professional agencies without keeping into account the functions served by these to achieve our national goals. We strive to attain an egalitarian society based on democracy, socialism, and secularism. Looking to the empirical evidence available with us, these organisations have served the interests of the ruling party either by directly providing them with vote banks or by playing sychophancy to the ruling elites. The corporate sector moves a step further. It does not toe the government approach. It rather dictates the government to toe its own line of working. Voluntary work to them is to create new areas of consumerism at the village side as did the colonial regime when it entered India as a corporate sector. In such a complex ideological situation, what has happened to the realisation of our cherished objectives for which we gave continuance to voluntary efforts by providing grant-in-aid and other priorities. The basic question which provides thrust to our argument is : have voluntary organisations been able to achieve some structural change in the rural society or are they just other rhetorics of the kind of government agencies ? We propose to examine the question in the light of two specific researches available with us. These are : professional volunteerism at Tilonia and rural development at Valod. We very much desired to examine third study on the volunteer effort done by the corporate sector. This being not accessible to us, we have taken the two approaches which are fairly representative of the present functioning of voluntary organisations.

Rural Development : Professional Volunteerism at Tilonia

Marcus Franda, as mentioned earlier has conducted a study of voluntary organisations in India at the instance of American Universities Field Staff in the capacity of scholarly reporter.[7] He has organised his data about voluntary organisations around four major topical clusters, namely, (1) Cottage Industries, (2) Voluntary Associations for Rural Development, (3) Education and Extension, and (4) Politics. He had collected data, it appears through personal interviews and observations. We shall dwell here only on two aspects of voluntary organisation, namely, its professional character and its achievements in terms of bridging social differentiation.

The voluntary organisation working at the village of Tilonia, near the town of Kishangarh, eighty kms. South of Jaipur, is called Social Work and Research Centre (SWRC) registered as a charitable organisation under a legislative act of 1860. Bunker Roy who is the Director of the Centre also associates his wife Aruna who resigned from the IAS in the task of rural development. Both Bunker and Aruna are committed professionals. The centre which started functioning since 1972 consists of a group of professionals of various kinds – doctors, engineers, geologists, soil-chemists, biophysicists, economists, teachers, and professional social workers along with a staff of about thirty people.

The centre besides working at Tilonia has its activities run in more than two dozen surrounding villages. One crucial objective of the functioning of centre is to change the villages. If the villages are not changed as a result of their work, they have failed, the Roys argue. The SWRC operates on its projects on a uniform basis at all its centres. The best strategy to effect rural development is to work with the villagers. "If a project is to succeed,...both planning and implementation must be done at the local level, by those who will be most affected."

The centre runs two kinds of programmes : (1) those generating income, and (2) others non-income generating ones. Among the income-generating programmes are included renting of the two tractors, drilling wells, selling medicines from the two dispensaries, and marketing village crafts in Delhi and Bombay. The non-income generating schemes consist of educational projects including adult education and functional literacy. Tilonia's groundwater survey is one of the most impressive achievements which surpasses any government endeavour.

The funding for the activities of SWRC is made primarily by the state and central government. Funds are also received from foreign agencies such as the OXFAM and Ford Foundation. The ultimate objective of the SWRC is to "introduce technology that will increase production and improve living standards for the poorer segments of village society."

Ideologically speaking, Tilonia's voluntary effort is heavily charged with secular-national-professional-bureaucratic character. There are no political overtones, anywhere. But what has this professional service organisation done to the rural social structure ? Has the structure moved towards anywhere in the neighbourhood of socialism ? To answer these questions, we should refer to the analysis provided by Franda. He is certain that SWRC has a distinct character compared to any missionaries or other relief or voluntary agencies. His assessment is that it can best be "understood as a modern nationalist, secular and vaguely socialist Indian organisation."

The major focus of development in the Tilonia voluntary effort is the eradication of poverty. This poverty relates to those who form the lowest economic groups of our society—the rural and the tribal. The centres both at Tilonia and the neighbouring villages have given projects which generate income, and improve local productivity. But it is found that a number of SWRC projects have given benefits "to those who are somewhat better off. Some seed distribution and agricultural extension programmes are aimed at the more progressive farmers." Actually Franda's conclusion is that the benefits of voluntary work have, by and large been cornered by the village leaders and the better-off segments. Then, he further informs that these better-off segments which are actually levers of power for rural change, resist any change that challenges their status quo.

The voluntary organisations are engaged in the development of rural poor at the cost of increasing social inequality, perhaps we shall have to redefine and restructure the total organisation of voluntary effort.

Gandhian Approach to Rural Development : The Voluntary Work by VIAS at VALOD

Ghanshyam Shah and H.R. Chaturvedi have evaluated the working of Vedchhi Intensive Area Scheme (VIAS) of Valod—a small taluka in Gujarat.[8] The voluntary organisation of VIAS owes its origin to the Gandhian movement. Its working is influenced by Gandhian approach to rural development. "Its guiding principles are individual morality, non-violence, harmony, self-sufficiency of village society and decentralisation of political power. In its attempt to utilize local resources and secure the participation of people in the development process, the VIAS experimented with decentralisation and planning from below."[9]

Valod lies in the Surat district in South Gujarat. The population of the taluka has two social groups—tribals and non-tribals. The tribals constitute more than seventy-three per cent of the general population. Valod was active quite like Bardoli in the satyagraha. It has a rich tradition of developing Khadi industry and participating in freedom struggle.

Constructive work on Gandhian ideology has been a part of the heritage of taluka.

Ideology

The Gandhian social order rests on moral ethical values. The Gandhians believe that the source of moral values in general lies in religion and Hindu scriptures like the *Upanishadas* and *Gita*, in particular. Gandhi believed in a society based on *Ram Rajya*, the kingdom of Lord Rama. For Gandhi, village is the unit of social order. He argues for decentralisation of social and political power for the real development of villages. The role of Gram Panchayat in such a scheme is crucial. Gandhi also pleaded for village self-sufficiency, and trusteeship. He believed that his ideal village society could be reconstructed with the help of voluntary organisations and dedicated workers.

Professionalism

Theoretically, VIAS denies any character of a professional organisation. "It is not just an implementing agency like a government department, or some rural development agencies sponsored these days by industrial and business houses. It has undertaken the task as a mission inspired by an explicit ideology. But at the level of functioning VIAS turns out to be a professional body. There are set rules of recruitment and promotion. The whole organisation is based on bureaucratic hierarchy. Rather salary differences in different cadres in the VIAS are striking. For instance, some workers get a salary as low as Rs. 250 per month without any fringe benefits. whereas a few set around Rs. 1000/- per month plus provident fund and other benefits. Nevertheless, there are regular grades and regular increments. Though VIAS has not gained professionalism as high as SWRC, it works on certain set down bureaucratic procedures. The missionary zeal of a voluntary organisation begins to disappear when people join such organisations not because of their commitments to values and ideological orientations but for more financial incentives and benefits.

Finances

The organisation in the beginning started with a meagre budget of Rs. 8,000 a year in the fifties. But slowly the flow of funds increased. It received financial support from Community Aid Abroad (Australia), Freedom From Hunger Campaign (FHC, Australia), NOVIB (Netherlands), OXFAM (Britain), Swiss Aid (Switzerland), and other Swedish and German organisations. At present (1983) its assets add upto about 400 thousand.

Achievements in Education and Agriculture

VIAS is credited to have worked considerably in the fields of education and agriculture. Through education new skills are imparted and qualities of leadership are developed. VIAS is keen to develop basic education on the model suggested by Gandhi. "But they had little option to work on those lines wholeheartedly. They worked out compromise model which provides opportunities to teachers and students to do some extension work in the villages. They have been able to build closer links between the school and the community." The VIAS runs five basic schools in different parts of the taluka. Besides these five schools, there is also a *nai talim* school in Vedohhi. The literacy in the taluka has gone up from thirty per cent in 1961, to forty-one percent in 1981. It is to the credit of VIAS that the literacy rate of Vedohhi is higher than the rate of literacy in the other tribal talukas of Gujarat.

In the field of agriculture also VIAS has sponsored some economic programmes to raise the income of the poor. Agricultural programmes included institutional change and modernisation of agriculture. It persuaded the farmers to use modern agricultural inputs and helped them to get loans for the purpose from various agencies. As a result of the working of VIAS, the cropping pattern of the whole taluka underwent change. The farmers have begun to take cash crops.

Other economic programmes taken up by the VIAS include dairy, poultry farming, fishing, neera and brick making. Financial support for these programmes was taken from the state government and other funding agencies. Dairying was financed partly by the Operation Flood, First programme of the National Dairy Development Board. The VIAS also set-up a mini paper factory at Vedohhi. It has followed modern management methods to make the factory viable.

Structural Outcome of VIAS Voluntary Work

It has been the thrust of our argument all through that the voluntary organisations in the aftermath of Independence have been toeing the line of government or playing sychophancy to it without operationally demonstrating their distinctive contributions. One can hardly make any differentiation in the programmes implemented by the government agencies and the voluntary organisations. There is no visible imprint of any moral or value stance. There might be some change in the approach but at the level of affecting the social structures, the practice is uniform. Our other argument has been that ideology plays an important part in determining the nature of voluntary effort. The organisations in a gleesome way pronounce their political neutrality but when proper opportunities come they cannot afford to sit on the hedge. VIAS makes no secret of its leanings towards Congress (I). Boldly, it must be observed on the basis of the two case studies cited above, that the voluntary organisations practise the ideology of capitalism. Invariably their source of funding does not lie in a substantial way with the masses, their consumers. The sources are beyond the target groups. And the logic is simple : those who control the funding sources control the ideology. Our third argument has been that the working of voluntary organisations has deepened the cleavages and gaps in the alreading existing social inequalities of the rural society.

The case of VIAS very clearly indicates that "the benefits of development programmes had gone only to either the upper strata of the tribals or the non-tribals."[10] There has been a marked increase in the farm productivity of Vedchhi as a result of agricultural modernisation but "the condition of small and marginal farmers remains deplorable. Despite all efforts, a larger number of these farmers do not even own a pair of bullocks, an iron plough and irrigation facilities. They do not get fertilizers and improved seeds regularly. Market prices are not always in their favour."[11] Even the economic programmes of dairy, poultry farming, brick making and fishing have gone in favour of the tribal better-off strata. Shah and Chaturvedi are honest when they strike their concluding observation: "However, the constraints of the dominant socio-economic system are so strong that the VIAS cannot really hope to improve the economic condition of the have-nots."[12]

If the socio-economic system of the monopoly houses and the government has an unrestrained constraint on the free working of the voluntary organisations, can we hope that the latter would be able to demonstrate "something" which is different from the former. Our argument is that we cannot think of the working of voluntary organisations in our country in isolation from the larger context which contains enough of capitalistic-bureaucratic-political party vested interests. If the larger society has run amuck of all normative and value constraints, can we think of the voluntary organisations following their specified path. We do not contest the idea that the modern voluntary organisations have become professional bodies. Neither we deny that they practise bureaucratic procedures and pretend to be rational. What we argue is that despite the voluntary organisations becoming modern in their structure and functioning, the end result of the processes releas-ed by them is a society which has assumed greater degree of inequality. Does it justify the survival and continuance of the voluntary organisations in contemporary India ?

NOTES AND REFERENCES

1. Kulkarni, V.M., *Voluntary Action in a Developing Society*, Indian Institute of Public Administration, New Delhi, 1969, p. 9.
2. *Ibid*, p. 11.
3. Gore, M.S., "Relative Roles of State and Voluntary Agencies in the Organisation of Social Services", *Proceeding of the Seminar on Social Administration in Developing Countries*, India International Centre, New Delhi, 1964, p. 84.
4. Franda, Marcus, *Voluntary Associations and Local Development in India : The Janta Phase*, Young Asia Publications, New Delhi, 1983, p. 11.
5. Verghese, B.G., "Voluntary Action : A New Mission for the New Missionaries", *Voluntary Action*, vol. XIV, no. 1, January-October, 1977, p. 4.
6. Windey, M.A., "A Rural Reconstruction Movement in India," *Voluntary Action*, vol. XVIII, no. 3-4, March-April, 1976, pp. 55-56.

7. *Op. cit.*
8. Shah Ghanshyam, and Chaturvedi H. R., *Gandhian Approach to Rural Development : The Valod Experiment*, Ajanta Book International, New Delhi, 1983.
9. *Ibid.*, p. 41.
10. *Ibid.*, p. 108.
11. *Ibid.*, pp. 108-109.
12. *Ibid.*, p. 110.

28

DANCE AS A PROFESSION : THE RELATIONSHIP OF VARIABLES UTILISED BY DANCERS TO MAINTAIN A POSITIVE SELF-IMAGE

MILDRED W. WEIL

The development of a strong self-image is necessary for performing any role in the theater or in dance. Self-image is to a great extent, the result of experience; however, the experience of most performers is repeated rejection making it difficult not to imagine oneself a failure. This paper explores self-image, focusing on how dancers in particular, keep "in face" and continue to see themselves as performers despite repeated rejections and long periods of professional unemployment.

Ten strategies dancers use to cope with failure are presented and the subject is viewed within the context of Weber's concept of rationalization[1] as well as Irving Goffman's two general face saving devices, the *corrective* and the *avoidance* process.[2]

According to Parsons, a major aspect of the dynamic system of development in Western society has been a particular form of Weber's concept of the "process of rationalization", with the occupational system probably the most important institutional "precipitate" of this process.[3] Through it, as well as other channels, it has been a fundamental part in structuring attitudes in our society and, therefore, is here considered in the world of dance.

Weber indicates that the process of rationalization structures attitudes, particularly when it comes to the ability to perform well and to hold one's own or excel in competition, one of the primary realistic tests of mature adequacy. Here, for performers, particularly dancers, probably the considerable majority, are destined to what they must feel to be an unsatisfactory experience. In addition, they may often feel they have been unjustly treated, because there is in fact much injustice in the realm of the performance world as well as in the nature of the society itself. However, in dance this may be a mixed blessing since to feel unjustly treated is not only soothing to one's sense of resentment, but is an excuse for failure, since how could one succeed if she/he is not given a chance ?

Here we can see Weber's description of rationality as a property of people's view of things, and as characterizing the person's orientation toward the world pertains. Weber does, however, in his work also use some variant of "rational" as synonymous with systematic, profitable, intellectualized, efficient, logical, accumulative, cognitively encompassing, disenchanted, and/or as any change from the status quo.

Considering these variants, rationalization introduces a method for viewing the fundamental structuring of the dancer's interests. Artists of any sort find it necessary to structure attitudes because of strain encountered in their sub-culture and in society itself but it should be noted that the restructuring itself can also contribute to role strain. Actually, beneath its apparently surface optimism, it may well be deeply pessimistic, and concerned only with giving some coherent shape to the despair.

The ideological definition of the situation in terms of the way it is structured by dancers never stands alone, it is also a part of the psychological process and the social expectations and realities of the situation that they must face.

The dancers chosen as the population for this study were trained in all four types of dance—ballet, modern, jazz and tap, with the majority having most of their training in ballet. In America, these dancers are known as "gypsies" ; trained in all types of dance, they look for a wide variety of jobs within the field including performing in companies, industrials,[4] dinner theaters and shows (the ultimate goal being to perform on Broadway). In their quest, they "travel" from performance to performance, face repeated rejection at auditions, and try to survive long periods of unemployment, while continuing to see themselves as performers.

Corrective and Avoidance Strategies

Face, as Goffman defines it, is the "image of self-delineated in terms of approved social attributes—albeit an image that others may share as when a person makes a good showing for his profession or religion by making a good showing for himself" and, in 1967, Goffman identified two general face saving devices, the *avoidance process* and the *corrective process*. The former strategy refers to the individual avoiding those contracts in which threats to his/her face are likely to occur. The corrective process operates when a person fails to prevent the occurrence of an event that is expressively incompatible with the image of social worth that he/she will try to correct for its effects and re-establish a satisfactory acting stage.

Some of the ten strategies presented in this paper can be classified as a part of the corrective process dancers use, as well as part of the avoidance process. An example of the avoidance process is in not giving a direct answer to the question about present theater employment, but rather substituting a description of conversation with a dance-instructor, which has been complimentary. However, this can also be described as a corrective mechanism as it also helps the dancer maintain self-worth.

Goffman used the term "ritual" to describe such behaviour because he is dealing with acts through whose symbolic components the actor shows how worthy he is of respect or how worthy he feels others are of it. The term equilibrium is also appropriate here because, according to Goffman, a person effectively claims a degree of respect designated as face by both his or her stance in an encounter and by other's reactions. Thus, face is an image of self in relationship to socially approved attributes which form the basis for treatment individuals can accept to receive. One of the ways Weber describes the process of rationalization is the deliberate adaptation to situations in terms of self-interests and because of its relationship to Goffman's concept of self-worth is here presented.

The Applicability of Weber's Concept of Rationalization

Parsons notes that the process of rationalization would scarcely have been of profound social importance if it had not affected large numbers of people in the immediate circumstances of their daily lives. But as an essential part of the same general cultural movement there has developed a tradition of "social thought" which, in a sufficiently broad perspective, can be seen to be highly distinctive in spite of its internal complexity.

One fundamental fact concerning rationalization is that the incidence of this process within the social structure is highly uneven that is, different elements of a population become "rationalized" in different degrees, at different rates, and in different people's personalities and orientations. It is the contention here that dancers (probably all performers) become "rationalized" to a great degree compared to other segments of the population, despite the variation of personalities found within the group, due to the combination of their expectations and the reality of the situations they have experienced.

The training of dancer takes years and is very demanding, requiring long hours and intense devotion in order to master very difficult techniques ; time for "normal" social activities is severely curtailed. This sacrifice (part of the necessary commitment) combined with the fact that students have difficulty in obtaining any of the few available positions for which they have so arduously trained, requires them to adapt certain attitudes and to learn various strategies which help maintain some type of security necessary for promoting their positive self-image.

As noted by Parsons there is considerable evidence that security is to a high degree a function of the stability of certain elements of the socio-cultural situation. This is especially true here because certain aspects of the situations dancers face are involved in the actual and, as they feel it, prospective fulfilment of their "legitimate expectations."[5] These expectations are, highly concrete so that any change, particularly if it is unfavourable, is apt to be disturbing and arouse a reaction of doubt and anxiety. When informal relationships in any of their working groups is disrupted, and expectations are unmet most of the time, dancers must work out coping mechanisms so that the created anxiety does not interfere with their self-image as performers. This change on the level of ideas and symbols is exceedingly important to the security and stability of their orientation.

The weight of evidence seems to be that the amount of such change when one is not being able to obtain work (to which even the best-integrated personalities cannot adapt without the possibility of upsetting the smooth functioning of personality) is rather limited. No matter what the personality type there tends to be a need for stability in these respects. The capacity to adapt to both kinds of change described is part of "emotional maturity," therefore, within this orientation, there must be serious limitations in the levels of emotional maturity which can be attained by dancers.[6] There seems to be little doubt that the continuing incidence of dynamic change in expectations through the process of rationalization is one major source of the generalized insecurity which not only characterizes our entire society, but the sub-culture of the dancer.

Techniques used to avoid the stigma of failure by unemployed dancers exhibit a pattern actually a character of what Weber calls "rationalization". Thus, by applying a Weberian perspective to strategies dancers employ to maintain a positive self-image, we can see a type of "internal logic" that can be used to study the artists in general and dancers in particular.

The strategies employed by dancers appear to be intellectualized, efficient, logical, and accumulative, which are some of the variations of "rational" Weber considers as synonymous with systematic.

In addition, Weber also conceives rationality not a property of things but of people's views of things; it characterized persons' orientation toward the world, not the world itself. Thus "increasing intellectualization and rationalization do not... include an increased and general knowledge of the conditions under which one lives."[7] Dancers indeed, do not or prefer not to see the reality of these conditions of their life, that is, they apparently deny the fact that few will find employment and if they do it will not be continuous. That is even if they become members of a dance company, or "get a show", the work is not continuous. With Weber's definitions of rationalization in mind the ten strategies identified utilized by the dancers will be presented.

As a dance student and member of a dance company for many years, the author was able to research through participatory-observation, the problems dancers have with their self-image, how they structure attitudes, and the mechanisms they adopt to avoid the stigma of being considered a failure by themselves, members of their sub-culture—dancers—and others in society at large.

Strategies

One of the effective strategies used to avoid the stigma of failure is obtaining a union card, such as an "Equity" card. This is not small achievement in itself. In order to go to an "Equity call" rather than an "open all" (also known as a cattle call) for an audition, a dancer must have an Equity card ; however, one can only become a member of Equity, if he/she has performed in "An Equity Show", and performing in an Equity show depends on success at an audition set-up for only members. This is the dancers' "catch 22." There are, of course, ways to "beat this system." One can "hang around the theater" after an audition (sometimes for as long as eight hours) until all union people have been seen and try to persuade the union representative (one must always be present) to allow him or her to audition. Or, a more effective method has been to perform in another type of union show such as S.A.G. (Screen Actors Guild) or A.G.V.A. (American Guild of Variety Artists), and once such membership was obtained, "buy" into Equity after waiting a prescribed amount of time, usually six to eight months. This latter method is presently being investigated by Equity and will probably be stopped.

Kadushin found in his study of music students, that the single highest predictor of musical excellence was union membership, followed by official class standing, and then professional performance. He states that union membership does not cause excellence, but rather is a requirement for the jobs to which music students aspired.[8] Thus having obtained the union card can be considered as a consequence of excellence. And so it is with dancers who must have that Equity card to audition for and obtain the positions for which they are trained. It is not just obtaining the card but sharing this information with others in the dancer's sub-culture that makes this technique effective. This strategy not only structures a positive attitude among the dancers using this mechanism but it utilized to structure such an attitude among the fellow dancers.

Related to this strategy is the one of *only auditioning for union shows*, and also another adopted technique, that of auditioning only for the most prestigious of the union shows again the effectiveness of both of these strategies ultimately depend on "talking" about these events especially with colleagues. A panel of dancers ranked shows according to their prestige value ?

1. Dance companies (also ranked)
2. Broadway shows
3. Off Broadway shows (which are rated from most to least prestigious)
4. Television series
5. Television performances
6. Industrials (ratings are based on whether they are for television consumption or use within a particular industry. Ranking is also on the basis of fame of fellow performers, director, producer and choreographer and who is sponsoring it, e.g. Dr. Pepper, and the channel on which it is shown)
7. Dinner theaters (also ranked).[9]

Expanding training to voice and theatre is the fourth mechanism used

This strategy is usually adopted after repeated rejection at dance auditions This may also be considered part of professional growth, especially when the dancer specifically has the goal of doing total theater. However, these performers are not dancers in the real sense of the word; they do not possess the total commitment to and involvement in *only* the dance.[10]

Training in the most prestigious schools and with the most prestigious instructors is the fifth and often used strategy. This includes enrolling in dance schools, schools of dramatic arts and studying with voice teachers. Kadushin reported that for music students, one of the major functions of the right school (Juilliard and Manhattan School of Music) is to encourage and control the development of self-image as a professional, allowing to develop at such time that it will provide motivation for transferring to a new situation without harming the perception of the current role. The schools develop excellence while, at the same time, permitting students to make use of their abilities in the professional world.[11]

In dance, the most prestigious schools for ballet are the American Ballet Theater, New York City Ballet, City Center, Harkness: for modern dance, Merce Cunningham's, Martha Graham's; and for Jazz, Phil Black's and Ron Farelli's. For training in dramatics, the high status schools are Herbert Bergdorf (Uta Hagen is the director), Actor's Studio (Strassborg Studio) American Academy, Stella Adler's, and in music Juillard and the Manhattan School of Music. A young dancer related in an informal interview: "This is also career building device, (not just a face savine one). The training is necessary for professional growth and provides additional opportunities for job placement (e.g. instructors have contacts and may be asked to supply actors/dancers for performances)."

Many of the other strategies adopted to "save face" are also devices which are used in building a successful career. Obtaining an Equity card, additional training in other areas, and performing a show case are part of career development, and may contribute to, as well as be a result, of professional excellence.

Performing in a show case, (non-paid theater performances) is the sixth device used by dancers. And, in addition to saving face, it provides the opportunity to dance, to be seen by agents, producers, directors and choreographers, and to add experience to one's resume. Show cases are rated on the basis of the status of the performers, directors and producers. Talking about these performances is also extremely important in employing this device. Goffman points out that the control if interaction is achieved largely by influencing the definition of a stiuation, and the definition of a situation is determined through the actor's (here the dancer's) expressing him or herself in such a way as to give others the kind of impressions that will lead them to act voluntarily in accordance with the dancer's own perception.

Being cut at an audition because of physical characteristics, or because of lack of other abilities such as singing or acting, provides gypsies with the seventh, ready-made face saving device. Being the appropriate type is something over which a dancer has little or no control ; for example, in chorus work all heights must be similar. Another example is the casting for *Fiddler on the Roof* which always results in the hiring of one redhead in addition to the brunettes hired to play the daughters. Thus, being "out" or "typed-out", or being judged on singing and/or acting, not on dancing alone, can be used as effective face saving devices. A frequent remark overheard in the dressing room is "they went with a singer who dances," rather than a "dancer who sings."

The eighth strategy observed is "*going commercial*," that is, auditioning for, and hopefully getting work in commercials, and industrials. This too is also part of career development. Moreover, "gypsies", as well as other people in show business, must pay the rent and buy the groceries. This type of employment not only serves this function, but is an excellent vehicle for doing what one is trained and for being seen by agents, directors, producers and choreographers. Here again, it is also a desirable activity as the dancer is given the opportunity to perform.

Exaggerating the prestige of the performance, that the describing the type of work as being more important and prestigious than it is another way of avoiding the stigma of failure. Thus, a show which may be so far off broadway that it is out of state is mentioned as "off broadway" to create an illusion. In reality this may not be dishonest, but a redefinition of the situation by gypsies as they succeed in convincing themselves, as well as others, of the importance of their work. Related to this is the withholding of some vital information related to the dancer's professional activities. A good example of this is the young woman who told me that she was with Alvin Ailey, thus leading me to think (which I readily did) that she was performing with the troupe. I later discovered that she was taking classes at the school and not a performer at all. This is more than redefining the situation ; here the dancer was, of course, intentionally conveying misinformation.

Discrediting others is the final technique employed. This involves playing down another person's achievement by noting (perhaps correctly) that "she/he got the job because : she/he has the "look" that's in ; the director owes his/her friend or mate a favour; or she spent the night with the choreographer, not because of his or her dancing ability.

All the techniques described indicate that these dancers not only structure their own attitudes but try to do this for others with whom they interact. In addition, they seemed to have developed a systematic and logical process to promote their individual self-interest. Moreover, these strategies also illustrate their masking the reality of their life situations as performers in general and dancers in particular are trained for jobs that, for the most part, do not exist.

Thus, no dancer will state, I am "unemployed" conveying the message "I am not performing because others were chosen because they are better," which may or may not be true. The techniques they have developed, some of which can be and are probably used in other occupations and some which are unique to this type of performing enables the dancers to cope with disenchantment. Actually, it permits them to cope, and these particular adaptations keep them from leaving the field. Systematizing their behaviour indicates that their actions help these dancers "keep in face." Of course, denial is also helpful not only to dancers but to those others who do not succeed in the American occupational scene. Thus, the mechanisms which are useful for the dancers observed, are also similar to those used by other professionals. Two important ideas adapted from Weber should be emphasized here. That is "calculation" implies a metric which permits the weighing of alternatives, the choice being whatever is thought most efficient. Moreover, "calculability" implies the capacity of freedom to weight alternatives. Thus, when Weber refers to rationalization as "deliberate adaption to situations in terms of self interest,"[12] his accent is on efficiency or the weighing of alternative courses of action.

SUMMARY AND FUTURE RESEARCH

"Participant-observation was the method used to collect" the preceding information, and provides a base for further data gathering on strategies dancers employ to avoid the concept of self-failure. In the second place of this research responses to a failure battery will be obtained and scored to give the respondent a "failure score", which will be related to the interweaving of the strategies used.[13]

The preceeding material illustrates that there are many "sign-vehicles" which allow dancers to convey information which presents the self in what is perceived as a desirous image not only as defined by the peer group, but by the larger society. The dancer succeeds in formulating and influencing the definition of the situation by expressing him or himself in such a way as to give others the kind of impression that will lead them to believe in and, presumably, to act in accordance with the dancer's plan. Moreover, "real" attitudes, beliefs and emotions of individuals can be ascertained only indirectly, that is, through what appears to be voluntary expressive behaviour of the individual. While the dancer can be calculating in his or her activities he/she can, at the same time, be relatively unaware that this is the case. In other words, he/she may be expressing him or herself intentionally or unintenationally while others are impressed in some way. This disposed control the dancer has in regard to the communication process "sets the stage for a kind of information game—a potentially infinite cycle of concealment, discovery, failure, revelation and rediscovery.[14]

It is important to note here, that Goffman points out that when the individual projects a definition of the situation in his/her interactions with others, no matter how passive the role of these others may seem to be, they themselves effectively project a definition of the situation by virtue of the response to the actor and by virtue of any lines of action they initiate to him or her. We have seen that Weber's reference to "rationalization" as a deliberate adaptation to situations in terms of self-interest is well exemplified by the coping mechanisms used by the dancer described. Weber sees people as variously aware of their choices in such a context and he differentiates between affectual and traditional actions which are a-rational because persons behave as if they are unaware of any choice in their behaviour, and rationality entering into what he describes as *wertrational* and *zweckrational* actions. In the first of these an "absolute commitment" is pursued by calculating any means possible ; in the latter, the ends as well as the means are weighed.[15]

While dancers certainly weigh or calculate within the means possible and obviously weigh these in terms of the desired end, it can be argued, that the dancers actions are both *wertrational* and *zweckrational* in that they are choosing means that are available in their sub-culture to achieve the desired end—conveying success to themselves and others with whom they interact and, most important, continue to see themselves as dancers so that they do not leave the field but pursue auditions. They are in a more limited manner *zweckrational* in that the means are not equally weighed or employed, that is the choice is not as clear-cut as Weber describes. For example, while dancers are aware of "choosing" the mechanisms employed they may not be consciously selected to communicate success to themselves, members of their sub-groups, and society itself, but thought of as only as career building devices (which indeed some are). Moreover, on a purely conscious level, most dancers may and probably would deny calculating any means among those possible to use as strategies.

Thus, while rationality obviously deals with this capacity or willingness to calculate means, end, and the relationship between them, it is difficult for these dancers to accept that essentially this is what they are doing. However, the calculation is there, and in Weber's "Science as Vocation" essay he notes that "the knowledge or belief that...there are no mysterious incalculable forces that come into play, but rather that one can, in principle master all things by calculatnoin,"[16] pertains here.

However, while the dancers described in this paper do not acknowledge the condition of failure which may eventually force them to leave performing, they are aware of choices to achieve ends despite their denial. When the decision to leave performing actually occurs, this is preceeded by disenchantment. However, this too is a means to an end, as they are leaving to pursue an occupation which hopefully can lead to success. In Weber's discussion of the four types of social action, he recognizes that human behaviour involves the use of means to an end, and he sees people as variously aware of their behaviours in this regard. Thus, individuals are not required to follow a pattern inexacably laid down in advance (radical determinism) so that rationalization applies in an interesting way in the artistic realm.

We have seen that the dancers studied are using mechanisms to control attitudes and responses of others and Tom Burns presents the argument that in all interaction, each participant is influenced by a common underlying theme, the desire to guide and control the responses made by others present.[17] Here we have been concerned with a specific kind of response and control, that is, with defining the nature of the relationship of those involved in interaction in which the dancer's success (or lack of it) is perceived as central.

When Weber refers to rationalization as "deliberate adaptation to situations in terms of self-interest," his accent is on efficiency or the weighing of alternative courses of action. But when he refers to rationalization as "substitution for the unthinking acceptance of ancient custom," his accent is on the freedom or capacity—intellectual and ethical—to weigh alternatives. The latter is Weber's theme of "disenchantment". Rationalization involves both themes, it is generally agreed,[18] and are applicable here.

Weber's analysis of social change focused on a double-barreled notion of rationalization. On one hand, he sought to understand the inhibiting factors—the "traditions" or "magical elements"—that prevent some alternatives from even becoming calculable and on the other hand, he sought to understand how people, to the degree disenchantment obtains, will calculate and systematize. No one wilfully chooses inefficiency. That is in this context chooses the idea of having failed.

To summarize, a common element found in Weber's writings whether it be bureaucracy, religion, economics, law, science or the arts is the role played by rational action, rationality, or rationalization. However, Weber, stated that rationalism means different very different things...The rationalization of life conduct with which we have to deal here can assume unusually varied forms. Also rationalization does not apply uniformally across a total society but proceeds instead at different rates in different institutional spheres.[19]

Using Weber's analysis, rationality then, depends upon the degree to which persons have knowledge about alternatives and have the capacity to act on them. Therefore, a central implication of the idea or rationalization is that a choice made at one time influences the knowledge and capability—and thus choice —at a latter time. So it is that many mechanisms dancers use here can be described as an "internal logic," an accumulative pattern in which, as new developments occur, subsequent developments seem almost to present themselves.

Thus, rationalization applies in the artistic realm of the dance even though no one performs in dance or any of the other of the arts to be efficient ; since by definition, the goal of performers is not only aesthetic but for these would be performers that of having the *opportunity* to perform, and if not performing creates the illusion that they are still dancers. Various techniques are employed to achieve the goal not only of obtaining eventual performances, but to continuously see oneself as a dancer. And, obviously dissatisfaction is frequent even for the employed due to continuos periods of unemployment and the uncertainty of when or where they will perform again. The rationalization process is part of the experience and condition of being a dancer and is exhibited not only in choices made in the mechanisms used to maintain a positive self-image, but in the systematizing that obviously preceeds and follows such choices.

There is little question but that the dancer has many motives for trying to control the impression others receive of the situation, but this paper has been concerned only with some of the common techniques or strategies that the "gypsy" employs to sustain impressions of success with some of the contingencies associated with employment of these techniques. Most of these are common to people in every profession, but some are institutionalized by those in dance profession : "The issues dealt with by stage craft and stage management are sometimes trivial but they are quite general ; they seem to occur everywhere in social life, providing a clear cut dimension of sociological analysis."[20]

Weber's concept of rationality as applied here, depends upon the degree to which the dancers had knowledge about alternatives and have had the capability to act on them. It also depends upon the fact these "gypsies" have denied the reality of their situation, enabling them to see existing alternatives in their life style, which help them keep "in face" and see themselves as performers. A central implication of the idea of rationalization is that a choice made at one time influences the knowledge and capability—and thus choice—at a later time. Also these many endeavours of these dancers exhibit an "internal logic," an accumulative pattern in which, as new developments occur, subsequent developments seem almost to suggest themselves, Moreover, Weber's description of rationalization as a striving for perfection, as an ingenious refinement of the conduct of life and the attainment of increasing mastery over the external world is applicable to this analysis.

While the author's observations indicate that emphasizing having an Equity card, auditioning for only Equity and prestigious performances, seeking additional training, going commercial, performing in show cases, exaggerating the quality of shows, attending prestigious schools, emphasizing being typed out, and discrediting others all appear to be inter-woven and related to self concept, the second stage of the research should provide the author with the additional data needed to substantiate the information provided by observation.

NOTES AND REFERENCES

1. While the concept of rationalization appears to be a central idea in Max Weber's analyses, however, he states that rationalization may mean different things.
2. Goffman, Irving, *Interaction Ritual*, Anchor Books, New York, 1967, p. 5.
3. Parsons, Talcott, *Essays in Sociological Theory*, The Free Press, Glencoe, Illinois, 1954, p. 314.
4. Industrials are shown which are sponsored by a manufacturer of a product and are presented live and/or on television. So called "superstars" apply for the lead roles if the sponsor is considered prestigious.
5. Parsons, *op. cit.*
6. *Ibid.*
7. Gerth, H.H., and C.W. Mills., *From Max Waber*, Oxford University Press, New York, 1948, p. 293.
8. Kadushin, Charles, Ronald M. Pavolko (eds.), *Sociological Perspectives on Occupations*, F.E. Peacock Publishers, Illinois, 1972, p. 168.
9. These rankings were done by a panel of five professional dancers.
10. Federico, Ronald Charles, "Ballet as an Occupation", Unpublished Ph. D. Dissertation, North-Western University, 1968.
11. Kadushin, *op. cit.* pp. 167-168.
12. Weber, Max, *Theory of Social and Economic Organization*, The Free Press, New York, 1947, p. 123.
13. Perinbanayagam, Robert S., *Failure and the Self*, An Exploratory Unpublished Doctoral Dissertation, University of Minnesota, December, 1967, pp. 103-105. Failure within this context refers to the responses to four questions used to measure self-definitions of failure constructed by Robert Parinbanayagam ; (1) What (identify and describe) was the experience in which you met with failure (in what Perinbanayagam describes as a "cherished enterprises")? The response to this item places the act of failure on the person ; (2) Why did this happen is a question used to elicit vocabulary of motives the subject would use to explain failure ; (3) What explanation did you offer your immediate circle of friends and/or relatives who were aware of this failure ? (this question was useful for the purposes of comparing two and three) ; and, (4) To what kinds of persons did you give the explanation, which is a continuation of item three ?
14. Goffman, Irving, *Presentation of Self in Everyday Life*, Doubleday, New Delhi, 1959.
15. Weber, Max, *op. cit.* p. 139.

16. *Ibid.*

17. Burns, Tom, "Friends, Enemies, and the Polite Fiction,': *American Sociological Review*, 1953.

18. Parsons, T., "Introduction to Weber's Theory of Social and Economic Organizations" *op. cit.*; Gerth, H.H., and Mills, C.W. "*Introduction*" in Weber, *From Max Weber, op. cit.*, Martindale *et al.*, Introduction in Weber *The Rational and Social Foundations of Music*"; Free Press, Carbondale, Ill, Southern Illinois 1958, XLVI, li-lii.

19. Weber, Max, *Protestant Ethic and the Spirit of Capitalism*, Allen and Unwin, London, 1930, p. 77.

20. Goffman, 1959, *op. cit.*

INDEX